MEDIEVAL
ROMANCES

MEDIEVAL ROMANCES

EDITED BY

Roger Sherman Loomis

AND

Laura Hibbard Loomis

THE MODERN LIBRARY · *New York*

Distributed by McGraw-Hill, Inc.

Contents

INTRODUCTION:

THE ORIGINS OF ROMANCE

Storytelling was for the Middle Ages a favorite form of entertainment. Today the theatre, the cinema, radio and television have largely taken its place, but our medieval ancestors, deprived of these blessings, were content to listen to tales of virgins and martyrs, rogues and heroes, giants and enchanters, fays and monsters. There was a vast appetite for narratives: humorous, sentimental, tragic, pious and romantic. To satisfy this appetite there was a large class of professionals who made a living by singing or reciting stories, and of wandering minstrels whose versatility rivaled that of Nanki-poo.

Among the Anglo-Saxons there were *scops,* who chanted to the accompaniment of the harp a poem of Sigemund the Dragon-slayer or of Wayland the Smith, and were rewarded for their skill with lands and gold rings. In Wales there was the bard who might be summoned to the queen's chamber to sing softly of Arthur's last battle at Camlan. About 1200 a count of Guines maintained at his castle near Calais three old men who on stormy evenings could recount the deeds of Roman emperors, the siege of Antioch, the loves of Tristan and Isolt, and the magic of Merlin. Every great festival—a marriage or coronation—brought a swarm of entertainers—jugglers, acrobats, musicians, dancers—and among them came *gestours* or *conteurs,* with a repertory of tales, to share in the distribution of largess. When Reynard the Fox, disguised as a minstrel, was asked about his accomplishments, he boasted that he knew Breton *lais* of Merlin, Arthur, Tristan, the Honeysuckle, and St. Brendan, and when further questioned whether he knew the *lai* of Lady Isolt, answered in English: "Ya, ya, God it wot!" As late as 1497, James IV of Scotland paid nine shillings to two fiddlers who sang the romance of *Graysteel.* Though we know from *The Decameron* and the *Canterbury Tales* that there were ladies and gentlemen, friars and nuns, even millers and carpenters who could spin good yarns to while away the time, nevertheless it is to the professionals that the major credit should go for collecting, elaborating and spreading, especially in the age before secular manuscripts became common, the vast mass of medieval fiction.

Of these storytellers some, as we have noted, enjoyed snug berths in the households of kings and barons and were regarded with high respect. Taillefer, the minstrel who rode before the advancing Norman host at Hastings and sang of Charlemagne, Roland, Oliver and the vassals who died at Roncevaux, was accorded by Duke William the high, though fatal, privilege of striking the first blow. But the great majority of these entertainers in the twelfth and thirteenth centuries seem to have been looked upon with condescension if not with contempt. The poet Chrétien de Troyes referred scornfully to those who earned their livelihood by storytelling and who in the presence of counts and kings mutilated the tale of Erec. A generation or so later another poet wrote of minstrels who went from court to court, were put up for the night, and in return told tales without rime and full of lies. Here we can detect a note of professional jealousy, and there can be no doubt that this anonymous multitude of oral reciters must have possessed some talent or they would have had no audiences. In fact, men of letters often paid them the compliment of plagiarism. Most of the Germanic, Carolingian and Arthurian legends were developed for centuries as the stock in trade of reciters and singers and had proved their worth before they were adopted as subjects for literature.

Once reduced to writing, these narratives not only were pored over by the solitary reader but also found a new class of auditors. Ladies read them aloud to a small circle; Chaucer himself implies again and again that his poems are addressed to listeners; and Froissart tells us how he read his romance of *Meliador*, night after night in the winter of 1388-89, to Count Gaston de Foix and his household at the castle of Orthez. Four of the narratives selected for inclusion in this book—*The Youth of Alexander, Aucassin and Nicolete, Havelok* and *Sir Orfeo*—give internal evidence that they were meant to be delivered orally, and the last two in all probability were actually composed by minstrels. The multiplication of manuscripts and the increased practice of reading gradually forced the professional storyteller out of the palace and the castle, and by the fourteenth century we find him usually catering to the unlettered, in the public square or the tavern. Chaucer parodied his crude rimes in "Sir Thopas." Semantics reveals the history of his degradation. The versatile *jongleur* of the twelfth century gave up the telling of tales, turned to conjuring tricks, and eventually became a juggler. The *gestour*, so called because he knew all the great *gestes* of heroes and conquerors, sank to retailing funny stories and making quips, and

so became a jester. But the work of the minstrels had long
since been done. By 1250 they had tapped all the main
sources of medieval fiction—classical, Byzantine, Celtic, Arabic, folk tales of beasts and birds, and cynical *fabliaux* from
India. The more sophisticated writers of the later Middle Ages
were largely content to recast, to amplify and to embellish
what had already been tried out in oral form by their humbler
predecessors. Only the allegory, of all the types of medieval
secular narrative, was of purely literary origin.

This volume contains some of the best of the medieval
stories that may be loosely classified as romances. In fact, the
word romance (French *roman*) was a broad term in origin
and was applied indiscriminately to any long narrative in
French verse—for example, the *Roman de Rou,* a chronicle
of Normandy; the *Roman de la Rose,* an allegory of aristo-
cratic courtship; the *Roman d'Alexandre,* the semifabulous
history of Alexander the Great. By the end of the Middle
Ages, however, the word *roman,* or *romance,* had become re-
stricted to something like its modern meaning: a tale of
knightly prowess, usually set in remote times or places and
involving elements of the fantastic or supernatural. So defined, the word would apply to all the eight stories in this
book. These eight examples of the type illustrate its range
and variety. Their authors were French, German and English;
two of them must be counted among the greatest geniuses of
their kind that the Middle Ages produced—Gottfried von
Strassburg and the composer of *Gawain and the Green
Knight.* Three texts survive in only a single manuscript,
Aucassin, Havelok and *Gawain and the Green Knight,* and
must have been little known in their day; whereas the romances of Perceval and Tristan and the episode of Alexander's celestial journey enjoyed an enormous popularity. The
same dark cloud of tragedy hangs over the star-crossed lovers
Tristan and Isolt as over Romeo and Juliet. Fate's ironies

determine the life and death of Balin with a Hardyesque rigor. On the other hand, in *Aucassin, Sir Orfeo* and *Havelok,* after trials and separations the lover or husband is rejoined to his lady and they live happily ever after. And humor, none too common in medieval romance, plays over the blunders of young Perceval, the precocious aeronautics of Alexander, and the adventures of Aucassin, while the comic spirit is not absent from the dialogues of Gawain with his temptress.

The translations are by divers hands, and, as the reader will recognize, there has been no attempt at achieving a uniform style throughout; indeed, a uniform style would not suit narratives so different. The editors are grateful for permission to use the rendering of *Sir Gawain and the Green Knight* by Mr. M. R. Ridley. As for Malory, there has happily been no need for modernization except, of course, in the spelling. We have allowed Miss Weston's abridgment of Gottfried's poem to stand; the *Youth of Alexander* consists of excerpts; and some of the diffuseness and awkwardness of *Havelok* has been remedied, we hope, by a tighter style. But these subtractions, we believe, have done no injustice to the original poems, and the reader can be assured that there have been no conscious additions or changes to alter the meaning, though, alas, we cannot assure him that any translation reproduces adequately the charm and the force of such masterpieces as the *Tristan* of Gottfried and *Gawain and the Green Knight.*

So we open the gate and bid the reader pass into the garden of romance with a quotation from Chaucer's *Parliament of Fowls* in mind:

> *This is the way to al good aventure.*
> *Be glad, thow redere, and thy sorwe ofcaste;*
> *Al open am I—passe in, and speed thee faste.*

ROGER SHERMAN LOOMIS
LAURA HIBBARD LOOMIS

MEDIEVAL
ROMANCES

PERCEVAL,

OR THE STORY OF THE GRAIL

by Chrétien de Troyes

FOREWORD

Of all the romances of the Middle Ages, those which celebrate King Arthur and the knights and ladies of his court may be considered the most typical, as they were—and still are, thanks largely to Tennyson and Wagner—the best known. Most English-speaking people will recognize allusions to Galahad and the quest of the Grail, to Perceval, the innocent fool, to the loves of Tristan and Isolt, and to the downfall of the Round Table.

Beginning about 1100, we get scraps of evidence that Western Europe was being invaded by minstrels with a new and fascinating repertory. They were referred to as *"fabulosi Britones et eorum cantores,"* Breton storytellers and singers. They spoke French as well as Breton and were devoted to the memory of their ancestral hero, Arthur, who had checked for a time the Anglo-Saxon conquest of Britain. They were laughed at for their belief that he was still alive, but their fantastic tales captivated the imagination, and by 1175 all Christendom, from Antioch in the southeast to Iceland in the northwest, was not only convinced of Arthur's prowess but was also eager to hear more about the adventures and loves of his knights. By 1200 the Matter of Britain, as it is called, had largely supplanted in popular favor the Matter of France, concerned with Charlemagne and his paladins.

This was primarily the accomplishment of the Breton minstrels and their imitators, but a learned cleric of Breton extraction, Geoffrey of Monmouth, supplemented their efforts with his Latin *History of the Kings of Britain* (ca. 1136), which represented Arthur as expelling the Saxons, conquering Western Europe and defeating the legions of Rome. Curiously enough, Geoffrey's influence on the French romancers who came shortly after him was slight.

The first of these was Chrétien de Troyes, who enjoyed the patronage of such powerful figures as Marie, Countess of Champagne, and Philip, Count of Flanders. Between 1160 and 1185 he composed in octosyllabic couplets five longish romances concerned with knights of Arthur's court—*Erec, Cliges, Lancelot, Ivain* and *Perceval.* Though the question of Chrétien's originality is still hotly debated, it is possible to show that he drew largely on genuine traditional materials which came to him indirectly from the minstrels and which ultimately went back to Welsh and even Irish story patterns. Two of his heroes, Erec and Ivain, bear Breton names, as do many of his minor figures. His account of the abduction of Guinevere and her recovery by Lancelot has many Celtic analogues. Perceval's riding on horseback into Arthur's hall and his reception there bear a marked resemblance to Kilhwch's arrival at the same court, as described in the Welsh *Mabinogion.* Scholars have pointed out that the early history of Perceval presents a marked parallelism to the Irish stories of the boyhood of Cuchulainn and Finn. Though thus derived from various remote Celtic sources, each of Chrétien's romances, with the exception of *Cliges*, seems to have followed in outline a single French prose narrative. This conclusion may detract from the poet's originality, but it also relieves him from blame for certain puzzling or inartistic features. For example, the adventures of Gawain that occupy the latter part of the romance of Perceval (omitted from the following translation), have no relation to the hero.

That Chrétien undertook with enthusiasm the composition of this, the last of his poems, seems evident. He refers to the story, which Count Philip had commissioned him to turn into rime, as the best ever told in a royal court. He imparts a feeling of vernal gaiety to his opening scene, and retells with spirit and a keen eye for comic effects the successive blunders and gaucheries of his ingenuous hero. He invests the meeting with the Fisher King and the mystifying events which followed with exactly the right atmosphere of awe and wonder, and he is equally successful in his treatment of the startling entrance of the Loathly Damsel and her violent denunciation of Perceval. The whole development of Perceval's character from boorish naïveté to knightly courtesy and from easy triumphs of physical strength to spiritual humiliation is traced with a fine, though not a flawless, art. Though the poet had an excellent outline to follow for the first 4700 lines, there is every reason to believe that he added greatly to its charm and vitality in his elaboration.

But with the sudden diversion of narrative interest to Gawain, and even more with Perceval's visit to the hermit, the attentive reader may be excused if he feels that something has gone seriously awry. With what justice did the hermit so severely rebuke Perceval for keeping silent in the presence of the Grail when he had done so in obedience to a wise counselor to whom he owed his induction into the order of knighthood and who had told him that loquacity was a sin: *"Qui trop parole péché fait"*? With what justice could Perceval be blamed for holding his peace when he had received not the slightest intimation of the direful consequences? More disconcerting still is the hermit's assertion that the Grail which the beautiful damsel bore through the Fisher King's hall contained a sacramental wafer intended for the King's father. Were not women strictly forbidden by church councils to administer the sacrament? Moreover, the word grail means a wide and rather deep dish, commonly used, as Chrétien implies, to hold a salmon or a lamprey. Neither ecclesiastical usage nor common sense would prescribe so large a vessel for a single Mass wafer. And if the Grail Bearer had performed her errand after one passage through the hall, why a repetition of the act with every course served to the Fisher King and his guest?

Though efforts have been made to explain away these violations of canonical practice and common sense, it is my belief that here, as elsewhere, Chrétien felt bound to follow his source in its aberrations as well as in its felicities. The Grail scene was to him a mystery, and the hermit's explanation of it as unsatisfactory as it is to us. The many and wildly inconsistent legends which later medieval authors produced about the miraculously food-supplying and youth-preserving vessel reveal their perplexity, and this diversity has made it possible for modern scholars to hold the most divergent theories about the origins of the tradition. It has been derived from Persia, Egypt and Constantinople, from the rites of Adonis, and from the heretical tenets of the Albigenses.

Too few in their recondite researches have noticed certain elementary facts. Perceval was a knight from Wales; the Welsh ate from *"scutellis latis et amplis,"* "wide and capacious dishes," whereas the word grail was defined soon after Chrétien's time as *"scutella lata et aliquantulum profunda,"* "a wide and rather deep dish"; Welsh medieval tradition records a dish which, like the Grail in several romances, miraculously provided whatever food one desired; the *Mabinogion* presents us with a King Bran, who held court in North Wales, was famous for his feasts, and was wounded with a lance in the foot in battle, whereas the French romances tell us that the Fisher King was named Bron and describe his sumptuous hospitality, and Chrétien himself informs us that he was wounded in battle with a javelin through the thighs.

There are numerous other links between the Grail legend and Wales, and the elements which we cannot find in early Welsh literature can be recognized in Irish sagas of the Dark Ages, particularly in those which Professor Dillon calls *echtrae* (adventure), tales of the visits of mortals to the palaces of the gods. In them we find venerable hosts, miraculous vessels of plenty, and a young hostess, who in other stories appears as a monstrous hag, like Chrétien's Loathly Damsel.

What, then, of the Mass wafer in the Grail? For the answer one must turn back again to Wales and to King Bran, so noted for his hospitality. He possessed a horn which produced whatever drink or food one desired—a counterpart to the dish of plenty. Translated into French, the word horn in the nominative case would be *corz* or *cors,* and since drinking horns were not common in France, it would suggest *cors,* "body." The Corpus Christi, the Body of Christ, was credited in Chrétien's time with miraculous nutritive powers. Once miraculous dish and miraculous wafer were associated, no wonder that one became a receptacle for the other, even in defiance of ecclesiastical ordinance and good sense.

This natural misinterpretation of the word *cors,* which Chrétien presumably took over from his source, was repeated in one form or another by successive romancers and led to the gradual Christianization of the legend, to the misconception of the Grail as a chalice, to the identification of the bleeding lance with the lance of Longinus which pierced the side of Christ, and to the substitution of the virgin Galahad for the amorous Perceval as the hero of the Grail quest. Seldom, if ever, has a misconception inspired a literature so vast, so beautiful, so strange; and Chrétien's poem, the first example of that literature, though it puzzles one as a consequence of that misconception, enthralls one by its strange beauty.

R. S. L.

He who sows little reaps little, and let him who wishes to reap scatter his seed on ground that will yield him a hundredfold, for on poor earth good seed dries up and dies. Chrétien sows the romance which he is beginning in so good a place that he cannot fail to gain great profit, for he does it for the worthiest man in the empire of Rome; that is, the Count Philip of Flanders, who is of greater worth than Alexander was. Though Alexander is said to be a model, I will prove that he did not equal the Count, for he gathered in himself all the sins and vices from which the Count is pure and free.

The Count does not listen to coarse buffoonery or insolent boasts, and grieves if he hears slander spoken of anyone. The Count loves justice, loyalty, and Holy Church, and hates all uncourtly behavior. His generosity is greater than anyone knows, for he gives without hypocrisy and without guile, according to the gospel, which says: "Let not thy left hand know what thy right hand doeth." Only they know his largess who receive it, and God, who sees all secrets and knows the inmost feelings of the heart and the bowels. Why does the Gospel say: "Hide thy good deeds from thy left hand"? The left hand, according to the story, means vainglory, which comes from false hypocrisy. What does the right hand mean? Charity, which does not boast of its good works but rather covers them up so that no one knows of them save Him who is called both God and charity. According to the text, God is charity, and whoever lives in charity—St. Paul says it and I have read it—abides in God and God in him.

Understand truly, therefore, that the gifts which the good Count Philip makes are gifts of charity; for no one persuades

* Translated by R. S. Loomis.

him but his generous, noble heart, which counsels him to do good. Is he not worth more than Alexander, who cared nothing for charity or any other virtue? Yes, without the slightest doubt. Therefore, Chrétien will not have toiled in vain when by the command of the Count he strives to put into rime the best tale which may be told in a royal court. That is the story of the Grail, of which the Count gave him the book. You will now hear how he acquits himself.

It was in the season when trees bloom, bushes put forth leaves, meadows turn green, birds sweetly sing in their language at dawn, and all things are aflame with joy, that the son of the widow lady of the lonely wild forest arose and easily saddled his hunter, took three javelins, and thus left his mother's manor, thinking that he would go to see his mother's harrowers, who were harrowing her oats with twelve oxen and six harrows. So he entered the forest, and at once his heart rejoiced at the sweet season and at hearing the warbling of the birds. All these things pleased him, and, filled with the sweetness of the calm weather, he took the bridle from his hunter and let him graze the fresh, greening grass. And the lad, who knew well how to cast the javelins that he carried, walked about casting them, now behind, now before, now low, now high, until he heard coming through the wood five knights, armed at all points. Their arms made a great crashing as they came, for the branches of the oaks and hornbeams struck them, the lances knocked against the shields, and all the coats of mail clinked. The wood of the shields and the steel of the mail cried out. The noble youth heard but did not see those who were approaching at a rapid pace; he wondered and said: "By my soul, the lady my mother told me the truth when she said that devils are the most terrible thing in the world and taught me that one ought to cross oneself against them. But I scorn her teaching and will not cross myself; rather I will strike the strongest with one of the javelins I am carrying, so that none of the others, I think, will dare to come near me."

Thus the youth talked to himself before he caught sight of them. But when he saw them clearly as they appeared out of the wood and observed the jingling coats of mail and the bright, gleaming helmets and the lances and the shields, such as he had never seen before, and when he descried the green and the vermilion catching the light of the sun, and the gold, blue, and silver, he was so delighted that he exclaimed: "Ah, Lord God, have mercy! These are angels that I see. Alas, now I was very wrong when I said that they were devils! My mother, who told me that angels were the most beautiful things there are, except God, who is more beautiful than everything else, was telling no lie. Here I see God himself, I think, for one of them is so fair to look at that the others, God keep me! have not a tenth of his beauty. My mother herself said that one must believe in God and adore, bow the knee, and honor Him. I will adore this one and all the others too."

At once he threw himself on the ground, reciting the creed and the prayers which his mother had taught him. The master of the knights saw him and said: "Stay back! For this youth has fallen to the ground for fear at sight of us. If we all went together toward him, it seems to me he would be so frightened he would die and he could not reply to anything I asked him."

They stopped, and the leader went quickly to the youth, greeted and reassured him, saying: "Young sir, do not be afraid."

"I am not afraid," said the youth, "by the Savior in whom I believe. Are you God?"

"No, by my faith."

"Who are you then?"

"I am a knight."

"I have never known a knight," said the youth, "nor have I seen one, nor ever heard talk of one. But you are more beautiful than God. If only I could be like you, so shining and shaped just so!"

At this word the knight drew near him and asked: "Have you seen in this glade five knights and three maidens?"

The youth had his mind set on asking about other matters. He put out his hand and took hold of the knight's lance, and said: "Fair dear sir, you who call yourself a knight, what is this that you hold?"

"Now you have given me very useful instructions, it seems!" said the knight. "I expected to get some information from you, my good friend, and now you want to learn something from me. But I will tell you; it is my lance."

"Tell me, does one cast it as I do my javelins?"

"Not at all, young sir, you are very foolish. One uses it to strike a blow."

"Then one of my three javelins that you see here is better, for, whenever I want to, I kill birds and animals with them as far away as a crossbow will shoot an arrow."

"Young sir, I have nothing to do with that. But answer my question about the knights. Tell me if you know where they are, and have you seen the maidens?"

The youth took hold of the edge of the shield and said: "What is this and what is it for?"

"Young sir, this is a trick to make me talk of things other than those which I asked about. So God help me, I expected you to give me news rather than to give instructions to you! Now you expect me to teach you! I will tell you, then, how this is managed, for you please me. This thing I carry is called a shield."

"Is called a shield?"

"Certainly, and I must never despise it, for it is so trustworthy that if anyone throws or shoots at me, it wards off all the blows. That is the service it renders me."

Then the knights who had remained behind rode up to their lord and said at once: "Sir, what does this Welsh lad tell you?"

The lord said: "He knows nothing of manners, so God help me, for he never answers properly any question I ask, but instead he asks the name of anything he sees and what it is good for."

"Sir, be assured that the Welsh are all by nature more stupid than beasts at pasture, and this one too is like a beast. It is a foolish man who stops to deal with him unless he wishes to trifle away his time."

"So God keep me, I do not know, but before I go farther, I will tell him whatever he wishes, and I will not depart otherwise." Then he asked again: "Young sir, do not be annoyed, but tell me if you have met or seen the five knights and the maidens."

The youth grasped and pulled the skirt of the coat of mail and said: "Tell me, good sir, what is this you are wearing?"

"Young sir, do you not know?"

"I do not."

"Young sir, it is my hauberk, and is heavy as iron."

"Is it of iron?"

"You see that it is."

"I know nothing about it, but, so God save me, it is very beautiful. What do you do with it and what use is it?"

"Young sir, that is easy to say. If now you wished to throw javelins or shoot arrows at me, you could do me no harm."

"Sir knight, God keep the hinds and the harts from wearing such hauberks, for then I could not kill any or chase them."

The knight repeated: "Young sir, so God help you, can you give me news of the knights and the maidens?"

The boy, who had little sense, said: "Were you born like this?"

"Not at all, young sir, no one can be born like this."

"Who, then, dressed you this way?"

"Young sir, I will tell you."

"Tell me then."

"Willingly. It is not yet five whole days since King Arthur knighted me and gave me all this armor. But now answer me; what has become of the knights who passed this way, escorting the three maidens? Were they riding slowly or were they in flight?"

The youth said: "Sir, now look at that very high wood which surrounds that mountain: there is the pass of Snowdon."

"And what of that, fair brother?"

"There are my mother's laborers who harrow and plow her fields, and if those people passed that way they would see them and tell you."

The knights agreed to go with him if he would lead them to the men who were harrowing the field of oats. The youth mounted his hunter and went where the laborers were harrowing. When they spied their lord, they trembled for fear. Do you know why? Because of the knights whom they saw accompanying him in arms, for they knew well that if the knights told him of their way of life he would wish to be one also, and his mother would go out of her mind. She had taken precautions to prevent him from ever seeing a knight or learning anything of knighthood.

The youth said to the ox-drivers: "Have you seen five knights and three maidens come this way?"

"They have been following the pass all this day," said the ox-drivers.

The youth said to the knight who had been conversing with him: "Sir, the knights and the maidens have taken this road. But now tell me more of the king who makes knights and where is he most often found."

"Young sir, I will tell you; the King is now at Carlisle. Five days have not passed since he was there, for I was there and saw him. If you do not find him there, there will be someone surely to direct you; he will not yet have gone so far that you will not hear news of him there."

At once the knight departed at a great gallop, so that he should not be too late to overtake the others. The youth was not slow to return to his manor, where his mother grieved in her heart for his delay. But she rejoiced the moment she saw him and could not hide her delight, and like a doting mother ran to him and called him "fair son, fair son" more than a hundred times. "Fair son, my heart has been torn by your absence. I have almost died of anxiety. Where have you been so long today?"

"Where, lady? I will tell you without any lies that I have seen something that made me very happy. Have you not often told me that the angels of our Lord God are so beautiful that Nature never made any creature so beautiful and that nothing in the world is more beautiful?"

"Fair son, I say it again; I said it truly and I repeat it."

"Hush, Mother! Did I not see just now the most beautiful things there are, passing through the wild forest? They are more beautiful, I think, than God and his angels."

The mother took him in her arms and said: "Fair son, I entrust you to God, for I am in terror for you. I believe you have seen those angels of whom everyone complains and who kill all they meet."

"I have not, Mother; truly I have not. They say they are called knights."

The mother swooned at the word when she heard him mention knights, and when she recovered she spoke like a woman in anger: "Alas, wretch that I am! Fair sweet son, I thought I would protect you so well from chivalry that you would never hear or see anything of it. You would have become a knight, fair son, if it had pleased God that your father and your friends had the care of you. There was no knight so honored and so feared, fair son, as your father was in all the isles of the sea. You can boast indeed that neither his lineage nor mine is a disgrace to you, for I am descended from the best knights of this country. In the isles of the sea there was no family better than mine in my time. But the best have fallen on evil days. One can see in many places that misfortunes overtake those who uphold honor and prowess. Wickedness, shame, and sloth prosper, for they cannot fall, but the good are doomed to ruin. If you do not know it, your father was wounded through the thighs so that he was maimed in body. The great lands and great treasures which he had won by his valor, all were lost and he fell into great poverty. After the death of King Uther Pendragon, the father of King Arthur, the noblemen were wrongfully impoverished, disinherited, and banished. Their lands were devastated and the poorer folk rendered destitute. Whoever could flee, fled. Your father had this manor here in this wild forest. He could not flee but had himself brought here hastily in a litter, for he knew no other refuge. You were a little suckling, scarce more than two years old. You had two very fair brothers. When they were big enough, they went by their father's counsel to royal courts to receive arms and horses. The elder went to the King of Escavalon and served him till he was dubbed knight. The younger took service with King Ban of Gomeret. On one and the same day both the youths were made knights, and on that day they started to return home, wishing to bring joy to me and their father, who never saw them alive, for they were both vanquished in combat and slain in combat. For this I suffer great anguish and grief. A strange thing happened to the elder: crows and rooks pecked out his eyes; thus people found them dead. Their father died of sorrow for his sons, and I have led a bitter life since his death. You were all the comfort and all the good I had, for all others were gone. God had left me nothing else to gladden my heart."

The youth hardly listened to what his mother told him, but said: "Give me something to eat. I do not know what you are talking about, but I want to go to the king who makes knights, and I will go, whomever it may displease!"

His mother detained and kept him as long as she could, and fitted him out with a large canvas shirt and breeches made in the fashion of Wales, where they make breeches and hose of one piece, I think; he had also a coat and hood of buckskin which fastened about him. Thus his mother equipped him. He stayed only three days; her caresses availed no longer to keep him.

Then his mother felt a strange grief; weeping, she kissed and embraced him, and said: "I feel a deep sorrow now that I see you depart, fair son. You will go to the court of the King and ask him to give you arms. There will be no refusal; I know he will give them to you. But when you try to use those arms, what will happen? How will you know how to do what you have never done before and never seen others doing? I fear you will do badly; you will be wholly unskilled, and it does not seem strange to me that one does not know what one has not learned. Rather is it strange when one fails to learn what one has often heard and seen. Fair son, I wish to teach you a lesson which you will do well to hear, and if it pleases you to remember it, great profit can come to you. You will soon become a knight, my son, if it please God, and I approve it. If, near or far, you find a lady who needs help, or a maiden in distress, do not withhold your aid if they ask for it; for in this all honor lies. He who does not yield honor to

ladies, loses his own honor. Serve ladies and maidens, and
you will receive honor everywhere. If you ask a favor of any,
avoid offending her and do nothing to displease her. He who
wins a kiss from a maiden receives much; if she permits you
to kiss her, I forbid you to take more if, for my sake, you are
willing to forego it. If she has a ring on her finger or a purse
at her girdle, and if for love or for entreaty she gives it to
you, it will be right and proper for you to wear her ring; I
give you leave to take the ring or the purse. Fair son, I would
tell you another thing: never on the road or at an inn keep
company long with someone before inquiring his name. Learn
his name, for by the name one knows the man. Fair son, speak
with noble men and go with them; a noble man never gives
bad counsel to those who frequent his company. Above
erything I beseech you to enter church and minster and pray
Our Lord to give you honor in this world and grant you so to
act that you may come to a good end."

"Mother, what is church?"

"A place where service is rendered to Him who made
heaven and earth and placed men and animals on it."

"And what is minster?"

"The same, my son; a beautiful and holy house, with relics
and treasures, where one sacrifices the body of Jesus Christ,
the holy prophet, whom the Jews treated so shamefully. He
was betrayed and wrongly condemned and suffered the agony
of death for men and women; for their souls, when they left
their bodies, went to hell, and it was He who delivered them.
He was bound to a pillar, scourged, and crucified, wearing a
crown of thorns. I charge you to go to the minsters to hear
Masses and matins and to worship that Lord."

"Then I will gladly go to churches and minsters from this
time on," said the youth; "I give you my promise."

Without further delay he took his leave, and his mother
wept. His saddle was ready, and he himself was equipped

after the Welsh fashion with brogues of rawhide. Wherever he went he was wont to carry three javelins, and he had intended to take them, but his mother made him leave two behind so that he would not seem too Welsh, and she would gladly have made him leave all three if it had been possible. He carried a willow switch in his right hand to whip his horse. Weeping, his mother kissed him whom she loved so dearly at his departure, and prayed God to keep him.

"Fair son," she said, "God give you wherever you go greater joy than remains with me!"

After the youth had ridden a stone's throw, he looked back and saw his mother fallen at the end of the bridge; she lay in a swoon as if she had dropped dead. But he applied his switch to the croup of his hunter, which went off without stumbling and carried him at high speed through the great dark forest. He rode from morning till evening, and lay in the forest that night till the bright day dawned.

The youth rose early, to the song of birds, mounted, and rode steadily till he saw a tent pitched in a fair meadow beside a spring. The tent was wonderfully beautiful; a part was scarlet, the other green, striped with gold embroidery. On top was a gilded eagle, on which the sun struck clear and red, so that the whole meadow was brightened by the brilliance of the tent. Around the tent, which was the most beautiful in the world, were arranged leafy bowers and Welsh lodges. The youth rode toward the tent, and before entering, said: "O God, it is Thy house I see. I should do wrong if I did not go and worship Thee. Surely my mother was telling the truth when she said that a minster was the most beautiful thing there is, and told me that if ever I found one I should go and worship the Creator in whom I believe. I will go pray Him to give me something to eat, for I need it badly."

Then he came to the tent, found it open, and saw, within,

a bed covered with a silk brocade. On the bed there lay alone a damsel sleeping. Her maidens were far away, for they had gone to pick fresh flowers with intent to strew them over the floor of the pavilion, according to custom. As the youth entered, his horse stumbled so heavily that the damsel heard it and awoke trembling. The youth spoke in his innocence: "Maiden, I greet you as my mother told me to do. My mother taught me to greet maidens wherever I met them."

The maiden quaked for fear of the youth, whom she took for an idiot, and she blamed her own folly for being discovered by him thus alone. She cried: "Young sir, go away! Flee, that my lover may not see you!"

"By my head," said the youth, "I will kiss you first, no matter whom it annoys, for my mother taught me to."

"I will not kiss you, indeed," said the maiden, "if I can help it. Flee, so that my lover will not find you, for if he does, you are as good as dead."

The youth had strong arms and embraced her clumsily, knowing no better, and stretched her out under him, and though she defended herself and struggled to escape as best she could, her effort was vain. For the youth kissed her willy-nilly twenty times without stopping, as the tale tells, until he saw on her finger a ring with a very bright emerald.

"My mother told me besides," said he, "to take the ring on your finger, but not to do anything more. Here, give me the ring; I want it."

"Indeed," said the maiden, "you will not have my ring, of that be assured, unless you snatch it from my finger by force."

The youth seized her hand, stretched out her finger by force, took the ring, slipped it on his own finger, and said: "I wish you well. I will go away now quite happy. Your kisses are much better than any handmaid's in my mother's household, for your mouth is not bitter."

She wept and said to the youth: "Do not take away my

ring, for I shall be in a sad state, and you will lose your life, sooner or later, I promise you."

The youth paid no attention to what he heard, but was dying of hunger because of his fast. He spied a leather bottle full of wine and beside it a silver goblet and on a bundle of rushes a new white towel. He lifted it and found underneath three good venison pasties, new made. This was a repast for which he felt no repugnance. Consumed with hunger, he broke one of the pasties before him and ate it with avidity, filled the silver cup with wine which was by no means bad, took big and frequent drafts, and said: "Maiden, I cannot finish these pasties today. Come and eat; they are good. One apiece will be enough for us, and there will be a whole one left."

All this while she wept, though he prayed and urged her. She answered not a word but wept piteously and loud and wrung her hands. He ate as much as he wished and drank till he had had enough. Then he covered up the remainder and promptly took his leave and commended her to God, though little it pleased her. "God save you," said he, "fair friend! For God's sake, do not be sorry for the ring I am taking, because I will repay you for it before I die. Now, with your leave, I am going."

She wept and refused to commend him to God, for on his account she was bound to endure such disgrace and trouble as no wretched woman ever had, and so long as he lived she would receive no help from him; let him understand that he had betrayed her.

Thus she remained in tears. Before long her lover returned from hunting in the wood. Seeing the hoof tracks of the youth who had gone his way, he was troubled, and when he found his mistress weeping, he said: "Damsel, I perceive by these signs that a knight has been here."

"No, my lord, on my faith. But there has been a Welsh lad, a rude, clownish fool, who drank all he pleased of your wine and ate one of your pasties."

"Why do you weep for that, my fair one? If he had drunk and eaten everything, I would have been willing."

"There was more, my lord," said she. "There was a struggle for my ring. He took it from me and carried it away. I would rather die than have him bear it away."

At that the man was disturbed and troubled in his heart. "By my faith," said he, "that was an insult! But since he has taken it, let him keep it. But I suspect that there was more; if there was, do not hide it."

"My lord," said she, "he kissed me."

"Kissed you?"

"Indeed, I tell you the truth, but it was against my will."

"Say rather that you took pleasure in it and refused him nothing!" said he, in a torment of jealousy. "Do you think that I do not know you? Surely, I know you too well and am not so blind or so squint-eyed that I do not see your falsity. You have started on a wicked path; you have taken a painful road. Your horse shall not have his feed of oats nor shall he be let blood until I am avenged. If he casts a shoe, he shall not be shod again. If he dies, you shall follow me on foot. The clothes which you are wearing shall not be changed, but you shall follow me on foot and naked until I have his head. No other punishment will I choose." He then sat down and began to eat.

Meanwhile, the youth rode on until he saw a charcoal-burner approaching, driving an ass before him. "Carl, you there, driving the ass, show me the shortest way to Carlisle. They tell me that there King Arthur, whom I want to see, makes knights."

"Young sir, in that direction there is a castle standing by the sea. If you go there, good friend, you will find King Arthur in the castle, both happy and sad."

"Now tell me what I want to know, how the King can be both happy and sad."

"I will tell you very quickly. King Arthur with all his army has fought with King Rion, and the King of the Isles was beaten, and it is that which makes King Arthur glad. He is angry with his companions who have gone back to their castles where they find it pleasanter to live, and he does not know what has happened to them. That makes the King sad."

The youth did not care a penny for the information, except that he took the road which the charcoal-burner had shown. He saw a splendid, strong castle well situated above the sea, and presently descried issuing from the gate an armed knight bearing a golden cup in his hand. With his left hand he held his lance, bridle, and shield, and the golden cup in his right. His arms, all scarlet, became him well. The youth, seeing the fresh, handsome arms, was pleased and said to himself: "By my faith, I will ask the King for these. If he gives them to me, I shall be well satisfied, and a curse on him who would want any others!"

At once, feeling impatient to reach the court, he rode rapidly toward the castle until he met the knight, who stopped him for a moment and asked: "Young sir, where are you going, tell me?"

"I am going to court to ask the King for these arms of yours."

"Young sir, it is right for you to do so. Go quickly and return. Tell the evil King if he will not hold his land as my vassal, let him yield it, or let him send someone out to defend it against me, for I declare that it is mine. Let him believe you by this token that just now I seized in his presence the cup I am carrying, with all the wine he was drinking."

The knight might better have found someone else to take the message, for the youth did not listen to a word, but hastened to the court where the King and the knights were seated at their repast. He rode into the hall, which was on the ground level, paved and as long as wide. King Arthur sat at the head of the table, sunk in thought; all the rest talked and amused themselves, save him who remained pensive and mute. The youth advanced, but he did not know whom to greet, for he did not recognize the King. Yonet, holding a knife in his hand, came to meet him. The newcomer said: "Young sir, you there, with the knife in your hand, show me who is the King."

Yonet was very courteous and replied: "Friend, behold him there."

The youth rode at once toward the King and greeted him as best as he knew how. The King remained brooding and uttered no word. Again the youth spoke; still the King brooded and uttered no sound.

"By my faith," said the youth then, "this King never made a knight! When I cannot drag a word out of him, how could he make a knight?"

Preparing to depart, the youth turned the head of his hunter, but, like an idiot, he had brought him so close to the King that actually the horse knocked the cap off his head onto the table. The King raised his head, turned toward the youth, and, dismissing his cares, said: "Good brother, welcome! Pray do not take it ill that I met your greeting with silence. Anger kept me from replying. My worst enemy, who hates and terrifies me most, has even here laid claim to my land, and is so mad as to threaten to take it, whether I will or no. He is called the Red Knight of the Forest of Quinqueroi. The Queen had come to sit with me in order to see and comfort these wounded knights. That knight would not have roused my anger, whatever he said, but he snatched the cup before

me and raised it so wildly that all the wine with which it
was filled poured over the Queen. That was a vile and churlish deed! Therefore the Queen, burning with sorrow and anger, has gone to her chamber, where she will die. So help me
God, I do not believe she can escape alive."

The youth did not care an onion for what the King said;
nor did his grief nor the Queen's humiliation make any im-
pression. "Make me a knight, sir King," said he, "because I
am eager to be gone."

The eyes in the countenance of the young barbarian were
bright and smiling. Though no one who saw him thought
him other than mad, all found him handsome and noble.
"Friend," said the King, "dismount and give your hunter to
this squire, who will care for it and perform your pleasure. I
vow to God that your request shall be granted, to my honor
and to your profit."

The youth answered: "The knights I met in the glade did
not dismount, and you want me to dismount? But knight me
quickly and then I will go."

"Ah," said the King, "dear good friend, I will do it gladly,
to your profit and my honor."

"By the faith I owe my Maker, good sir King," said the
youth, "I will never be a knight unless I am a red knight.
Give me the arms of the man I met outside the gate who
was carrying away your golden cup."

The seneschal, who was wounded, was angry at what he
heard and said: "Friend, you are right. Go at once and take
away his arms, for they are yours. You were no fool when you
came here to get them."

"Kay," said the King, "in God's name, I beg you. You are
too ready to mock and do not care who is the butt. It is un-
becoming a gentleman. If the youth is simple-minded, he is
still, I think, well born. If he has been thus trained by a
boorish master, he may yet prove brave and wise. It is churlish

to make a jest of others and to promise without giving. A gentleman should not promise anything that he cannot or will not bestow, for he earns the ill will of him who, but for that promise, would be his friend and who, after the promise is made, expects it to be kept. You should learn that it is better to refuse outright than to rouse vain expectations. To tell the truth, he mocks and deceives himself who promises and does not fulfill, for he loses the heart of his friend."

Thus the King rebuked Kay. As the youth departed, he noticed a fair maiden and greeted her. She returned his greeting and said, laughing: "Young sir, if you live long enough, I believe in my heart that in all the world there will not be, nor will there be acknowledged, a better knight than you. This is my faith and firm belief."

Now this maiden had not laughed for more than six years, and she spoke so loudly that all heard her. Kay, touched to the quick by these words, leaped up, and with the palm of his hand dealt her tender face such a stout blow that he stretched her on the ground. After striking the maiden, he was about to return to his seat when he came upon a fool, standing by the fireplace, and kicked him into the flames in anger because the fool had often declared: "This maiden will never laugh till she sees him who will win the lordship of knighthood." The dwarf screamed, the maiden wept, but the youth did not pause and, without asking counsel of anyone, rode after the Red Knight.

Yonet, who knew all the shortest passages and was eager to bring news to the court, ran alone through a garden beside the hall and descended through a postern till he came to the road just where the Red Knight was waiting for a knightly adventure. The Welsh youth now approached at high speed to seize his arms. The knight, while waiting, had set down the golden cup on a block of brown stone. As soon as the youth came within hearing, he cried: "Lay down your weapons! Carry them no longer, for King Arthur sends you this order!"

The knight inquired: "Young sir, does no one dare to come here to uphold the King's cause? If so, do not hide it from me."

"What the devil! Are you jesting with me, sir knight, that you have not yet stripped off my arms? Take them off at once, I command you."

"Young sir, I ask you whether anyone is coming on the King's behalf to fight with me."

"Sir knight, take off the arms at once, or I will take them off myself, for I will not let you keep them longer. Understand me, I will strike you if you make me talk any more about it."

Then the knight was furious, raised his lance with both hands, and gave the youth a blow across the shoulders with the butt, so that he made him crouch over the neck of his horse. The youth, enraged in his turn when he felt himself bruised by the stroke, aimed as well as he could at the knight's eye and let fly a javelin. It struck him through the eye and brain, so that he saw and heard no more, and the blood and brains oozed out at the nape of his neck. With the agony his heart stopped, and he fell full length to the earth. The youth alighted, laid the lance aside, took the shield from his neck, but could not remove the helm from his head, for he did not know how to grasp it. He sought to ungird the sword, but he did not know how, and he could not draw it from the sheath, but grasped the sheath and pulled and pulled.

Yonet began to laugh when he saw the youth so occupied. "What is it, friend?" he said; "what are you doing?"

"I do not know. I thought your King had given me these arms, but I will have to cut up the dead man for chops before I can get any of them, for they stick so to the body that the inside and the outside seem to be of one piece; they hold together so fast."

"Do not vex yourself," said Yonet, "for I will separate them if you wish."

"Do so then at once," said the youth, "and give them to me without delay."

Yonet promptly stripped the body, even down to the toes, removing coat and hose of mail, helmet, and every other piece of armor. But the youth would not take off his own garments, nor, in spite of anything Yonet said, would he put on the comfortable padded silk tunic which the knight had worn under his coat of mail; nor would he remove the brogues from his own feet, but said: "What the devil! are you mocking me? Change my good clothes that my mother made for me the other day for the clothes of this knight? Do you wish me to put off my thick shirt of hemp for this soft thin one, and my jacket that keeps out the water for this that will not stop a drop? Shame on his neck who would exchange his good clothes for another's bad ones!"

It is a hard task to teach a fool. The lad would take nothing but the arms and would heed no request. Yonet laced the mail hose on his legs, attached the spurs to his brogues, then put on the coat of mail so that none ever looked better, fitted the helm over the padded skullcap becomingly, and showed how to gird on the sword so that it swung loosely. Then he placed the lad's foot in the stirrup and made him mount the war horse. The youth had never seen a stirrup before and was not used to spurs but only to whip or willow switch. Yonet brought the shield and lance and handed them over to him. Before Yonet departed, the youth said: "Friend, take my hunter and lead him away, for he is a very good one. I give him to you because I have no more need of him. And take the cup to the King and greet him for me. And tell the maiden whom Kay struck on the cheek that if I can, before I die, I hope to cook him such a dish that she will be well avenged."

Yonet replied that he would return the cup to the King and carry the message faithfully. So the two parted. Yonet entered through the door the hall where the barons were gathered, bringing the cup back to the King, and said: "Sire, rejoice now, for your knight who was here returns your cup to you."

"Of what knight do you speak?" said the King, who was still in a rage of anger.

"In God's name, sire," said Yonet, "I speak of the youth who but now departed."

"Do you speak," said the King, "of the Welsh youth who asked me for the red colored arms of the knight who has many times done all he could to humiliate me?"

"Sire, indeed it is he."

"How did he recover my cup? Did the knight love him or prize him so much that he yielded it of his free will?"

"Nay; rather, the youth made him pay dearly, for he killed the knight."

"How was that, good friend?"

"Sire, I know only that the knight struck the youth a painful blow with his lance, and the youth struck him back with a javelin through the eyehole so that the blood and the brains flowed out behind, and hurled him dead to the earth."

Then the King said to the seneschal: "Ah, Kay, what harm you have done me today! By your evil tongue, so ready with idle chatter, you have driven away a knight who this day has done me great service."

"Sire," said Yonet to the King, "by my head, he sent a message by me to the Queen's handmaid, whom Kay struck in hatred and scorn, that he would avenge her if he lives and if the chance offers."

The fool, who was sitting beside the fire, heard these words, leapt to his feet, came before the King, and skipped and danced for glee, saying: "Lord King, so God save me, your adventures now begin, and often you will find them perilous and hard. I pledge you that Kay will surely regret his feet and his hands and his stupid, churlish tongue. Before forty days have passed, the young knight will have avenged the kick Kay gave me, and the buffet he gave the maiden will be well paid back, for his right arm will be broken between the elbow and the shoulder, and he will carry it slung from his shoulder for half a year; he can escape it no more than death."

At this speech Kay was so enraged that he almost burst with malice and anger and could hardly keep from killing the fool before the whole court. But he did not attack him because it would displease the King. The King exclaimed: "Ah, ah, Kay, how you have offended me today! If anyone had taught and trained the youth a little about the arms so that he would know how to defend himself, and likewise about his shield and lance, he without doubt would have been a good knight. But the youth knows little of arms or anything else, for he could not even draw a sword if there were need. There he is sitting on his horse; he will meet a knight who will not hesitate to maim him for the sake of his horse. He will speedily be left dead or crippled. He is so simple-minded and brutish that he will soon have played his last stake."

Thus the King mourned for the youth and looked down-cast, but there was nothing to be gained by that, and he fell silent. Meanwhile, the youth without a pause went spurring through the forest till he came to a plain bordering a river which was wider than a crossbow shot, for all the water of the countryside flowed through its bed. He crossed a meadow toward the great rushing river but he did not descend into it, for he saw that it was very deep and black and swifter than the Loire. So he followed the bank. Opposite, there was a tall cliff whose base was washed by the stream, and on the side which sloped toward the sea there stood a noble, strong castle. Where the river entered the bay the youth turned to the left and saw the towers of the castle, which seemed to him to grow out of the castle. In the middle stood a huge and mighty keep. Toward the bay, where the river fought with the tide, stood a strong barbican, and the waves beat against its foot. At the four corners of the walls, built of hard stone, there were four low turrets, strong and fair. The castle was finely situated and well furnished within. In front of a round outwork a bridge of sandstone and limestone was built across the river, strong, high, with battlemented parapets, and in the middle a tower. At the near end was a drawbridge, fitted for its purpose, to serve as a passageway by day and as a closed gate by night. The youth proceeded to the bridge.

On it a lord, clad in an ermine robe, was pacing for his pleasure, and he waited the approach of the newcomer. He was holding for dignity's sake a short staff, and near him were two squires without mantles. The newcomer remembered well his mother's lesson, for he bowed to the lord and said: "Sir, my mother taught me that."

"God bless you, fair brother!" said the lord, who perceived that the stranger was uncouth and silly of speech, and he added: "Fair brother, whence have you come?"

"Whence? From King Arthur's court."

"What did you do there?"

"The King made me a knight, good luck to him!"

"A knight? God save me, but I did not think that at this time his mind was on such things. I thought rather that he was concerned with other matters than making knights. Now tell me, gentle brother, who gave you these arms?"

"The King gave them to me."

"Gave them? How?"

The youth related what you have already heard; to retell it

would be tedious and futile, for no story gains by repetition. The lord then asked what he did with his horse.

"I make him run up hill and down dale, just as I used to make the hunter I had in my mother's house."

"Tell me also, fair friend, what you can do with your arms."

"I know well how to put them on and take them off, just as the squire did who put them on me and took them off the knight whom I had killed. And they are so light to wear that they do not tire me at all."

"By God's soul," said the lord, "that I am glad to hear. Now tell me, if it does not annoy you, what errand brought you here."

"Sir, my mother taught me to go to men of rank to get their advice and to trust it, because good comes to those who believe them."

The lord replied: "Fair brother, blessed be your mother, for she gave you sound counsel. But have you more to say?"

"Yes."

"What?"

"Only this and no more, that you give me lodging tonight."

"Gladly," said the lord; "but grant me a favor which will bring you much good."

"What is it?"

"That you take your mother's advice and mine."

"By my faith, I grant it."

"Then dismount."

The youth dismounted, and one of the two squires who had come up took his horse and the other removed his arms, so that he stood in his rude costume, with the brogues and in the ill-made and ill-fitting coat of buckskin which his mother had given him. The lord then had the sharp steel spurs which the youth had brought attached to his own feet, mounted the horse, hung the shield by the strap around his neck, grasped the lance, and said: "Friend, now take a lesson in arms and watch how to hold a lance, and how to spur and check a horse."

Then he displayed the pennon and showed how to hold the shield, a little forward so that it touched the horse's neck. He laid the lance in rest, and pricked the horse, worth a hundred marks, which no other surpassed for ardor, speed, and strength. The lord was skilled in the management of shield, horse, and lance, since he had been trained in it from boyhood. All that he did delighted the youth, and when he had finished his expert tilting before the youth, who had watched it closely, he returned with his lance upright, and inquired: "Friend, would you too like to know how to manage lance and shield and how to spur and control a horse?"

The youth answered at once that he did not care to live another day or to own wealth or lands before he had learned how to do the same. The lord said: "Dear good friend, what one does not know one can learn if he will take the pains. Every profession demands effort, heart, and practice; every knowledge comes by these three. But since you have never done these things nor seen others do them, you cannot be shamed or blamed if you do not know how."

Then the lord caused the youth to mount, and he began to carry lance and shield as adroitly as if he had passed all his days in tourneys and wars and had journeyed throughout the world seeking battle and adventure. For it came to him by nature, and when Nature teaches and the heart attends, nothing can be too hard. With the aid of these two, the youth performed so well that it greatly pleased the lord, and he said in his heart that if his pupil had devoted all his life to arms, he would have become a master. When the youth had carried out the exercise, he returned to the lord with his lance erect as he had seen it held, and said: "Sir, did I do well? Do you think that I will learn it if I take pains? My eyes have never seen anything that I am so eager to master. I long to know as much about it as you do."

"Friend," said the lord, "if you set your heart on it, you will learn without any difficulty."

Three times the lord mounted and three times showed all he knew of the handling of arms till he thought it was enough, and three times he made the youth mount. After the last he said: "Friend, if you met a knight and he struck you, what would you do?"

"I would strike him back."

"And if your lance broke?"

"Then there would be nothing to do but to attack him with my fists."

"Friend, never do that."

"What should I do?"

"You must use your sword and fence with him."

Then the lord planted the lance in the ground, for he wished to teach him how to defend himself with the sword or to attack with it, as circumstances required. He grasped the sword and said: "In this way you should defend yourself if anyone assails you."

"As for that, so God save me, no one knows more than I, because I have often practiced on cushions and shields at my mother's house until I was tired out."

"Then let us go inside," said the lord, "for there is no other lodging, and, whoever may object, you will enjoy no mean hospitality tonight."

Then, as the two went in, side by side, the youth said to his host: "Sir, my mother taught me that I should never be long in the company of anyone without knowing his name; so, as my mother taught me, I would ask your name."

"Fair sweet friend," said the lord, "my name is Gornemant of Gohort."

They entered hand in hand, and as they mounted the steps

a squire of his own accord came running with a short mantle, which he cast over the youth that he might not, after the heat of exercise, take a bad cold. The buildings of the lord were rich and large, his servants pleasant to look upon, and an excellent meal was prepared. So the knights washed and sat down to eat. The lord seated the youth beside him and caused him to eat from the same dish. I will not say how many courses they had or what they were, but they had plenty to eat and drink; I do not need to tell more of the repast.

When they had risen from table, the courteous lord besought the youth who had sat beside him to stay a month; indeed, he would gladly keep him a whole year if he wished, and he would meanwhile teach him such things as would help him in case of need. The youth replied: "Sir, I do not know whether I am near the manor where my mother lives, but I pray God to guide me so that I may see her again, for I saw her fall in a swoon at the end of the bridge before her gate, and I do not know whether she is alive or dead. But I do know that she fainted for sorrow at my leaving her, and so until I know how she is I cannot stay here long. I must leave tomorrow early."

The lord perceived that prayers would be of no avail, and held his peace. Without more debate they retired to rest, for the beds were already made. Early on the morrow the lord arose and went where he found the youth lying in bed, and brought him as a present a shirt and breeches of fine linen, hose dyed red, and a tunic of indigo silk woven in India. He told him to put them on, saying: "Friend, if you trust me, dress yourself in the clothes you see here."

The youth answered: "Fair sir, surely you could give me better advice, for the clothes that my mother made me, are they not better than these, and yet you wish me to put these on?"

"Young sir," said the lord, "by my head, they are worse.

You promised me, good friend, when I brought you here that you would obey all my orders."

"I will do so," said the youth; "I will not oppose you."

Without a pause he donned the new clothes and left those of his mother. The lord, bending over, fastened on his heel the right spur, such was the custom for him who made a knight. Many squires were present, and each, as opportunity offered, helped in the arming. The lord took the sword, girded it on the youth, kissed him, and said that with the sword he had given him the highest order that God had made and decreed—namely, the stainless order of knighthood. He continued: "Remember this, fair brother, I pray you: if it happens that in combat with a knight you gain the upper hand and he is unable to defend himself longer, have mercy on him and do not kill him wittingly. Beware also of talking too much and of gossiping. No one can talk too much without saying something rude. The wise man declares: 'He who talks too much commits sin.' Therefore, fair brother, I forbid you to talk overmuch. Moreover, I beg you, if you find man or woman, whether damsel or lady, in distress, advise them so far as you can and if you have the power to help. One more thing I would have you learn, and do not despise it, for it is not to be scorned. Go to the minster and pray to Him who made all things, to have mercy on your soul and to keep you a good Christian in this earthly life."

The youth said to the lord: "Good sir, may you be blessed by all the Apostles of Rome! That is what I once heard my mother say."

"Now, fair brother," said the lord, "hereafter do not keep saying that your mother taught you this or that. Till now I do not blame you at all, but, begging your pardon, I ask that henceforth you correct yourself, for if you persist, you will be taken for a fool. So I pray you, avoid it."

"What shall I say then, good sir?"

"You may say that the vavasor who buckled on your spur taught you so."

The youth promised that he would never as long as he lived utter a word of any other master, for he saw clearly that the lord's teaching was good. His host then made the sign of the cross over him and, with hand uplifted, said: "Fair sir, God preserve you! Adieu, and may He guide you, for the delay is irksome to you."

The new knight departed from his host, and he was impatient to go to his mother and find her alive and well. He plunged into the wild forests, where he was more at home than on the level lands, and he rode till he saw a strong, well-placed castle, but outside the walls there was nothing but sea and water and ravaged fields. Hastening toward it, he arrived at the gate, but before he could enter he had to cross a bridge so feeble that he doubted whether it would hold up under him. But he mounted it and passed over without any harm or humiliation. When he arrived at the gate, he found it locked. He did not knock softly or call in a low voice, but struck so hard that presently there appeared at a window of the hall a thin and pale maiden. She asked: "Who is it calls there?"

The youth looked up at the maiden and said: "Fair friend, I am a knight and I ask you to let me in and give me lodging for the night."

"Sir," said she, "you will have it, though you may not be pleased with our entertainment; nevertheless, we will do the best we can."

Then the damsel withdrew, and he who was waiting at the gate feared that he might be kept too long and resumed his knocking. Soon, four servants, bearing great axes on their shoulders and girded with swords, came and opened the door saying: "Sir, enter."

In better days the servants would have been handsome fellows, but through lack of food and sleep they were wonderfully changed, and if the fields outside were ravaged and stripped, it was no better within. Wherever the new knight passed, he found the streets empty and the old houses tumbled down, and there was neither man nor woman about. There were two abbeys in the town, one of terrified nuns, the other of helpless monks, and the buildings were not in a good state, and the walls were cracked and the towers roofless and the gates open both night and day. No mill was grinding or oven baking in the whole town; there was no bread or cake or even a penny's worth of anything for sale. The knight found the castle so desolate that there was no bread, pastry, wine, cider, or ale.

The four servants led him to a slate-roofed hall, there caused him to alight, and removed his arms. Promptly a squire descended the steps of the hall bearing a gray mantle and fastened it round his neck, while another stabled his horse in a stall where there was no grain or hay and only a little straw; there was no more in the house. The other squires made him ascend the stairs before them, and in the stately hall two lords and a maiden advanced to meet him. The hair of the lords was grizzled but not white, and they would have been at the peak of their ardor and strength if they had not suffered hardship.

The maiden approached, more gracious and glowing with life than sparrow hawk or parrot. Her mantle and her gown were of a dark silk, starred with gold and trimmed with fine ermine, and the collar of the mantle was of black and gray sable, neither too long nor too wide. And if ever I have described the beauty with which God endowed the body and the visage of a woman, I will try again without varying from the truth by a word. Her tresses flowed free and the beholder would mistake them, if it were possible, for fine gold, they were so lustrous. Her forehead was high, white, and smooth, as if it had been carved of marble or ivory or fine wood; her eyebrows dark and wide apart; her eyes smiling, bright, and large; her nose straight and regular; the red glowed on her white skin more charmingly than vermilion on silver. To steal away the minds and hearts of men, God made of her a wonder, and never before or since has He made her equal.

When the knight saw her, he greeted her, and she and the two attendant knights responded. The damsel took his hand courteously and said: "Fair sir, our lodging tonight will not be such as a man of rank deserves. If I tell you at once of our condition, you may think perhaps that I speak out of hostility, to induce you to leave. But may it please you to remain and to accept our hospitality, such as it is, and may God grant you a better tomorrow."

Then she led him by the hand into a fair, wide, and long chamber with a vaulted ceiling, and there they seated themselves on a couch, spread with a coverlet of samite. Knights entered in groups of four, five, and six, and sat down but said not a word, looking at the guest who sat silent beside their lady. And he refrained from speaking because he remembered the charge which Gornemant had laid upon him. Then all the knights began to whisper among themselves. "By God," said each, "I wonder if this knight is dumb; it would be a great pity, for never was so handsome a knight born of woman. How well he looks beside my lady, and she beside him, if only they were not both so silent. They are both so beautiful that never knight and maiden looked better together. It seems as if God had made each for the other in order that he might join them."

They all continued to talk together, while the damsel waited for her guest to address her. Perceiving at last that he would not speak unless spoken to, she said courteously: "Sir, whence did you come today?"

"Damsel," said he, "I lay last night at the castle of a nobleman, where I had good lodging. There were five towers, exceeding strong, one big and four little ones. I cannot tell you all about it and I do not know what the castle is called, but I know well the name of the nobleman, Gornemant of Gohort."

"Ah, fair friend," said the maiden, "well have you spoken and courteously. May God the King reward you for calling your host a nobleman. You have never uttered a truer word, for he is a noble man, by St. Richier; that I can vouch for. Know, then, that I am his niece, but it is long since I have set eyes on him. Surely, since you left your home, you have not met a nobler man, to my thinking. As a noble and gracious host, powerful and prosperous, he must have given you cheerful and joyous entertainment. But here there are only six loaves, which a holy prior, my uncle, has sent me for supper tonight, with a bottle of boiled wine. There is no other provender except a buck which one of my servants shot with an arrow this morning."

She ordered the tables to be set up, and when this was done, all sat down to supper. They did not linger long at the meal but ate ravenously. Afterwards those remained who had kept watch the night before and who were now due to sleep, while fifty servants and squires whose duty it was to keep watch that night over the castle went out. The rest busied themselves in making their guest comfortable, and those who attended to the bedding spread fair sheets and a costly coverlet and laid a pillow at the head. The youth enjoyed that night in his bed all the comfort and pleasure imaginable except the delight of a maiden's or a lady's company, if it had pleased or been permitted him; but of that he knew and thought nothing, and free from care he went promptly to sleep.

But his hostess, who was shut in her chamber, did not rest.

While he slept peacefully, she, who had no defense in the struggle which went on within her, brooded, turning and tossing, till at last she donned a short mantle of scarlet silk over her shift, and set out on a bold enterprise. It was no trifling matter; rather she planned to go to her guest and tell him something of her plight. Leaving her bed, she issued from her chamber, perspiring and trembling in every limb with terror. She came to the bed where the knight was sleeping, wept and sighed deeply, and knelt so that the tears wetted his face; she did not dare to be bolder. At last he woke, startled and wondering how his face was so wet, and found her on her knees beside the bed and her arms around his neck. He had the courtesy to embrace her in turn, and drew her toward him, saying: "Fair lady, what do you wish? What has brought you here?"

"Ah, gentle knight, have mercy! I implore you for God's sake and for His Son's not to take me for a vile thing because I have come to you thus, and though I am nearly nude, I have no light, wicked, or coarse design. In the whole world there is no living creature so wretched and poor that I am not more so. I have nothing to cheer me; every day is a grief. I shall never see another night nor another day than tomorrow, but I will kill myself with my own hand. Of three hundred and ten knights who garrisoned this castle, only fifty are left. Forty-eight have been led away and either killed or imprisoned by an evil knight, Anguingueron, seneschal of Clamadeu of the Isles. I grieve as much for those who are in prison as for the dead, for I know that they will die too, for they can never escape. So many brave men have been killed for my sake that I have a right to mourn. For a whole winter and a summer Anguingueron has laid close siege to us, and while his forces increase, ours dwindle, and our provisions are spent, so that there is not enough to feed a bee. Tomorrow, unless God wills otherwise, this castle must surrender, for it can no longer be defended, and I with it. But surely, before Anguingueron takes me alive, I will kill myself, and he will have only my corpse. Then little shall I care, though Clamadeu, who hopes to possess me, gain his end, for he will have the body without life and soul. I keep in my casket a knife of fine steel, which I intend to plunge into my body. I have said enough. I will now go back and leave you to your rest."

Here then was an opportunity for the knight to win fame if he had the courage, for the maiden had come and shed tears over his face for no other purpose than to inspire him to do battle, if he dared, in defense of her land and herself. He spoke: "Dear friend, be of good cheer tonight. Take comfort, stop crying, come close to me, and wipe the tears from your eyes. God, if He pleases, will do better by you tomorrow than what you have told me. Come and lie in this bed beside me, for it is wide enough for us both. Do not leave me now."

She replied: "If it pleases you, I will do so."

Then, holding her in his arms, he kissed her and drew her softly under the coverlet, and she did not resist his kisses and I do not think that they displeased him. Thus they lay that night beside each other, mouth to mouth, until dawn approached. That night gave him so much delight that they slept together mouth to mouth, in close embrace. When day came the maiden returned to her chamber and dressed herself without the aid of her women, who were not yet awake. The guards who had watched through the night, as soon as they saw daylight, woke those who were sleeping and made them rise from their beds without delay. The maiden herself went back to her knight and said courteously: "Sir, God give you good day! I do not expect that you will make a long stay or find anything to do here; it would be of no use, and I will not take it ill if you go, for it would not be polite of me. We have done nothing for your ease and comfort. But I pray

God to arrange better lodging for you and more bread, wine, salt, and every provision, than you have found here."

He answered: "Fair maiden, I will not look today for any other lodging, but if I can I will restore peace to all your land. If I find your enemy yonder outside, I shall not be happy if he stays longer, for he has no right to torment you. But if I defeat and kill him, I will ask you to be my love as a reward. I will take no other pay."

She courteously replied: "Sir, it is a poor and contemptible thing you now request of me, but if I refuse, you will think me proud, and therefore I will not deny you. Nevertheless, do not say that I become your love on condition that you go forth to die for my sake; that would be outrageous. Be assured that you have not the strength or the age to hold your own in battle against a knight so big and hardy as he who waits outside yonder."

"You will see today," said he, "for I will go and fight with him. I will not stop for anyone's advice."

Thus she warned him against a plan which she wished him to execute. Often, when one sees a man eager to carry out a wish, one hides one's real desire in order to make him more ardent. So she behaved shrewdly, rebuking Perceval for doing what she had put it in his heart to do. He called for his arms, and when they were brought, and the gate was opened, attendants armed him and had him mount a caparisoned steed, in the open square. Everyone showed signs of grief and said: "Sir, God give you aid this day, and bring to an evil end Anguingueron, the seneschal, who has destroyed this country."

Thus both men and women wept as they accompanied him to the gate, and when they saw him sally from the castle, they said with one voice: "May the true cross, on which God allowed His Son to suffer, protect you this day from mortal peril and from prison and bring you back safe to the place where you may have peace and joy!"

Thus they all prayed. Meanwhile the besiegers saw him coming and pointed him out to Anguingueron, who was sitting before his tent, confident that the castle would be surrendered before nightfall or that someone would come out to meet him in bodily combat. He had already had his mail hose laced, and his men were exulting at the thought that the castle and the land were as good as conquered. When Anguingueron saw the knight, he hastily completed his arming, rode swiftly toward him on a strong, heavily built charger, and called: "Young sir, who has sent you? Tell me your purpose. Have you come to seek peace or battle?"

"But you, tell me first what you are doing in this land," said the youth. "Why have you killed the knights and ravaged all the country?"

Arrogant was the reply: "I demand that this day the castle be vacated and the keep surrendered; it has been defended too long. And my master must have the maiden."

"A curse on this answer and on him who makes it!" said the youth. "It is you, rather, who must give up all claims against her."

"You are plying me with lies, by St. Peter," said Anguingueron. "Many a man pays the penalty who never committed the fault."

The youth grew restive, laid his lance in rest, and each spurred against his opponent as fast as his horse could carry him. Furiously and with mighty blows they reduced what remained of their lances to splinters. Anguingueron fell from his saddle, painfully wounded in the arm and side. The youth, not knowing how to deal with him on horseback, sprang to the ground, drew his sword, and laid on again. I cannot describe all the strokes, but they were heavy and the fight lasted long, until Anguingueron fell. The youth still attacked him fiercely till he begged for mercy, but the youth declared that he would grant none. Then he remembered that

Gornemant had taught him never wittingly to slay a knight after he had vanquished him, and the seneschal cried: "Fair friend, do not be so cruel as to refuse me mercy. I acknowledge that you have the best of me and are a very great knight but no one who knew us both and had not seen it would ever believe that you alone had killed me in battle with your arms. But I will bear witness that you have fairly overcome me in battle, in the sight of my people before my tent, and my word will be accepted and your glory will be known; no knight ever had greater. Think, too, if you have a lord who has shown you favor and whom you have not yet repaid, send me to him and I will go and report how you have defeated me and give myself up as a prisoner to do with what he pleases."

"A curse on him who would expect more! Do you know where you must go? To that castle yonder, and say to the beautiful maiden who is my ladylove that never in all your life will you do her harm and that you put yourself wholly at her mercy."

Anguingueron replied: "Then kill me, for so she would have me killed, and she desires nothing so much as my ruin and death. I was at the death of her father, and this year I have slain or imprisoned all her knights. To send me to her would place me in a dungeon cell, and nothing could be worse. If you have no other friend, man or woman, send me to someone who bears me no grudge. This lady, if she had me in her power, would not fail to take my life."

Then the youth commanded the seneschal to go to the castle of a nobleman and told him the name, and described the architecture as well as any mason in the world. He praised the river, the bridge, the little towers, the keep, and the outworks so well that the seneschal recognized that he was to be sent as captive to the place where he was hated most. "Good sir," he said, "if you send me there, I shall be no safer. God help me, but you are bent on putting me on a fatal journey into fatal hands. In this war I slew one of that lord's brothers, and you slay me too, good friend, if you force me to go to him. It will be my death."

"Then," said the youth, "you shall go as a captive to King Arthur. Greet him, and ask him for my sake to show you the maiden whom Kay the seneschal struck when she laughed on seeing me. Give yourself up to her and tell her, if you please, that I pray God not to let me die before I have avenged her."

Anguingueron replied that he would gladly do this service, and then the victor returned to the castle. His prisoner departed, caused his banner to be borne away, and lifted the siege, so that no one of the host, be his hair dark or light, remained. The men of the castle sallied forth to meet the returning hero, but they were disgusted that he had not taken the head of the vanquished knight and given it to them. With great joy they caused him to dismount at a horseblock and disarmed him, saying: "Sir, since you have not brought Anguingueron back, why did you not bring his head?"

The knight answered: "Sirs, by my faith, that would not have been right. Because he killed your relatives, he would have had no warrant for his safety, and you would have killed him in spite of me. There would be little left of my honor if, after getting the best of him, I had not granted his plea for mercy. Do you know what I granted? He will go, if he keeps his promise, as a prisoner to King Arthur."

Just then the damsel arrived and made great joy of him and led him to her chamber to rest and take his ease. Nor was she coy with her kisses and embraces, but they amused themselves thus and in gracious talk, instead of in drinking and eating.

Meanwhile Clamadeu was indulging in foolish anticipations as he traveled toward the castle, thinking at last to take it without resistance. A squire met him on the road, lamenting loudly, and gave him the news of his seneschal, Anguingueron. "In God's name, lord," said the squire, tearing his hair in distress, "the worst has happened."

Clamadeu replied: "What is that?"

"Lord," said the squire, "on my faith, your seneschal has been overcome by arms and has gone to give himself up to King Arthur."

"Who, tell me, squire, has done this and how could it happen? Whence could the knight have come who could make so noble and valiant a man surrender?"

The squire answered: "My dear lord, I do not know who the knight was; I know only that I saw him come out of Belrepeire, wearing red arms."

"What do you advise, squire?" said his master, who was nearly out of his mind with rage.

"What, sire? It is best to turn back, for if you proceed you will gain nothing."

At this word there came forward a grizzled knight, who was the counselor of Clamadeu, and said: "Squire, you do not speak wisely. It is best to follow more sensible advice than yours. If he takes yours, he will act like a fool. My counsel is to go on." Then he added: "Sire, would you like to know how to capture the knight and the castle? I will tell you how, and it will be easy. Within the walls of Belrepeire there is neither drink nor food, and the knights are weak, while we are strong and hale, and, suffering neither thirst nor hunger, we can put up a stout fight. If the defenders dare to make a sally and engage in battle outside, let us send twenty knights to offer battle before the gate. The knight who is dallying with Blancheflor, his sweet mistress, will be eager to undertake feats of arms beyond his powers and will be captured or slain. The other knights will be so feeble that they can give

him little aid, and our twenty will retreat before them until
we burst upon them through this valley and surround them."

"By my faith, I commend the plan that you propose," said
Clamadeu. "We have here picked men, five hundred fully
armed knights and a thousand well-equipped foot, and it will
be like capturing a troop of dead men."·

Clamadeu sent accordingly twenty knights toward the gate,
with their various gonfalons and banners unfurled to the
wind. When those within the castle saw them, they opened
the gate wide, for the youth willed it so. He himself rode out
at their head to encounter the foe, and attacked them all
boldly and fiercely. Those he met did not take him for an ap-
prentice in arms. That day his lance head was felt in many a
gut. One he pierced in the chest, one in the nipple, of one he
broke the arm, of one the collarbone. Him he killed, him he
maimed, him he unhorsed, him he captured. He turned
over the captives and the horses to those who were charged
with the duty of taking them.

Now the troops who had ascended the valley came in sight
of the battle, and they were five hundred knights by count,
besides a thousand foot. The defenders were staying close to
the open gate, and when the new arrivals saw their own comrades maimed and dead, they made a wild and disorderly rush
toward the gate. The defenders, however, held their ranks at
the gate and bravely met the onslaught, but they were few
and weak. The attackers were now reinforced by the foot
soldiers who had followed them, so that the defense was
obliged to withdraw into the castle. Archers posted over the
gate shot into the dense mass which was struggling ardently to
make an entry. At last a small body forced its way in. But
the defenders dropped a portcullis which killed and crushed
all those whom it struck in its fall. Clamadeu never saw anything that made him sadder, for many of his men were slain

at the portcullis and he himself was shut out. There was nothing to do but take a rest, for another hasty assault would only be wasted effort.

His counselor advised him: "Sire, it is no wonder if a wise and worthy man sometimes fails. As God wills, good and evil fortune come to every man. You have lost the battle, that is plain; but there is no saint who does not have a feast day. You have been struck by a storm; your men are crippled, and the defenders have won the day. But, rest assured, their turn will come to lose. Pluck out both my eyes if they hold out two more days. The castle and the keep will be yours, and they will all place themselves at your mercy. If you stay only today and tomorrow, the castle will be in your hands, and the maiden who has refused you so long will implore you in God's name to take her."

Then those who had brought tents and pavilions pitched them, and the others camped as best they could. The men of the castle disarmed the knights they had captured, but did not put them in dungeons or in irons, but only made them pledge on their honor as knights not to attempt an escape and never to do them injury again. So it was arranged within the castle.

Now that very day a high wind drove a barge, heavily laden with wheat and other provisions, across the sea and, as God willed, brought it safely before the castle. When the besieged saw it, they sent to inquire who the new arrivals were and what they wanted, and descending to the barge they asked what sort of people they were, whence they came, and whither they were bound. The answer was: "We are merchants, bringing food for sale, bread, wine, salt bacon, and, if there is need, oxen and swine for slaughtering."

The men of the castle exclaimed: "Blessed be God, who lent strength to the wind and brought you here under full sail! Welcome! Come ashore, for your whole cargo is already sold at as high a price as you wish, and take your payment at once, for you will have plenty to do, counting and carrying away the gold and silver ingots that we will give you for the wheat, and you may, if necessary, require a cart to load the meat and wine."

So those who bought and those who sold made a good bargain. They saw to the unloading of the ship and had everything carried up for the relief of the castle. When those within spied the bearers of the food approaching, you can imagine their delight, and with all speed they hastened to prepare a meal. Clamadeu, who was idling away the time outside, might now have long to wait, for the besieged were provided with oxen, swine, and salt meat in plenty, and wheat enough to last till harvest. The cooks were not sluggish; the kitchen boys lighted the fires for the roasts. Carefree, the youth may now disport himself with his love; she embraces him, he kisses her, and thus each gives joy to the other. The hall was no longer quiet, but was full of noise and gaiety. Everyone was merry over the repast, which they had craved so long, and the cooks worked fast and made those sit down to eat who had the greatest need. When they had finished, they rose to give place to others.

Clamadeu and his men, however, who had heard news of the good fortune which had come to the besieged, were dismayed, and there were those who said it was best to depart, because the castle could not be starved out and the siege had been undertaken for nothing. But Clamadeu, mad with rage, sent a message to the castle without asking counsel of anyone, informing the red knight that until noon the next day he could be found on the plain ready to meet him in single combat, if he dared come out. When the maiden heard this challenge delivered to her lover, she was torn with grief, but he returned answer that, since Clamadeu had demanded battle, he should have it. This only aggravated the maiden's sorrow, but it was of no avail. All the others, men and women, besought the youth not to go out to fight with one who had never yet met his match in battle.

"Sirs," said the youth, "you would do well to be still, for I will not be stopped for anything or for any man in the world."

Thus they had their answer, and dared speak no more, but retired to bed and slept till the sun rose on the morrow. They grieved that their prayers had not succeeded in persuading their lord to heed their advice. The same night his love pleaded with him not to go out to battle but to rest in peace, for the besieged no longer cared a whit for Clamadeu and his men. It was all in vain; and that was strange, for her blandishments were very sweet to him, and with every word she kissed him so tenderly that she placed the key of love into the lock of his heart. Nevertheless, she could not dissuade him from his purpose. He called for his arms, they were quickly brought, and as he donned them, both men and women lamented. He commended them all to the King of Kings, then mounted a steed from Norway which had been led up, and rode away, leaving them in their grief.

When Clamadeu saw his adversary approaching, he felt a foolish confidence that he would soon make him void his saddle. The heath was fair, level, and empty except for the two combatants, for Clamadeu had sent back all his people. Each laid his lance in rest and spurred against the other without shouting a defiance. Each had a thick but manageable lance of ash wood, with a sharp head; the horses were swift; their masters were strong and hated each other with a mortal hatred. They struck each other so that the shields and the lances were broken, and they were both thrown to the earth. But they quickly sprang up and renewed the combat on foot with their swords, and long the issue hung in the balance. If I wished I could describe it fully, but I will not, since one word is as good as twenty. At last Clamadeu was forced to beg mercy, and promised everything, except that, like his seneschal, he would not be imprisoned at Belrepeire, nor would he go for all the empire of Rome to the nobleman who possessed the castle so grandly placed, but he would consent gladly to become the prisoner of King Arthur, and would deliver the message to the maiden whom Kay had brutally struck—namely, that the youth would avenge her in time if God gave him the power, in spite of anyone's displeasure. The youth made him promise also that the next day before dawn all the prisoners in his towers would be allowed to return freely, and that if ever in his life an army laid siege to Belrepeire he would disperse them if he could, and that never would he or his men do injury to its mistress.

So Clamadeu departed to his own land, and when he arrived, he commanded that all the prisoners be freed, and so by his orders they departed, unhindered, with all their equipment. Clamadeu himself took the road alone. It was the custom of that country, as we find it written, that a vanquished knight was allowed to proceed to the place of his captivity with such arms as he was wearing, neither less nor more. So equipped, Clamadeu followed the road Anguingueron had taken to Dinasdaron, where the King was said to hold court.

But there was great rejoicing at Belrepeire when those who had long suffered vile imprisonment returned. The hall and the quarters of the knights resounded with mirth. The bells in the chapels and minsters rang out gaily, and there was no monk or nun who did not render thanks to the Lord. Men and women danced through the streets and market places. Throughout the castle and town there was exultation that the war was over.

Anguingueron meantime had completed his journey, and Clamadeu, following, put up three nights in the same lodgings, as he knew by his traces, and arrived at Dinasdaron in Wales, where King Arthur was holding high feast in his halls. They saw Clamadeu approaching, fully armed, as was his right. Anguingueron had already the evening before delivered his message, and had been asked to remain as one of the King's household and council. When he saw his lord stained with blood, he recognized him and exclaimed: "Sirs, sirs, behold a wonder! The youth with the red arms, believe me, has sent here that knight whom you see. He must have conquered him, I am certain, because he is covered with blood. I recognize his shield and the man himself, for he is my lord and I am his man. His name is Clamadeu of the Isles, and I believed that there was no better knight in the empire of Rome. But many a mighty man comes to grief."

"So Anguingueron spoke as Clamadeu approached, and then each ran to meet the other. It was the feast of Pentecost, and the Queen was sitting at Arthur's side at the head of the dais, and there were counts, dukes, kings, queens, countesses in plenty, and they had come from hearing all the masses at the minster. Kay walked through the hall, without mantle, in his right hand a small staff, a cap of goodly stuff on his head, his blond hair twined in a single tress. There was no handsomer knight in the world, but his evil speech detracted from his good looks and his prowess. His tunic was of rich colored silk. About his waist was a girdle finely wrought, with a buckle and ornaments of gold, as the story testifies. Everyone got out of his way as he came through the hall, they so dreaded his raillery and his malicious tongue. For it is a sensible man who fears public slander, whether in jest or earnest. So no one spoke to Kay, and he walked up to where the King was sitting and said: "Sire, if you please, you may eat at once."

"Kay," the King replied, "leave me in peace, for by the eyes in my head, I will not begin eating at a high feast such as this until some new tidings are brought to my court."

As they talked, Clamadeu entered, in arms, as was proper, to give himself up as a prisoner; and he said: "God save and bless the best king living, the most generous and courteous, as all those bear witness who have heard of his great deeds! Now harken, good lord, to the message that I would deliver. Though it pains me, I will nevertheless confess that I was sent here by a knight who conquered me, and must surrender to you, for I cannot do otherwise. If asked what his name is, I must admit my ignorance, but will report that his arms are red and that he says you gave them to him."

"Friend," said the King, "so may God keep you, tell me truly whether he is well and vigorous?"

"Yes, you may be quite sure, dear good lord," said Clamadeu; "he is the most valiant knight whom I have known. Furthermore, he told me that I should speak to the maiden who laughed when she saw him and whom Kay struck shamefully on the cheek, and tell her that he will avenge her, if God grants him the power."

The fool, hearing this speech, leapt for joy and cried: "Lord King, so may God bless me, she shall be well repaid for the buffet; and do not take it for a jest, for Kay will have his arm broken and his collarbone put out."

Hearing these words, Kay took them for utter nonsense, and if he let them pass, it was not because of cowardice but from respect for the royal presence. The King shook his head, saying: "Ah, Kay, I am sorely distressed that the youth is not here among us. It was you and your foolish tongue that drove him away, to my sorrow."

At these words Giflet rose and Sir Ivain, who shed refinement on all those about him, and the King told them to lead Clamadeu to the chambers where the Queen's damsels were making merry. The knight bowed and was led to the chambers, where the maiden was pointed out to him. There he gave her the tidings she was eager to hear. Though she had recovered from the blow on her cheek, she had not forgotten the shame of it. It is very wrong to forget shame or injury. Pain passes, but shame lasts in a strong and steadfast man; while in an evil man it cools and dies. Clamadeu had now performed his errand, and the King retained him the rest of his life in his household.

Now he who had contested with Clamadeu the maiden Blancheflor and her land took his ease and delight with his fair love, and the land would have been entirely his if his mind had not turned elsewhere. He thought again of his mother, whom he had seen falling in a swoon, and he yearned to see her more than anything else. He did not dare to take leave of his love, for she forbade it and sent all her folk to beseech him to stay. But their prayers availed only to win a promise that if he found his mother alive, he would bring her back with him and would then take over the land, and if she were dead, he would return likewise. Thus he set out on the promise of return, but he left his gracious lady angry and sorrowful, and her people also. As he rode out of the town, there was such a procession as on Ascension Day or on a Sunday. All the monks had gone out, clad in silken copes, and all the veiled nuns, and both monks and nuns pleaded: "Sir, you who have delivered us from exile and restored us to our houses, it is no wonder if we mourn when you leave us so soon. Our grief is such that it could not be greater."

He replied: "Weep no longer; it is not fitting. I will come back, if God keeps me. Tears are worth nothing. Do you not believe that it would be good for me to see my mother, who used to live in that wood which is called the Wild Forest? I will come back, whether she lives or not, for my mind is set. If she is alive, I will make her a veiled nun in your church; if dead, I will arrange a service for her soul every year that God may place her in Abraham's bosom among the pious souls. Reverend monks and you, fair ladies, this ought not to cause you sorrow, because I will make great provision for her soul if God brings me back."

Then the monks, nuns, and all the others went their ways, and Perceval set forth, lance in rest, armed at all points as he had come there. All day he journeyed without meeting earthly creature or Christian man or woman to direct him. He did not cease to beseech the Lord, the sovereign Father, if it were His will, to grant that he might find his mother in life and health. He was still praying when he came at the bottom of a hill to a river. Gazing upon the deep and rapid water, he did not dare to descend into it but said: "Ah, Almighty God, if I could cross this stream, I believe I would find my mother, if she is still alive."

So he rode along the bank till he came to a cliff washed by the stream, so that he could not pass. Then he caught sight of a boat floating downstream and two men in it. He waited, expecting them to come up to him. But they stopped in the middle of the river and dropped anchor. The man in the bow had a line and was baiting his hook with a fish somewhat larger than a minnow. The knight, not knowing where to find passage, greeted them and asked: "Sirs, tell me if there is a ford or a bridge on this river?"

The fisherman answered: "No, brother, on my faith there is not for twenty leagues up or down a boat larger than this, which would not carry five men, and one cannot cross on horseback, for there is no ferry, bridge, or ford."

"Then tell me, in God's name, where I may find shelter."

The fisherman replied: "Indeed you will have need of that and more. I will myself give you lodging tonight. Ride up by the cleft in this rock, and when you have reached the top, you will see before you in a valley a house where I dwell, near the river and near the wood."

Without further pause the knight ascended, and at the top of the hill he gazed long ahead without seeing anything but sky and earth. He exclaimed: "What has brought me here? Stupidity and trickery. God bring shame on him today who sent me here! Truly he put me on the right path when he said that at the top I would spy a house! Fisherman, you foully deceived me if you spoke out of malice!"

At that instant he spied before him in a valley the top of a tower. One might seek as far as Beirut without finding one as noble or as well situated. It was square, built of dark stone, and flanked by two lesser towers. The hall stood in front of the tower, and before the hall an arcade. As the youth descended he confessed that the fisherman had given him good directions, and praised him and no longer called him a treacherous liar, since now he had found harborage. So he proceeded to the gate, before which there was a drawbridge lowered. As he crossed, four squires came to meet him; two removed his arms; a third led his horse away to give him fodder and oats; the fourth clad the youth in a scarlet mantle, fresh and new. Then they led him to the arcade, and be assured that none as splendid could be found as far as Limoges. There he waited till the lord of the castle sent two squires to fetch him, and he accompanied them to the square hall, which was as long as it was wide. In the middle he saw, sitting on a couch, a handsome nobleman with grizzled locks, on his head a sable cap, black as a mulberry, with a crimson lappet below and a robe of the same. He was reclining on his elbow, and in front of him a great fire of dry branches blazed between four columns. Four hundred men could seat themselves comfortably around it. The four strong columns which supported the hood of the fireplace were of massive bronze.

The squires brought the youth before his host and stood on

either side of him. When the lord saw him approach, he promptly greeted him, saying: "Friend, do not take it amiss if I do not rise to meet you, but I cannot do so easily."

"In God's name, sire, do not speak of it, for, as God may give me joy and health, it does not offend me."

The nobleman raised himself with difficulty, as much as he could, and said: "Friend, draw nearer; do not be abashed but sit here at my side, for so I bid you."

As the youth sat beside him, the nobleman inquired: "Friend, from what place did you come today?"

"Sire, this morning I left the castle called Belrepeire."

"So help me God," exclaimed the nobleman, "you have had a long day's ride. You must have departed before the watchman blew his horn at dawn."

"No," the youth answered, "prime had already been rung, I assure you."

As they talked, a squire came in at the door, a sword suspended from his neck. He handed it to the rich host, who drew it halfway from the sheath and observed where it was forged, for it was written on the blade. He saw too that it was of such fine steel that it could not break save only in one peril which no one knew but him who had forged and tempered it. The squire who had brought it announced: "Sire, the fair-haired maiden, your beautiful niece, sends you this gift. You have never seen one lighter for its length and breadth. You may present it to whom you please, but my lady would be glad if you would bestow it where it would be well employed. He who forged it made only three, and he will die before he can make another."

At once the lord, taking the sword by the hangings, which were worth a great treasure, gave it to the newcomer. The pommel was of the best gold of Arabia or Greece, and the sheath was covered with Venetian gold embroidery. This richly mounted sword the lord gave to the youth, saying:

"Good sir, this was destined for you, and I desire you to have it. Gird it on and then draw it."

The youth thanked him and fastened the girdle so that it was not too tight. Then he drew out the naked blade from the sheath and after holding it a little put it back. Rest assured that it became him well hanging at his side, and better still when gripped in his fist; and it surely seemed that it would do him knightly service in time of need. Looking about, he noted standing behind him around the brightly burning fire some squires, and he entrusted the sword to the keeping of the one who had charge of his arms. Then he returned to his seat beside the lord, who showed him great honor. The light of the candles was the brightest that one could find in any mansion.

While they were talking of this and that, a squire entered from a chamber, grasping by the middle a white lance, and passed between the fire and those seated on the couch. All present beheld the white lance and the white point, from which a drop of red blood ran down to the squire's hand. The youth who had arrived that night watched this marvel, but he refrained from asking what this meant, for he was mindful of the lesson which Gornemant gave him, warning him against too much speech, and he feared that if he asked, it would be considered rude. So he held his peace.

Then two other squires came in, right handsome, bearing in their hands candelabra of fine gold and niello work, and in each candelabrum were at least ten candles. A damsel came in with these squires, holding between her two hands a grail. She was beautiful, gracious, splendidly garbed, and as she entered with the grail in her hands, there was such a brilliant light that the candles lost their brightness, just as the stars do when the moon or the sun rises. After her came a damsel holding a carving platter of silver. The grail which preceded her was of refined gold; and it was set with precious

stones of many kinds, the richest and the costliest that exist
in the sea or in the earth. Without question those set in the
grail surpassed all other jewels. Like the lance, these damsels
passed before the couch and entered another chamber.

The youth watched them pass, but he did not dare to ask
concerning the grail and whom one served with it, for he kept
in his heart the words of the wise nobleman. I fear that harm
will come of this, because I have heard say that one can be
too silent as well as be too loquacious. But, for better or for
worse, the youth put no question.

The lord then ordered the water to be brought and the
cloths to be spread, and this was done by those whose duty
and custom it was. The lord and his guest washed their hands
with moderately warm water. Two squires brought a wide
table top of ivory, which, according to the story, was all of a
piece, and they held it a moment before the lord and the
youth, till two other squires came bringing trestles. The wood
of which they were made possessed two virtues which made
them last forever. Of what were they made? Of ebony. What
is the property of that wood? It cannot rot and it cannot
burn; these two dangers it does not heed. The table top was
placed on the trestles, and the cloth was laid. What should I
say of the cloth? No legate, cardinal, or even pope ever ate
on one so white.

The first course was a haunch of venison, peppered and
cooked in grease. There was no lack of clear wine or grape
juice to drink from a cup of gold. Before them a squire carved
the peppered venison which he had set on a silver carving
platter, and then he placed the slices on large pieces of bread
in front of them.

Meanwhile the grail passed again before them, and still the
youth did not ask concerning the grail, whom one served with
it. He restrained himself because the nobleman had so gently
charged him not to speak too much, and he had treasured

this in his heart and remembered it. But he was silent longer than was proper, for as each course was served, he saw the grail pass before him in plain view, and did not learn whom one served with it though he would have liked much to know. Instead he said to himself that he would really ask one of the squires of the court before he departed, but would wait till the morning when he took leave of the lord and his attendants. So he postponed the matter and put his mind on eating and drinking; in no stingy fashion were the delicious viands and wines brought to the table. The food was excellent; indeed, all the courses that king or count or emperor are wont to have were served to that noble and the youth that night.

After the repast the two passed the evening in talk, while the squires made up the beds for the night and prepared the rarest fruits: dates, figs, nutmegs, cloves, pomegranates, electuaries, gingerbread of Alexandria, aromatic jelly, and so forth. Afterwards they had many draughts of piment without honey or pepper, mulberry wine, and clear syrup. At all this the youth wondered, for he had never experienced the like. At last the nobleman said: "Friend, it is time to go to bed, and do not take it ill that I depart to my chamber to sleep. And when you please, you may lie here. Because of my infirmity I must be carried."

Four nimble and strong servants came out of a chamber, took hold by the four corners the coverlet of the couch on which the nobleman was lying, and carried him away. Other squires remained with the youth to serve him as was needed. When he wished, they removed his hose and other clothing and put him to bed in white linen sheets.

He slept till break of day, but the household had already risen. When he looked about, he saw no one, and was obliged to get up alone; though he was annoyed, he rose since he must, drew on hose without help, and took his arms, which he found at the head of the dais, where they had been brought. When he had armed himself well, he walked past the doors of chambers which he had seen open the night before. But all in vain, for he found them closed. He shouted and knocked. No one opened; there was no response. When he had called long enough, he went to the door of the hall, found it open, descended the steps, and found his horse saddled and his lance and shield leaning against the wall. He then mounted and searched about the courtyard, but saw neither servant nor squire. He rode to the gate and found the drawbridge lowered, for it had been so left that nothing should prevent him from passing it freely at any hour. Then he thought, since the bridge was down, that the squires must have gone into the forest to examine the nets and traps. So, having no reason to wait longer, he said to himself that he would follow after them and learn, if possible, from one of them why the lance bled and whither the grail was carried. He passed out through the gate, but before he had crossed the drawbridge, he felt that the feet of his horse were rising, and the animal made a great leap, and if he had not done so, both he and his rider would have come to grief. The youth turned his head to see what had happened and perceived that someone had raised the drawbridge. He called out, but no one answered.

"Speak," said he, "you who have raised the bridge! Speak to me! Where are you, for I do not see you? Show yourself, and I would ask you a question."

Thus he wasted his words, for no one would reply. So he rode toward the forest and entered on a path where there were fresh hoofprints of horses. "This is the way," said he to himself, "which the men I am seeking have taken."

Then he galloped through the forest as long as the tracks lasted, until he spied by chance a maiden under an oak tree, crying and lamenting in her distress. "Alas, wretch that I am, in an evil hour was I born! Cursed be that hour and that in which I was begotten! Never before has anything happened to enrage me so. Would that God had not pleased to make me hold my dead lover in my arms! He would have done better to let me die and let my lover live. O Death, why did you take his soul rather than mine? When I see him whom I loved best dead, what is life worth? Without him I care nothing for my life and my body. Death, cast out my soul that it may, if his soul deigns to accept it, be its handmaid and companion."

Thus she was mourning over the headless body of a knight which she clasped. The youth did not stop when he saw her, but approached and greeted her. She returned his greeting with head lowered, but did not cease her lament. The youth asked: "Who killed this knight who lies in your lap?"

"Good sir," the maiden replied, "a knight killed him this very morning. But one thing I see which amazes me. For people say that one may ride twenty-five leagues in the direction from which you came without finding an honest and clean lodging place, and yet your horse's flanks are smooth and his hide is curried. Whoever it was who washed and combed him, fed him on oats and bedded him with hay, the beast could not have a fuller belly and a neater hide. And you yourself look as if you had enjoyed a night of comfortable repose."

"By my faith, fair lady," said he, "I had indeed as much comfort last night as was possible, and if it appears so, there is good reason. If anyone gave a loud shout here where we are, it would be heard clearly where I lay last night. You cannot know this country well, for without doubt I have had the best lodging I ever enjoyed."

"Ah, sir, did you lie then at the dwelling of the rich Fisher King?"

"Maiden, by the Saviour, I do not know if he is fisherman

or king, but he is very rich and courteous. I can say no more than that late last evening I met two men floating slowly in a boat. One was rowing, the other was fishing with a hook, and he directed me to his house and there gave me lodging."

The maiden said: "Good sir, he is a king, I assure you, but he was wounded and maimed in a battle so that he cannot move himself, for a javelin wounded him through the two thighs. He is still in such pain that he cannot mount a horse, but when he wishes to divert himself, he has himself placed in a boat and goes fishing with a hook; therefore he is called the Fisher King. He can endure no other pastime, neither hunting nor hawking, but he has his fowlers, archers, and huntsmen to pursue game in his forests. Therefore he enjoys this place; in all the world no better dwelling could be found for his purposes, and he has built a mansion befitting a rich king."

"Damsel," said he, "by my faith, what you say is true, for last evening I was filled with wonder as soon as I came before him. I stood at a little distance, but he told me to come and sit beside him, and bade me not think that he did not rise out of pride, for he had not the strength."

"Surely he did you a great honor when he seated you beside him. Tell me, when you were sitting there, did you see the lance of which the point bleeds, though there is no flesh or vein there?"

"Did I see it? Yes, by my faith."

"Did you ask why it bled?"

"I said nothing about it."

"So help me God, learn, then, that you have done ill. Did you see the grail?"

"Yes, indeed."

"And who held it?"

"A maiden."

"And whence did she come?"

"From a chamber."

"Whither did she go?"

"Into another chamber."

"Did no one precede the grail?"

"Yes."

"Who?"

"Only two squires."

"What did they hold in their hands?"

"Candelabra full of candles."

"Who came after the grail?"

"Another maiden."

"What did she hold?"

"A little carving dish of silver."

"Did you not ask anyone where they were going?"

"No question came from my mouth."

"So help me God, that was worse. What is your name, friend?"

Then he who did not know his name divined it and said that his name was Perceval of Wales. He did not know whether he told the truth or not, but it was the truth though he did not know it. When the damsel heard it, she rose and faced him, saying angrily: "Your name is changed, good friend."

"What is it?"

"Perceval the wretched! Ah, unfortunate Perceval, how unlucky it was that you did not ask all those things! For you would have cured the maimed King, so that he would have recovered the use of his limbs and would have ruled his lands and great good would have come of it! But now you must know that much misery will come upon you and others. This has happened to you, understand, because of your sin against your mother; she has died of grief for you. I know you better than you know me, for you do not know who I am. I was reared with you in the house of your mother long ago. I am

your first cousin and you are mine. I grieve no less because
you have had the misfortune not to learn what is done with
the grail and to whom it is carried than because of the death
of your mother or because of this knight whom I loved dearly,
seeing he called me his dear mistress and loved me as a brave
and loyal knight."

"Ah, cousin," said Perceval, "if what you say is true, tell me
how you know it."

"I know it," the damsel answered, "as truly as one who
saw her laid in the earth."

"Now may God of his goodness have mercy on her soul!"
cried Perceval. "It is a sorrowful tale you have told. Now that
she is laid in earth, what is there left for me to seek? For I
was journeying only to see her. I must now take another road.
If you are willing to accompany me, I should be pleased. He
who lies dead here can no longer serve you, I warrant. The
dead to the dead, the living to the living. Let us go together,
for it seems very foolish for you to watch here alone over
this body. Let us pursue the slayer, and I promise and swear
that, if I overtake him, either he will force me to surrender,
or I will force him."

She, unable to suppress the great woe in her heart, said:
"Good friend, I cannot go with you or leave my lover until
I have buried him. If you listen to me, follow this paved road,
since it is by this way that the evil, insolent knight who killed
my sweet lover departed. So help me God, I have not said
this because I wish you to pursue him, though I wish him as
much harm as if he had slain me. But where did you get the
sword which hangs at your left side and which has never
drawn blood and has never been unsheathed in the hour of
need? I know well where it was forged and by whom. Do not
trust it, for it will betray you in battle and fly in pieces."

"Fair cousin, one of the nieces of my good host sent it to
him last evening, and he gave it to me, and I was well

pleased. But you terrify me if what you have said is true. Tell me now, if you know: if the sword should break, will it ever be repaired?"

"Yes, but with much hardship. If one could find the way to the lake which is near the Firth of Forth, he could have it hammered, tempered, and made whole again. If chance should take you there, go to a smith called Trebuchet, because he made it and will reforge it; it can be done by no other man."

"Surely," said Perceval, "if it breaks, I shall be in grievous peril."

Then he went his way, and she remained, unwilling to part from him whose death wrung her heart. Perceval followed the tracks until he came up with a lean and weary palfrey, which was walking ahead of him and by its wretched appearance seemed to have fallen into bad hands. It was travel-worn and starved like a hired horse which has been ridden hard all day and poorly cared for at night. It was so gaunt that it trembled as if with a distemper. The neck was shrunk, and the ears drooped. Its bones were covered only with hide, so that mastiffs and hounds would have expected to make a meal of it. There was a saddle on its back and a bridle on its head such as befitted such a beast.

The rider was a maiden. No one ever saw a more wretched, though she would have been beautiful if her fate had been happier. She was in such evil case that not a palm's breadth of her dress was whole and her nipples showed through the rents. Here and there it was fastened together with knots and rude stitches. Her skin seemed to be scratched, as if with a lancet, and it was tanned with heat and cracked with hail and frost. Her hair was loose, she wore no mantle, and on her face were the ugly traces of tears which ceaselessly flowed down to her breast and over her dress to her knees. Well might the heart feel anguish when the body suffered such pain.

As soon as Perceval perceived her, he rode up swiftly. She drew her robe about her to cover her skin, but as soon as she closed one hole, she opened a hundred others. Perceval approached her in her discolored and pitiful state and heard her bitterly complaining of her sorrow and pain: "O God, may it please Thee to end my life! I have suffered too long and too grievously, and I have not deserved it! O God, since Thou knowest well that I am innocent, send, if it please Thee, someone to free me from this misery, or do Thou deliver me from him who makes me live in such shame. I find no mercy in him. I cannot escape from him alive, nor will he kill me. I do not understand why he desires my company in this manner unless he enjoys my disgrace and woe. Even if he were certain that I deserved this usage, even if I am not dear to him, he ought to have pity on me since I have already paid so heavily. But it is sure that he does not love me when he puts this humiliation on me and shows no concern."

Then Perceval said: "Fair lady, God save you!"

When the damsel heard him, she bowed and said in a low voice: "Sir, for your greeting may you have all that your heart desires, and yet I have no cause to say this."

Perceval changed color for shame and replied: "In God's name, fair friend, what do you mean? Surely I do not know that I have ever seen you before or done you any wrong."

"You have indeed," said she. "You have made me so wretched that no one should greet me, and I sweat with fear when anyone stops me or looks at me."

"Truly," said Perceval, "I was not aware that I had injured you. I did not come here to do you shame or harm, but was following my road. Since I caught sight of you so poorly and scantily clad, I cannot be happy until I learn what chance has brought you to this sorrowful state."

"Ah, sir," said she, "have pity! Say no more but flee and leave me in peace. You do wrong to tarry. Be wise and flee!"

"I must know," said he, "for what danger or what threat I should flee when no one is pursuing me."

"Sir," said she, "be not offended, but flee while you can, before the Proud Knight of the Glade, who seeks nothing but strife and battle, finds us together. If he discovers you, he will kill you at once. He is so furious when anyone stops me that no one can depart with his head who is caught with me. It is but a short while since he killed a man. First, however, he tells each one why he holds me so vile and treats me so cruelly."

While they were talking, the Proud Knight came out of the wood and, raising a cloud of sand and dust, rode up like thunder, shouting: "In an evil hour did you halt to converse with the maiden! I would have you know that your end has come because you made her pause for a single step. But I will not kill you before I have told you for what misdeed I have put her to such shame. Listen and you will hear the story. One day I had gone hunting and had left this damsel, whom I loved more than all else, in my tent, when by chance a Welsh youth came there. I do not know what happened except that he kissed her by force and she has confessed it. If she lied, what harm was it? If he kissed her against her will, did he not afterward have all his desire? No one would believe that he would kiss her without doing more, for one deed leads on to another. One who kisses a woman and does no more when they are alone together is a faintheart. A woman who grants her mouth easily gives the rest; that indeed is what she intends. Beyond a doubt, as everyone knows, though a woman may defend herself, she has no wish to be victor in this struggle. Even when she takes a man by the throat and scratches, bites, and half kills him, she wishes to be overcome, however much she defends herself and delays. She is reluctant to surrender, for she prefers to be forced, and then she shows no gratitude. Therefore I believe that the youth lay with her. Besides he seized a ring that she wore on her finger and carried it away, and sorely it vexes me. And before that he drank some strong wine and ate one of three pasties I had ordered kept for me. But now my mistress is doing a noble penance, as you see. Whoever indulges in folly, let him pay for it so that he may beware of repeating it. When I returned and learned the truth, imagine my anger. I swore—and I was right—that her palfrey should have no oats nor be bled nor be shod again, and that she herself should wear no other tunic or mantle than the one she was then wearing, until I should have the best of him who had forced her, killed him and cut off his head."

When Perceval had heard this, he replied: "Friend, I assure you that she has done her penance. I am the youth who kissed her against her will and to her distress; I took her ring from her finger, but that was all. And if I ate one and a half of the three pasties and drank my fill of wine, I swear it was merely my stupidity."

"By my head," said the Proud Knight, "it is a wonderful thing to hear your confession! If it is true, you have richly deserved death."

"Still, my death is not as near as you think," said Perceval.

Without another word they gave their horses the spur and met with such fury that they splintered their lances and were hurled from their saddles, but they sprang up at once, drew their swords and exchanged great blows. The combat was stern, but it would be wasted time to say more than that they fought till the Proud Knight of the Glade surrendered and begged for mercy. Perceval, who never forgot the nobleman who had charged him not to kill any knight who begged for mercy, said: "Knight, I will have mercy on you only when you pardon your lady. She has never deserved, I swear, the harsh treatment you have given her."

The knight, who really loved the maiden more than the apple of his eye, said: "Good sir, by your counsel I will make amends to her. You cannot command anything that I am not ready to do. My heart is sombre with grief for the suffering I have caused her."

"Go then," said Perceval, "to the nearest manor you own hereabouts, so that she may bathe and rest till she is well again. Then make ready and take her, suitably garbed, to King Arthur, greet him for me, and place yourself at his mercy, equipped as you are here. If he asks who sent you, you will say: he whom he made a red knight at the advice of my lord Kay, the seneschal. And the suffering and the wrong you have done to your damsel, that you must rehearse before all the court so that all may hear it, including the Queen and her fair maidens. Of these I prize one above all. Kay struck her on the cheek and stunned her, merely because she laughed with pleasure at seeing me. Seek her out, I command you, and give her this message, that I will not be moved by any plea to join King Arthur's court till I have so avenged her that she will rejoice."

The Proud Knight replied that he would go and say everything that Perceval had enjoined, and that he would not delay except such time as was needed for his damsel to rest and make ready. He invited Perceval also to stay with him till his wounds healed. But Perceval said: "Go your way and may you have good adventure. But I have other plans and will seek shelter elsewhere."

Without further words they parted. That evening the Proud Knight arranged that his mistress should be bathed and richly robed, and thereafter saw that she was so well cared for that her beauty returned. Then they both took the direct road to

Caerleon, where King Arthur was holding court, but it was a small assemblage, for there were only three thousand valiant knights. Before them all the knight came, bringing his damsel, that he might surrender to King Arthur, and addressed him thus: "Sire, I am your prisoner to do with what you will. It is right and reasonable since that is the command of the youth who asked and obtained red arms from you."

As soon as the King heard this, he understood its meaning and said: "Disarm yourself, good sir. Joy and good adventure be his who has sent you as a gift to me, and you yourself are right welcome. For his sake you will be cherished and honored in my household."

"Sire," said the knight, "before I disarm, I have one thing more to say. I would ask that the Queen and her maidens come to hear the news that I have brought, for it will not be disclosed till she comes who was struck on the cheek because of a single laugh; that was her only offense."

He ceased, and the King, hearing what was required, sent for the Queen, and she came with all her maidens, two by two and hand in hand. When the Queen was seated beside her lord King Arthur, the Proud Knight of the Glade spoke: "Lady, a knight whom I honor highly and who overcame me in combat sends you greeting. I have no more to say of him save that he sends you this maiden, my mistress."

"Friend," said the Queen, "he has my great thanks."

Then the knight related all the cruelty, shame, and suffering he had long inflicted on her, and the reason for his behavior—all without concealment. Then the damsel whom Kay the seneschal had struck was pointed out to him, and he said: "He who sent me here, maiden, asked me to give you his greeting, and not to stir a foot hence till I had told you this. he will never, so may God help him, enter King Arthur's court till he has avenged you for the buffet you received on his account."

When the fool heard this, he leapt to his feet and cried: "Lord Kay, may God bless me, you will surely pay for that injury, and that right soon."

After the fool, the King spoke: "Ah, Kay, that was not courtesy when you mocked the youth. By your jest you robbed me of him so that I never expect to see him again."

Then the King caused the knight, his prisoner, to sit before him, freed him, and bade him disarm. Sir Gawain, who was sitting at the King's right, asked: "In God's name, sire, who can it be who, alone, vanquished by his arms as good a knight as this? In all the isles of the sea I have not heard of a knight, nor have I seen or known one, who could compare with him in arms and chivalry."

"Good nephew," said the King, "I do not know who he is though I have seen him; but when I saw him, I failed to ask. He demanded that I make him a knight on the instant, and, seeing him handsome and comely, I said: 'Brother, I will do so, but dismount till someone brings you gilded arms.' He refused to take them or to alight till he had red arms. He added other strange things, saying that he would accept no arms but those of the knight who had carried off my golden cup. Kay, who was and is and always will be ill-mannered and who never says a good word, spoke to him: 'Brother, the King gives you the arms; go take them at once.' The youth, who did not understand the jest, thought that Kay was telling the truth, followed the Red Knight, and killed him with the cast of a javelin. I do not know how the fight began, but only that the Red Knight of the Forest of Quinqueroi struck him, I know not why, with his lance, in contemptuous fashion. The youth then hit him in the eye with his javelin, killed him, and took his arms. Since then he has done me such good service that, by my lord St. David, to whom men pray in Wales, I will never lie two nights in the same chamber or hall till I see him, if he is alive, whether on sea or land, but I will start presently to seek him."

When the King had sworn this oath, all understood that the time had come to depart. One could have seen men packing bedclothes, coverlets, and pillows, filling chests, trussing pack horses, loading a large train of carts, stowing tents and pavilions. A clever and well-lettered cleric could not describe in a whole day all the baggage and provisions that were promptly got ready. Thus the King departed from Caerleon as if he led an army, and his barons followed, while the Queen, with equal pomp and majesty, took her whole retinue and left not a maiden behind. That night they camped in a meadow near a forest. Before morning there was a heavy fall of snow.

That same morning Perceval had risen early, according to custom, to seek adventure, and came to the meadow, covered with frost and snow, where the royal host had camped. But before he came to the tents, he saw and heard a flock of wild geese, which had been blinded by the snow and were flying with a clamor before a pursuing falcon. When one of them became separated from the flock, the falcon pounced on her and struck her to the ground, but since it was too early, left her without feeding. Perceval galloped toward the spot. The goose had been wounded in the neck and had shed three drops of blood which spread on the white snow like a natural color, but she was not injured so badly that she could not leave the earth, and before Perceval arrived, had flown away. When he saw the snow where the goose had lain beaten down and the blood drops around it, he leaned on his lance to gaze at the spectacle. The blood melting into the snow reminded him of the fresh hues of his lady's face, and he mused till he forgot himself. For so did the red of her cheeks stand out against the white as the three drops of blood stood out against the white snow. The sight pleased him so much that he seemed to behold the fresh color of his fair lady.

Perceval mused upon the drops of blood while the morning passed, until the squires, issuing from the tents, saw him in a reverie and thought that he was asleep. Returning, they encountered before the royal tent, where the King was still sleeping, Sagremor, who was called the Hothead because of his hot temper.

"Tell me," he cried, "and conceal nothing! Why are you in such haste?"

"Sir," they answered, "outside this camp we have seen a knight sleeping on his steed."

"Is he armed?"

"In faith, yes."

"I will go to speak with him," said he, "and bring him to the court."

At once Sagremor ran to the King's tent and waked him, saying: "Sire, on the heath yonder there is a knight sleeping."

The King bade him go and fetch the knight if he consented to come. Without delay Sagremor ordered his horse to be led out and his arms brought. His command was obeyed and, being promptly and fully armed, he rode out from the camp and approached the knight, saying: "Sir, you must come to the court."

Perceval did not move and seemed not to hear. Sagremor spoke again, and, when the other did not stir, he grew angry and shouted: "By St. Peter the apostle, you will come willy-nilly. I am sorry that I asked you, for I wasted my breath."

Then he unfurled the pennon wrapped round his lance, took his position, and then gave spurs to his horse, warning his adversary to beware, for he would strike him if he did not defend himself. Perceval looked and saw Sagremor charging at full speed. Emerging from his reverie, he spurred against him. At the encounter Sagremor's lance shattered, but Perceval's did not break or bend but struck his opponent with such force that he was hurled to the ground. The steed fled, head up, toward the tents, where those who were just rising saw it with great dismay. Kay, who could never refrain from mockery, said in jest to the King: "Good sir, see how Sagremor is returning. He is leading the knight by the bridle and bringing him against his will."

"Kay," said the King, "you do not well to make a mock of brave men. Go now and let us see whether you will fare better than he."

"Sire," said Kay, "I am very glad that you wish me to go. I will bring him back by force, whether he will or no, and make him tell his name."

Then he had himself armed, mounted, and rode toward him who was so absorbed in contemplating the three drops that he was oblivious to everything else. From a distance Kay shouted: "Knight, knight, come to the King! By my faith, you shall come, or you will pay dearly."

Hearing the threat, Perceval turned the head of his horse and pricked him with his steel spurs into a gallop. Both adversaries were eager to do their best and drove at each other in earnest. Kay splintered his lance in the shock, as if it had been a piece of bark. And Perceval was not slack but hit Kay above the boss of his shield and hurled him onto a rock, so that his collarbone was dislocated and his right arm was broken between the elbow and the armpit like a dry stick, just as the fool had foreseen and often described it. The lackwit's prophecy proved true. Kay fainted with the pain, and his horse trotted rapidly away toward the tents. The Britons saw it returning without the seneschal; squires rode to meet it, and ladies and knights bestirred themselves. When they found the seneschal in a swoon, they felt sure that he was dead and set up a loud lamentation, both men and women.

Perceval returned to gaze on the three drops, leaning on his lance.

But the King was deeply concerned over the seneschal's injury and sorrowed until he was informed that he need not be distressed, because Kay would recover, provided that he had a leech to restore the collarbone to its place and to set the broken arm. So the King, who had a tender feeling for Kay, sent a wise leech and three maidens trained in his school, who restored the collarbone and bandaged the arm so that the broken bone would knit together. Then they brought him to the King's tent, comforted him, and told him that he need not be anxious, for he would be cured. Sir Gawain addressed the King: "Sire, so help me God, it is not right, as you know and have always said, for one knight to disturb another's thoughts for any cause, and this your two knights have done. I do not know that they were wrong, but that they came to grief is certain. Perhaps the knight was brooding over some loss or was cast down because his lady had been stolen from him. Now, if it is your pleasure, I will go to observe him, and if I find that he has stopped brooding, I will request him to come to you here."

At these words Kay broke out in anger: "Ah, Sir Gawain, you expect to lead the knight here by the hand, even if he is reluctant. That will be a gallant deed, if he permits you and yields the upper hand to you. Many a prisoner you have won in this way. When a knight is weary and has had his fill of fighting, that is a fit time for a gallant knight to ask permission to go forth and subdue him! A thousand curses on my neck, Gawain, if you are not so wise that one can take lessons from you! You know how to make your fine, polished words pay! You would speak proud and insulting words to him? A curse on him who believed or believes that. Indeed you could carry out that errand in a silken gown, without drawing sword or breaking lance. You may well pride yourself that if your tongue is able to say: 'Sir, God save you and give you joy and health!' he will do your will. I do not speak for your instruction, for you know quite well how to smooth him down as one strokes a cat. Then people will say: 'Now Sir Gawain is waging a fierce battle!'"

"Ah, Sir Kay!," said Gawain, "you could surely speak more kindly. Do you think to get your revenge by pouring out your fury on me? In faith, good friend, I will bring him back, and without a broken arm or a dislocated collarbone, for I do not like such wages."

"Go now, nephew," said the King; "you have spoken with courtesy. Bring the knight if you can, but take all your arms, for you must not go defenseless."

Gawain, who was renowned for all the virtues, had himself armed speedily, mounted a strong and spirited horse, and came straight to the knight, who was still leaning on his lance and enjoying his reverie. But the sun had now melted away two of the drops of blood in the snow, and the third was disappearing, and so the knight was not so deep in thought as he had been. Sir Gawain approached him quietly, at an amble, without any hostile show, and said: "Sir, I would have greeted you if I had known your heart as I do my own; but I may say this, that I am a messenger of the King, who sends and begs you through me to come and speak with him."

"Two men have already been here," said Perceval, "who drove away my joy and the happy thoughts which absorbed me, and who treated me as if I were a captive. Anyone who tried to make me leave this place was not seeking my welfare. Before me were three drops of fresh blood which brightened the snow, and, looking at them, I seemed to see the fresh color in the face of my lovely mistress, so that I would never seek to leave."

"Truly," said Sir Gawain, "that was no boorish fancy, but right courteous and sweet. He who took your mind from it was a fool and overbold. But now I would gladly know what you intend to do. If it would not displease you, I will readily bring you to the King."

"Tell me first, dear good friend," said Perceval, "is Kay the seneschal there?"

"In faith, he is; and you may know that it was he who jousted with you but now, and the joust cost him a broken right arm and a dislocated collarbone."

"Then," said Perceval, "I have well avenged the maiden for the blow he gave her."

When Sir Gawain heard that, he gave a start in his amazement, and said: "Sir, God save me, it is you for whom the King is searching. What is your name?"

"Perceval, sir; and what is yours?"

"Sir, believe me truly that I received in baptism the name of Gawain."

"Gawain?"

"Indeed, good sir."

Perceval, filled with joy, said: "Sir, I have heard speak of you in many places, and I would greatly desire your acquaintance, if it would not displease you."

"Be assured," said Sir Gawain, "that it would not please me less than you, but rather more."

Perceval replied: "In faith, I will gladly go wherever you will, for it is right, and I shall regard myself more highly now that I am your friend."

They met and embraced; then they began to unlace helms, coifs, ventails, drew down the mail from their heads, and departed, making great joy. Squires who had witnessed their delight from an outpost ran to the King, exclaiming: "Sire, sire, in faith, Sir Gawain is bringing the knight, and they are rejoicing together."

There was no one who heard the news but left his tent and went to meet them. Kay said to his lord, the King:

"Now the honor belongs to Sir Gawain, your nephew. The fight must have been right stiff and dangerous, if I do not lie, because he is returning as whole and sound as he went out, as if he had never received a blow nor given one. He uttered no word of defiance. So it is right that he should have the glory and that men should say that he has accomplished what we others could not, in spite of all the strength and effort we put into it."

So Kay said his say according to his wont, whether right or wrong. Sir Gawain did not wish to bring his companion to court all armed, but had him disarmed in his tent, and a chamberlain drew a robe out of his chest and presented it to Perceval to wear. When he had donned a tunic and a fine, becoming mantle, the two proceeded hand in hand to the King, who was sitting before his tent. "Sire, sire," said Sir Gawain, "I bring you the knight whom you have wished to see this fortnight past. It is he of whom you have spoken much, it is he whom you set out to find. I present him to you, for here he is."

"Good nephew, many thanks!" said the King, rising to his feet in honor of the newcomer. "Good sir, you are right welcome! Pray tell me what I should call you."

"In faith, good lord King," said Perceval, "I will not hide my name. It is Perceval of Wales."

"Ah, Perceval, sweet good friend, now that you have come to my court, you shall not leave it by my will. I have been much troubled since I first saw you, not knowing the amends which God had destined for you. It was foreseen clearly by the maiden and the fool whom Kay the seneschal smote, so that all my court was aware of it. You have indeed fulfilled their prophecy in every point, so that no one can doubt it, for I have heard the truth about your exploits."

As he spoke, the Queen arrived, having heard tidings of the newcomer. When Perceval saw her and learned who she was, and recognized the damsel who followed her as her who laughed for joy at sight of him, he went to meet them, saying: "God give joy and honor to one who, by the testimony of all the eyes who see or have seen her, is the most beautiful and the best lady alive."

The Queen replied: "You are most welcome, as a knight whose high and noble prowess has been well proved."

Then Perceval greeted the maiden who had laughed, and embraced her, saying: "Fair one, if there is ever need, I would gladly be the knight whose aid will never fail you." And for this the maiden thanked him.

Great was the joy which the King, the Queen, and the barons made over Perceval of Wales. They returned that evening with him to Caerleon, and the rejoicing lasted that night and through the morrow. On the third day they saw a damsel come riding on a tawny mule, with a scourge in her right hand. Her hair hung in two black twisted braids, and if the book describes her truly, never was there a creature so loathly save in hell. Her neck and hands were blacker than any iron ever seen, yet these were less ugly than the rest of her. Her eyes were two holes, as small as those of a rat; her nose was like that of a monkey or a cat; her lips were like those of an ass or an ox; her teeth resembled in color the yolk of an egg; she had a beard like a goat. In the middle of her chest rose a hump; her backbone was crooked; her hips and shoulders were well shaped for dancing! Her back was hunched, and her legs were twisted like two willow wands. Her figure was perfect for leading a dance!

Into the King's presence the damsel urged her mule; never had such a creature come to a royal court. She gave a general greeting to the King and all the barons, but, seated on her tawny mule, she addressed Perceval alone, in these words: "Ah, Perceval, Fortune is bald behind, but has a forelock in front. A curse on him who greets or wishes you well, for you did not seize Fortune when you met her. You entered the dwelling of the Fisher King; you saw the lance which bleeds. Was it so painful to open your mouth that you could not ask why the drop of blood sprang from the white point of the lance? When you saw the grail, you did not inquire who was the rich man whom one served with it. Most unfortunate is he who when the weather is fairer than usual waits for even fairer to come. It was you, unfortunate man, who saw that the time and the place were right for speech, and yet remained mute. You had ample opportunity, but in an evil hour you kept silence. If you had asked, the rich King, who is now sore troubled, would have been wholly cured of his wound and would have held his land in peace—land which he will never hold again. Do you know what will happen if the King does not hold his land and is not healed of his wound? Ladies will lose their husbands, lands will be laid waste, maidens, helpless, will remain orphans, and many knights will die. All these calamities will befall because of you!"

Then, turning to the King, she said: "Oh King, I depart, and may it not offend you, for this night I must take my lodging far from here. I do not know if you have heard speak of Castle Orgulous; it is there that I am bound to go tonight. In that castle are five hundred and sixty-six knights of fame, and be assured that none but has a ladylove with him, noble, courteous, and fair. I tell you this because no one goes there without finding joust or battle; he who would perform feats of chivalry will not fail of his purpose if he seeks there. But if any would have the supreme glory of the world, I know the place, the very spot, where he may best win it, if he dares. On the hill which stands below Montescleire a damsel is besieged. Great would be the honor he would win who would raise the siege and deliver the maiden. All praise would be his, and if God grants him that good fortune, he will be able to gird on without fear the Sword with the Strange Hangings."

After saying all it pleased her to say, the damsel ceased and departed without another word. Sir Gawain then leapt up and vowed that he would go to Montescleire and do all in his power to rescue the lady. Giflet, son of Do, in turn announced that, if God aided him, he would make his way to Castle Orgulous. Kahedin spoke: "And I will ascend Mount Dolorous, and will not pause till I arrive."

But Perceval spoke otherwise, and vowed that henceforth he would not lie two nights in the same lodging, nor avoid any strange passage of which he might hear, nor fail to engage in combat with any knight who claimed to be superior to every other or even two other knights, until he could learn whom one served with the grail, and until he had found the lance that bleeds, and had heard the true reason why it bled. He would not give up the quest for any suffering. Thus as many as fifty arose and swore, one to another, that they would not fail to pursue any adventure or seek any marvel of which they heard, even though it were in the most perilous land. [Here Chrétien inserted adventures of Gawain.]

Perceval, as the story tells, had so lost his memory that he had forgotten God. Five times April and May had passed, five whole years indeed, since he had entered a minster or worshipped God or His cross. But for all that he did not cease to pursue chivalry, and sought out strange and stern adventures and proved his mettle and undertook no exploit from which he did not emerge triumphant. Within the five years he sent sixty knights of fame to Arthur's court as prisoners. Throughout this time he did not think of God.

Toward the end he was journeying, all armed as was his wont, through a wilderness, when he came upon three knights and ten ladies walking shoeless, in woolen gowns, their heads deep in their hoods. The ladies, who for the salvation of their souls were doing penance on foot for their sins, were astonished to see Perceval coming all armed, holding lance and shield. One of the three knights stopped Perceval and said: "Dear good sir, do you not believe in Jesus Christ, who wrote the new law and gave it to Christians? It is surely not right but rather a great sin to bear arms on the day that Jesus Christ died."

Perceval, who gave no heed to day or hour, answered: "What day is this then?"

"What day, sir? Do you not know? It is the holy Friday, the day when every man should adore the cross and weep for his sins, for today He who was sold for thirty pence was hung upon the cross. He who was clean of all sin saw the sins in which the whole world was bound and befouled and became a man for our sins. In truth He was both God and man, for the Virgin bore a Son, conceived by the Holy Ghost. In Him God received flesh and blood, so that His deity was concealed in human flesh. This is a certainty, and whoever does not believe it will never see His face. He was born of the Virgin Lady and took the form and the soul of man, together with the holy Deity. On this day He was crucified and delivered His friends from hell. Right holy was that death which saved the living and restored the dead to life. The wicked Jews, whom one should kill like dogs, in their hatred wrought their own harm and our good when they raised Him on the cross. Themselves they destroyed, and us they saved. All who believe in Him ought to spend this day in penitence. Today no man who believes in God should bear arms on field or road."

"Whence do you now come?" asked Perceval.

"Sir, we come from a good man, a holy hermit, who dwells in this forest, and, so great is his sanctity, he lives by the glory of heaven alone."

"In God's name, sirs, what were you doing there? What did you ask for or desire?"

"What, sir?" said one of the ladies. "We asked counsel for our sins and made confession—the highest work which a Christian can do who would draw near to God."

Hearing them, Perceval was moved to tears, and determined to go speak with the holy man. "I would go to the hermit," he said, "if I but knew the path or the road."

"Sir," was the answer, "whoever would go there should follow this path by which we have come, through this thick, scrubby wood, and let him watch for the twigs which we knotted with our hands as we came. We left such signs in order that no one seeking the holy hermit would lose his way."

Then they commended each other to God, without further inquiry. Perceval started on the path, sighing from the bottom of his heart because he felt that he had sinned against God and was deeply repentant. So, weeping, he traversed the wood and came to the hermitage. There he dismounted, removed his arms, and tethered his horse to a hornbeam. Entering a little chapel, he found the hermit, a priest, and another ministrant about to begin the highest and the sweetest service that can be celebrated in a church. As soon as Perceval entered the chapel he fell on his knees, and the good man called to him, seeing that he was humble and that the water flowed from his eyes to his chin. Perceval, who greatly dreaded that he had offended God, grasped the foot of the hermit, bent before him, and with joined hands begged for counsel of which he had great need. The good man bade him make his confession, for unless he were confessed and repentant, he could have no remission.

"Sir," said Perceval, "for five years I have not known where I was. I did not love God nor believe in Him, and I have done nothing but evil."

"Ah, good friend," said the worthy man, "tell me why you

have done so, and pray God to have mercy on the soul of His sinner."

"Sir, I was once at the house of the Fisher King, and saw the lance of which the point truly bleeds, but concerning that drop of blood which I saw hanging from the white steel, I did not ask, and ever since I have fared ill. Nor do I know whom one serves with the grail which I saw, and since then I have endured such sorrow that I would willingly have died. I forgot God, and have not implored His mercy and have done nothing, to my knowledge, to obtain pardon."

"Ah, good friend," said the worthy man, "tell me your name."

The other replied: "Perceval, sir."

At this word the worthy man, who recognized the name, sighed and said: "Brother, a sin of which you know nothing has wrought this harm. It was the sorrow you caused your mother when you left her, for she fell swooning to the earth at the end of the bridge before her gate, and died of that grief. Because of the sin you then committed it came to pass that you failed to ask concerning the lance and the grail. Thus many evils have befallen you, and know that you would not have endured so long if she had not commended you to God. But her prayer had such power, that God for her sake has preserved you from death and from prison. Sin cut off your tongue when you saw before you the bleeding point which never has been staunched, and did not ask the reason. And great was your folly when you did not learn whom one served with the grail. It was my brother, and his sister and mine was your mother. And believe me that the rich Fisher is the son of the King who causes himself to be served with the grail. But do not think that he takes from it a pike, a lamprey, or a salmon. The holy man sustains and refreshes his life with a single Mass wafer. So sacred a thing is the grail, and he himself is so spiritual, that he needs no more for his sustenance than the Mass wafer which comes in the grail. Fifteen years he has been thus without issuing from the chamber where you saw the grail enter. Now will I enjoin penance on you for your sin."

"Good Uncle," said Perceval, "with all my heart will I perform it. Since my mother was your sister, rightly should you call me nephew, and rightly I should call you uncle and love you the better."

"It is true, good nephew. But now listen: if your soul is seized with pity, you are indeed repentant, and for atonement go to the minster every day before any other place, and it will be for your good. Do not neglect it for any cause, but if you are in any place where there is minster, chapel, or parish church, go there when the bell rings, or earlier if you are already risen. Never will you regret it, but rather will your soul be benefited. If the Mass is begun, it will be all the better, and stay until the priest has finished his prayers and chants. If you choose to do so, you can still advance in worth and enjoy both honor and paradise. Believe in God, love God, worship God. Honor good men and good women. Rise in the presence of a priest; it is a service which costs little and God in truth loves it because it comes from humility. If a maiden asks your help, or a widow or an orphan girl, give it, and yours will be the gain. Such service is the highest. Aid them, and on no account weaken in welldoing. This is what I would have you do to atone for your sins and to recover all the graces which once were yours. Tell me now if you assent."

"Yes," said Perceval, "right gladly."

"Now I pray you that you stay two whole days with me and as a penance take only such food as mine."

Perceval agreed, and the hermit taught him an orison and repeated it till he knew it by heart. In this prayer were many names of our Lord, and they were so great that mouth of man ought not to utter them save in the fear of death. So after teaching the prayer, he forbade Perceval to say it except in great peril, and Perceval said: "Sir, I will not." So he remained and heard the service with great delight. After the service he adored the cross, wept for his sins, and repented of them heartily. Thus he meditated, and for supper that night he ate what the holy hermit pleased to give him, herbs such as chervil, lettuce, and cress, bread of barley and oats, and clear water of the spring, while his horse had straw and a basin full of barley, and was properly groomed and stabled.

Thus Perceval learned how God was crucified and died on a Friday, and on Easter Day he received the communion. Of him the tale tells no more at this point.

[The rest of the poem is occupied with the adventures of Gawain and ends at verse 9234 without returning to Perceval. Within the next two generations several poets in succession continued the narrative and brought Perceval back to the Grail castle more than once.]

TRISTAN AND

ISOLT

by Gottfried von Strassburg

Not many years ago Denis de Rougemont published a book which in America bore the title *Love in the Western World,* and which not only pretended to analyze this vast and subtle subject but also to set forth the history and esoteric meaning of the Tristan "myth." From a reading one deduces that the legend was a compound of druidic mythology, Albigensian heresy, courtly love and the wish for death. One is actually invited to believe that Tristan and Isolt did not love each other and that they never missed a chance of parting. This of the most famous lovers of medieval romance, who over and over again risked death to meet in secret embrace!

As a matter of fact, we now know, thanks to Bédier, Miss Schoepperle and other scholars, a great deal about the history of that legend and it bears almost no resemblance to de

Rougemont's speculations. It begain with a historical king of the Picts, Drust or Drustan, who reigned about 780. To him was attached a tale somewhat like that of Perseus and Andromeda, the outline of which was borrowed and incorporated in an Irish saga, the *Wooing of Emer*. In that outline one still finds a Drust, though demoted to a subordinate role, and one can recognize clearly certain elements of the medieval romance of Tristan. From Pictland, which bordered on Lothian (the Lyonnesse of Tennyson), the legend passed south to Wales, where Mark, Isolt and the elopement of the lovers to the forest were added; thence again southward to Cornwall, where Cornish raconteurs chose the romantic castle of Tintagel, whose ruins we see today, as the seat of Mark's court. Again southward across the Channel to Brittany, where we find that in about 1100 Breton boys were being christened Tristan, and where presumably storytellers added accounts of the sad birth and the tragic death of the hero. (Gottfried's "Parmenie" is now regarded as a corruption of Armorica, that is, Brittany.) Here, too, certain non-Celtic elements may well have been absorbed into the expanding legend—for instance, Tristan's marriage to Isolt of the White Hand, also localized in Brittany and derived from the Arab love story of Kais and Lobna. Thus a highly elaborated biographical romance came into being, full of crudities but full of vitality.

Once included in the repertory of Breton minstrels, as has been noted in our account of the origins of romance, it achieved a prodigious oral circulation. There is some curious dovetailing evidence that a Welshman, Bleheris or Breri by name, adopted this Breton version and made a sensation on the Continent by his recital of it in French. About 1154 the famous troubadour, Bernard de Ventadour, in a poem addressed to Eleanor of Aquitaine, declared that he suffered more pain for his lady than "Tristan l'amador" for Izeut. Some scholars believe that before this time a French poet had composed a long romance which was the source, direct or indirect, of all the full-scale histories of the lovers. Others are not so certain, because of the many differences between the three earliest versions, hard to explain if the three were directly dependent on a single written source. Nevertheless, all critics would agree that the tragic history of Tristan had crystallized in either an oral or a written form before 1150.

All would, we think, agree also that one reason for the success of the romance at that particular time was that it embodied, more by accident than design, cardinal doctrines of the new cult of "courtly love," of which Eleanor of Aquitaine and her daughter, Marie Countess of Champagne, were the high-priestesses. Whether this cult arose as a revolt against the sordidness of feudal marriage and the subservience of women, or as an offshoot from the Arabic idealistic cult of love as exemplified in the romance of Kais and Lobna, its principal tenets—the repudiation of holy matrimony and the concept of the mistress as inspirer of an all-absorbing devotion, as well as of courtesy and valor—could have found no more fitting and powerful narrative expression than the romance of Tristan and Isolt. Their moving story, as reflected in the arts, far surpassed in popularity all other secular subjects and is illustrated in the museums of London alone by medieval representations on four caskets, a German and a Sicilian embroidery and several English tiles.

The tile designs were based on a poem written about 1170 in England by a court poet, Thomas, perhaps for the delectation of Eleanor of Aquitaine, Henry II's queen. Thomas was probably a cleric; his education surely included a familiarity with the Latin classics, and one can trace in his poem the influence of *Apollonius of Tyre*. He insisted not only on the courtly accomplishments of his hero, such as hunting and harping, but also on his training in the liberal arts—a training which enabled Tristan to impart his knowledge to the Princess Isolt and make of her a learned heroine. One may well be skeptical of Thomas's invocation of the authority of Breri, but, whatever his sources, he endeavored to improve on them, to refine them. He seems to have dropped the repulsive episode in which Mark turned Isolt over to the lepers, and in general treats Mark with some sympathy though his heart is with the lovers. Indeed, at the end he tells us that he wrote for lovers, and through analysis, soliloquy and debate he sets forth with finesse and deep feeling the emotions of his chief characters. In the final scene of the *Liebestod*, however, he is content to abandon all subtlety and prolixity and to give us simply Isolt hastening up the steep street, the wonder of the people, the tolling of the bells and the last despairing words over Tristan's body.

Owing to Time's ravages, only fragments of Thomas's poem have reached us, but three redactions, in Norse, English and German, happily survive. The third is a poem composed by Gottfried von Strassburg about 1210 at the height of the German poetic Renaissance, and there are many critics who regard it as the greatest of all medieval romances. At any rate, Gottfried's own declaration and a comparison with his source reveal him as a conscious and conscientious artist, clear as to his aims and proud of his attainment. He carries much farther and higher the process of rationalizing and refinement begun by Thomas. He carefully notes the inconsistencies and improbabilities of his source and corrects them, and supplies motivation where it is lacking. He refines the manners, for example, making Tristan give the potion to Isolt before drinking himself.

The most significant and original change is the sublimation of the feeling of Tristan for Isolt, and hers for him. For Thomas that feeling, though sensual, was dignified by its intensity and lastingness; the potion did not, as in other versions, lose its power with the passage of time. It was Thomas from whom Gottfried borrowed the famous couplet: *"Isolt ma drue, Isolt m'amie, En vous ma mort, en vous ma vie!"* But this was not enough for Gottfried. Love, though it leads to sin and grief, is somehow above them both. Without *Minne* (romantic love) there is no honor, and in *Minne* grief becomes bliss. All is stale and unprofitable that is not love, and love is spiritualized till it resembles the mystic union of the soul with Christ.

This concept finds its supreme expression in the lyrical de-

scription of the life of the lovers in the wilderness, banished
from the comforts and the companionship of the court. It is
symbolized in the Love-Grotto which became their home and
their temple of Goddess *Minne.* As the poet expounds the
features of the grotto, in a passage not included in the following translation, it is obvious that he had in mind the sym-
bolic interpretation of a Christian church. To quote from Professor Closs: "The rounded vault represents the single-hearted-
ness of love, the breadth love's boundless power, the height
noble-mindedness, the white wall purity, the floor constancy;
through the three windows (kindness, humility, good breeding), the light of honor shines into the house of love. Entrance is granted only to *edeliu herzen,* who possess delicacy of
feeling. No German poet has gone further than Gottfried in
making a religion of love." Indeed, according to the poet God
himself approves it.

The poem remained unfinished, ending shortly after
Tristan's marriage to Isolt of the White Hand. It was supplied
with two inferior conclusions, one by Heinrich von Freiberg,
the other by Ulrich von Türheim. Miss Jessie Weston's translation, published in 1899, is rather freely abridged and is not
intended to be literal; the lyrical style of the original defies
such treatment. The conclusion she based mainly on Heinrich,
with the exception of the dramatic meeting of the two Isolts,
based on Ulrich.

R. S. L.

THE STORY *

I have undertaken a task to please the world and to delight
lofty spirits; that is, the spirits whom I love and the world
into which my heart gazes. I do not mean the everyday world,
of which I have heard it said that it can bear no grief. This

* Translated and abridged by Jessie L. Weston. First published
by David Nutt (London, 1899).

world and mine stand far apart. It is another world that I mean, which bears in one heart at the same time the bitter-sweetness and the misery of love, its heart's love and its yearning misery, its life of love, its death of misery, its death in love, its life in sorrow.

In the olden days there lived in the land of Parmenie[1] a young knight of royal birth named Rivalin, who held his land of a certain duke named Morgan. He was fair both of face and limb; rich, freehanded, bold and faithful. Now when he had been three years a knight, and was well practiced in all knightly skill (whether because his lord had wronged him, or because he longed to try his fortune in war, the chronicle does not say), he raised an army and marched into Morgan's land, and laid siege to his castles, many of which fell into his hands. On his side Morgan gathered his men together and did much harm to Rivalin; and many valiant deeds of knighthood were done, and the land wasted with fire and sword, before they made a year's truce with each other, and Rivalin returned home glad at heart, and with much booty which he shared freely among his knights.

But the time was weary to him that he was not fighting, and he longed to win more honor; so, since he had heard men speak of the young King of Cornwall, Mark, that he was both courteous and valiant, he bade them make ready a ship, and provision it well, and set sail southward, that he might pass the year of truce at King Mark's court. For it seemed to Rivalin a wise and fitting thing for a prince to learn the customs and courtesies of other lands. And while he should be absent from his kingdom he gave his lands and all that he had into the care of his marshal, Rual, whom men called the Faith-keeper, for he knew he might trust him well; and with no more than twelve companions he set sail for Cornwall.

When Rivalin came to the Cornish land he heard that

[1] A corruption of Armorica, i. e., Brittany.

King Mark held his court at the castle of Tintagel, and he and his men clad themselves in their richest robes and made their way thither; and Mark received them so courteously that the young knight thought to himself, "I have done well in coming to this folk. All that I heard of Mark is true; he is a good and gracious king." Then he opened all his heart to his host, and told him wherefore he had come; and Mark answered him, "Body and goods, all that I have are at thy service to do even as thou wilt with them." So Rivalin dwelt at the court, and all men loved him.

Now the time for the yearly high feast came round; for every year through the month of May Mark held high court, and the knights from Cornwall and England came and brought their ladies with them, and all was mirth and rejoicing. The tents were pitched in a meadow nigh to Tintagel, where there was everything to delight eye and ear: the birds sang in the thicket, the green grass was studded with flowers, a stream rippled through the meadow, and the linden boughs waved in the soft summer wind. The guests lodged each one as it pleased him best: some in pavilions of silk, some in bowers woven of the green summer boughs; they rode knightly jousts, and danced, and made merry all the day long.

But of all the fair maidens there was none so fair as the king's sister Blanchefleur; the sight of her face made many a noble heart beat high for gladness. And of all the knights there were none so valiant as King Mark and his guest Rivalin. All who saw the young knight praised his courage and skill and fair appearance; and as the maiden Blanchefleur watched the knightly sport, the love of the stranger prince crept into her heart, and though she hid her secret from all men, yet she knew him to be her chosen lord.

And one day he saw her as she sat alone, and greeted her, saying, "God keep thee, sweet lady."

"Gramercy," said the maiden, and spoke shyly. "God give

thee all good fortune, Sir Knight; and yet methinks I have somewhat against thee."

"Ah, sweetest lady, what have I done?"

And she said, "Thou hast made me sorrowful for a friend, the best I ever had."

Then the knight thought to himself, "What is this? What can I have done to lose her favor?" For he thought that surely she spoke of some kinsman or friend whom perchance he had overthrown and wounded in a knightly joust. But the maiden was thinking of her own heart. And as the young knight thought upon her words, how she spake, and how she looked, love was kindled in his heart too, and though no word passed between them, yet their eyes told the tale, and each knew that they loved the other more and more as the days went on.

When the feast had come to an end and the guests had gone to their own homes, tidings came to King Mark that one of his foes had ridden into his land and was laying it waste with fire and sword. Then Mark collected a great army and rode against him, and in a great battle defeated him with such slaughter that he might well account himself fortunate who escaped with his life. But Rivalin was wounded in the side with a spear, and his men bare him back to Tintagel, as they deemed, dying. At first the rumor went about the court that he was slain, and great lamentation was made, for all men thought it a great pity that so fair and brave a knight should die so young, and Blanchefleur in her chamber wept, and tore her hair, and was ready to die for grief. She sent for the mistress of her court, and prayed her to order things so that she might see Rivalin once more, even though he were already dead.

Then the mistress thought, "Little harm can come of this; though the knight be not dead, yet if he live to the morning 'tis all he may do, and if I give my lady her will now she will love me the better henceforward." So she said, "Dear princess, I will do all that I may, have no doubt of that; but it will be better that I go first alone and see how the matter stands."

Then she went her way to Rivalin's chamber, as if she had come to tend him, and secretly she told him that her lady desired to see him; and it rejoiced the knight greatly. Then she gave out that she would bring a wise woman—one skilled in the virtue of herbs—to wait on the wounded prince; and going her way to Blanchefleur, she dressed her in a waiting-woman's robe and hid her face in a veil, and so brought her, none knowing it was the princess, to Rivalin's side. And when the maiden saw her love lie there, pale and to all seeming lifeless, she fell down swooning. Then she raised him in her arms and kissed him over and over again, till her kisses brought him back to life and her love gave him strength to live.

So Rivalin recovered; but the two still kept their love secret, for they had little hope that Mark would give his sister to a stranger, and none but the princess's faithful lady knew of the matter, or deemed how often the lovers met.

But alas! news came to Rivalin that his foe, Morgan, had broken the truce and marched into his kingdom, and Rual prayed that his lord would return in haste and defend his lands. So he went his way to tell Blanchefleur the ill tidings, and she fell to weeping piteously.

"Alas, alas!" she said, "woe is me! What may I do, left here alone? For when my brother learns, as he surely will do some time, that I have given my love without his will, he will disinherit me and take all my lands and money from me!"

"What wouldst thou have me do, sweetheart?" said Rivalin. "Shall I abide here with thee, and lose my kingdom? Or wilt thou fly with me now by night to mine own land? I will do whatever shall please thee best."

"Then will I come with thee," said Blanchefleur. So that evening, when Rivalin went to bid farewell to King Mark, the princess disguised herself, and stole down through the twilight to the ship—and they set sail and fled together from Cornwall.

But when they came to Rivalin's country they found that Morgan had gathered together a vast army, and all the land was in terror for him. But first, ere he gathered together his men and went forth against his foeman, by Rual's counsel Rivalin wedded the princess with great state in the minster, in the presence of all his nobles, so that if harm should befall him in the war all should know that Blanchefleur was his wedded wife and their liege lady. And for a time they were happy in each other's love. But when the army was raised, then Rivalin must needs go forth with it; and the war was fierce and terrible—till at last a great battle was fought, in which many a valiant knight was slain, and, alas! among them the brave and gallant Rivalin. And when they brought the news to Blanchefleur she spake no word and shed no tear, but for four days she lay without speaking, and on the fourth day she bare a fair son, and died.

And when the faithful marshal Rual saw that both his lord and his lady were dead he knew he must needs make peace with Morgan, yet he feared greatly lest he should harm the child who was rightful heir to the lands. So he caused it to be proclaimed abroad that the babe had died with its mother, and secretly he bare it to his wife, and said that she had borne him another son.

So Rivalin and Blanchefleur were buried in one grave, and all thought that their child lay with them; but the babe was safe in Rual's care, and he named him *Tristan*, and brought him up as his own son.

Till he was seven years old Tristan dwelt with the wife of the marshal, and had no thought save that she was his mother, for she loved him well; and when he was seven Rual gave him into the charge of a wise and learned man named Kurwenal, that he might journey with him into foreign lands, and there learn the lore of books, and foreign tongues, and all the skill that should befit a prince. For seven years did he dwell abroad, and when he came again to his own land all men were loud in his praise, he was so well grown a lad, so fair to look upon, and courteous in his speech and bearing.

Now, after Tristan had dwelt some time in his home, a ship from Norway, laden with all kinds of merchandise, put in at the port, and the men displayed their wares before the castle. News was brought to Tristan that there were some goodly falcons on board, and his brothers, Rual's sons, prayed him to go with them to their father and win leave to go down to the ship and themselves see the birds, and if need were, purchase them. And inasmuch as Rual never denied Tristan anything on which he had set his heart, he said that he himself would go with the lads, and see what the merchants had brought. So they all went together to the ship and found there all that heart could desire—jewels, silk, and fair raiment. Nor was there any lack of birds; peregrines, merlins, and sparrow hawks—all that could be needed for the chase—and Tristan bade them purchase hawks for himself and also for his brothers.

When they had bought all they desired and were about to leave the ship, as ill luck would have it, Tristan spied a chessboard that hung on the wall, and beside it chessmen cunningly carved in ivory. Then he turned to the master of the ship and said in the man's own tongue, "What, noble merchant, canst thou play chess?"

The merchants looked keenly on the youth when they heard him speak in their tongue, which but few folk in that land knew, and they thought they had never seen a fairer lad, nor one of more courteous manner, and one of them answered,

"Yea, friend, there are many among us who are skilled in the game; if it so please thee, I myself will play a match with thee."

Tristan answered, "Let it be so," and the two sat down to the board.

Then said the marshal, "Tristan, I will e'en return to the castle; if thou wilt thou canst remain here; thy brethren shall come with me, and I will leave Kurwenal to guard thee."

So the marshal and his folk went back to the shore, and Tristan and his governor remained alone on the ship. And, if the story tells true, never was there a nobler lad than Tristan, or one of truer heart and more courteous bearing; and Kurwenal himself, who had taught the boy all he knew, was a good man and true.

Thus Tristan sat and played chess with the strangers, and they looked upon him, and marveled much at his gentle and courteous ways, and yet more at his skill in tongues, for scarcely might they tell of what land he came, so many foreign tongues he spake. All the terms of chess fell readily from his lips, and he taught them much they knew not before. Also he sang to them strange sweet melodies, with a cunning refrain, till the strangers, listening, thought it would be a good thing for them could they take the boy with them; his skill would bring them both gold and honor. So secretly they bade the oarsmen draw up the anchor, and put to sea, and this they did so quietly that neither Tristan nor Kurwenal knew aught of the matter till they were a good mile from shore.

At last Tristan won the game, and looked up and took note of what was around him, and when he saw how he had been entrapped, never was any lad more sorrowful. He sprang to his feet, crying, "Ah, noble merchant, what means this? What will ye do with me? Whither are ye taking me?"

Then one of them spake: "See, friend, thou canst do no

otherwise but must even come with us. Be at ease and make merry."

But Tristan began to weep and lament, and Kurwenal with him, till the merchant and the crew waxed wrathful. So they took Kurwenal and placed him in a little boat, with oars and food, and bade him go where he listed, but Tristan should stay with them. So they set him adrift, and by good hap the current bare him homeward, and he came to the marshal and told him what had chanced; and Rual and his wife were sorely distressed, and ran, weeping, with all their folk to the sea shore. And as night fell, and they could see nothing, and knew not whither the ship had taken its course, they cried, lamenting, "Fair Tristan, courteous Tristan, we commend thy fair body and soul to God; may He guard and protect thee!"

Thus the men from Norway bare Tristan away with them, and deemed they had got all their will. But as they sailed there arose a great tempest, and a mighty storm wind blew the ship hither and thither, so that they could not hold on their course, but drifted even as the wind drove them. And the great waves now tossed them up to the heavens, now drew them down to the depths, so that none might stand on his feet. This they did for eight days and eight nights, and at length one spake, and said, "Surely this is God's doing, and a judgment on us for stealing Tristan from his friends"—and the others answered of a truth they deemed it was even so.

So they took counsel together, and determined if the wind and the waves would abate so that they might put into any port, whatsoever it might be, they would touch at the first land they came to, and there set Tristan ashore, to go whither he would. And even as they had made their compact the winds fell, and the sea grew calmer, and the sun shone once more.

Now, in their eight days' drifting they had come nigh to the coast of Cornwall, and, seeing they were near to land, they drew in, and set Tristan ashore, and gave him bread and other food, saying, "Friend, God give thee good fortune." Thus they blessed him and went on their way.

Now what did Tristan do? At first he sat him down and wept, for he was but a boy and all alone in a strange land. Then he knelt down and held up his hands to heaven, and said, "Dear God, I pray Thee that Thou wouldst look upon me, and be gracious to me, and show me how I may come where I shall find folk. Here I am all alone, with no living soul near me, and I fear me much for this great wilderness, for I see nothing but wild rocks and sea, and I fear for the wolves lest they devour me, for the day draws toward eventide."

Then he bethought him that he would climb one of the cliffs which were near at hand, if by chance from the summit he might see something of human life, or see some shelter where he might pass the night. Now Tristan was richly dressed in a robe and mantle of silk, green as the grass in June, and furred with white ermine. He drew up his robe higher through his girdle, and folded his mantle, laying it across his shoulders, and so set out inland.

The way was rough, and there was neither path nor road; hand and foot were both needed to make his way. So he climbed over stock and stone till he came out upon the hilltop and found a curving path, narrow and overgrown with grass. He followed this down to the valley, and it brought him out on a fair road, wide and good for traffic.

The boy sat him down by the roadside and wept, for he was weary and lonely, and his heart turned back to his friends and his country, where he knew the folk and loved them. "Ah, God," he said, "I have lost both father and mother. Alas! had I but left my foolish chess, which I shall hate for evermore! Ill luck betide ye all, falcons, hawks, and merlins! Ye have taken me from my father, my kin, and all who wished me well, and now are they all in sorrow for me. Sweet Mother, I know well how thou art mourning, and thou, too, Father! Could I but let them know that I am living and in good health! But I know well that neither they nor I may be joyful till we have tidings one of the other!"

As he sat thus lamenting he saw coming toward him two pilgrims, well on in years, with long hair and beard. They were clad in linen garments, with a hood, and scallop shells and suchlike tokens sewn upon them. They were barefooted, and held staves in their hand, and on their back were palm branches; and as they went they chanted their prayers and psalms. As they drew near to Tristan, and he saw what manner of men they were, he said joyfully, "Now thanks be to Thee, O God. Of these good folk need I have no fear." He waited till they were so close they needs must see him, and then went toward them courteously, with outstretched hands.

The pilgrims greeted him in kindly wise: "God save thee, fair friend, whoever thou mayst be."

Then Tristan bowed to the old men, and said, "God bless such holy company"; and they looked on him and said, "Dear child, whence art thou, and who has brought thee hither?"

Now Tristan was wise and prudent for his years, and he thought it might be well not to say what had really chanced. "Dear sirs," he answered, "I am a native of this land, and this morning I rode forth hunting in the wood with my comrades, and outrode huntsmen and hounds. They knew the wood paths better than I, and so it chanced that I took a path that led me astray. I came over this hill, and thought to lead my horse downward, but he wrested the bridle from my hand, and fled back into the wood. Then I struck this path that led me hither, but now I know not where I am, nor whither I should go. Good sirs, tell me whither ye may be bound?"

"Friend," they answered, "we hope tonight to sleep in the city of Tintagel."

Then Tristan courteously prayed them to let him go with them.

"Dear child," said the pilgrims, "come with us an thou wilt."

So he turned with them, and they went on together, and Tristan talked with the old men, and answered them so readily and so courteously, that they wondered much, seeing his fair face and his rich dress, and said within themselves, "Who may this lad be, who has such courteous manners?" Thus they walked on a mile or so.

Now, even as they went, it chanced that the hounds of King Mark had that morning chased a stag and slain it by the roadside. The hunters had come up with them, and were blowing gaily on their horns. When Tristan saw them, he said to the pilgrims, "Sirs, these be the hounds, the stag, and the folk I lost earlier in the day. With your leave I will rejoin them."

"God bless thee, lad," they answered. "Thou goest to good fortune wherever thou goest."

"Fair thanks, good sirs, God keep you," said Tristan courteously, and turned toward the hunt.

When he came up they were even about to quarter the stag.

"Halt!" cried Tristan; "what woodcraft is this?"

" 'Tis the custom of our land," said the huntsmen. "Canst thou show us a better?"

"Yea, forsooth," said Tristan. "In my land we skin the stag and take out the entrails ere we cut it up."

The huntsman looked on the lad and saw he was richly clad and of noble bearing, and being himself courteous, he said, smiling, "See, if thou wilt, thou canst show us how these things are done in thy land. I and my fellows will gladly aid thee."

Then Tristan laid aside his mantle, and rolled up his sleeves, and tucked his flowing curls behind his ears, and bent down over the stag, and showed the huntsman how in his northern land they skinned the quarry and cleaned it, and cut it up into its several parts. And when he had finished, he bade them lay all the pieces in order on the skin, and take the head in their hand, and so bear it to their lord. Then because they were mightily pleased with his skill and courtesy, they prayed him to ride with them to court, and Tristan said, "That may I well do. Take up the stag, and let us hence."

As they rode together the huntsmen asked him who he was and whence he came. And Tristan said, "Far to the north lies a land, Parmenie— There my father is a merchant, and hath riches sufficient to live right well in merchant wise. A brave man and good is he, too, and made me learn all that I might. Often there came to us merchants from foreign lands, and I learned their speech and their ways, till at last a desire came upon me to see the folk and the countries of which I had heard, and I thought thereon early and late, till at last I ran away from my father and came hither with merchants. Now ye know all."

" 'Twas well done lad," said the huntsmen, "for life in a strange land teaches men much. Surely that land is blest of God where a merchant bears such a son as thou art; no king could have trained his son better. Tell us, fair youth, how did thy father call thee?"

"Tristan," he answered. "Tristan is my name."

"Nay," spake another, "what made him call thee thus? Surely thy fair and smiling youth might have been better named."

Thus they rode on, talking together, till they came in sight of the burg. Then Tristan brake two boughs from a linden, and wove them into chaplets for himself and the chief huntsman.

"Tell me," he said, "what is yon castle?"

"Tintagel," said the other.

"God keep thee well, Tintagel, and all the folk within thee," quoth Tristan.

"A good wish, fair lad, and may fair befall thee within our walls."

As they came near to the castle gates Tristan bade them ride in order, two and two, and give him a horn that he might blow a blast thereon. So they passed through the gateway in fair order, and Tristan blew a melody on his horn the like of which they had never heard before, and all joined in, so that the courtyard rang again.

When the king and his courtiers heard the strange notes, they were startled, and made their way to the palace door to see who this folk might be, and marveled much to find that they were but their own people. And when King Mark saw Tristan his heart went out to him, though he knew not that he was of his own blood and his own kindred, and he greeted him kindly; and Tristan answered again in such wise that Mark wondered, and called up the huntsmen, and said, "Who may this lad be who speaks thus courteously?"

"Lord," answered the other, "he is a Parmenois, and he says his name is Tristan, and his father a merchant, but that I may not believe, for what merchant would ever have brought up his son in such courtly wise? He is learned in the chase, too, and hath shown us how to skin and divide the quarry in such cunning fashion as we never knew before."

Then the king bade the younger courtiers fetch Tristan into the palace and bring him before the throne, and he said, "Tristan, thou must needs do me a favor, and I will not have it otherwise."

"It shall be as thou wilt, my lord."

"Thou shalt be master of my hunt, Tristan."

Then all around laughed gaily, and the lad answered, "Command me as thou wilt, lord. Huntsman and servant will I be to the best of my power."

"Then let it be so," said King Mark.

Thus Tristan, all unknowing, had come to his own people and his mother's home, and yet deemed himself a stranger in a strange land.

King Mark bade the men of his court treat the lad kindly, which they were willing enough to do, and he himself loved him dearly, and wherever he went would have Tristan at his side.

One even after meat they sat in the hall, and a harper sang a lay before the king. Tristan listened to the sweet notes till he could no longer keep silence.

"Master," he said, "thou harpest well, 'tis even so that the lay should sound; 'twas made by Bretons of Gurûn and his lady."

The harper said nothing till the lay was ended, and then he turned him to the lad and said, "What dost thou know of the lay, fair youth? Canst thou sing it?"

"Yea, good master," said Tristan; "I was taught it aforetime, but so little skill have I, I dare not play before thee."

"Nay, friend," said the harper, "take this harp, and let us hear how men play in thy land."

"Is it thy will that I play?" said Tristan.

"Yea, fair comrade, harp on."

So Tristan took the harp in his hands that were well skilled to such a task, and struck the notes softly, and sang the lay of Graalent and his proud lady; and Mark sat on his throne and listened, and marveled much at his skill, for indeed, as the old romances tell us, there was no knight in those days who could touch the harp or make songs and sing them as Tristan could; and even to this day we have some of the lays he sang. All the courtiers came into the hall and drew near to hearken, for they knew not which was the sweetest, his harping or his singing. And they said, each to the other, "Who is this lad who is dwelling among us? For none other is there in all this land who can be compared with him."

And King Mark said, "Tristan, may he be honored of God who taught thee this skill, and thou with him. Thou shalt play to me when the night falls; it will keep thee from slumber, and rejoice us both."

"That will I gladly," said the lad.

"And canst thou speak all these tongues in which these lays are made?" said Mark.

"That can I of a truth," said Tristan.

Then all the strangers at court drew near—men of Norway, Scotland, and Ireland, Danes and Germans—and to all of them Tristan spake in their own tongue.

Then King Mark said, "Tristan, in thee is all that I need in my friend; henceforth will we be comrades. Robes and horses, as many as thou wilt, canst thou have, and take here this bracelet and this golden horn; dwell here with us, and be joyful."

So Tristan abode at King Mark's court, and was loved of all men. And meanwhile the marshal, Rual, sought through the wide world to find him.

For Rual, the marshal, the Faith-keeper, had set sail, with much money in his ships, vowing he would not return till he might bring back his young lord, Tristan. He came to Norway, and went through the whole land, seeking for the boy, but could hear no tidings of him. Then he sailed to Ireland, and sought him there, but in vain; and when he found his money was well-nigh spent, he sent his folk home, and sold his horses, and went himself on foot through the country, till at last, when he had spent all he had, he was forced to beg his bread from place to place. Yet he never rested, but wandered on from land to land, ever hoping to find the boy.

At length, in the fourth year, he came to Denmark, and as he went from town to town, asking all he met if they had seen his young lord, he fell in with the two pilgrims whom Tristan had met in Cornwall, and they told him how they had seen even such a lad as he described; and they told him the time they had seen him, and how he was clad, the fashion of his dress, his face and his speech, and Rual knew well it could be none other than his foster son. And when he heard where they had parted from him, in Cornwall, and nigh to Tintagel, he said to himself, "This surely is the hand of God, for if Tristan be indeed in Cornwall, then has he come to his own land and his own folk, for Mark, the king, is his uncle, his mother's brother. Now God prosper my journey, for I must needs seek Cornwall without delay."

So he bade farewell to the pilgrims, thanking them for their good tidings, and took his journey to the sea coast, scarce resting on his way. But when he came thither, there was no ship bound for Cornwall, and he must needs wait a while. And when he found a ship it took him not into Cornwall, but to Britain, and he had a long journey on foot before he found the place he sought.

It was on a Saturday, early in the day, that he came to Tintagel, ere the folk went to Mass, and he took his stand outside the minster. He would fain have asked tidings of the folk around him, but deemed they would disdain him, being so worn and travel-stained.

Then King Mark came with a goodly following to Mass; and Rual looked well on them, and saw not him whom he sought. So he took courage, and when the king left the minster he spake to an old man of courtly bearing, and said, "Sir, of thy good will I pray thee tell me if there be here at court a boy named Tristan?"

"A boy?" said the other. "Nay, but there is a young squire, shortly to be made a knight, whom the king loves much. He is courteous and skilled in all knightly ways; a well-grown youth with brown curling hair and fair face, a stranger, and we call him Tristan."

"Sir," said Rual, "art thou of the court?"

"Yea," said the other.

"Then I pray thee of thy courtesy do this thing for me. Say to Tristan that a poor man, one of his fellow-countrymen, would fain speak with him."

So the courtier went his way and told Tristan, and he came swiftly, and when he saw who it was that sought him, he cried, "Now, blessed be God, Father, that I see thee once more!" and laughing for joy, he ran to him and kissed him, even as a son should; and, indeed, no father on earth might do more for his son than Rual had done.

"Tell me, Father," said Tristan, "how fares it with my mother? And my brothers, are they well?"

"In sooth, my son, I know not, for since the day I lost thee I have not set foot in mine own land, nor seen any whom I knew."

"What dost thou mean, Father? And now I see thee thou art thin and worn, and poorly clad."

" 'Tis for thy sake, son, and for seeking thee."

"Then will I repay thee all thy toil. Come now to the court with me."

"Nay, son, that may I not. Thou seest well I am clad in no courtly wise!"

"Nevertheless thou must needs come, that my lord the king may see thee."

Then Rual thought within himself that when King Mark heard all that he could tell him, and knew Tristan to be his nephew, he would care little for his torn clothing; a messenger who bears good tidings is ever well clad! So the two went together to the court, and King Mark said to Tristan, "Say, Tristan, who may this man be?"

" 'Tis my father, sire," said Tristan.

"Is that so?" asked the king.

"Yea, of a truth."

"Then shall he be welcome here."

And with that all the courtiers came and greeted him kindly, for they saw that though Rual's clothes were torn and threadbare, yet he was tall and stately to look upon, and had the manner of one well used to courts.

The king bade them give him fitting robes, and made him sit and eat at his own table, and bade Tristan wait upon him; but Rual's greatest pleasure was to look on the lad whom he had found again. Then after meat the king questioned Rual as to how he had come thither, and of his country.

"Lord," said Rual, " 'tis four years and a half since I left my own land, and since then I have asked tidings of nothing save of that which I sought, and which hath brought me hither."

"And what may that be?"

"Tristan, my lord, whom thou seest here. And in sooth I have three sons, by God's grace, at home, who are dear to me as sons may be; were I at home now they would all be knights, yet had I suffered for these three one-half of what I have suffered for Tristan, who is no son of mine, I had done much."

"No son of thine?" said the king. "How may that be? He calls himself thy son."

"Nay, lord, mine is he not, yet I am his, for I am his servant."

Tristan gazed at him, startled at his words, and Mark said, "Tell us, why hast thou left thy wife and thy children, and suffered so much for him if he be not thy son?"

And Rual hesitated, wondering if he might dare tell the truth, and said, "I might indeed tell thee that which should make thee marvel much, yet know not if I dare."

"Speak on, good friend," said Mark kindly. "Say who *is* Tristan."

Then Rual spake: "Sire, dost thou remember Rivalin, who came from afar, and dwelt in this court, and how he won the love of thy sister Blanchefleur, and she fled with him? They were wedded indeed, as I know well, for I was Rivalin's man, and should be now were he living. But, alas! he fell in fight with his foe, Duke Morgan, as thou hast doubtless heard. And when the tidings came to my lady her heart brake, and she bare a son, even Tristan who stands here, and died." And Rual burst into tears and wept as he thought of all the bygone sorrow.

And King Mark himself wept when he heard of his sister's death; but Tristan grieved most to think that he might no longer call Rual his father.

Then the marshal went on to tell them how he had hidden the truth that his young lord lived for fear lest Morgan should slay the child, and how he had named him *Tristan* for his mother's sorrow, and brought him up as his own. And he told them how he had sent him to foreign lands to learn all that befitted a prince, and how he had been stolen by the merchants, and had come, without knowing, to his mother's land. Then he drew from his finger a ring, and gave it to Mark, and when the king saw it he knew it again as one that his father had given him, and that he had given to his sister Blanchefleur, and he said, "Tristan, come hither and kiss me. So long as I live will I be a father to thee, and thou shalt be mine heir. And for thy father and mother, God rest their souls, they were true lovers."

Then he praised and thanked Rual for his fidelity, and all the courtiers strove to show him honor, but Tristan himself was but ill pleased.

"This is a wonder, and no great pleasure," he said. "I hear my father say my father is long since slain, so now am I fatherless who had two fathers. Today I rejoiced, thinking I had found my father, and now he whom I had found robs me of two—of himself and of him whom I had never seen!"

"Nay, nay, my son," said Rual, "thou hast lost nothing. I am thine as I ever was, and thou hast gained a father in my lord thine uncle. I would pray that he make thee knight speedily, and help thee to win back thine own lands."

Mark thought this good counsel, so he made a great feast, at which Tristan and thirty of his comrades were made knights, and bade him go back to his own land, and win it again from Morgan, and then return to Cornwall.

So Tristan sailed again northward, and all the folk were indeed joyful when they saw their lord return with his son, and still more joyful when they knew the truth that Tristan was indeed their rightful prince, and son to Rivalin, whom they had loved.

Then Tristan and his comrades dealt cunningly, for they learnt where Morgan was to be found, and then they rode forth as if to hunt, but under their hunting dress they were well armed, and Rual and his men-at-arms were not far from them. And as they had purposed, they met the duke, and Tristan told Morgan who he was, and prayed him to yield up the lands he had taken. But this Morgan was no ways minded to do, and he answered Tristan scornfully, saying he was no rightful prince, for his father and mother had not been lawfully wedded. At this insult, which he knew for a lie (since Rivalin and Blanchefleur had been wedded in the minster before Rual and all the nobles), Tristan waxed wrathful, and drew his sword upon Morgan, and smote him through helmet and head, so that he fell dead from his steed. Then Morgan's men attacked Tristan fiercely, but Rual came to his master's aid, and they beat back Morgan's men, and so Tristan became lord of his own lands once more.

But now his heart was torn in two, for he loved Rual and his own country, and yet he longed for Cornwall and his mother's folk. And he thought how he had promised to go back to his Uncle Mark, and be to him son and heir, and it seemed him well that he should give Parmenie to Rual to be his and his son's after him. And though his people prayed him to abide with them, yet he held to his purpose; but ere he sailed away he made Rual's two elder sons knights, and commended them to the loyalty of his vassals, but Kurwenal and twelve of his comrades would he keep with him, and so he took ship again for Cornwall.

Now, when Tristan came again to his uncle's kingdom he found all the land in dismay, for Morolt, a mighty champion from Ireland, had landed in the country, and demanded from King Mark the tribute due to Gurmun, King of Ireland.

The story of the tribute was this: Gurmun of Africa had, with the favor of the Romans, won Ireland, and defeated the men of England and Cornwall while Mark was yet a youth. As tribute from the defeated lands he claimed the first year a hundred marks of tin, the second year a hundred marks of silver, and the third a hundred of gold. The fourth year came Morolt, Gurmun's brother-in-law, and demanded thirty lads of noble birth, or else a champion to fight with him in mortal combat. But since Morolt was known far and wide as the fiercest warrior of his time no man was willing to fight with him. King Mark sent an embassy to Rome to pray counsel of the senate, but they could give him no aid. So whenever it pleased Morolt to come into Cornwall and demand this tribute, little as Mark liked it, the lads were forced to go.

Tristan had heard tell of this when he dwelt in Cornwall, and now, when he came back to Tintagel, he found all the city in mourning, for the nobles had been summoned to court to cast lots and see on whom the tribute should fall. So when Tristan came they had but little heart to give him welcome, for all, from the king downward, were overcome with grief.

But for that Tristan cared little; he made his way boldly into the hall to where men drew the lot, and King Mark and Morolt sat side by side. "My lords," he said, "all ye here who draw lots and sell your own children, have ye no shame for the disgrace ye bring on this land? Nobles are ye all by birth and bearing; your country should be honored rather than dishonored by your deed. Yet here have ye bound yourselves foot and hand with this shameful tribute. Your children, who should be your joy and delight, ye give and have given for slaves and servants, and can show but *one* man who forces you to this! For no other necessity is there—yet not one of you can be found to risk his life upon the chance of a combat! For see, if ye die, death is but short, and soon over, but this shame and sorrow are enduring, so the two may not be weighed the one against the other. And if ye conquer and the wrong is vanquished, then have ye the greater reward in heaven and the greater honor on earth. Surely a father should give his life for his child, who is his own life? 'Tis dead against God's law that he should sell his child into slavery that he may himself live in freedom! If ye take my counsel, following the laws of God and of honor, ye will choose out a man from among you to fight for you, and leave the issue of the combat to God. Morolt may indeed be strong and skillful, but God never yet forsook the man who fought in a rightful cause! Do not this dishonor to your country and your noble birth."

"Ah, sir," said they all, "but this man is not as others: none may prevail against him."

Then Tristan answered, "Let such talk alone! Do ye forget that ye are all of noble birth, the equals of king and kaiser, that ye sell and barter your noble children, who are even as ye are, to be body slaves and thralls? But if indeed there be no man among you who dares to fight for the right in God's name against this one man, and ye care to leave the chance to God and to me, then will *I* set my life on this venture. If I fall no man of you is one jot the worse, your need is neither less nor more than it was; and if I conquer, then may ye thank God and not me. For with God and the right on my side are we three against one, and though I know not much of knighthood, yet I trow I may well hold my own!"

Now, Morolt heard all this as he sat beside King Mark, and was angered at heart that Tristan, who looked such a youth, should speak so valiantly, and he hated him bitterly.

Then Tristan said again, "Speak, lords all, what is it your will that I shall do?"

"Sir," they said, "if it might be that the chance ye have given us come to good, it would profit us all greatly!"

"Then, since it seems good to you, I will e'en try my fortune, and see if God favoreth me or no."

Then King Mark rose up and came to him, and prayed him not to risk his life on so dangerous a venture; but Tristan would hearken neither to commands nor to prayers; he turned to Morolt as he sat, and spake aloud: "Sir, tell me what dost thou desire here?"

"Friend," said Morolt, "what need to ask? Thou knowest well what I do here, and whom I demand."

Then Tristan said, "Listen, my king and ye lords. Sir Morolt, thou art right—I know well why thou art come hither, and hold it for a shame and a disgrace. The tribute has been paid overlong. In the days when thy folk wasted our lands and destroyed our castles and slew our men, it might not be otherwise; but now are our lands flourishing, and our men many, and we can come with our armies and take back that which hath been taken from us. If my counsel be followed, all that thy king holds of ours shall be restored to the last ring; yea, our tin shall be paid back in gold! Stranger things and more unforeseen have come to pass ere this! God grant me this, for in His name do I demand it, and with mine own hand, if need be, will I carry this banner into Ireland."

But Morolt said scornfully, "Sir Tristan, the less thou sayest the better for thee. Brave words may be spoken here, but they shall not hinder us from taking that to which we have a right." Then he turned to the king and said, "King Mark, and all ye who are here present to settle with me the tribute, say, am I to take the words Sir Tristan has spoken as your will, and your answer to my claim?"

Then they all answered, "Yea, Sir Knight, what he shall say or do, that is our will, our pleasure, and our counsel."

Quoth Morolt, "Ye have broken the compact, and the oath sworn to my king and to me!"

"Nay," said Tristan, "thou speakest ill, Sir Knight; no faith is broken here. An oath and a compact was there that tribute should be sent yearly to Ireland, or that the matter should be settled by single combat or by battle. So long as the compact be kept by tribute or by combat are we within our rights. Now, Sir Morolt, say, shall the matter be settled between us by single combat or by our armies? Choose which thou wilt: *the tribute* shalt thou have no longer."

And Sir Morolt said, "Sir Tristan, my choice is swiftly made. Few men have I with me, too few to fight a pitched battle. I came here peaceably, as I have come aforetime, and deemed not that matters should go otherwise than of yore. I thought to go hence in all good will, and with what was rightfully mine. Now hast thou challenged me to battle, and for that am I unprepared. But I am no child to be terrified by thy rough words and threats. Such pride and boasting have I heard full often; we two will fight it out here, and settle whether thou or I be in the right."

Then Tristan drew off his glove and gave it to Morolt, saying, "My lord King Mark and all ye here present are witnesses that I demand this combat. I will maintain with my hand and sword that neither Sir Morolt here, nor his king who sent him hither, nor any other, hath a right to demand tribute of this kingdom; and may God avenge on this knight here all the shame and dishonor which this land hath suffered."

Then from many a noble heart there went up prayers to heaven that God would look upon their sorrow and need, and free them from their trouble. But though they took the combat thus seriously, it seemed to Morolt but a small matter. With haughty countenance he proffered his gage to Tristan; in truth the combat was much to his liking, for he held himself bound to come off victor.

The time was fixed for the third day, and as the news spread through the country the folk came from far and near, till it was as if the city were girded about with a mighty army. But King Mark was sad at heart; rather would he have paid the tribute all the days of his life than that Tristan should be slain, yet he scarce saw how he might escape. And when the day came he himself, with Kurwenal's aid, would arm his nephew for the fight. They clad him all in white armor, and gave him a shield white and shining as silver, with the device of a black boar upon it, and they brought him a gallant steed, with trappings all of glistening white, like the armor. So he came to the place fixed for the combat; 'twas a little islet in the sea, near enough to the city for the folk to see what went on, but none save the two champions might set foot upon it. There were two small boats ready, each of which might carry an armed man and his steed. Morolt had already entered one, and taking the helm sailed over to the island. Landing, he made fast the boat, and mounted his steed, making it prance and caracole on the strand.

Then Tristan came to his boat, and stepped in, holding shield and spear. "King Mark," he said, "sorrow not so sore; here must we trust in God. It will help us naught to be downcast; our victory lies not in the chances of knighthood and warlike skill, but in the hand of God. Trouble not for me, for I may well be victor, I feel so strong of heart. Be thou the same. Full often things fall out other than one forebodes. And however it may be, thy folk and thy land which thou hast entrusted to me, thou hast trusted them rather to God who goeth with me. He will bring right to the right. It is not I, but God who goeth to conquer, or to be conquered."

With that Mark gave him his blessing, and he pushed off from land. As he came to the shore he let his boat float whither it would, and mounted his steed, careless of its fate.

"What doest thou?" said Morolt. "Why hast thou set thy boat adrift?"

"Why?" quoth Tristan. "Here of a truth be two men and but one boat, but it may be we shall both abide here, and if not both, of a surety *one* shall lie here dead, and methinks he who remaineth victor shall find the boat that brought thee over enough for his return!"

"Of a truth," said Morolt, "if the fight go on it may not be otherwise, but if thou wilt withdraw thy challenge, and yield me my right of tribute over this land, so that we leave this island as friends at peace with each other, it will be to thy profit. Otherwise I shall slay thee, and that were a pity, for never saw I a knight who pleased me better."

Then the valiant Tristan answered, "If we are to be at peace the tribute must no longer be paid."

"Nay," said the other; "I will have no peace at such a price; the tribute must go with me."

"We waste o'ermuch time in idle talk," quoth Tristan. "Morolt, since thou art so certain of slaying me, look well to thyself, for fight we must."

With that they set spurs to their steeds, and with lance in rest rode straight at each other, and each smote the other so full on the shields that the spears splintered into a thousand pieces, and the knights drew forth their swords, and fought fiercely even as they were on horseback. Each had as it were the strength of four men, and but for his good shield Tristan might scarce have escaped Morolt's onslaught. As it was, in defending himself he held the shield too high, and Morolt's sword cut through the armor, and laid Tristan's thigh bare, so that the blood spurted forth.

"How now?" said Morolt. "Wilt thou yield? See'st thou one cannot defend the wrong, and thou art in the wrong, as this wound well shows. Think, too, how thou wouldst be cured of thy hurt. For I tell thee, Tristan, this wound shall be thy death, for the sword was poisoned with a deadly poison, and no leech nor leechcraft can heal thee, saving only my sister Isolt, the Queen of Ireland. She knoweth the virtues of all plants, and many secrets of healing; she can heal thee, but none other on earth can. Yield thee to me, and grant my right to the tribute, and my sister the queen shall heal thy wound, and I will share with thee, as a true comrade, all that I possess, and refuse thee nothing on which thou mayst set thine heart."

But Tristan spake: "My truth and my honor will I give up neither for thee nor for thy sister. I have here, in my free hand, the freedom of two lands; they shall go hence with me, or I must first suffer greater harm, or even death. I am not driven to such straits by one wound alone that I should yield me here and now! The strife between us is yet undecided, and the tribute is thy death or mine—nor may it be otherwise."

Then, confident in God and the right, Tristan's courage waxed anew: he spurred his horse against Morolt, and smote him with such force that knight and steed fell to the ground; and as he strove to rise Tristan was on him, and smote his helmet from his head. But Morolt was strong and skillful, and he sprang free from the fallen steed, and ran to Tristan and smote his horse a blow that brought it to the earth, for he thought to give himself time to remount and rehelm. So he cast his shield on his back and took his helmet in one hand, and with the other he caught hold of the saddlebow, and set his foot in the stirrup to mount. But ere he could do so Tristan

was upon him, and smote him so fiercely that the hand tha'
held the sword fell with a clang of metal to the ground, and he
smote him again on the head, so that the sword clave through
the steel cap, and as he drew it back with a mighty heave a
piece of the blade brake, and remained sticking in the skull,
the which afterwards brought much sorrow to Tristan, and
had well-nigh been his death. Morolt staggered and fell, weaponless and powerless.

"How now? How now?" said Tristan. "Say, Morolt, dost
know the token? Methinks thou art sorely wounded; it goeth
ill with thee, I ween! However it may be with *my* wound, *thou*
needest good leeching! Whatever skill thy sister Isolt may have,
thou hast need of it all wouldst thou recover. God hath shown
the right, and made manifest thy wrong; let the rest be in His
care, but now is thy pride fallen." With that he came nearer,
and took his sword in both hands, and smote off Morolt's head.

Then he gat him to the shore, where he found Morolt's boat;
he entered and rowed toward the haven and the folk who
awaited him. There by the sea he heard great joy and great
lamentations—joy for his victory, for it was a blessed day to
the men of Cornwall. They clapped their hands, and praised
God, and sang hymns of victory to heaven. But the stranger
folk, they who had come with Morolt from Ireland, they wrung
their hands, and wept aloud for grief. They thought them
'twas time to betake them to their ships; but as they came to
the haven they met Tristan, and he said, "Sirs, turn aside, and
take the tribute ye see yonder on the meadow. Bear it with you
to your king, and say that my uncle, King Mark, and his land
send him this present, and therewith make known to him that
if it be his will to send his messengers hither for such tribute,
we, on our part, will not let them return empty-handed, but
will send them hence with such honor as we have done to
Morolt." And as he spake he held his shield so that the bloody

signs of his wound were hidden from the strangers—and that hereafter stood him in good stead.

So the men of Ireland departed from the land, and sailed first to the island, where they found but a mutilated corpse for their lord, and they took up the doleful gift they were bidden to bear to their king, Morolt's body, his head and hand, and with wailing and lamentation set sail for their own country. When they came to Ireland they delivered the corpse to King Gurmun, even as they were bid, and the king was wroth, and sorely grieved, for in this one man he had lost heart and courage, strength and counsel. But the queen, Morolt's sister, her grief and lamentation were even greater; she and her daughter Isolt mourned even as is the way of women when they have a sorrow that goeth near to their heart. They kissed the head and the hand that had made so many lands tributary to them, and looked well on the deadly wound in the head. And as they looked the wise queen saw the splinter of the sword yet fast in the skull, and she drew it forth, and she and her daughter wept over it, and laid it aside in a little casket—and that same splinter thereafter brought Tristan in deadly peril. So Morolt was buried, and the King Gurmun caused a decree to be published throughout all Ireland that whoever should land on the Irish shores from Cornwall, man or woman, should be slain; and though they should offer gold as a ransom for their life, no ransom should be taken; yet that was little use, since Morolt lay dead, and no decree might bring him to life again.

Now when Tristan set foot again on the shore the people came to meet him in their thousands, on horse and afoot, and welcomed him gladly; 'twas the fairest day king and kingdom had ever known, for their sorrow and shame were done away, and he had won them honor in their stead. And they lamented over the wound that Morolt had given him, but Tristan made light of it and said it would soon be healed. So they led him into the palace, and disarmed him, and laid him on a soft couch and sent for physicians to heal him. But to what end? Though they summoned the most skillful leeches from all the lands around, not one of them had skill enough to aid him, for the poison was of such subtle venom that they could not bring it from the wound, but it spread all over his body, and his color and his look were so changed one might scarce know him.

Little by little Tristan learnt the truth of Morolt's words, and indeed he had heard aforetime of the beauty and wisdom of Queen Isolt, for the fame of her had spread into all countries, and men spake of her as *"Isolt the fair, Isolt the wise, bright as the dawn in eastern skies."*

So Tristan began to turn the matter over in his mind: he saw well if he were to be cured it could only be by the skill of the Irish queen, and yet how he might in safety come to her he knew not. Yet though he knew 'twould be a question of his life, he said to himself, "Better be in peril, or even dead, than live in this misery and torment." So he set his mind firmly that he would seek the queen, let hap what might. Then he sent for his uncle, King Mark, and told him everything, from beginning to end, as a friend does to his friend, and told him how he purposed in his heart to take Morolt's counsel, and seek healing at the hand of Queen Isolt. And the king liked it both ill and well, for one must put up with trouble if needs be, and of two evils a man will choose the least; but they were at one mind between them as to what it were wisest to do if he took this journey, that they should keep it secret that he went to Ireland, and say that he had gone for a while to Salerno, and would abide there till his wound was healed.

Then they sent for Kurwenal, and told him what they purposed, and Kurwenal thought it good, and said he would go with Tristan, and die with him if need be. So when it was evening they made ready a barque for the journey, and provisioned it well, and bare Tristan to the ship with many tears, and as much secrecy as they could, so that few knew anything of his going. He commended all his folk to the care of his uncle, King Mark, and bade him see that none departed ere tidings came of how he had fared, and he took his harp with him and nothing more.

So he set sail, with but eight men who had set their lives upon the venture; and Mark looked long and sadly after them, for all the joy of his life had sailed hence with Tristan.

Then Tristan sailed night and day, till they drew near to the shores of Ireland; and when the land was well in sight he bade the captain steer for the chief city, Dublin, for there he knew the queen had her dwelling. And when they were near enough to see it well the captain spake: "Master, I see the city: what dost thou counsel?"

And Tristan said, "Let us anchor here till evening be past and the night well advanced." So they cast anchor and rested through the evening.

When night came he bade them row closer to the city, and when they were but half a mile from shore Tristan bade them clothe him in the poorest garments they could find in the ship, and set him in the little boat they had brought with them, and give him his harp and enough victuals to last three or four days. And when all this was done he called Kurwenal and the sailors to him, and said, "Friend Kurwenal, take thou this ship and this people for thine own, and care for them well and kindly for my sake, and when thou art come again reward them well, and bid them keep secret what has happened here. And do thou return home, and greet my uncle, and tell him that I am living, and trust, by God's grace, to be made whole. He shall in no wise grieve for me, for if all go well I shall see him again within this year. But say in the court and abroad that on the way hither I died of my sickness. And as for my folk who are there, see thou keep them together, and wait for the year's grace, and if I come not in that time then take my men and get thee home to Parmenie, to Rual, my dear father. Tell him from me that I pray him to reward my love and faith in him by his love to thee; and for all that have served me faithfully pray him to give them thanks and reward according to their service. Now, dear friends, I commend you all to God; go your way and set me afloat; I must throw myself on God's grace. 'Tis time ye save life and limb by flight, for it draweth near to morning."

So with many tears and lamentations they set him afloat on the wild sea; never was there a sadder parting! He who has won and lost a faithful friend will know how deep was Kurwenal's sorrow; yet, though his heart was heavy, he must needs sail homeward even as his lord bade him.

And Tristan was left all alone, floating hither and thither till the morning light; and when the day broke and the men of Dublin saw the rudderless boat tossing on the waves they bid men put out from the haven and see what it might be. When they drew near there was no man to be seen, but from the boat came the sound of harping and the sweetest singing they had ever heard, and they rested on their oars to hearken. Yet, sweet as the song was, Tristan's heart was not in it, but he sang as a martyr, out of his sorrow and suffering.

When the music stayed the ship drew nearer, and the men caught hold of the little boat, and looked, and saw him lying therein, ill clad and worn with sickness, and marveled much that he could make such sweet music; and they greeted him kindly, and prayed him to tell them who he was and how he came thither.

Then Tristan said, "I was a minstrel, and well skilled in all kinds of music, and in such jests and sport as are the manner of courts, and thereby I won much money, and having much, desired yet more. So I turned my thoughts to merchandise— which thing has undone me. For I took a comrade, a rich merchant, and we two loaded a barque in Spain and would sail to Brittany; but on the sea a robber ship assailed us, and slew my comrade the merchant, and all our people, great and small, so that I alone escaped, living, but with this wound. And this was by virtue of my harp, for when I told them how that I was but a minstrel they gave me for my prayers this little boat and food whereon I have lived till now. Forty days and forty nights have I floated, in much pain and suffering, wherever the winds drove me or the waves bare me, and I know not where I may be, nor what it were best to do. Now, sirs, I pray you help me, and may God reward you."

"Friend," said the messengers, "thy sweet voice and thy music shall bring thee to profit; thou shalt no longer float without comfort or counsel. Whatsoever hath brought thee hither, whether it be the guidance of God or the chance of wind and wave, we will bring thee to where thou shalt find folk." And so they did, for they towed him into the harbor, and made the boat fast, and said, "Sir Minstrel, look well on this castle and this fair town beside it; dost know what town it is?"

"Nay, sirs, I know not what it may be."

"So will we tell thee; thou art at Dublin in Ireland."

"Then praises be to God, who hath brought me to a kindly folk, for surely there will be some among you who will aid me in my need."

With that the boatmen began to tell their fellows all that had chanced; how, as they drew near to the boat, they had heard so sweet a harping and song that the choirs of heaven could scarce be sweeter, and how it was but a poor minstrel, wounded even to death. "Ye may see from his look he can scarce live over the morrow, and yet in all his suffering he has so brave a courage that one might search through all lands without finding a heart that would bear so heavy a misfortune as if it were so light a matter."

So the citizens went and spake with Tristan, and he answered them even as he had answered the sailors, and they prayed him to sing to them, and he did after their bidding. And when they saw how, in spite of his deadly wound, he could yet play and sing so sweetly, they were moved with pity, and they bade bring him from his ship and bear him to a physician, and say that he should take him into his house and do all he might for his healing, and they would pay the cost. And this they did; but though the physician put forth all his skill it helped Tristan but little.

Now, the tale of the coming of the minstrel, of his deadly wound and his sweet singing, was spread abroad through all the city, and among those who came to see the stranger was a certain priest who was himself skilled in all manner of music, and knew many a foreign tongue. He was of the queen's household, for he had taught her from her youth, and from him she had learned much of her skill, and she would now have him to teach the Princess Isolt, her only child. When he saw how courteous Tristan was, and what a skilled musician, he pitied his suffering, and went his way to the queen, and told her that there was a minstrel in the town, sorely wounded, and dead even while he lived, yet that never man born of woman might equal his skill in music, or his courage.

"Ah, noble queen," he said, "could we but bring it about that thou shouldst see him, for 'tis nothing but a marvel that a dying man can harp and sing with such sweetness when he knows that no skill or counsel can aid him. For cured he may not be; the physician who has had him in his care has now ceased to do aught for him— Skillful as he is, 'tis a case beyond his wisdom."

"See," said the queen, "I will tell my chamberlain, if he may still bear it, and can endure that man handle him and move him, that he have him carried up here to us, and we will see if any skill can aid him, or if he be past cure."

This was done even as the queen commanded; and when she saw Tristan, and beheld his wound and his appearance, she knew the poison, and cried, "Ah! poor minstrel, thou art wounded with a poisoned weapon!"

"I know not," said Tristan; "I cannot say what it is; but hitherto no skill of leechcraft has profited me. I know not what I can do more, save commit myself to the care of God while life may last. But may He reward all who show me kindness in this my need, for indeed I need help sorely. I live, and yet am dead."

Then the queen asked him, "Minstrel, what is thy name?"

"Lady, my name is Tantris."

"Tantris, now trust thyself to me; I myself will be thy physician; be of good courage, and thou shalt do well."

"I thank thee, sweet queen. May thy lips ever be young, and thy heart never know sorrow; may thy wisdom endure to give help to the helpless, and thy name be honored on earth."

"Tantris," said the queen, "if thou are not too feeble, which would be no·marvel, wounded as thou art, I would fain hear thee play on the harp; in that I have heard thou art most skillful."

"Nay, lady, my wound hinders me not; I will do right willingly what becomes thy servant."

With that they brought his harp, and sent for the fair young Princess Isolt that she might hear this skillful minstrel; and indeed Tristan played and sang better than ever he had done before, for he hoped that now his suffering was wellnigh at an end; and he sang with such a good courage and so brave a spirit that he won the hearts of all who heard him.

Then the queen said, "Tantris, it may be that I can heal thy wound, and on my side I would ask somewhat of thee. Here is my daughter Isolt; she is but young, but already has she learnt some measure of skill in music and poetry. Teach her what thou knowest, for thou canst do so better than her master or I can, and I in payment will give thee back life and limb, whole and sound, for both are in my hand."

"Yea," said the minstrel; "if it be so that I may be healed by my singing, then, by the help of God, healed I will be! Fair queen, if it be indeed thy will that I should teach thy daughter, then I think I shall do well, for I have read much, and I know well that no other minstrel of my years is as skilled in many instruments as I. What thou desirest of me is done, so far as lies within my power."

So the queen prepared for him a chamber, and therein every day she caused him to be carefully tended and nursed. And now Tristan profited by the wisdom and foresight that had bidden him hide his wound beneath his shield from the eyes of the strangers, so that none of Morolt's men when they sailed from Cornwall had any thought that he was wounded. For if they had known the truth of his wound, as they knew of that which slew Morolt, it had scarce gone so well with the knight!

The wise queen set all her thought and her skill to work to see how she might bring about Tristan's healing. She tended him day and night, and yet she hated him more than she loved her own life. But she had no thought that this was her foe, and the man who slew her brother; had she known she would rather have helped him to death than to life.

Thus, not to make my tale too long, within twenty days the poison had gone forth, and the wound was healing; and every day the young Princess Isolt came and sat beside the minstrel's couch, and learned of him all he might teach of music and song. And the princess knew much already; she could speak both French and Latin, beside her own Irish tongue, and play on the lute and harp and sing sweetly, but under Tristan's teaching she grew daily more skillful, and more learned in courteous ways; till by the time he had dwelt among them half a year all the land spake of the beauty and wisdom and courtesy of the Princess Isolt; and all the strangers who came to her father's court listened in wonder to her sweet singing, for there was no secret of song or carol, pastoral or roundelay, in which she was not versed.

But now Tristan's wound was healed, and his strength and beauty had come back to him, and day by day he was vexed with fears lest some one of the Irish should know him again; and he turned it over in his mind how he might with courtesy take leave of the queen and princess, for he misdoubted him much that they would not let him go, and yet he knew that he only abode there at risk of his life. So he determined what he would do, and one day he went and knelt courteously before the queen, and said, "Dear and gracious lady, may God in His eternal kingdom reward thee for all the help and aid thou hast given me. Thou hast dealt with me so well and kindly that wherever I may be I will sing thy praises, and be thy servant as long as I may live. And now, my queen, let me with thy good will go forth to mine own land, for my matters stand so that I dare no longer be absent."

The queen laughed, and said, "Thy flattery goeth for naught, Tantris; I will not grant thee leave. Know that I let thee not hence till the full year be sped."

"Nay, noble queen, bethink thee of the rights of marriage and of true love; for I have at home a wedded wife, whom I love as my own soul, and I know well that she deems me of a surety to be dead, and what I fear is, lest, thinking me to be dead, she be wedded by her parents to another; then shall all joy and gladness be over for me."

"Of a truth," said the queen, "Tantris, thou hast cause for care, and it doeth thee honor; husband and wife none should part. Loath as I am to lose thee, yet I may not withhold my consent; go freely, and I and my daughter Isolt will ever be thy friends; and for thy journey will we give thee two marks of good red gold."

Then the minstrel folded his hands in homage, to both mother and daughter. "God give you both favor and honor"; and without more words he left them and took ship for England, and from England he made his way home to Cornwall.

Now when Mark his uncle, and all the folk of the land, knew that Tristan had returned safe, and healed of his wound, there was great joy and gladness throughout the kingdom.

The king asked him how it had chanced, and he told him all the story from beginning to end, and they laughed and made great jest over his journey to Ireland, and his healing at the hand of his enemy, and said 'twas the most marvelous tale they had ever hearkened. And when they had laughed over it well they asked him of the Princess Isolt.

"Isolt," he said, "she is so fair a maiden that all that we hear of beauty is but as an idle tale compared to her. No child or maiden of woman born was ever so fair to look upon. Erewhile I read that Aurora's daughter, and her child fair Helen, were the fairest of all women, that in them was gathered all beauty, as in a flower. Such a tale do I believe no longer. Isolt has robbed me of all faith in it. The sun of beauty dawned not in Greece, it hath risen in our own day, and the hearts and eyes of all men turn to Ireland where the sun is born of the dawn—Isolt, daughter of Isolt. From Dublin doth it shine forth to gladden all men. Nor does her beauty lessen that of other women; rather, through her fairness is all womankind honored, and in her fame all women are crowned."

And all who heard Tristan speak felt their heart refreshed within them, even as the May dew refreshes the flowers.

So Tristan took up his life again, for it was as if new life had been granted to him, and he was as a man new born. But little by little envy crept into the hearts of the courtiers, and they waxed jealous of the honor and love in which Tristan was held, and a whisper went round among them that he was a sorcerer, and his victory over Morolt and his good luck in Ireland had been brought about by magic.

"Tell us," they said, "how did he escape from so fierce a foe as Morolt? How did he deceive Isolt, the wise queen, so that she tended him diligently with her own hand till his wounds were healed? A sorcerer is he who can thus blind the eyes of men and bring to a good ending everything to which he sets his hand!"

So they took counsel together, and besieged Mark early and late with their prayers, beseeching him to take to himself a wife, so that he might have an heir, whether son or daughter.

But Mark said, "God hath given us a valiant heir already; may he live long! Know ye that while Tristan is alive there shall be neither queen nor lady at this my court."

Then was their envy and hatred greater than before, so great that they could no longer hide it from Tristan, but often threatened him by word and gesture, till he feared for his life at their hands. And at last he spake to his uncle Mark, saying he would do well to give the lords their will, else sooner or later they would surely slay him by treachery.

But the king said, "Be silent, nephew Tristan; that will I never do. I ask no heir but thee; and as for thy life, have no fear of that. What is their ill will to thee? Such is ever the lot of a brave man. For worth and envy, they are even as mother and child, the one must needs give birth to the other. Who is more hated than the lucky man? 'Tis a poor fortune that never saw envy! Go thy way, and know thou shalt never be free from envy: if thou wouldst have the bad love thee, then must thou sing their song and deal their dealing, so will they cease to hate thee! Counsel me no more to that which may turn to thine own harm; in this will I follow neither them nor thee!"

"Lord and Uncle," said Tristan, "give me leave to withdraw from court, for in sooth I see not how to shield myself from their ill will, and rather than have a kingdom the holding of which shall cost me so much care and thought will I be land-less!"

Then when Mark saw he was fully in earnest, he said, "Nephew, I had fain have kept faith with thee, but thou wilt not have it so. Now, whatever chances hereafter, shalt thou hold me guiltless. I am ready to do all thou wilt; say, what dost thou require of me?"

And Tristan said, "Call together thy council, who have aided thee hitherto, ask them what they deem good for the present need and do after their advice."

So this was done, and the lords came together and took counsel among themselves, and said that the king should wed the Princess Isolt, for by the fame that had gone abroad of her wisdom and beauty they deemed her a fitting wife for their king. Then they chose a spokesman who should declare their wishes, and he said, "Sire, we have heard tell of the Lady Isolt of Ireland, how that she is a maiden in whom all wom-anly beauty finds its crown. Yea, thou thyself hast heard how she is perfect alike in soul and body. If it may so be that she become thy wife and our queen, we ask nothing better on earth."

And King Mark said, "How may that be, my lords? Even if I desired her as a wife, how might it be brought about? Ye know well how matters stand between the two countries: Gurmun hates me from his heart, and with good reason, for so do I hate him. How then may there be so close an alliance between us?"

"Lord," they said, "it doth often happen that when two lands are at strife peace is brought about through the children, and a great friendship groweth from a bitter enmity. Think the matter over, for it may well be that Ireland becometh thine. There are but the three there; the king and queen have no heir save Isolt; she is their only child."

Then Mark answered, "Of a sooth Tristan has made me think much of the maiden; since he praised her so she has often been in my mind, and 'tis true that the thought of her pleases me above all other maidens. I swear if I may not have her to wife I will have no other woman on earth!" Now, Mark said this not because he really desired Isolt, but because he thought there was little chance that the marriage should be brought about.

Then the councilors spake further: "My lord king, if it please thee that Sir Tristan here, who knows the court of Ireland well, serve as thy messenger, then the matter will surely be brought to a good end. He is wise and skillful in such matters, and, what is more, fortunate in all he takes in hand. He knows all tongues, and will bring to an end what should be ended."

"Ye counsel ill," said Mark; "ye are too jealous for Tristan's peril and hurt. He has been well-nigh dead once for you and your children, and ye would now slay him again. Nay, men of Cornwall, go ye yourselves; I send my nephew no more!"

"Sire," said Tristan, "herein they do not speak amiss. 'Twere fitting that I should be more ready and willing to such a task than another man, and 'tis right that I should go. Uncle, bid me go, and none will do thine errand better than I. But do thou command that these lords, too, go with me, that together we may watch over thine interest and thine honor."

"Nay; since God hath sent thee home safely, thou comest no more into the land or the power of thy foes."

"Uncle, it must needs be so; and whether for good or for ill these lords must needs go with me and see if it be *my* blame that thy kingdom is without an heir! Bid them make ready, and I will myself be steersman and guide them to that happy Ireland, and to Dublin, whence shines forth the sun in which the joy of many a heart is hid. Who knows if the maiden be ours? And, sire, if thou dost win fair Isolt 'twill be little loss to thee if we all die on the quest."

When Mark's councilors heard how Tristan spake, never in their lives were they so sorrowful; but 'twas too late: the thing was and must be so. Tristan bade them choose twenty of the king's most valiant knights, and of the folk of the land and strangers he hired sixty, with twenty lords of the council, so that the whole company numbered one hundred; and they provisioned the ships well, and set sail over sea.

But the barons were ill pleased at the journey, and heavy at heart. Many a time they wished that they had said no word of Ireland and the Princess Isolt, for now their own lives were in danger, and they saw no way of escape. They had but the choice of two things: to carry the matter through either by daring or by cunning; and they liked neither. Nor could they think of any fitting ruse, but they said among themselves, "This Tristan hath wisdom and courage enough, and good luck too. If he will but put a curb on his blind rashness he may escape, and we with him. Yet is he so bold and so daring, he cares not a jot either for our lives or his own. Still, our best chance is in his good fortune; his wit must find a way out of this peril."

Now they drew near to the coast of Ireland, and one told them that the king abode in the harbor of Wexford. So Tristan bade them cast anchor far enough from the haven to be out of bowshot; and the lords prayed him earnestly to tell them how he would set about his wooing, for their lives were in danger, and they would fain know what was in his mind.

And Tristan said, "Have a care that none of you be seen by the landsfolk, save the serving men and seamen only; they must remain on deck, but do ye abide in the cabin and keep hidden. I will show myself, for I know their tongue; the citizens will send out and question us, and I must lie to them as

I best can, for if ye be seen, then shall we have strife straightway, and none of us will get to land. And while I am absent on the morrow, for I think to ride forth early and see what may chance, Kurwenal, and another who knows the tongue, will keep guard over you. But mark this: two days, or perchance three, shall I be absent; after that, if I come not, wait no longer, but flee away over seas and save yourselves, for I shall have paid for my wooing with my life. Then can ye counsel your lord to wed as ye may like— This is my thought and my purpose."

Now the marshal of the King of Ireland, under whose care both town and haven lay, came down in full armor, with a body of men, as the decree bade him, that he might ask of all newcomers to the haven if they were from King Mark's land or no, and if they were, to put them to death. When Tristan saw them he put on such a hood as a man might wear on a journey, that his face might be the better hidden, and took a cup of red gold, worked in the English fashion, and entered a little boat, with Kurwenal to row him, and made for the shore, greeting them with courteous gestures.

When the folk saw the boat they all ran together, shouting, "To land! to land!"

Tristan put into the harbor, and said, "Good folk, what mean this roughness and these threatening gestures? I know not what I have done amiss. If there be any one in authority here, I pray that he will speak with me."

"Yea," said the marshal, "here am I, and I must needs know whence ye come and whither ye go?"

"Of a sooth," said Tristan, "an thou wilt bid this folk keep silence so that I may be heard, I will tell thee mine errand gladly." And when they were silent, he went on: "Sir, we are merchants, I and my fellows, and come from Normandy. Our wives and children are with us in the ship, and we go hither and thither, from land to land, buying such things as we have need of. Within this thirty days I and two other merchants set sail to go to Spain, and about an eight days agone a storm arose which separated us, and drave me northwards. I know not how the others have fared, whether they be living or dead; I had much ado to escape with my life. Yesterday at noon the wind fell, and I knew the look of the coast, so came hither to rest me. And at daybreak I made for Wexford, for I know the town, and have been here aforetime with merchants. But if this folk will not be at peace with me I must perforce set sail again, though I have much need of rest. Yet if thou wilt let me land, then what good fortune I may find will I freely share with thee, that I and mine may remain in peace while I seek my friends ashore, and see if I may here do some trading. Bid thy men be at peace, for they are all putting off in boats, wherefore I know not. Otherwise, I go back to my men, and fear ye all not one straw."

Then the marshal bade his men return to land, and said to the stranger, "What will ye give the king if I protect your lives and goods in this land?"

"Sir, whatever our gains may be, I will give a mark of red gold for each day we sojourn in the land; and thou thyself shalt have this golden cup, if indeed thou art able to assure me of safety."

"Yea," said they all, "that can he, for he is the king's marshal."

Then he gave them the cup, and the marshal thought it a rich and precious gift, and bade him come ashore, and sware that he and his should be in peace and surety. And for that did they win rich payment in royal red gold—red gold for the king's tribute, red gold for the messenger's fee—and 'twas good too for Tristan, since it won him peace and favor.

Now, the story tells us that there was at that time in Ireland a monstrous dragon which devoured the people and wasted the land; so that the king at last had sworn a solemn oath that whoever slew the monster should have the Princess Isolt to wife; and because of the beauty of the maiden and the fierceness of the dragon many a valiant knight had lost his life. The land was full of the tale, and it had come to Tristan's ears, and in the thought of this had he made his journey.

The next morning, ere it was light, he rose and armed himself secretly, and took his strongest spear, and mounted his steed and rode forth into the wilderness. He rode by many a rough path till the sun was high in the heavens, when he turned downward into a valley, where, as the *geste* tells us, the dragon had its lair. Then he saw afar off four men galloping swiftly over the moor where there was no road. One of them was the queen's seneschal, who would fain have been the lover of the Princess Isolt, but she liked him not. Whenever knights rode forth bent on adventures the seneschal was ever with them, for nothing on earth save that men might say they had seen him ride forth, for never would he face the dragon, but would return swifter than he went.

Now, when Tristan saw the men in flight, he knew the dragon must be near at hand, so he rode on steadily, and ere long he saw the monster coming toward him, breathing out smoke and flame from its open jaws. The knight laid his spear in rest, and set spurs to his steed, and rode so swiftly, and smote so strongly, that the spear went in at the open jaws and pierced through the throat into the dragon's heart, and he himself came with such force against the dragon that his horse fell dead, and he could scarce free himself from the steed. But the evil beast fell upon the corpse and partly devoured it, till the wound from the spear pained it so sorely that it left the horse half eaten, and fled into a rocky ravine.

Tristan followed after the monster, which fled before him roaring for pain till the rocks rang again with the sound. It cast fire from its jaws and tare up the earth around, till the pain of the wound overcame it, and it crouched down under a wall of rock. Then Tristan drew forth his sword, thinking to slay the monster easily, but 'twas a hard strife, the hardest Tristan had ever fought, and in truth he thought it would be his death. For the dragon had as aids smoke and flame, teeth and claws sharper than a shearing knife; and the knight had much ado to find shelter behind the trees and bushes, for the fight was so fierce that the shield he held in his hand was burnt well-nigh to a coal. But the conflict did not endure overlong, for the spear in the vitals of the dragon began to pain him so that he lay on the ground, rolling over and over in agony. Then Tristan came near swiftly, and smote with his sword at the heart of the monster so that the blade went in right to the hilt; and the dragon gave forth a roar so grim and terrible that it was as if heaven and earth fell together, and the death cry was heard far and wide through the land. Tristan himself was well-nigh terrified, but as he saw the beast was dead, he went near, and with much labor he forced the jaws open and cut out the tongue; then he closed the jaws again, and put the tongue in his bosom. He turned him again to the wilderness, thinking to rest through the day, and come again to his people secretly in the shadows of night; but he was so overcome by the stress of the fight and the fiery breath of the dragon that he was well-nigh spent, and seeing a little lake near at hand into which a clear stream flowed from the rock, he went toward it, and as he came to the cool waters the weight of his armor and the venom of the dragon's tongue overpowered him, and he fell senseless by the stream.

But the seneschal, who would fain be the princess's lover, as he rode homeward, heard the death cry of the dragon, and bethought him what it might mean; he said to himself, "The beast is either dead or sorely wounded; now is my chance if I work warily." So he stole away from his companions, and rode quietly down a hill to the valley; then he turned his bridle toward the place whence the sound came, and rode swiftly till he found the carcass of Tristan's horse, and there he halted, for his heart misgave him. Then as he heard and saw nothing he took courage and rode, still fearful and trembling, along the track made by the grass and broken underwood, and ere he knew he came right on the dragon lying dead. Overcome by terror at the sight, he turned his bridle so swiftly that horse and man alike stumbled and fell over a little hillock, and when he sprang to his feet he was so terrified he durst not wait to remount, but fled on foot. But as he found the dragon did not move he took heart, and stole back, trembling; he led the horse to a fallen trunk and remounted, and then rode with caution nearer to the dragon to see whether it were alive or dead. And when he saw that the monster was in truth dead, he cried aloud, "Now by God's grace I have come hither in a happy hour!"

With that he laid his lance in rest and rode gaily toward the dragon, crying, "Now art thou mine, my Lady Isolt!" and smote with such force that the spear went through the dragon's jaws, and remained there. This he did out of pure cunning, for he thought: "If the knight who has slain the dragon be living he will not be able to deny that I have aided him." Then he turned, and sought all about to find the knight, for he thought if he were, as well might be, sorely wounded, then he could fight with him, and slay and bury him, and no man be aught the wiser. And when he found him not he said, "Well, let him go; whether he be living or dead I am the first here, and I have kinsmen and friends enow, so that if any man would take the credit of this deed he shall but lose by it." So he rode back to the dragon, and with his sword he gashed the carcass here and there. He had fain hewn off the head, but the neck was so thick he might not come at it. Then he took his spear, and brake it in two over the trunk of a tree, and stuck the pointed end in the monster's jaw, as if it had been broken in a joust.

Having thus as he deemed made all safe, he rode back to Wexford, and bade them go with a waggon and four horses to bring back the head of the dragon, and told every one what he had done, and the sore peril he had been in. "See, see," he cried, "what a man of brave heart and steadfast courage can do for the sake of the lady he loves. I marveled, and marvel still, how I escaped the danger which beset me; had I been as soft as was another man, I had never done it. I know not who he was—an adventurer, who for his cowardice, ere I came up, had met with an evil end. Both man and horse are dead and devoured; the horse still lies there half eaten. I have dared more for the love of a woman than ever a man before me!"

Then he called his friends together, and went again to the dragon, and bade them look again on the wonder, and bear testimony to what they saw. The head they cut off and brought again in the waggon, and he fixed a day for them to ride together with him to the court, and claim the fulfillment of the king's promise.

Now, the tale was speedily brought to court, and told in the women's chambers, and never were tidings more unwelcome! To that fair maid the Princess Isolt it was bitter as a deathblow; never had she seen a sadder day. But her mother spake: "Nay, sweet daughter, nay, let it not trouble thee so; we will see first whether this be truth or a lie. God forbid that the thing should be so! Weep not, my daughter; thy bright eyes should never be reddened for so small a grief!"

"Ah! Mother," said the maiden, "insult not thy birth and thyself; ere I be that man's wife I will thrust a knife through my heart. Neither wife nor lady shall he have in Isolt, unless he have her dead."

"Nay, nay, fear not, sweet daughter; whatever the truth may be, thee has he lost, for if all the world were to swear it thou shouldst never wed the seneschal."

When the night fell, the queen wove cunning spells, the virtue of which she knew well, for her daughter's sorrow, so that in a dream she saw all the truth and knew that the seneschal had dealt falsely; and as the day began to dawn she spake to Isolt: "Daughter, art thou waking?"

"Yea, Mother mine."

"Then let thine heart be at peace: I have good tidings for thee. The seneschal slew not the dragon. 'Twas a stranger knight—I know not what brought him hither—who did the deed. Come, let us go thither quickly, and we will see for ourselves how the truth may be. Brangoene, rise up softly and bid the squire Paranise saddle our horses; we must ride forth, we four: I and my daughter, thou and he. Bid him bring the horses as quickly as may be to the little postern where the orchard opens on to the moorland."

When all was ready, the little company mounted and rode to the spot where they had heard that the dragon was slain, and there they found first the carcass of the horse, and beheld the trappings, and knew that never in Ireland had they seen the like; and they said to each other that whoever the man might be who rode the horse, 'twas he and no other who slew the dragon. Then they rode further and came on the monster as it lay, and it looked so grim and so ghastly in the dim morning light that the women grew pale with dread. The queen said to her daughter, "Now of one thing am I sure: our seneschal never dared face that monster! We may lay aside all care; and, daughter, whether the man be living or dead, methinks he is hidden somewhere near by; let us go and seek him. God grant we may find him, and with his aid overcome the dread that oppresses thine heart."

So they parted asunder and began to seek hither and thither, but 'twas the Princess Isolt who first found that which they sought, for she saw a helmet shining from afar, and called to her mother, saying, "Hasten hither, Mother, for I see something gleaming there beyond: I know not what it may be, but methinks 'tis like a helmet."

"So think I," said her mother. "I ween we have found that which we sought."

With that they called the other two, and rode forward together. But when they came nearer and saw how the knight lay they deemed he was dead, and Isolt cried, "We are undone! the seneschal hath treacherously murdered him and borne him to this bog!"

They dismounted, and all four drew him out of the water to land; they did off his helmet and the steel cap beneath, and the wise queen saw that he yet lived, but that his life hung by a single hair.

"He is living," she said; "let us disarm him quickly. If he be not mortally wounded all may yet be well."

Then the three fair women bent over the knight and began to disarm him with their white hands, and behold, the dragon's tongue fell out from his breast. "What may that be, Brangoene, fair kinswoman, say?"

"Methinketh 'tis a tongue!"

"Thou speakest true, Brangoene—a tongue it is, and I think me well 'twas once in the dragon's mouth! Sweet Isolt, daughter mine, of a truth we have come on a happy journey. 'Tis the venom of this tongue that has bereft him of his senses."

When they had disarmed the knight and found no wound upon him, they were all joyful, and the queen took an antidote to the poison and poured it between his lips, and when she saw signs of life, "The man will recover," she said; "the venom of the tongue is yielding; he will speedily regain sight and speech." And in sooth, ere long Tristan opened his eyes and looked around him.

When he saw the fair women bending over him, he knew them, and said in his heart, "Now God hath surely thought upon me, and hath sent me the three fairest lights the world doth hold—Isolt the sun; her mother, Isolt the fair dawn; and Brangoene the stately moon." With that he sighed softly: "Ah! who are ye? and where am I?"

"Canst thou speak, knight?" said the queen. "We are aiding thee in thy need."

"Yea, sweet lady, but I know not how my strength should have vanished in so short a time."

The younger Isolt looked on him; " 'Tis the minstrel Tantris, if ever I beheld him!" said she.

"Is it thou indeed, Tantris?" asked the queen.

"Yea, lady, 'tis I."

"Then say, whence hast thou come hither, or what dost thou seek here?"

"Sweetest lady, I am yet so feeble I cannot tell thee all as it were fitting, but bid them bear me to some shelter where I may abide in secret a day and a night, and when I have once more recovered my strength, then will I gladly tell thee all that it behoves thee to know."

Then between them they helped Tristan on to a steed, and brought him secretly to the palace, by the postern door, so that none knew of his coming, and made ready for him a couch and all he needed. Nor did they forget the dragon's tongue, nor his harness, but brought all with them.

And the following morning the queen said to him, "Tantris, thou knowest I have ever been thy friend; I tended thee and healed thee of thy wound; tell me truly by the faith thou owest to thy liege lady, when didst thou come to Ireland and how didst thou slay the dragon?"

"Lady," said he, " 'tis three days since that I came to Ireland with other merchants, and as we came to the harbor, robbers boarded us, and, had I not bought them off, would have taken my life and my goods. Then, since we wished to dwell here in this strange land, and I had heard the tale of the dragon, it came into my mind that as the people were but ill disposed toward us, if I could but slay the monster I should find favor and peace in the sight of this folk."

"Favor and peace shalt thou have to thy dying day," quoth the queen; "thou hast come hither in a happy hour for thyself and us. Ask whatever thou desirest of my lord or of me, and it shall be done."

"I thank thee, lady. I would put myself and my ships in thy protection. I prithee let me not rue the day that I trusted life and goods to thy faith."

"Nay, forsooth, Tantris, have no care for thy life or thy goods: see, I give thee mine hand upon it that none shall touch thee or thine in Ireland as long as I live, and all thou askest of me will I do. But now I would take counsel with thee on a matter that nearly touches mine honor and my happiness."

With that she told him of the seneschal, how he would fain lay claim to the princess's hand, and how with lies and falsehood he made believe to have won her.

"Dear lady," said Tristan, "have no care. Thou hast given me back life and strength, both are at thy service to withstand all danger at thy will."

"God reward thee, Tantris. Gladly will I take thine aid, for if this thing should come to pass 'twould be the death of me and of my daughter Isolt."

"Have no fear, lady. But tell me, what of the tongue that was in my bosom, didst thou leave it there, or what?"

"Nay, I have it here; my fair daughter Isolt and I, we brought all that belonged to thee with us."

" 'Tis well," said Tristan. "Now, sweet queen, trouble no more, but help me to my strength, and all shall go as thou desirest."

Meanwhile the comrades whom Tristan had left on the ship were in much trouble and sorrow when he came not again at the end of the three days, and they heard the tale of the dragon—how it had slain a stranger knight and his horse. They said, "Of a truth this must be Tristan; were he alive he had returned ere now." So they took counsel, and sent Kurwenal ashore that he might see the carcass of the horse; and when he came there he knew the steed and the trappings for Tristan's, but of Tristan himself there was no sign. He found the remains of the dragon, but not a sign of his lord's armor or of his raiment, and he knew not what to think. "Ah, Sir Tristan," he said, "art thou living or dead? Alas, Isolt, that the fame of thy beauty ever came to Cornwall, if it have brought so noble a knight to so evil a fate!"

Then he returned, weeping, to the ship, and told his comrades what he had seen, and they were sorrowful at the tidings, though, in their heart, some of them were not ill pleased. Thus the twenty lords who had come with him were of one accord that they would wait his coming no longer, for they were in haste to be gone from Ireland, but the others would not listen to their counsel, but said they would not leave the land till they knew whether their lord was really dead, and that they would await him for at least two days longer, and the twenty lords must needs yield to their will.

Meanwhile the day had come that King Gurmun had set for redeeming his pledge to the seneschal, and all the knights were gathered together for counsel, and the queen had also come thither, for the king trusted much to her wisdom. And before the council he spake with her in secret: "What counsel canst thou give, my wife? For 'twere bitter as death to give our daughter to the seneschal."

"Be at peace," said the queen; "that will we never do; I have well foreseen the matter."

"How, lady? Tell me quickly, that we may rejoice together."

"See thou, our seneschal never slew the dragon as he saith; but I know well who did, and when the time is ripe I will declare the matter. Go thou to thy lords, and say that when thou art well assured of the truth of the seneschal's word thou wilt be ready to keep thine oath. Then sit thou on thy judgment seat, and bid thy knights to judge with thee, and let the seneschal bring his plea and say as he will, and when the time is ripe then will I come with Isolt, and will speak for thee, for her, and for myself. I will now seek her, and come again swiftly."

So the king went back to the palace and sat on the judgment seat, with all the barons round him, and a great company of knights and nobles, for all were fain to know what should be the end of the matter. And when the queen and princess entered they said among themselves, " 'Twere good fortune for the seneschal who hath never had good fortune to win such a maid as this! All men might well envy him."

Then the seneschal came forth and stood before the king, and Gurmun arose, and said kindly, "Speak, what dost thou require of me?"

"Lord king," he answered, "I pray only that thine honor and thy plighted word be not broken. Thou didst swear that whosoever slew the dragon to him wouldst thou give thy daughter Isolt to wife, and this oath of thine hath slain many. But I recked little since I loved the maiden, and I risked my life more often and more valiantly than any man, till at length fortune befriended me, and I slew the monster. See there the head where it lies, I brought it for a token. Now fulfill thy pledge, for the king's word and the king's oath, they should be holy."

"Seneschal," said the queen, " 'tis too much, by my troth, to desire so rich a prize as my daughter Isolt, when thou hast not won it!"

Quoth the seneschal, "Thou doest ill to speak thus, lady. My king, *he* shall decide. He can speak for himself; let him answer me."

But the king said, "Lady, do thou speak for thyself, for Isolt, and for me."

"That will I, my lord. Seneschal, thy love may be true, and thou be a valiant man, worthy a woman's love; but he who claimeth a great reward which he hath never merited doeth ill, I trow. Thou hast taken to thyself a deed and a manhood that, as I am well advised, belong not to thee."

"Lady, I know not what thou sayest; I have here a proof of my words."

"Thou hast brought a head, so might another man if he thought to win Isolt by it; but she is not to be so lightly won."

"Nay," said the younger Isolt; "it needeth greater labor for my winning."

"Ah, princess!" said the seneschal, "dost thou count as naught all the perils I have dared for love of thee?"

"That thou hast loved me may perchance be reckoned to thee for good, but I never loved *thee,* nor looked on thee with favor—nor shall I ever."

"Yea," said the seneschal, "I know well thou doest as all women do: they love those who hate them, and hate those who love them; the crooked they account straight, and the straight crooked. Love is the most uncertain game a man may play at, and he is but witless who risks his life for any woman if he hold not a pledge from her first. And yet whatever thou or my lady the queen may say, the thing must go according to my word, or the king hath broken his oath."

But the queen spake: "Seneschal, methinks thou knowest women so well thou hast become as one of them, for see, thou thyself lovest one who hateth thee, and desirest one who will naught of thee. If that be but the way of women, why dost thou even as they? Deal thou rather as a man, and love the maiden who loveth thee, and desire her who desireth thee. We have heard overmuch of thy love for Isolt; she loveth thee not, and that perchance she hath from me, for I loved thee never! And as for the king's oath, I tell thee thou didst never slay the dragon; another slew it; and if thou askest me, 'Who was he?' I answer that I know him, and will bring him hither at the fitting time."

"Lady, there is no man shall falsely deprive me of my right and my honor. If he lay claim to it, then must he stake life and limb upon it, hand to hand, before this court, ere I waive a tittle of my right."

" 'Tis well," spake the queen. "I will myself be his surety; the knight who slew the dragon will I bring hither on the second day from now."

Then the king and the council said, " 'Tis enough. Seneschal, go thou and take measures for the fight, and, my lady the queen, do thou see to thy champion." Then the king took pledges from either side, and they made fast the fight for the third day.

So the queen and the princess went their way and told all to their minstrel, for by now Tristan's health and strength had come back to him; and the ladies looked upon him, and secretly they thought it a strange thing that one so fair in face and so noble in bearing should be but a wandering minstrel, seeking his bread from land to land; and they said between themselves, " 'Twere more fitting that he should be king and lord of some country; many a folk has a less kinglike ruler. Of a sooth, his looks and his lot match each other but ill." The queen bade her squire, Paranise, look well to the knight's harness, and see that it was well polished and in fair order; and this he did and laid all the pieces together. Now, as chance would have it, the princess came and looked upon the armor as it lay, for her heart was heavy within her for the coming conflict, and she took up the sword and drew it out of the scabbard, and gazed on it long and earnestly, and as she did so her eyes fell on the splinter that was lacking. She thought within herself, "Now God help me! I ween that the splinter that should be here is in my keeping." Then she ran to the casket wherein lay the splinter that her mother had drawn from Morolt's skull, and fetched it, and laid it on the blade, and lo! it fitted as if it were but one, as in truth it had been not two years back.

Then the maiden's heart grew cold within her, and her color changed from red to white, and she said, "Ah, unhappy that I am! How came this fatal weapon hither from Cornwall? With this sword was my Uncle Morolt surely slain, and 'twas Tristan slew him. Who gave it to the minstrel Tantris?" And as she thought, suddenly it was as if she saw the name before her, *Tantris, Tristan,* and she knew the one was but the other read backwards, and she cried aloud: "Ah! my heart forbode this falsehood and this treachery, for since I have looked upon him well and marked his face and bearing, I have known he must be of noble birth. But how dared he come hither with his deadly wound? And we have cherished and healed him! *Healed?* Nay, not yet, for this sword shall be his death! Hasten, Isolt, avenge thy wrongs. If he be slain with the sword that slew thine uncle thou hast repaid him well!"

Then she took the sword in both hands and ran swiftly to Tristan's chamber, and stood over him as he sat in a bath. "Yea," she said, "art thou *Tristan?*"

"Lady, nay, I am Tantris."

"That I know well— Tantris and Tristan they are but one traitor. The wrong Tristan did me shall be avenged on Tantris; thou must pay for my uncle's death."

"Nay, nay, sweetest lady, what wouldst thou do? Think of thine own honor and thy fair name. Thou art woman and maid. If men may accuse thee of murder, thy beauty will be for ever dishonored, the Sun of Ireland that rejoices so many hearts will have set. A sword becomes not those white hands!"

As he spake, the queen her mother entered. "How now?" she cried. "What meaneth this? What doest thou, my daughter? Are these womanly ways? Art thou beside thyself? What wouldest thou with that sword? Is this jest or anger?"

"Ah, lady mother, 'tis our heart sorrow. See, this is the murderer Tristan, who slew thy brother; now may we avenge ourselves. Let us smite him through with this sword. A better chance shall we never have."

"This *Tristan?* How dost thou know, daughter?"

"I know it well. He is Tristan. This sword is his; look well on it, and see here the splinter, see how the two fit together! As I laid one on the other I saw well they were but one blade."

"Ah!" cried the queen, "Isolt, what hast thou told me? If this indeed be Tristan, then have I been sorely betrayed!"

Isolt lifted the sword again, and drew nearer. "Stay, Isolt, stay!" cried the queen. "Dost thou not remember how I am pledged to him?"

"I care not; he shall die."

"Mercy, fair Isolt!" quoth Tristan.

"No mercy shalt thou have, traitor!" said the maiden. "I will have thy life."

"Not so, daughter," said the mother. "We may not take vengeance on him lest we break our troth and our honor. He is under my protection, life and limb, with all that belongeth to him. I have taken him into my peace, come what may."

"I thank thee, lady," said the knight. "Forget not that I entrusted myself and all I had to thine honor; my life is in thy keeping."

"Thou liest!" said the maiden. "I know well what passed, and life and shelter did my mother never swear to *Tristan.*" With that she would have raised the sword again, but her mother stayed her hand. And in sooth even had Tristan been bound and alone with her she would scarce have slain him, for her womanhood fought hard with her anger, till at length her gentle heart conquered, and she cast the sword from her, and fell a-weeping. "Alas!" she cried, "that ever I saw this day!"

But her mother said, "Daughter mine, thy sorrows are my sorrows, and even heavier are they for me. Morolt was my brother, nearer to me than to thee, and he is dead. That was my sorest sorrow; but now I have another. I tremble for *thee,* daughter, and in that sorrow I forget the first; better one grief than two. How of that wretched man who claims thine hand? If we have no champion to overcome him, then thy father and I are dishonored with thee, and may never more be joyful."

Then Tristan said, "Fair ladies both, it is true I have caused you sorrow, yet it was forced upon me. If ye will, as ye may, remember it, then know I was in peril of death, and a man defends his life as he best may. For the present, as concerns the seneschal, I can bring that to a good end, if ye will let me live. Queen Isolt, and Princess Isolt, I know you well, that ye are wise and gracious; if I might speak freely, and ye would moderate your wrath against me and this ill will ye have so long borne to Tristan, I would tell you good tidings."

The queen looked upon him, and her eyes filled with tears. "Ah!" she cried, "now I hear and know of a truth that thou art Tristan. I doubted me much before, but now hast thou owned the truth unasked. Alas, alas! Sir Tristan, that ever thou camest in my power, since I may not use that power as were most fitting. 'Tis a manifold thing, this royal power, and I ween I might use it against my foe if I would, and do evil against the evil. Shall I withhold my hand? I trow so."

As she spake Brangoene came into the chamber with a smiling face, and saw the sword lying on the ground, and the women with tearful eyes. "What is this?" she said. "What troubles you all three, and what does the sword here?"

"Brangoene, kinswoman," said the queen, "we have been

tricked and betrayed, we have cherished the serpent for the nightingale; our foe who deserved death at our hands have we tended as our friend. This is none other than Tristan! Say, may we avenge ourselves?"

"Nay, nay, lady; thine honor is worth more than the life of thy foe. Avenge thyself thou canst not, but leave him now, and take counsel as to what we may best do."

So the three went apart, and the queen spake: "Tristan said even now, that if we would lay aside the ill will we had borne him, he would give us good tidings— What may that mean, Brangoene?"

And Brangoene answered: "Perchance he may mean well by you both. One must turn one's mantle as the wind blows, and who knows but what he be come hither for your honor? We may well be thankful that God brought him hither at this time to prove the seneschal's falseness. Had we not found him when we did it had been the worse for thee, my princess! Treat him kindly, for he is nobly born, and both wise and courteous: whatever thine heart may feel toward him, let thy speech be gentle, for 'tis no light matter that hath brought him hither again."

Then the three went back to Tristan, and when he saw them he knelt before them, saying, "Peace, fair ladies. I pray you grant me my life, since 'tis but for your honor and profit I have come hither."

The queen bade him rise, and each proffered him the kiss of peace, though Isolt the princess did it but unwillingly, and they sat down together.

"My queen," said Tristan, "wilt thou be my good friend, and aid me to persuade thy daughter, whom thou lovest, to take as husband a noble king, one well fitted to be her lord; fair, and free of hand; a valiant knight, of a royal race, and richer than her father?"

"Were I sure of the truth," said the queen, "I would even do my best."

"Yet it is so, lady, for since I was here aforetime I have spoken ever in praise and honor of thee and thy daughter to my uncle King Mark; and 'tis he who hath sent me hither, for we are both at one accord to pray that thy daughter become his wife and lady, and Queen of Cornwall and England."

"Yea, but if I counsel my husband to make peace with King Mark, shall I not do ill?"

"Nay, lady, he must needs know all the tale, only I prithee see that he be friends with me."

"Of that have no fear," said Queen Isolt.

Then the queen sent for the king, and prayed of him a boon, saying it lay near to her heart and to that of her daughter.

"Thou shalt have what thou desirest," said the king.

"Then, lord, I pray thee to pardon Tristan, who slew my brother Morolt; he is here in my keeping."

"Nay, that is more thy matter than mine. Morolt was *thy* brother. If thou hast pardoned Tristan, then so have I."

Then the queen told her lord the whole matter, and Gurmun thought it good, and bade Tristan come before him; and he came and knelt, saying, "Grace, my lord the king."

"Rise, Sir Tristan," said Gurmun, "and kiss me, for though I were unwilling to pardon thee, yet since my wife hath done so I may not do otherwise."

"Lord," said Tristan, "with me thou dost pardon my king and both his realms?"

"Yea, sir," said Gurmun.

Then the king bade Tristan sit beside him, and asked him of his errand; and Tristan told him all he had told the queen, and of his fight with the dragon and all that had chanced.

"How may I know, Sir Tristan, that thou speakest truth?" asked Gurmun.

"My lord, I have twenty of King Mark's barons with me; they will be surety enough."

Then Tristan bade Paranise go to the ship, and seek out Kurwenal, and bring him to the palace in secret. And when Kurwenal saw his lord he was greatly rejoiced: "Sir, we feared thou wast slain, and with great difficulty did we keep the lords here; they have sworn to sail hence tonight."

"That they must not do," said Tristan. "Go hence, tell them I have done all for which I came hither, and bid them tomorrow clothe themselves in their richest attire, and make ready to ride to court whenever I send a messenger to summon them."

So Kurwenal departed and told the barons the good tidings; but they in their envy said, "Now surely this man is a sorcerer, see how he brings to a lucky end everything to which he sets his hand."

Now the day had come on which the single combat was to be fought, and a great folk had come together, for all wondered who should fight with the seneschal for the maiden Isolt; and each man asked his fellow, "Who may he be who claims to have slain the dragon?" and the question was passed from one to another, but none could give an answer. Meanwhile Tristan's comrades had come from the ship clad in their finest raiment, and he himself robed him as became his royal birth; and when the queen and Princess Isolt saw him they said to themselves, "Truly this is a gallant knight; methinks our cause is in good hands." Seats were set for the barons in the halls, and the people gazed on them, and marveled at their rich attire and their silence, for there was not one of them that knew the speech of the country.

Then a messenger came from the king to call the queen and the princess to the court, and she spake: "Rise, Isolt, and we will go. Sir Tristan, do thou abide here, and when I shall send for thee, come thou with Brangoene."

"Gladly, my lady queen."

So came Queen Isolt, leading with her her daughter, even as the dawn that brings with it the rising sun. With measured pace the maiden walked beside her mother, clad in a robe of brown samite and a flowing mantle furred with ermine, which she held together with the fingers of her right hand. On her head was a circlet of gold, set with jewels, and but for the gleaming stones one would scarce have known that the circlet was there, so golden were her shining locks.

So the fair women passed up the hall, greeting all as they came, the mother with word, the daughter with gesture. When they had taken their seat by the king, the seneschal stood forth, and said, "My lord the king, I demand my right of battle. Where is the man who thinks to deprive me of mine honor? My friends and kinsmen are here, and my cause is so good that if this council do justice all must go well with me. Nor do I fear force, that be far from thee."

"Seneschal," said the queen, "if this combat may not be averted, I scarce know what I may do. 'Twere well if thou wouldst leave thy claim on my daughter,. and set her free; 'twould be to thy profit as well as to hers."

"Free?" said the seneschal; "yea, lady, thou wouldst fain throw up a game that is already won! But I should have put myself in much peril for little profit if I now gave up thy daughter. Lady, let there be an end of it— I will wed the princess, or do thou bring forth the man who slew the dragon."

"Seneschal, I hear what thou sayest, and I will prove my truth." She signed to her squire: "Bring hither the man."

All the nobles looked one on the other, and a murmur ran round the hall, question and answer— All asked who the man might be, but none could tell. But now Brangoene entered, tall and stately, leading by the hand Sir Tristan. He was richly clad in a robe of purple silk, all inwoven and embroidered with gold, that glittered as he moved, and on his head was a gold and jeweled circlet. His bearing was frank and fearless, and, as he drew nearer, all made way for him. But when the men of Cornwall saw him they sprang to their feet, and came forward, greeting him joyfully; and taking him and Brangoene by the hand, they led them up to the high dais where sat the king and queen, and Tristan bowed low before them. Then as the folk clustered round, gazing at the strangers, the hostages from Cornwall saw that these were verily their kinsmen, and they made their way through the crowd, laughing and weeping, and greeted them gladly.

The king bade Tristan take his place beside him, and commanded silence to be made, and when all were still, he said, "Seneschal, what dost thou demand?"

"Sire, I slew the dragon."

The stranger rose and spake: "Sire, he slew it not."

"Sire, I did, and I will prove it here."

"What proof dost thou bring?" said Tristan.

"See this head, I brought it hither."

"My lord king," said Tristan, "since he brings the head as proof, bid them look within the jaws; if the tongue be there, I withdraw my claim and renounce the combat."

Then they opened the jaws, and found nothing therein; and, as they marveled, Tristan bade his squire stand forth with the tongue. "See, now, if this be the dragon's tongue or no." And all looked, and saw that it was in truth the tongue—all save the seneschal, who stood there and knew not what to say, nor whither to turn.

"Lords all," said Tristan, "mark this marvel. I slew the dragon, and cut this tongue from out the jaws, yet this man afterward smote it a second time to death!"

And all the lords said, "One thing is clear: he who came first and cut out the tongue was the man who slew the monster." And never a man said nay.

Then when the truth was clear, Tristan said, "My lord the

king, I call thy covenant to mind; thy daughter falleth to me."

And the king said, "Sir Knight, thou hast redeemed thy pledge; I will fulfill mine."

But the seneschal cried, "Nay, he speaketh falsely! Sir King, I demand my right of combat ere I be robbed of mine honor."

"Why should he fight with thee, seneschal?" quoth the queen. "He has won what he would of my daughter. He were more foolish than a child did he fight with thee for nought."

"If he think I have done him wrong, lady," said Tristan, "I will fight with him; let him but go and make ready, and I will arm myself."

When the seneschal saw it would come to a combat he called his friends and kinsfolk aside to take counsel with them, but he found little comfort, for they thought the matter a shameful one, and they said, "Wherefore fight in an unrighteous cause? 'Twere but foolish to throw thy life after thy lost honor. Since the devil hath tempted thee to thine undoing, keep thy life at least."

"What would ye have me do?"

"Go thou, and say to the king that at thy friends' counsel thou dost withdraw thy challenge."

Then he did as they bade him. And the queen said mockingly, "Seneschal, never did I think to see thee give up a game that was already won." And throughout the palace, from the highest to the lowest, all made sport of the seneschal, till he scarce durst show his face for shame; so his falsehood brought him to an evil end.

Now when the matter was ended, King Gurmun made known to all his nobles the errand on which Tristan had come, and how he had granted his prayer, and solemnly in their presence he gave his daughter to Tristan's care, that he might lead her to Cornwall as bride to his uncle King Mark.

Then in the face of them all did Tristan take the princess by the hand, and he spake: "King, since this lady is now my queen and my liege lady, I pray thee to deliver to her all the hostages thou dost hold of Cornwall, for now they are become her subjects, and 'tis but fitting that they should journey with her to her kingdom."

And Gurmun was willing; so with much joy the hostages were released.

Then Tristan bade them prepare a ship, such as should please both Isolt and himself, and assemble together all the men of Cornwall who were in the land, that they might set sail with him.

The while that Tristan and his folk made them ready for the journey did the wise Queen Isolt, with much thought and care, prepare a love potion of such power and magic that did any two drink thereof they must needs, without will of their own, love each other above all things from that day forward; death and life, sorrow and joy, were sealed within that little flask of crystal. Then the queen took the drink and spake softly to Brangoene: "Brangoene, my kinswoman, let not my words grieve thee: thou must go hence with my daughter; therefore hearken and heed what I say unto thee. Take thou this flask with the drink within it, and keep it in thy care. Treasure it above all thy treasures, see that none know of it, above all that none taste of it; but when Isolt and King Mark be come together, then do thou pour out the drink as if it were wine, and see that the twain drink of it. Nor shalt thou share in it thyself, for 'tis a love potion, forget not that. I commend to thy care Isolt, my dearest daughter; my very life doth hang on her. She and I alike are entrusted to thee on peril of thine eternal welfare; methinks I have said enough."

"My very true and dear lady," said Brangoene, "if this be

the will of you both, then will I gladly go with Isolt, and watch over her honor and her welfare as best I may."

Then Tristan and his folk departed with much joy for the haven of Wexford, and for the love of Isolt, king and queen and all their household accompanied them thither. Weeping, her steadfast friends surrounded the princess; her father and mother filled the short space left to them with their lamentations; many eyes were red and tearful, and many hearts weighed down with sorrow for the loss of their life's delight, fair Isolt.

But the two Isolts, the sun and her rosy dawn, and the stately moon, fair Brangoene, when they three must part asunder, the one from the twain, then indeed was woe and wailing! Sad was the severance of such true companionship. Many a time and oft did the queen mother kiss them both.

Now they of Cornwall, and the men of Ireland, the young queen's followers, were already aboard, and had taken their leave; Tristan was the last to enter the ship, leading by the hand the fair young Queen Isolt, the flower of Ireland; sad and sorrowful she went with him. Then the two bent in greeting toward the land, and prayed God's blessing be on it and on its folk. They pushed off from the shore, and with a loud voice one and all sang, "So sail we forth in the name of God." Thus they departed from Ireland.

By Tristan's counsel they set apart a private cabin for the queen and her maidens, wherein none might join them, save only at times Tristan, who now and again would go thither to comfort the young queen as she sat and wept, for she bemoaned herself sorely that she must thus perforce part from her land where she knew all the folk, and from the friends who were dear to her, and journey with an unknown folk to a land she knew not. Then Tristan would comfort her as he best could, and take her in his arms gently, even as a knight might his liege lady and the wife of his lord. But as often as he laid his arm around her, fair Isolt would bethink her of her uncle's death, and chide with him, saying, "Let be, sir; take thine arm away, thou art a wearisome man; wherefore dost thou touch me?"

"Do I then vex thee so sore, fair lady?"

"Yea, forsooth, since I hate thee."

"But wherefore, sweetest lady?"

"Thou didst slay mine uncle."

"For that have I made my peace."

"May be, yet I love thee not, for ere I knew thee had I neither sorrow nor care: thou alone with thy craft and courage hast brought this sorrow upon me. What brought thee from Cornwall to Ireland, to my hurt? They who brought me up from my childhood, from them hast thou reft me, and bearest me I know not whither! What price hath been paid for me I know not, nor what shall befall me."

"Nay, nay, fair Isolt, be at peace; wouldst thou not rather be a rich queen among strangers than poor and weak among thine own kin? Honor and wealth in a strange land, and shame in thy father's kingdom—they weigh not equal."

"Yea, Sir Tristan," said the maiden; "but say what thou wilt, I would have the lower lot with love and pleasure, rather than displeasure and trouble with great riches."

"Thou sayest true," answered Tristan; "but where one may have riches and pleasure alike, the two good things pass better together than either of the twain alone. But say, were it come to that that thou must needs have taken the seneschal for thine husband, what then? I wot well that would have made thee glad! Hast no thanks for me that I came to thine aid and freed thee from him?"

"Too late," quoth the maid. "I might well have thanked thee then, when thou didst deliver me from him, but since then hast thou heaped such sorrow upon me that in sooth I had liefer have wedded the seneschal than have sailed with thee! How worthless soever he may have been, had he dwelt but a short while with me then had he laid aside his evil ways; for this I know of a truth, that he loved me well."

Spake Tristan: "This tale seemeth me overstrange; 'twere great labor indeed for a man to act worthily against his nature. The world holds it for a lie that a worthless knight should do worthy deeds. Be content, fair lady; in a short while will I give thee for lord a king in whom thou shalt find henceforth virtue and honor, riches, joy, and fair living."

So they sailed onward with a favoring wind and a fair sea; but Isolt and her maidens were not wont to be exposed to the water and the wind, and ere long they were sorely in need of rest. Then Tristan bade them put to land for a little space, and as by good luck they came near a haven, they ran the ship therein and made it fast, and the more part of the folk went ashore to refresh themselves. But Isolt remained aboard, and Tristan went into the cabin to greet his liege lady, and sat him down beside her, and the twain spake of this thing and of that, till Tristan became thirsty and bade them bring whereof he might drink.

Now, besides the queen was there no one on board save little maidens, and one spied the flask where Brangoene had laid it, and said, "See, here is wine in this flask." But it was not wine that was therein, though like unto it, but bitter pain and enduring sorrow of heart, of which the twain at last lay dead. Yet the little maiden might know nought of this, so she took the flask from its hiding place and brought it to Tristan, and he gave forthwith of the drink to Isolt. She drank of it unwillingly enough, and after a space passed the cup to Tristan, and he too drank of it, and neither knew that it was other than wine. And even as it was done Brangoene entered, and saw well what had chanced. For very terror she became white as death. Cold at heart, she took that vessel of ill chance, and bearing it forth flung it into the wild and stormy sea. "Woe is me," she said within herself, "that ever I was born into this world! Miserable that I am, I have lost mine honor and failed in my trust. Would to God I had never come on this journey. I must ever bemoan that death took me not ere I pledged myself to sail with Isolt on this evil voyage. Alas, Tristan and Isolt, for this drink shall be your death!"

Now, when the man and the maid, Tristan and Isolt, had drunk of the potion, Love, who never resteth but besetteth all hearts, crept softly into the hearts of the twain, and ere they were ware of it had she planted her banner of conquest therein, and brought them under her rule. They were one and undivided who but now were twain and at enmity. Gone was Isolt's hatred; no longer might there be strife between them, for Love, the great reconciler, had purified their hearts from all ill will, and so united them that each was clear as a mirror to the other. But one heart had they—her grief was his sadness, his sadness her grief. Both were one in love and sorrow, and yet both would hide it in shame and doubt. She felt shame of her love, and the like did he. She doubted of his love, and he of hers. For though both their hearts were blindly bent to one will, yet was the chance and the beginning heavy to them, and both alike would hide their desire.

When Tristan felt the pangs of Love, then he bethought him straightway of his faith and honor, and would fain have set himself free. "Nay," he said to himself, "let such things be, Tristan; guard thee well, lest others perceive thy thoughts." So would he turn his heart, fighting against his own will, and desiring against his own desire. He would and would not, and, a prisoner, struggled in his fetters. There was a strife within him; for ever as he looked on Isolt, and Love stirred his heart and soul, then did honor draw him back. Yet he must needs follow Love, for his liege lady was she, and in sooth she wounded him more sorely than did his honor and faith to his uncle, though they strove hard for the mastery. For Love looked smiling upon his heart, and led heart and eyes captive; and yet if he saw her not, then was he even more sorrowful. Much he vexed himself, marveling how he might escape, and saying to his heart, "Turn thee here or there, let thy desire be other, love and long elsewhere." Yet ever the more he looked into his heart the more he found that therein was nought but Love—and Isolt.

Even so was it with the maiden: she was as a bird that is snared with lime. When she knew the snare of Love and saw that her heart was indeed taken therein, she strove with all her power to free herself, yet the more she struggled the faster was the hold Love laid upon her, and, unwilling, she must follow whither Love led. As with hands and feet she strove to free herself, so were hands and feet even more bound and fettered by the blinding sweetness of the man and his love, and never half a foot's length might she stir save that Love were with her. Never a thought might Isolt think save of Love and Tristan, yet she fain would hide it. Heart and eyes strove with each other; Love drew her heart toward him, and shame drove her eyes away. Thus Love and maiden shame strove together till Isolt wearied of the fruitless strife, and did as many have done before her; vanquished, she yielded herself body and soul to the man, and to Love.

Shyly she looked on him, and he on her, till heart and eyes had done their work. And Tristan, too, was vanquished, since Love would have it none otherwise. Knight and maiden sought each other as often as they might do so, and each found the other fairer day by day. For such is the way of Love, as it was of old, and is today, and shall be while the world endures, that lovers please each other more as Love within them waxeth stronger, even as flowers and fruit are fairer in their fullness than in their beginning; and Love that beareth fruit waxeth fairer day by day till the fullness of time be come.

Love doth the loved one fairer make,
So love a stronger life doth take.
Love's eyes wax keener day by day,
Else would love fade and pass away.

So the ship sailed gaily onward, even though Love had thus turned two hearts aside; for she who turneth honey to gall, sweet to sour, and dew to flame, had laid her burden on Tristan and Isolt, and as they looked on each other their color changed from white to red and from red to white, even as it pleased Love to paint them. Each knew the mind of the other, yet was their speech of other things.

In right maidenly wise Isolt questioned Tristan of his doings; they spake of how he came aforetime, wounded in a barque, to Dublin, how her mother had taken him in her care, and how Tristan had taught her Latin and the lute. And much she praised his valor when he slew the dragon, and she told how she had known him in the marsh for the minstrel Tantris, and later for Tristan. Then they spake together and Isolt said, "Ah, how was it that I thought better of my purpose, and slew thee not, that day? Had I known then what I know now, methinks it had been thy death."

"Wherefore," he said, "fair Isolt? What troubleth thee? What dost thou know?"

"What I know, that troubleth me; what I see doth bring me sorrow. Sky and sea weary me, life weigheth heavily on me."

She stirred a little, and leant against him, and the springs of her heart sorrow rose to her lips and weighed down her head.

Then Tristan laid his arm around her gently, and spake softly: "Ah, fair and sweet, tell me what troubleth thee. Of what dost thou make thy plaint?"

And Isolt spake, riddling: *"L'Amer,"* she said, "doth trouble me, it weigheth down my soul, and bringeth me sorrow."

Then Tristan bethought himself of her words, and saw well

how she spoke with a threefold meaning. *L'Amer* might alike mean love and bitterness, and the sea; and of the first would he say nothing, so he made answer: "I ween, fair Isolt, that the sea and the wind troubleth thee; the sea, and the salt sea wind; thou dost taste them, and they are alike bitter to thee."

"Nay, nay, what sayest thou? I taste nor wind nor sea. *L'Amer* alone doth trouble me."

And Tristan whispered, "Of a sooth, sweetheart, so doth it me. *L'Amer* and thou, ye are my sorrow! Heart's lady, sweet Isolt, thou and the love of thee have turned my heart aside; so far have I wandered that nevermore may I find the right path. All that mine eyes behold is but weariness and sorrow, weakness of spirit and heaviness of heart; in all the world is there nought that my heart doth love save thee only."

Isolt spake: "Even so is it with me."

So the twain made their confession of love each to the other; he kissed her, and she him; and each drank of the sweetness that the heart may offer. Yet they kept the matter secret, that none in the world might know their hearts' desire. 'Twas enough that each knew the will of the other.

But the wise Brangoene, she watched them in silence, and saw well what they would fain keep hid, and she thought within herself, "Alas! now see I well how love doth begin." And when she saw how day by day trouble of heart wrought upon them so that they grew pale and thin, a fear came upon her that this love might in truth be their death; and she said in her heart, "Now be of good courage, and learn what may be the truth of this."

So as they sat together one day she spake, saying, "Here is no man save we three alone; tell me, ye twain, what doth ail you? I see you hour by hour sigh and weep and make lamentation."

"Lady," said Tristan, "an I dared, I would tell thee."

"Speak on, Sir Knight; tell what thou wilt."

"Nay, that may I not, saving that thou dost first swear an oath to be a friend to us; otherwise are we lost."

Then Brangoene sware an oath that she would truly and faithfully do their bidding.

"Dear lady," quoth Tristan, "have pity alike on me and on the princess; what hath chanced to us we know not, but a madness hath come upon us; we die of love! Aid us, we pray, for our life and death are in thine hands."

Then Brangoene spake to Isolt: "My princess, is it even as Sir Tristan saith?"

And Isolt answered, "Yea, friend of my heart."

Brangoene quoth, "Woe is us, for the devil hath made sport of us! Now see I well that I must deal for mine own sorrow and your shame; for so must it needs be if I would not let you die. Yet hear my counsel: let this shame be kept secret between us three; it strikes at your honor, and if another know it ye are lost, and I with you. Heart's mistress, sweet Isolt, thy life and thy death, they rest with thyself alone. Have no fear of me, but do even as thou thyself shalt think best."

And that night Love, the physician, led Tristan to Isolt's side, and bound the twain together with such master skill and wondrous power that nevermore in all their lives might the bond between them be loosed.

So they sailed on their journey, blissful in each other's love, yet fearful lest any should espy their secret; and sad at heart when they thought how fair Isolt must needs be the bride of one whom she loved not. When they saw the coast of Cornwall and all on board were joyous that their voyage was well-nigh ended, Tristan and Isolt were heavy at heart, for if they might have had their will, never again would they have looked on land, but sailed the seas together for evermore.

As they drew near to shore, Isolt bethought her of a ruse. She sought out Brangoene, and prayed her that she would, on the marriage night, take the place of the queen—for Brangoene was fair and a maiden, and Isolt had it in her heart to belong to none but to her lover Tristan. So she spake on this wise to Brangoene, who kept silence a space, and then answered, "Dear lady, thy mother, my liege lady and queen, committed thee to my care; 'twas my part on this ill-fated voyage to have kept thee from this very sorrow. Through my carelessness have sorrow and shame come upon thee, so may I not complain if I must needs share the shame with thee; 'tis but right that I should take my part therein. Ah, God! how came I to be thus forgetful?"

"Dear cousin," said Isolt, "wherefore reproach thyself? I know not of what thou speakest."

"Lady, 'twas but the other day I cast a crystal flask into the sea."

"'Tis true, but why should that so trouble thee?"

"Alas! that same flask, and the drink that was therein, 'twas the death of ye both!"

"How may that be? What is this wild tale?"

Then Brangoene told the twain the story, from beginning to end, even as it had chanced.

"Now in God's name," quoth Tristan, "were it death or life, the poison was sweet! I know not what may come of it, but such death it pleaseth me well! Shall fair Isolt indeed be my death, then would I die daily!"

And yet, however sweet love may be, a man must at whiles bethink him of his honor, and Tristan knew well that he owed both faith and honor to Mark, who had sent him to fetch his bride, and the twain fought hard with his love, and vexed heart and soul between them; yet was it of no avail, for since he had chosen Love, Honor and Faith alike must needs be put to the worse.

Then Tristan sent messengers in two boats to the land, to bear tidings of the coming of the fair Princess of Ireland; and Mark sent forth a thousand messengers through all the kingdom, to bid his knights prepare a fitting welcome for their comrades and the strangers who came with them, and Mark himself received the twain even as a man welcomes that which he holds the dearest upon earth.

Then King Mark bade all his barons assemble at court within eighteen days, to witness his wedding with Isolt, and they came together, many a fair company of knights and ladies, all eager to behold fair Isolt, of whose beauty they had heard such tales. And when they had looked upon her, there was but one thought and one voice among them: "Isolt the fair is the marvel of all the world. 'Tis true what we have heard of her; she is even as the sun rejoiceth the hearts of men; never did any kingdom win so fair a maiden."

So King Mark and Isolt of Ireland were wedded, and the kingdoms of Cornwall and England were laid in her hands, with the pledge that if she bare no heir to Mark, then should Tristan inherit them, and so was homage done to her.

When night fell, then were matters wrought even as Isolt had planned. When the queen put out the lights in the bridal chamber, then Brangoene, in the royal robes, lay down beside the king; but when the king asked for wine, that men were wont to drink on the bridal night, Brangoene arose, and when Tristan bare the lights and the wine, 'twas Isolt sat beside the couch. But the drink that she and Mark should have shared had been drunk long since, and the flask lay in the depths of the sea.

King Mark and all his folk, and the people of the land, loved and honored Queen Isolt, for the grace and the courtesy that they found in her, and no man but spake her praises; and none knew how the matter stood betwixt her and Tristan, or thought evil of them. With that there came a thought into the queen's mind: since none but Brangoene knew aught of the deceit that she had practiced toward King Mark, might it not be for her safety that she should live no longer? Were she no longer there, there would be little fear of any man discovering aught against the queen's honor. And if it were so that Brangoene had any love or friendship for King Mark, might it not be that she would reveal his shame unto him? And in this did the queen make clearly manifest that men fear shame and mockery more than they fear God, for she sent for two squires, strangers of England, and made them swear an oath, on peril of their lives, to do her bidding without question. And when they had sworn she said, "Now mark well my mind; I will send a maiden with you, and ye three shall ride swiftly and secretly till ye be come to some wood, near or far, even as ye shall deem best, but apart from all dwelling place of man. There shall ye smite off the maiden's head. And mark well all her words, and what she saith, that shall ye tell me, and bring me back her tongue. And be ye sure of this: if ye do my bidding well, on the morrow will I make you knights and give you lands and riches so long as ye shall live." And all this did they swear to do.

Then Isolt took Brangoene aside, and said, "Brangoene, look at me well; am I not pale? I know not what aileth me, but mine head doth pain me sorely. Thou must go forth and seek me herbs and roots, and we must take counsel, else I fear for my life."

The faithful Brangoene answered, "Lady, thine illness grieveth me sore; let us not delay. But say, where may I find that which may do thee good?"

"See, here are two squires; ride with them; they will guide thee aright."

"Gladly will I go, lady."

Thus the three rode forth together, and they came to a wood, where was great plenty of herbs, roots, and grass, and Brangoene dismounted from her steed. Then the squires led her deeper into the wild woodland, and when they were far from all haunts of men, the two seized the faithful maiden and threw her on the ground, and drew forth their swords to slay her.

Brangoene was so terrified she lay still on the ground, trembling in every limb. Fearful, she looked up to them: "Sirs, of your pity, what will ye do to me?"

"Thou shalt die here!"

"Alas! wherefore? Tell me, I pray you."

And then one said, "What hast thou done to anger the queen? She bade us slay thee, and it must needs be so. Isolt, our lady and thine, she hath commanded thy death."

Brangoene folded her hands, and spake, weeping: "Nay, sirs, for God's sake, of your mercy delay a while, and let me live till I have answered you; after that slay me if ye will. Know yourselves, and hereafter tell my lady the queen that I have done nought to lose her favor, or that should bring her hurt, save perchance this one thing, and that I scarce believe it may be. When we twain sailed from Ireland we had each of us a garment white as snow, fairer and better than our other garments. When we were on the sea so great was the heat of the sun that the queen might not bear her robes, but did on this white robe, and ware that only, and she ware it till it was soiled and stained and its whiteness marred. But I had hid my garment within my coffer, and its white folds were all unsullied. And when my lady came hither, and took my lord the king for her husband, on the bridal night would she wear her white robe, but 'twas no longer so fair as she would have it, so prayed she the loan of mine. Yet at first I forgot my duty and refused it to her, but at the last did I do even as she prayed. If it be not this that hath angered her, then I know not what it may be. God knoweth never at any time did I transgress her will and her command. Now do what ye will with me. Greet my lady from me as is fitting from a maiden

to her mistress. May God in His goodness preserve her in life
and in honor, and may my death be forgiven her. I commend
my soul to God and my body to your will."

Then the squires looked pitifully the one on the other; they
had compassion on the maiden and her bitter weeping, and
repented them much that they had sworn to slay her, for they
could find no fault in her, nor anything that was worthy of
death. They took counsel together, and determined, happen
what might to them, they would let her live. So they bound
the maiden to a tree, high up, that the wolves might not touch
her before they could come to her again, and took one of their
hounds and slew it, and cut out its tongue, and rode thence.

Then they told Queen Isolt how, with sorrow and pain, they
had obeyed her commandment, and showed her the tongue,
and said it was that of the maiden. And Isolt said, "Now tell
me, what did the maid say to you?"

Then they told her all from the beginning, even as Brangoene had told them, and forgat no word.

"Yea," quoth the queen, "said she no more?"

"Nay, lady."

Then Isolt cried, "Alas for these tidings! Wretched murderers, what have ye done? Ye shall hang, both of ye!"

"Lady," they said, "most gracious Queen Isolt, what dost
thou say? Didst thou not beseech us, and lay pressure upon us,
that we should slay her?"

"I know not what ye say of prayers. I gave my maiden
into your care that ye should guard her on the road, that she
might bring me back that which I desired. Ye must restore
her to me or your lives are forfeit. Cowardly death-dealers, ye
shall hang, both of you, or be burnt on a pyre!"

"Nay," spake one of them, "lady, thy heart and thy mind,
they are not pure and single; thy tongue is double indeed! But
rather than lose our lives we will give thee thy maiden again,
whole and in good health."

Then Isolt spake, weeping bitterly: "Lie to me no more: doth Brangoene live, or is she dead?"

"She liveth, gracious Isolt."

"Ah! Then bring her back to me, and I will keep the promise I sware to ye."

"Lady, it shall be done."

Isolt bade one squire remain with her; the other rode thence to the spot where he left Brangoene, and brought the maiden again to Isolt. And when she came into the queen's presence, Isolt clasped her in her arms, and kissed her lips and her cheek over and over again. To the squires she gave for payment seventy marks of gold on the promise that they should keep the matter secret.

Now that Queen Isolt had tested Brangoene, and found that she was faithful and true, even to death, and that her courage was steadfast, even as gold tried in the furnace, the twain were henceforth so one in heart and mind that nought could befall the one but it touched the other as nearly. The court was full of Brangoene's praise, all loved her, and she bore ill will to no man. She was trusted alike by king and queen; nought was done in the council chamber but Brangoene knew it. Also would she serve Isolt and her lover Tristan even as they might command her. But this was done so secretly that no man in the court had any suspicion. None dreamed what were the thoughts and words of Tristan and the queen.

And as the days passed on they learnt, even among the folk around them, to speak to each other by glances and hidden words, as is the way of lovers. And as they grew bolder, even through their open speech there ran a meaning, known but to themselves, love working in their speech, even as a gold thread running through silken tissue. None saw more in their words than was fitting betwixt near of kin, for all knew the love and confidence that were betwixt Tristan and King Mark.

Yet even that love and confidence turned to the king's un-doing, for therewith did Love play her hidden game, and Mark held their yea was yea, and their nay, nay; but alas! 'twas far otherwise.

So they passed the hours gaily, sometimes glad, sometimes sad, as lovers are wont to be. At whiles they were wroth with each other, but without ill will; for so the way of Love—she kindleth anger in the hearts of lovers, but the pain of anger is swiftly forgotten in the bliss of pardon, when love is as it were new born, and trust greater than it was before. Ye all know well how anger ariseth and how peace is made for but little cause, for lovers are lightly prone to think that there is another nearer and dearer than they, and a small suspicion they make occasion for great anger; out of a little grief they win a rich atonement. Thus did Tristan and Isolt, even as all lovers have done before them and shall do while the world en-dures.

Now, Tristan loved all valiant deeds of knighthood, but when such might not be had he would spend his days in hunt-ing and hawking, and often ride far afield—as it chanced even at this time.

For in these days a ship came to Mark's haven in Cornwall, and there landed from it a knight, a noble baron of Ireland, named Gandîn; he was rich, handsome, and courteous; so manly and strong of limb that all Ireland spake of his valor.

Fairly clad, without shield or spear, he came riding to the king's court. On his back he bare a lute adorned with gold and precious stones, and strung as a lute should be.

He dismounted, and entered the palace, and greeted Mark and Isolt in fitting wise. Many a time and in many ways had he served the queen in her own land, through his knighthood and the great love he bare her, and for her sake had he jour-neyed hither from Ireland.

Then Isolt knew him, and greeted him courteously: "God save thee, Sir Gandîn."

"Gramercy, fair Isolt, fair, and fairer than gold in the eyes of Gandîn!"

Isolt spake softly to the king, saying who the knight was and whence he came; and Mark hearkened, wondering much why he bare a lute, and in sooth so did all the folk, for such was not the wont of wandering knights. Nevertheless would Mark do him all the honor he might, both for his own sake and for that of Isolt, since he was the queen's countryman; so he bade the stranger sit beside him, and spake to him of his folk and land, and of knightly deeds.

When the feast was ready, and water was brought round to the guests to wash their hands, then did the courtiers pray the stranger to play the lute before them. The king and queen said nought; they would leave it to his own will; and when he took no heed of their prayers, the courtiers mocked him, calling him "The Knight of the Lute," "The Prince with the Penance"; and Gandîn said nought, but sat beside King Mark, and ate and drank, and heeded them not.

When the feast was over and the tables borne away, then King Mark prayed him, an he could, to pleasure them awhile with his skill on the lute; but Gandîn answered, "Sire, I may not, save that I know what my reward may be."

"Sir Knight, what meanest thou? Dost thou desire aught of my possessions? If so, 'tis granted; let us but hearken thy skill, and I will give thee whatever thou desirest."

"So be it," spake the knight of Ireland.

Then he sang a lay which pleased them all well, so that the king desired him to sing another. The traitor laughed in his heart. "Tell me," he said, "what thou wilt, that I may play even as shall please thee."

Now, when he had sung another lay, Gandîn arose and

stood before the king, holding the lute in his hand. "Sir King," he said, "bethink thee of what thou didst promise me."

And Mark answered, "Of good will will I do it. Tell me what wilt thou?"

"Give me Isolt," quoth the knight.

"Friend," said Mark, "whatever else thou desirest thou shalt have, but this may not be."

"Verily, Sir King," said Gandîn, "I will neither much nor little, but Isolt alone."

The king spake: "Of a truth that shall not be!"

"Sire, wilt thou then break thy promise? If thou be thus forsworn, henceforth shall men hold thee unworthy to be king of any land. Bid them read the right of kings, and if this be not so, then will I renounce my claim. Or dost thou, or any other, say that thou didst *not* swear to give me what I asked, then will I assert my right against thee, or against whomsoever the court may choose. My body shall be overcome with fight ere I renounce my claim. Choose thou a knight to ride in the ring against me, and I will prove by combat that fair Isolt is mine."

The king looked all about and on either side if he might find one who would dare to uphold his cause; but there was no man who would set his life on such a wager, nor would Mark himself fight for his queen, for Gandîn was so strong and valiant that none durst take up his challenge.

Now, Tristan had ridden forth to the woods to hunt, and as he came homeward to the court, he heard on the way the news of what had chanced. 'Twas all true; Gandîn had led the queen, weeping and lamenting bitterly, from the palace to the sea shore. On the shore was pitched a tent, rich and costly, wherein he led the queen that they might wait till tide and river rose and floated the barque, which now lay high on the sand.

When Tristan had heard the tale from beginning to end, he mounted his horse and took his harp in his hand, and rode swiftly, even to the haven. There he turned aside, secretly, to a grove, made his horse fast to the bough of a tree, and with his harp in his hand took his way to the tent. The knight of Ireland sat there, armed, beside the weeping queen, whom he strove hard to comfort, but little might it avail, till she saw Tristan and his harp.

He greeted Gandîn, saying, "God save thee, fair minstrel!"

"Gramercy, gentle knight."

"Sir," he said, "I have hastened hither. Men have told me thou art come from Ireland; I too am from thence. I pray thee, of thine honor, take me back to mine own land."

The Irish knight made answer: "That will I do; but sit thee down, play to me, and if thou canst comfort my lady, whom thou seest weeping so sorely, I will give thee the fairest garment that is in this tent."

" 'Tis a fair offer, Sir Knight," said Tristan. "I have good hope that I may do so; an her grief be not so great that it will stay not for any man's playing, she must needs be consoled."

Therewith he harped so sweetly that the notes crept into Isolt's heart and bare her thoughts so far hence that she ceased weeping, and thought but of her lover.

Now, when the lay was ended, the water had come up to the barque, and it floated, so that they on board cried to the haven, "Sir, sir, come aboard; if my lord Tristan comes whilst thou art yet ashore, we shall have but an ill time! Folk and land alike are in his power—also he himself, so they say, is of such wondrous daring, so valiant and strong, he will lightly do thee a mischief."

This was unpleasing to Gandîn, and he said angrily, "Now may heaven hate me if I stir hence a moment earlier for that! Comrade, play me the lay of Dido; thou dost harp so sweetly that I must needs love thee for it. Now, play and banish my lady's sorrow. Out of love for thee will I bear thee hence with her and me, and will give thee all I have promised thee, yea, and more!"

"So be it," quoth Tristan.

The minstrel touched his harp again; and he played so sweetly that Gandîn listened eagerly, and Isolt was all intent on the music. And when it had ended, the knight took the queen by the hand, and would lead her aboard, but by now was the tide so high, and running so strong, that no man might reach the barque save on horseback. "What shall we do now?" asked Gandîn; "how may my lady come aboard?"

"See, Sir Knight," quoth the minstrel, "since I am sure thou wilt take me home with thee, I think but little of what I have here in Cornwall. I have a horse near by; I ween he shall be tall enough to carry my lady, thy friend, over to the barque without the sea wetting her."

Gandîn said, "Good minstrel, haste, bring thy horse hither, and take also the robe I promised thee."

Tristan fetched his horse swiftly, and when he came back he swung his harp behind him, and cried, "Now, knight of Ireland, give me my lady, I will carry her before me through the water."

"Nay, minstrel, thou shalt not touch her; I will carry her myself."

"Nay, sir," said fair Isolt, " 'tis needless to say he shall not touch me. Know of a truth I go not aboard save the minstrel bear me."

Then Gandîn led her to Tristan. "Comrade," he said, "have a care of her—carry her so gently that I shall be ever grateful to thee."

Now, as soon as Tristan held Isolt he spurred his steed forward, and when Gandîn saw it he spake in wrath: "Ha, fool, what dost thou?"

"Nay, nay, fool Gandîn," quoth Tristan, " 'tis thou who art

befooled; what thou didst steal from King Mark by thy lute, that do I bear away with my harp. Thou didst betray, now art thou betrayed. Tristan has followed thee till he has befooled thee! Friend, thou hast indeed given me a rich garment, even the richest that thy tent did hold!"

With that Tristan rode his way, leaving Gandîn beyond measure sorrowful; his loss and his shame cut him to the heart; mourning, he returned overseas.

Tristan and Isolt rode homeward, rejoicing in their love; and when they came to the palace Tristan led the queen to King Mark, and spake bitterly: "Sire, God knoweth if thou dost hold thy queen so dear as thou sayest; 'tis a great folly to give her up lightly for mere lute or harp play! The world may well mock! Whoever saw a queen the chattel of a lay? Henceforth bethink thee, and guard my lady better!"

In these days had Tristan a companion, a noble knight, who held his lands from the king, and was chief seneschal at court; he was named Marjodo. The same bare Tristan love and honor for the sake of the queen, whom he loved secretly, though no man was ware of it.

The two knights had their lodging in common, and were fain to be of each other's company. It was the seneschal's custom to have his couch spread by Tristan's at night, that they might speak freely to each other, and he be solaced by Tristan's fair speech.

One night it chanced that the two had spoken long together ere Marjodo fell asleep, and when at length he slept soundly, the lover Tristan arose softly, and stole secretly on the track that led to much sorrow for him and the queen. He thought himself unmarked as he trod the path that had often led him gladly to Isolt's side; snow had fallen, and the moon shone clear, but Tristan had no care to conceal his steps.

When he came to the queen's chamber Brangoene took a

chessboard, and leant it against the light so that the chamber
was darkened, and then she laid her down to sleep; how it
chanced I know not, but she left the door undone, whereof
came sorrow and trouble.

Now, as the seneschal Marjodo lay and slept, he dreamed
that a fierce boar came out of the forest and ran into the
palace, foaming, and gnashing his tusks, and oversetting all
in his way, so that no man durst withstand him. Thus he
came even to the king's chamber, and burst open the door and
tare the couch to pieces, tossing it hither and thither; and
Mark's men beheld, but none dare lay hands upon him.

With that the seneschal awoke, and would fain tell Tristan
his dream; so he called on him by name, and when he answered not he called again, and felt with his hands, and knew
the bed to be empty. Then he bethought him that Tristan was
gone forth on some secret errand; not that he had any
thought of his love for the queen, but he was somewhat
vexed that, such friends as they were, Tristan had not told
him his secret. So he arose and did on his garments, and
stole forth softly, and looked around, and saw the track
made by Tristan in the snow.

He followed the path through a little orchard, till he came
to the door of the queen's chamber. There he stopped,
trembling, for a strange doubt fell on him when he found the
door undone. He stood awhile and gazed on Tristan's foot-
prints, and thought now one thing, now another. One moment
he deemed that Tristan had come hither for the love of one
of the queen's maidens; and then again he deemed 'twas
surely for love of the queen herself; so he wavered 'twixt one
thought and another.

At last he went forward softly, and found neither taper
nor moonlight; a taper was burning, yet he saw but little of it
for the chessboard that was set over against it. Yet he went
forward still, feeling with his hands against the wall till he

came near the queen's couch, and heard the lovers as they spake softly to each other.

Then was Marjodo sorrowful at heart, for he had ever loved and honored Queen Isolt, but now his love was overcome of anger. He hated and envied the twain, yet knew not what he might do in the matter. He bethought him of this and of that; he was so wrathful for the treachery that he fain had revealed it, but the thought of Tristan, and the dread of his anger should he do him a hurt, restrained him. So he turned him about, and went his way back, and laid him down again as one who had been sorely wronged.

In a short space Tristan came back softly, and laid him to bed again. He spake no word, nor did Marjodo, which was little his custom. From his silence Tristan misdoubted him, and bethought him to keep a better watch over his speech and actions; but 'twas too late, his secret was his no longer.

Then Marjodo spake secretly to the king, and told him how a rumor went about the court touching Tristan and the queen, that was but ill pleasing to the folk, and he counseled the king to look into the matter, and do as should best beseem him, for 'twas a thing that touched his wedded honor. But he told him not the true story as he himself knew it.

The simple-hearted king, who was himself true and faithful, was much amazed and heard him unwillingly, for the guiding star of his joy in Isolt would he not suffer lightly to be belied. Yet in his heart was he ill at ease, and could not but watch them secretly to see if he might find aught unfitting in their speech and bearing; yet could he find nought, for Tristan had warned Isolt of the seneschal's suspicions.

Then the king bethought him of a ruse, and one evening when he was alone with the queen he spake on this wise: "Lady, I have a mind to go on a pilgrimage and may be long on the road; in whose care wilt thou that I leave thee?"

"My lord," answered Isolt, "wherefore ask me? In whose

care shouldst thou leave thy folk and thy land save in that of thy nephew Tristan? He is valiant and wise, and can guard them well."

This saying misliked the king, and he watched even more closely, and spake to the seneschal of his suspicions; and Marjodo answered, "Of a truth, sire, 'tis as I say. Thou canst thyself see that they may not hide the love they bear to each other. 'Tis a great folly thus to suffer them. Much as thou dost love thy wife and thy nephew, thou shouldst not for thine honor endure this shame."

The matter vexed Mark much, for he could not but doubt his nephew, yet might he find no ground for his doubt.

But Isolt was joyful, and told Brangoene, laughing and with much glee, of her lord's pilgrimage, and how he had asked her in whose care she would be left. Then Brangoene said, "My lady, lie not to me, but tell me truly—whom didst thou choose?" And Isolt told her all, even as it had chanced.

"Ah, foolish child!" said Brangoene, "why didst thou say so? Of a truth 'twas but a ruse, and the counsel was the seneschal's—herewith he thought to take thee. If the king speak to thee again on the matter, do as I shall tell thee, and answer thus and thus." So she counseled the queen.

When now king and queen were alone, Mark took Isolt in his arms, and kissed her many times on her eyes and on her lips, and spake: "Sweetest, I love nought beside thee, and now that I needs must leave, God knoweth it lieth heavy on my heart."

Then the queen said, sighing, "Alas and alas, my lord! I deemed thy speech was but in sport; now I see thou wert in very earnest." And she began to weep so bitterly that the simple king felt all his doubts vanish; he could have sworn that she spake from her heart (for in sooth women can weep without cause, and without meaning, so oft as it seemeth them good so to do).

Then, as Isolt still wept, Mark said, "Dearest, tell me what vexeth thee, why dost thou weep?"

"Well may I weep, and much cause have I to lament. I am but a woman, and have but one body and soul, and both have I so given over to thee and to thy love that I can care for none beside. And know for a truth that thou dost not love me as thou sayest, or thou couldst not have the heart to journey hence and leave me all alone in a strange land; by this I know thou lovest me not, and I must needs be sorrowful."

"But wherefore, fair Isolt? Thou hast folk and land in thine own power; they are thine even as they are mine; thou art mistress, and what thou dost command, that shall be done. And while I am on my journey shalt thou be in the care of one who can guard thee well, my nephew Tristan: he is wise and of good counsel, and will do all he may for thine honor and happiness. I trust him well; thou art as dear to him as I may be; he will guard thee alike for thy sake and mine."

"Tristan!" said fair Isolt. "I were liefer I were dead and buried than left in his care. He is but a flatterer who is ever at my side telling me how dear he holds me! Yet I know well wherefore he doeth so: he slew my uncle and doth fear my hatred! For that alone doth he ply me with flatteries, thinking to win my friendship, but it helpeth him little! 'Tis true, I have spoken to him oft with lying lips and friendly glances, and laid myself out to please him, but I did it for thy sake, and lest men should bring against me the reproach that women aye hate their husband's friend. Ofttimes have I deceived him with my friendly words, so that he would have sworn they came from my heart! Sir, leave me not in the care of thy nephew Tristan, no, not for a day, if I may persuade thee!"

Thus Isolt by her soft words soothed Mark's heart, and laid his doubts to rest; and he told the seneschal how that the queen had contented him. But Marjodo would not rest till he had persuaded the king to test Isolt once more.

So on an even, as they sat in their chamber, Mark said, "My lady queen, since I must journey hence I would fain see how a woman may rule a kingdom. All my friends and kinsmen who owe aught to me must needs treat thee with all honor, but any who have not found favor in thine eyes will I send out of the land; I will no longer love those whom thou lovest not. Otherwise live free and happy, and do as shall best please thee. And since my nephew Tristan displeaseth thee, I will shortly send him hence; he shall return to Parmenie, and see to his own land; 'tis needful alike for him and the country."

"I thank thee, sire," said Isolt; "thou dost speak well and truly. Since I know now that thou art so swiftly displeased with those who trouble me, it seemeth to me that I should strive, in so far as I may, to honor those who are pleasing in thine eyes. 'Tis neither my mind nor my counsel that thou shouldst banish thy nephew from court; so were I dishonored, for all the folk would say that I had counseled thee to do it, in revenge for the death of mine uncle, and that were shame to me and small honor to thee. Also bethink thee well, who shall guard thy two kingdoms? Shall they be safe in a woman's hand? I know none who may guard them so well as thy nephew Tristan; he is thy nearest of kin, and shall be best obeyed. Should he be banished, and war come upon us, as may chance any day, and we be put to the worse, then would men reproach me, saying, 'If Tristan had been here, then should we not have had such ill success;' and all will blame me; so shall I forfeit alike my honor and thine. Sir, bethink thee better; either let me go with thee, or bid Tristan guard the kingdom; however my heart may be toward him, 'tis better he guard us than another shame us."

Now the king saw truly that Isolt's heart was set on Tristan's honor, and he fell again into doubt and anger. Isolt also told Brangoene all that had passed, and it vexed the wise maiden that she had spoken thus; so she counseled her again as to what she should say. And when the king held her in his arms and kissed her, she said, "Sire, wast thou in very earnest when thou didst speak of sending Tristan hence for my sake? If it were true, then would I be grateful to thee, and in sooth I know I should trust thee; yet my mind misgave me that thou saidst it but to try me? If I might know certainly that thou dost hate all who are my foes, then should I be assured of thy love for me. Of a truth had I thought thou wouldst hearken, I should ere now have made my request to thee to send thy nephew hence to his own land, for I misdoubt me much, should evil befall thee on thy journey, that he will take from me the kingdom; he has the power to do so. If then thou wert in earnest, it might indeed be well to send him to his own land, or to take him with thee on thy journey and bid the seneschal Marjodo guard me while thou art absent. Or if thou wilt but let me journey with thee, then mayest thou commit the land to whomsoever thou wilt." So she caressed and flattered her lord till she had driven all doubt from his soul, and he held the queen for innocent, and the tale of her love for Tristan a dream, and Marjodo himself but a liar; yet had he spoken the truth.

When Marjodo saw he could not bend the king to his will, then he tried in other wise. There was a dwarf at court, named Melot of Aquitaine; the tale went that he was learned in hidden lore, and could read the stars, but I will say nought of him save what is writ in the book, and that telleth nought save that he was clever, cunning, and ready of speech. He was in the king's confidence, and had free entrance to the queen's apartments. With him Marjodo took counsel, and prayed him when he was in the company of the women to take close heed of Tristan and the queen, and if he were so fortunate as to find sure proof of the love betwixt them, then would he win great reward from King Mark.

So Melot went his way, and dealt cunningly. Early and late he watched the two, till he saw well, by their sweet ways to each other, that they were lovers. Then he went his way to King Mark, and told him what he had seen, and the three, Mark, Melot, and Marjodo, counseled whether it were not better to forbid Tristan the court.

Then the king prayed his nephew, on his honor, to refrain from visiting the queen's apartments, for he said tales went about the court, and 'twere well he should be careful, lest perchance slanders should arise concerning him and the queen. From henceforth Tristan avoided any place where the queen and her maidens chanced to be alone. But the courtiers were not slow to note his altered bearing, and spake of him in no friendly wise; so that his ears were full of their chatter.

The time passed but sadly for the lovers. They were sorrowful for Mark's suspicions, more sorrowful that they might no longer meet and converse together as of yore. From day to day each began to lose heart and strength, and to wax pale and thin. The one suffered for the other, Tristan for Isolt, Isolt for Tristan. Nor was it great marvel, for they had but one heart and soul betwixt them; their sorrow, their joy, their death and their life, they were interwoven the one with the other. The sorrow of heart they bare in common was so manifest on their faces that few might doubt their love who saw the whiteness of their cheeks.

When this had endured so long that Mark knew surely they would seek to meet did he but give them occasion thereto, he laid his plans warily, and commanded that the huntsmen should make themselves ready, and announced in the court that he would ride forth hunting for the space of twenty days, and that all who loved the sport, or would ride with him for pastime, should make them ready. Then he took leave of the queen, and bade her do according to her own pleasure, and be joyful and glad at home; but secretly he commanded the dwarf, Melot, to keep watch upon Tristan and Isolt, and, if it might be, aid their meetings. So he departed to the wood with a great company.

But Tristan abode at home, saying to his uncle that he was sick—in sooth he thought to hunt other game! He and Isolt cast about in their minds how they might meet secretly, so that none should know of it, but at first they could think of no way. Then Brangoene went to Tristan, for she knew well what ailed him, and they made great lamentation together.

"Ah, dear lady," he said, "canst thou find no counsel in this pass? For surely if we may not meet, 'twill be the death of Isolt and myself!"

"What counsel may I give?" quoth Brangoene. "Would to God we had never been born! We have all three lost our joy and our honor; never again shall we be free as of yore. Alas, Isolt! Alas, Tristan! Would that mine eyes had never seen you, for all your sorrow is my doing! I know neither ease nor counsel whereby to aid you, yet I know 'twill be your death and mine if this endure longer. See, since it may not better be, do this: take the twig of an olive, and cut it lengthwise; mark nothing thereon save on the one side a T and on the other an I. Then go thy way into the orchard. Thou knowest the little stream that floweth from the spring hard by the queen's chamber? Throw thy twig therein, and let it be carried past the chamber door—there do we sit ofttimes and weep, the queen and I. When we see the twig float past, then shall we know that thou art by the spring, beneath the olive tree; there wait till Isolt may come to thee, my lady and thy beloved, and I with her, if it be thy will. The while I have to live am I thine and my lady's; might I but buy you one hour of joy by a thousand hours of life, I would pledge all my days to lessen your sorrow!"

"I thank thee, fair lady," said Tristan. "I doubt me not of thy truth and honor; never were the twain more deeply planted in any heart. Should any good fortune chance to me, then should it turn to thy gladness."

With that he kissed her on the cheek. "Farewell, lady," he said. "Do as shall seem best to thee, and commend me to my queen, fair Isolt, and bear us in thine heart."

"That will I, Sir Knight. But now would I go hence; do as I have counseled thee, and grieve not too sorely."

With that Brangoene departed, sad at heart.

Then Tristan did even as Brangoene bade him, and threw the twig into the streamlet, and he and his lady Isolt met by the spring and under the shadow of the tree with such secrecy that they had met eight times in eight days ere any was ware of it.

But it chanced one night as Tristan went thither that Melot spied him (I know not how it so fell out) and crept after him. And he saw him go to the tree; and ere he had stood there long a lady came to him, and he took her in his arms; but who the lady might be, that could not Melot tell.

The next day, a little before noon, Melot came secretly to Tristan with falsehood on his lips, and said, "Alas, my lord! With peril have I come to thee; thou art so beset with spies that I have had much pain to steal hither, but my heart is heavy for Isolt, the noble queen; she sorrows sore for thee, and hath sent me to thee since she would have none but me to know of the matter. She greets thee, and prays thee to come to her at the place where thou didst meet her of late (I know not where that may be), and at the same hour at which thou art wont to come. I know not of what she would warn thee; but wouldst thou believe me, never did I grieve for any one's sorrow as for thine, Sir Tristan. An thou biddest me, I

will take what message thou wilt to her, but I dare not stay
with thee, for if the courtiers knew mine errand harm would
befall me. They believe of a sooth that all that has chanced
'twixt thee and the queen has come about through me, yet
was it none of my counsel."

"Friend, thou dreamest!" quoth Tristan. "What fable
wouldst thou tell me? Are the courtiers mad? What have I
and my lady done? Out! To hell with thee! Know in truth
that an I did not think it beneath mine honor to touch thee,
thou shouldst have no chance of telling thy dreams in court
henceforward!"

Then Melot gat him swiftly to the woodland to King Mark,
and told him that he had at last found out the truth and of
the tryst by the spring. "Thou canst see the truth for thyself,
sire, an thou wilt. Ride with me at nightfall, 'tis the better
way; they will surely meet tonight, and thou canst thyself see
their doings."

So the king rode with Melot to await his sorrow, and they
came to the orchard at nightfall, but they saw no place where
they might well hide themselves. Beside the spring was an
olive tree, none too high, yet with spreading branches; thither
they betook themselves, and climbed into the branches, and
there they sat and held their peace.

As it grew dark Tristan stole forth into the orchard; he
took his messenger in his hand and dropped it where the waters gushed forth, and saw it float away. 'Twas token enough
to Isolt that her lover was at hand. Then Tristan crossed the
spring where the shadow of the tree fell on the grass, and
stood there, awaiting her who was his secret sorrow.

And as he stood there it chanced that he spied the shadows
of Mark and Melot, for the moon shone through the
boughs so that he could well distinguish the shadows of the
two men; and a great terror fell upon him, for he saw their
ruse and his danger.

"Ah, God," he thought, "protect us! If Isolt see not the shadows in time she will come to me, and if she do 'twill be sorrow and shame for us both. Have us in Thy keeping, guard Isolt's footsteps, warn my queen betimes of the trap they have laid for us, ere she speak or act so that men think evil of her. Have mercy on us both, our life and our honor are in Thy hands tonight!"

Meanwhile Isolt the queen, and Brangoene, awaited his summons in the little garden where they had so oft bewailed their woe. They walked up and down, Isolt speaking ever of her love sorrow. Then Brangoene saw the token floating in the stream, and signed to her lady, and Isolt took the twig and looked on it, and saw the T and I on either side. With that she took her mantle, and drew it over her head, and stole through grass and flowers to the olive tree beside the spring.

But when she came so nigh that each could see the other, Tristan stood still, which he was never wont to do, for never aforetime did she come toward him but he went to meet her.

Now, Isolt wondered much what this might mean, and her heart grew heavy within her. Timidly, with head bent down, she came toward him, fearing much for what she was doing. As she drew thus slowly nearer the tree, her eyes on the ground, she espied the shadow of three men, and knew there should be but one. With that she understood her danger, and the meaning of Tristan's bearing toward her.

"Ah, murderers!" she thought; "what may this be? Wherefore this ambush? I fear me my lord is hidden near at hand. I see well we are betrayed. Blessed Trinity shield us! Help us to depart hence with honor, he and I!" Then she thought again, "Doth Tristan know this ill chance or not?" and again she felt assured he knew it by his bearing.

Then she stood afar off and spake: "Sir Tristan, it grieveth me much that thou shouldst so count on my simplicity as to deem I would come and speak with thee here! That thou shouldst guard well thine honor as against thine uncle and myself, that indeed would befit thee well, and would better accord with thy faith and my honor than to pray of me so late and so secret a meeting! Now say, what wouldst thou? I came here with fear and trembling, for Brangoene would not have it otherwise. When she left thee today she prayed and counseled me to come hither and hear thy plaint; yet have I done wrong in that I have followed her counsel. 'Tis true that she sitteth near at hand, yet, though I know myself to be safe, for fear of evil tongues I would give one of my fingers from off my hand ere any should know that I have met thee here. Folk have told such tales of us twain! They sware that we were sick and sorrowful by reason of our treasonable love to each other! The court is full of such fables. God knoweth how my heart standeth toward thee. I will say no more save that I speak the truth of my feeling toward thee, and that God is my witness I never gave my heart to any man, heretofore, or today, save to him to whom I gave the first blossom of my maidenhood. My lord King Mark doeth ill to suspect me for thy sake, Sir Tristan, for he himself well knoweth my mind toward thee. They who whisper such tales of us in his ear are but evil counselors. A hundred thousand times have I shown thee a friendly bearing through the love I bear to him whom I ought to love—never for falsehood! Whether he were knight or squire, 'twas but right I should show kindness to one who was my lord's kinsman. Now men will turn that to my hurt! Yet will I not hate thee for their lies. Sir Knight, what thou wouldst say to me, that say, and let me go hence; I may not stay here longer."

"Dearest lady," spake Tristan, "no doubt had I as to thy feelings toward me. I knew well thou wouldst do as befitted thine honor. Give no ear to the liars who have slandered thee and me, and brought us, innocent, out of our lord's favor; God reward them! My lady queen, I pray thee counsel my lord that the wrath and rancor he beareth against me be hidden, and that he be courteous to me for but eight days more—till now have ye both borne yourselves as if ye loved me—so will I within that time make ready to depart hence. We shall be dishonored, the king, thou, and I alike, if ye bear yourselves thus toward me ere I depart, for all men will say, 'Of a truth was there somewhat in that tale. Mark ye how Sir Tristan has fallen out of the king's favor, and is departed hence?' "

"Sir Tristan," said Isolt, "I would rather die than that I should pray my lord to do aught against thee for my sake. Thou knowest well that because of thee he has this long while past been ill disposed toward me; did he know that I had met thee here, alone and by night, henceforth would he show me neither love nor honor. If things may so chance, alas! I know not. But I wonder much how my lord came thus to suspect me? I know not who hath slandered us, but matters stand ill enough for us both. May God look upon the thing and better it. Now Sir Knight, give me leave, I must go hence; do thou, too, depart. Much do I grieve for thy sorrow and trouble; I had much against thee, yet will I not count it to thy wrong that I should hate thee; sorry enough am I that thou shouldst thus be troubled for no cause. I will think the matter over; and, Sir Knight, when the day comes that I must go hence, then may the Queen of Heaven have thee in her keeping. If I thought there were any power in my prayers or my counsel, then would I do all I might for thee, though it should bring me ill. Yet, since thou hast thought no treason against me and my lord, will I do thy bidding as best I may."

"I thank thee, lady," said Tristan; "if thou winnest favor or not, I pray thee let me know straightway. But if I hear nought, and must needs go hence without delaying, so that I see thee not again, whatever be my lot, gracious queen, thou must needs be blessed, for a truer lady never trod this earth. My queen, I commend thy soul and body, thine honor and thy life, to the care of God."

Thus they parted. The queen went her way, sighing and lamenting, sorrowing secretly in heart and soul. Tristan also departed, sad and weeping. But King Mark who sat up in the tree grieved even more. It went to his heart to think that he had so sorely wronged his nephew and his wife, and a thousand times with heart and lips he cursed those who had brought him to this pass. Bitterly he reproached the dwarf Melot for having deceived him and slandered the innocent queen. They descended from the tree, and rode back to the hunt heavy at heart—Melot, that he had ever meddled in the matter, and Mark for the suspicion which had wronged his nephew and his wife, and his own self yet more, and which had caused such ill talk in the land.

In the morning the king bade the rest of his company continue the hunt, but he himself returned to the court, where he sought Isolt. "Say, lady queen, how hast thou passed the time in mine absence?"

"Sire, my idleness was undeserved sorrow; my labor, harp and lyre."

"Undeserved sorrow?" quoth Mark. "What was that, and how did it chance?"

Isolt smiled a little. "However it chanced, it chanced and doth chance today and every day. Sorrow and vain reproaches are my lot and that of all women; therewith cleanse we our hearts and enlighten our eyes. Yet ofttimes do we make a great sorrow of nought, and forget it as quickly." Thus she mocked him.

But the king marked her words and said, "Now, lady, tell me, does any one here, or dost thou, know how matters are with Tristan? They told me he was sick when I departed."

" 'Twas true, sire."

"How dost thou know? Who told thee?"

"I know nought, save that Brangoene spake to me of his sickness a while back. She saw him yesterday, and prayed me that I would make his plaint to thee, and pray thee not to think aught against his honor, but hide thy displeasure for these eight days longer, when he will make him ready so that he may leave thy court and thy land in all honor. That he prayed of us both."

So she told him all Tristan's will even as he had spoken it by the spring, and as Mark himself had overheard.

But the king said, "My lady queen, ill luck may he have who caused me to think ill of Tristan; I repent me sore of it, for in these last days have I learnt his innocence, and my ill will is at an end. Dear lady, by the love thou dost bear to me, I pray thee to lay aside thine anger; do as thou wilt, but make peace betwixt me and him."

"Nay, to what good, my lord?" said the queen. "For even if thou dost lay aside thy suspicion today, tomorrow wilt thou take it to thine heart again."

"Nay, of a truth, lady, never more. I will never again think aught against his honor and thine, my queen. Show favor to him if thou wilt." Thus he swore to her.

Herewith Tristan was sent for, and the suspicion laid to rest between them. Isolt was commended to Tristan's care, that henceforth he should be the keeper of the queen's chamber.

So for a while Tristan and his lady Isolt led a happy life; their joy was full, their desire was granted them after much sorrow. But not for long might it endure, for do as they might Tristan and Isolt might not guard themselves so well but that the king should find fresh matter for suspicion. Again Mark knew not what to think: he suspected both, yet would suspect neither; he thought them true, yet deemed they lied to him; he would not have them guilty, yet would not speak them free of guilt. This was a heavy load on the heart of the doubter.

At last he bethought him he would call his lords together, and take counsel on the matter; so he summoned all those in whom he might trust, and laid all his trouble bare to them, telling them of the tale which went about the court, and which so nearly touched his honor, and how, do what he might, he could not lay his doubts to rest. But now was the tale so spread abroad in the land that it seemed to him alike for his sake and the queen's 'twas time that her innocence should be made clear in the sight of all men. He besought their counsel as to how the matter should be cleared up.

Then the lords, his friends, bade him assemble a great council at London, in England, and there make known to all the bishops, who knew well the law of the church, the doubt and sorrow in which he found himself. The council was therefore summoned without delay to meet at London, after Pentecost, on the last days of May. Of priests and lay folk a great number came together by the king's command, and thereto came King Mark and Isolt his queen, heavy at heart, and in much fear and trembling: Isolt feared greatly lest she lose her life and her good fame, and Mark also feared lest his gladness and his honor be shamed through his wife Isolt.

Then Mark sat at the council, and laid bare to all the princes of his land how he was troubled and perplexed by this tale or scandal, and prayed them earnestly for God's sake that they would bethink them of some means by which the matter might be fairly judged, and, for good or for ill, an end put to it. And some said one thing and some another, till many men had spoken their minds.

Then there stood up one of the princes, who by his age and wisdom was well fitted to give good counsel; a man noble and ancient, gray-haired and wise, the Bishop of Thames. He leaned on his staff and spake: "My lord king, hear me. Thou hast called us princes of England together that we may aid thee by our counsel as thou hast need. Sire, I am one of these princes, and well advanced in age; I think I may well take upon me to speak my mind in the matter; if thou thinkest my counsel good, thou canst follow it. My lady the queen and Sir Tristan are suspected by many of having betrayed thee, yet can nought be proved against them—so do I understand the matter. How then mayst thou pass judgment on thy nephew and thy wife, since none have found them offending? No man can accuse Tristan of it but he is ready with an answer to the charge; even so is it with the queen. Thou canst prove nought. But since the court holdeth them so strongly in suspicion, I counsel thee that thou forbid the queen thy bed and thy board till the day that she can show herself free of offense against thee and against the land. The tale is spread abroad, and men speak of it daily, for alas! to such scandals, be they true or false, men's ears are ever wont to be open, and whatever evil be in the story, of that will they make the worst. But whether true or false, the mischief and the scandal are so widespread they must needs injure thee and be held amiss by the court. Therefore I counsel thee to call the queen hither that all present may hear her answer to the charge, and see if she be ready to give open proof of her innocence."

This counsel seemed good to King Mark, and he bade them summon Queen Isolt, and she came to the council chamber. When she was seated, the gray-haired Bishop of Thames arose, and spake as the king bade him: "Lady Isolt, gracious queen, be not wrathful at my speech; the king my master hath bid me speak, and I must needs obey him. God is my witness, I would fain say nought that could reflect on thine honor and on thy fair fame. My lady queen, thy lord and husband hath bid me speak to thee of a charge openly brought against thee. I know not, nor may he know, how it hath come about; he knoweth only that court and country alike couple thy name with that of the king's nephew, Sir Tristan. I pray God, my lady queen, that thou art innocent of this sin—yet doth the king doubt, the court is so full of the rumor. My lord himself hath found in thee nought but good; 'tis not his thought but the talk of the court that hath brought this suspicion upon thee. Therefore doth he call thee hither that his friends and councilors may hear thee, if perchance by their aid an end may be put to this slander. Now methinks it were well that thou shouldst make answer to the king in this matter, here, in presence of us all."

Then Isolt, the quick-witted queen, seeing that it fell to her to speak, arose and answered: "My king, my lord bishop, lords of the land and all ye courtiers, ye shall all know well that I deny my lord's shame and mine, and I shall deny it both now and at all times. Ye lords all, I know well that this accusation hath been brought against me—it is now over a year—both at court and abroad; yet ye yourselves know that no man may be so fortunate that, however well he may live, evil shall never be spoken of him. Therefore I marvel not if such chance should also befall me. I may never be left in peace; I must ever be slandered and misjudged since I am here a stranger, and have neither friend nor kinsfolk in the land—there are but few here whom my shame may touch. Ye all and each, whether rich or poor, believe readily in my misdoing! If I knew now what I might do, or what counsel I might follow whereby I might prove mine innocence, and win again your favor and my lord's honor, I would readily agree to it. What would ye have me do? Whatever judgment may be passed upon me, thereto will I readily submit, that your suspicions may be laid to rest, yet even more that mine honor and that of my lord may be maintained."

Then the king spake: "My lady queen, hereby shall the matter be set at rest. If I may pass judgment upon thee as thou hast prayed us to do, thus shalt thou give us certainty: submit to the ordeal by red-hot iron, as we here counsel thee!"

This the queen did; she sware to undergo the ordeal even as they should ordain, six weeks hence, in the town of Caerleon.

Thus the king and the lords departed from the council.

Isolt remained alone, sorrowful and sore dismayed at heart, for much she feared that her unfaithfulness must now be made manifest, and she knew not what to do. So with prayer and fasting she made supplication to heaven to aid her. And a thought came into her mind. She wrote a letter to Tristan, bidding him be at Caerleon early on the morn of the day she must arrive there, and await her on the shore. And this Tristan did, journeying thither in pilgrim's guise, his face stained and soiled, and his appearance changed.

Now, Mark and Isolt came thither by water, and as they drew to shore the queen saw Tristan and knew him. As the ship cast anchor in the stream Isolt commanded they should ask the pilgrim if he were strong enough to carry her to shore, for on that day she would have no knight to bear her.

Then all the folk cried, "Come hither, thou holy man, and bear our lady the queen to land."

Tristan came at their call, and took the queen in his arms and bore her to the shore; and as he held her Isolt whispered in his ear that as he set foot on land he should fall with her. And this he did; as he stepped out of the water onto the shore, the pilgrim sank down on the earth as if he could not help himself, so that the queen fell from his clasp and lay beside him on the ground.

Then the folk came swiftly with sticks and staves, and

would do the pilgrim an harm. "Nay, nay, let be," cried Isolt; "the pilgrim could not help himself; he is sick and feeble, and fell against his will."

Then they all praised her much that she was not wrathful with the pilgrim, but Isolt spake, smiling a little: "Were it then so great a wonder if the pilgrim had thought to mock me?" And as Mark stood near and hearkened, she spake further: "Now I know not what shall befall me, for ye have all seen well that I may not swear that no man save the king ever held me in his arms or lay at my side!"

Thus they rode gaily, jesting the while of the palmer, till they came into Caerleon. There were many nobles, priests, and knights, and of lesser folk a great crowd. Bishops and prelates were there, ready to do their office and bless the ordeal. They had all things in readiness, and the iron was brought forth.

The good Queen Isolt had given in charity her silks and her gold, her jewels and all she had—horses and raiment— praying that heaven would look favorably on her, forgive her what she had done amiss, and preserve her honor. Herewith she came to the minster with good courage to face her ordeal.

She wore next her skin a rough garment of hair; above it a short gown of woolen stuff, a hand's breadth above her ankles; her sleeves were rolled up to her elbows, and her hands and feet bare. Many hearts and many eyes beheld her with pity.

Herewith they brought forth the relics, and bade Isolt swear her innocence of this sin before God and the world. Now had Isolt committed life and honor to heaven; so hand and heart did she proffer reverently to the relics and the oath.

Now were there many there who would fain from ill will have had the queen's oath turned to her shame and downfall. The envious seneschal, Marjodo, strove to harm her in every way he might; while there were many who honored Isolt,

and would fain see her come off scatheless; so there was
great strife among them as to the manner of the queen's oath.

"My lord the king," spake Isolt, "whatever any may say, I
must needs swear in such wise as shall content thee. Say
thyself what I shall speak or do. All this talk is too much.
Hearken how I will swear to thee. No man hath touched this
my body, hath held me in his arms, or lain beside me other
than thou thyself, and this man whom I cannot deny, since
ye all saw me in his arms—the poor pilgrim! So help me God
and all the saints, to the happy issue of this ordeal! If this be
not enough, my lord, I will better mine oath as thou shalt bid
me!"

"Lady," said King Mark, "methinks 'tis enough. Now take
the iron in thine hand, and God help thee in thy need."

"Amen," said fair Isolt. Then in God's name she seized the
iron, and carried it, and it burnt her not.

And so, had men but known it, they might have seen that
God at whiles doth let the wrong triumph, since He turned
not this oath, which was true in the letter yet false in spirit,
to the confusion of the queen, but ruled matters so that she
came forth from the ordeal victorious, and was held in
greater love and honor by Mark and his people than ever before; all his thoughts and all his heart were truly set upon her,
and his doubts had passed away.

Now Tristan, when he had borne Isolt to the shore at
Caerleon, departed secretly from England, and came to
Wales, to the court of Duke Gilân. He was a noble prince,
unmarried, young and rich, free, and light of heart. There
was Tristan a welcome guest, for Gilân had heard great
marvels of his valiant and knightly deeds, and did all in his
power to honor him and give him pleasure; but Tristan was
ever sorrowful, plunged in thought over his ill fortune.

One day it chanced that Tristan sat by Gilân, sad, in deep

thought, and sighing often; his host noticed this, and bade men bring him his little dog, Petit-criu, his heart's delight and the joy of his eyes, that erewhile came to him from Avalon. As he bade, so was it done: a rich purple cloth was laid upon the table, and the dog placed upon it. 'Twas a fairy dog, as I have heard tell, and had been sent to the duke from the land of Avalon, as love token, by a fay.

No tongue could tell the marvel of it; 'twas of such wondrous fashion that no man might say of what color it was. If one looked on the breast, and saw nought else, one had said 'twas white as snow, yet its thighs were greener than clover, and its sides, one red as scarlet, the other more yellow than saffron. Its under parts were even as azure, while above 'twas mingled, so that no one color might be distinguished; 'twas neither green nor red, white nor black, yellow nor blue, and yet was there somewhat of all these therein; 'twas a fair purple brown. And if one saw this strange creation of Avalon against the lie of the hair there would be no man wise enough to tell its color, so manifold and changing were its hues.

Around its neck was a golden chain, and therefrom hung a bell, which rang so sweet and clear that when it began to chime Tristan forgot his sadness and his sorrow, and the longing for Isolt that lay heavy at his heart. So sweet was the tone of the bell that no man heard it but he straightway forgat all that aforetime had troubled him.

Tristan hearkened, and gazed on this wondrous marvel; he took note of the dog and the bell, the changing colors of the hair, and the sweet sound of the chime; and it seemed to him that the marvel of the dog was greater than that of the music which rang ever in his ears, and banished all thought of sorrow.

He stretched forth his hand and stroked the dog, and it seemed to him that he handled the softest silk, so fine and so

smooth was the hair to his touch. And the dog neither
growled, nor barked, nor showed any sign of ill temper,
however one might play with it; nor, as the tale goes, was it
ever seen to eat or to drink.

When the dog was borne away, Tristan's sorrow fell upon
him as heavy as before, and to it was added the thought
how he might by any means win Petit-criu, the fairy dog, for
his lady the queen, that thereby her sorrow and her longing
might be lessened. Yet he could not see how this might be
brought about, either by craft or by prayer, for he knew well
that Gilân would not have parted with it for his life. This
desire and longing lay heavy on his heart, but he gave no
outward sign of his thought.

As the history of Tristan's deeds shows us, there was at
that time in the land of Wales a giant named Urgan, who
had his dwelling by the sea shore. Gilân and his folk were under the lordship of this giant, and must pay him tribute
that they might dwell in peace. In these days tidings were
brought to the court that Urgan had come and demanded his
tribute of cattle, sheep, and swine.

Herewith Gilân began to tell Tristan how this tribute
had been laid upon him by force at the first.

"Now tell me, friend," said Tristan, "if I can help thee in
such wise that thou shalt shortly be free of this tribute for all
the days of thy life, what wilt thou give me?"

"Of a truth," said Gilân, "I will give thee whatever I possess."

Tristan spake further: "Sir Duke, if thou wilt swear that,
then will I on my part promise shortly to free thee for ever
from Urgan, or to lose my life in the trial."

"Of a truth, Sir Tristan, I will give thee whatever thou dost
desire," said Gilân. "What thou askest, that shall be done,"
and he gave him his hand upon it.

Then Tristan sent straightway for horses and armor, and

bade the folk tell him whither that devil's son, Urgan, would journey with his spoil. Then they showed him how that the way of the giant lay through a wild wood which bordered on his own lands, and by a bridge over the which he must needs drive the cattle.

The giant came thither with his spoil, but Tristan was before him, and would let the cattle go no further.

When Urgan saw there was a foe on the bridge, he came swiftly, with a long steel staff in his hand, which he brandished aloft.

But when he saw the knight so well armed, he spake, saying, "Friend on the horse, who art thou? Why dost thou not suffer me and my cattle to pass? Since thou hast so done thou must die, or yield thee captive."

Then the knight on the horse answered, "Friend, men call me Tristan, know that well; and I fear neither thee nor thy staff a straw! Turn thee aside, for know surely thy spoil goeth no further."

"Yea," said the giant; "Sir Tristan, thou vauntest thee of having slain Morolt of Ireland, with whom thou didst most unjustly fight, and whom thou didst slay by thy pride. Nor is it with me as with that knight of Ireland whom thou didst mock, and stole from him that fair lady Isolt, whom he rightly claimed. Nay, nay, this shore is mine, and I am Urgan; out of my path swiftly!"

Herewith he dealt a sweeping blow at Tristan, and had taken his aim so well that had he smitten him he had been slain forthwith.

Tristan swerved aside, yet not so swiftly but that the giant's blow fell on the steed and cut it in twain.

The monster shouted aloud, and cried, laughing, to Tristan, "God help thee, Sir Tristan! Ride not away, but grant me my prayer, if I may make request unto thee. Let my tribute pass in peace and honor!"

Tristan, seeing his horse was slain, dismounted, and took his spear in his hand, and smote Urgan with it so that he wounded him in the eye; and as the giant stretched out his hand to take his staff again, Tristan drew his sword, and smote off his hand so that it fell to the earth. Then he smote him another blow on the leg, and drew back. But Urgan seized the staff in his left hand, and ran upon Tristan, and chased him hither and thither under the trees.

But now was the flow of blood from his wound so great that the giant feared his strength would fail him. He left the knight and the cattle, and took up his hand as it lay on the grass, and fled to his fortress.

Tristan stood alone in the wood with the spoil, not a little troubled that Urgan had departed thence alive. He sat him down on the grass, and bethought him what it were best to do. For the regaining of the tribute alone he cared not a jot; if the giant lived he might scarce claim the fulfillment of Gilân's promise. So he turned him about, and followed the bloodstained track which Urgan had left on grass and shrubs. Thus he came to the castle, and entered, and sought Urgan hither and thither, but found neither him nor any living man, for the tale saith that the giant had laid his severed hand on the table in the hall, and gone forth from his castle in the valley to the mountain to seek herbs of healing for his wound. For he knew well their virtue, and that if he could lay the hand to his arm skillfully, ere it grew cold, he should be healed.

But this might not be; for Tristan came thither and spied the hand, and as he found no man there, he took it and bare it away with him.

When Urgan came back, and saw he had lost his hand, he was wrathful indeed, and casting aside the healing herbs, he pursued after Tristan, who had already crossed the bridge, and knew well that the giant was on his track. He took the hand

and hid it 'neath the trunk of a tree, and for the first time he began to fear the monster, for he saw well that the matter must be the death of one or other of them. Then he turned him back to the bridge, and met Urgan, and smote him with his spear so fiercely that it brake in two; and as he did so the giant struck at him with his staff. Had the blow fallen on Tristan he must have perished, had he been made of brass; but in his wrath and haste Urgan overreached himself, and the blow fell beyond Tristan, and ere he might draw back his staff, Tristan had smitten him in the other eye.

Then Urgan laid around him fiercely on all sides, as a blind man may, and Tristan fled from him, and let him deal blows all around. At last he came within reach, and the knight put forth all his might, and with both hands thrust him off the bridge, so that he fell, and was crushed by his own weight on the rocks below.

Then the victor, Tristan, took the giant's hand, and fared homeward, and full soon he met Gilân the duke riding toward him, for it had grieved him much that Tristan had taken this venture on himself, for he had little thought that he might escape as he had done. When he saw him running toward him, he cried, "Welcome, welcome, gentle Tristan. Say, friend, how is it with thee? Art thou whole and unwounded?"

Forthwith Tristan showed him the dead hand of the giant, and told him how good luck had been his portion.

At this Gilân was greatly rejoiced. He rode straightway to the bridge and saw the shattered corpse of the giant, even as Tristan had told him, and marveled much at it. Then they returned gaily, driving the cattle before them; and the tale went abroad through all the land of Wales, and men praised Tristan, so that never more in that land did men win a third part of the praise that was sung and spoken of him.

But Tristan and Gilân returned to the duke's palace; and as they spake of their good fortune Tristan said, "My lord duke,

I would remind thee of thy promise and of the oath that was sworn betwixt us ere I set forth."

And Gilân answered, "That oath will I keep willingly. Tell me, what dost thou desire?"

"Duke Gilân, I pray thee, give me the dog, Petit-criu."

Quoth Gilân, "I would counsel thee better."

"Let me hear what thou wouldst say."

"Leave me my little dog, and I will give thee my fair sister, and with her the half of my kingdom."

"Nay, nay, my lord duke, bethink thee of thine oath. 'Twas *I* should choose, and neither land nor riches will I have. I slew Urgan the giant for nought else but to win Petit-criu."

"Alas! my lord Tristan, if that be indeed thy will, I will keep faith with thee and do thy pleasure. Neither craft nor cunning am I minded to use. Though it be greatly against my will, yet what thou desirest that shall be done."

Herewith he bade them bring the little dog. "See," he spake, "I will tell thee, and swear to thee on my eternal bliss, that I have nothing and may win nothing so precious (save life and honor) that I would not rather give thee than this my dog. Now take him, and God grant it may be for thy happiness. Thou hast in truth taken from me the greatest delight of mine eyes, and much of my heart's joy."

But Tristan was more joyful at having won the little dog than if Rome and all its riches, nay, all the kingdoms of the world, had been his. In comparison with Petit-criu he held them all not worth a straw. Never had he been so glad, save when with Isolt.

Then secretly he called to him a minstrel of Wales, and counseled him how he should bring joy to the Queen Isolt. He hid the little dog cunningly within a lute, and bade the minstrel bear letters to the queen, telling her why and by what means he had won the dog for her.

The minstrel went his way, even as Tristan had commanded,

and came without misfortune or ill hap to King Mark's castle
at Tintagel. There he sought out Brangoene, and gave letter
and dog into her charge, that she might bear them to Isolt.
The queen marveled much at the little dog, and gave the
minstrel for reward ten marks of gold. She also wrote a letter
that he might bear back to Tristan, telling him that King
Mark was well disposed toward him, and had never held him
in greater favor than now. She had so managed the matter that
he might well return to court.

Tristan did as she prayed him and returned forthwith; king
and court, folk and land, held him in honor even as heretofore;
never had he been in higher favor, even so much so that both
Marjodo and the dwarf Melot must perforce show him honor
—if that may well be said to be honor that cometh not from
the heart, but from the lips only.

Now Isolt the queen told her husband that the dog had
been sent to her by her mother, the wise Queen of Ireland.
She bade them make for it a fair little house, of gold and
cunning work, with a rich silk whereon it might lie, and ever,
night and day, would she have it in her sight. Wherever she
went, whether on horse or afoot, there the dog must be with
her. Yet she did this, not for the lessening of her sorrow, but
for the love of Tristan who had sent it to her. In sooth no
other profit might she have of it, for when the dog was first
brought to the queen, and she heard the bell ring softly, and
through the sweet chime forgat her grief, she bethought her
how her lover Tristan was still weighed down with sorrow for
her sake, and she said to herself, "Alas, alas! and shall I be
joyful? 'Twere faithless indeed did I rejoice the while *he*
sorrows, who hath given over life and happiness to grief and
heaviness for my sake! How may I smile when Tristan knowe-
eth no gladness apart from me? He hath nothing in life save
my love. Can I live glad and joyful while he is sad? God for-

bid that I should know happiness apart from him." Herewith she brake off the bell, leaving the chain round the dog's neck. But when the bell was thus broken off it lost all its magic power; it might ring henceforth, but never might it bring peace to the heart of man more. Yet so had Isolt willed it, that true and faithful lover, apart from Tristan would she not be joyful, for all her heart and life had she given unto him.

So were Tristan and Isolt once more together; once more held in honor by all the courtiers, and beloved by King Mark; and once more it behoved them to keep their secret hidden from all, in so far as love might do so, for it is but blind— and was their companion at all times.

But now are the seeds of love and suspicion alike: where they be sown, there they take root, and bud, and bring forth fruit; and thus suspicion began ere long to make sport of Tristan and Isolt; in their looks and gestures men saw the assurance of their love. For however lovers may guard their speech, yet are they gladly in each other's presence; the eye follows the heart, the hand the pain. Thus they built up suspicion by many a soft glance and stolen handclasp. And King Mark watched them closely, and saw their love written in their faces, though otherwise he might find but little assurance of it.

Yet their glances were so soft, so sweet, so full of longing, that they went to his heart, and such anger awoke therein, such hatred and envy, that his senses were bewildered, and he knew not what to do. For the thought that his heart's beloved, Isolt, should love another better than himself wrought in him deadly rage. However wrathful he might be, Isolt was dearer to him than his life, and yet, dearly as he loved her, he could think of nought but his anger. So betwixt the two was King Mark sore perplexed, till at length, for very anger, he cared not a jot which side the truth lay.

Thus blinded by passion, he summoned them both to the

palace court, where all the courtiers were met together, and he spoke thus to Isolt: "My Lady Isolt of Ireland, 'tis well known to all the folk and the land that for long while, and at many times, thou hast been under heavy suspicion with my nephew Tristan. Many ways have I tried, openly and in secret, to lead thee for my sake to put aside this folly, yet to no purpose. I am not so foolish nor so besotted but that I can see that openly and secretly thine eyes and thine heart are set upon my nephew. Thou showest greater kindness to him than to me; by thine actions and bearing I see well that he is dearer to thee than I. No precautions I may take toward thee or toward him may avail; all I do is done in vain. I have separated you in body so long 'tis a marvel your hearts are yet so at one. Your sweet glances have I severed, yet I may not sever your love. I have borne it too long; herewith will I make an end. The shame and scandal ye have brought upon me will I share with you no longer. I suffer this dishonor no more from henceforth. Yet will I not revenge myself upon you, as I well have the right to do. Nephew Tristan, my wife Isolt, that I should put you two to death, or do you any hurt, for that do I love you too well. But now since I see clearly that ye each hold the other dearer than ye do me, so be ye with each other henceforth, nor have further fear of me. From this time forward I meddle with you no more. Take each other by the hand and leave my court. If ye wrong me, I will neither see nor hear it. We three can no longer keep companionship. I loose me from the bond and leave you twain. Such fellowship is ill—the king who knowingly doth company with lovers doeth foolishly. Go forth, ye two, love and live as it shall please ye; of our fellowship are ye no more."

'Twas done even as King Mark said. Tristan and his lady Isolt, cold at heart, bowed to the king their lord, and to the courtiers; then the faithful lovers took each other by the hand, and passed from the court. They bade farewell to their friend

Brangoene, and bade her abide at court till she might hear
how matters went with them. Tristan took twenty marks of
the queen's gold for their needs, and bade men bring him
what he desired for the journey—harp and sword, crossbow
and horn, and one of his hounds called Hiudan, which he had
chosen from among the others. He commended his men to
God, and bade them return to their own land, to Rual his
father, save Kurwenal only; him would he take with him. He
bade him carry the harp, while he himself took crossbow, horn,
and dog (Hiudan, not Petit-criu). Thus the three rode from
court.

Brangoene abode alone; the sorrow and grief of their ill
venture and the parting from her friends went so near to her
heart 'twas a marvel she died not of sorrow. Tristan and Isolt,
too, grieved much at parting from her, yet they hoped that her
wit might find means to make peace once more betwixt them
and King Mark.

So the three rode toward the wilderness, two days' journey,
through woods and over moorland.

Now, Tristan aforetime knew of a cave in a wild hill, which
he had once chanced upon while hunting. This same cavern
in the old days of heathendom, when giants were lords of the
land, had been hewn by them in the hillside. 'Twas there they
were wont to resort secretly for love dalliance, and when
any such were found they were shut in with brazen doors and
named Love Grottoes.

The cavern was round, wide, and lofty; the walls snow-
white and smooth; the vault above bare in the center; at the
keystone, a crown richly wrought in metal work and adorned
with gems; the floor below was of polished marble, its hue
green as grass.

In the center was a couch, carved out of a crystal stone,
with letters engraven all around, saying 'twas dedicated to the
Goddess of Love. High in the wall of the cavern were little

windows hewn in the rock, through which the light might enter. Before the entrance was a brazen door, and without there stood three lindens and no more; but all around the hill and toward the valley were countless trees, whose boughs and foliage gave a fair shade. On one side was a little glade and a spring of water, cool and fresh and clear as sunlight, and above the spring were again three lindens, which sheltered it alike from sun and rain; and all over the glade the bright blossoms and green grass strove with each other for the mastery; each would fain overcome the brightness of the other.

In the branches the birds sang sweetly, so sweetly that nowhere else might one hear the like. Eye and ear alike found solace. There were shade and sunshine, air and soft breezes.

From this hill and this grotto for a good day's journey was there nought but rocks—waste and wild and void of game. Nor was the road smooth and easy; yet was it not so rough but that Tristan and his true love might make their way thither and find shelter in the hill.

Now when they had come to their journey's end, and thought to abide there, they sent Kurwenal back, bidding him say at the court that Tristan and Isolt, with much grief, had sailed thence to Ireland to make their innocence plain to all; and he had thought it best to return straightway to court. Then they bade him seek out Brangoene and give her tidings of her friends, and learn from her how it stood with King Mark, and if he had lent an ear to evil counsels, and purposed any treachery against the life of the lovers. He was thus to watch how matters went for Tristan and Isolt, and once in every twenty days bear them tidings from the court.

What more shall I say? Kurwenal did as he was bade, and Tristan and Isolt remained alone to make their dwelling in this wild hermitage.

Many have marveled wherewith the twain might support their life in this wilderness, but in truth they needed little save each other; the true love and faith they bare the one to the other, such love as kindles the heart and refreshes the soul, that was their best nourishment. They asked but rarely for other than the food which giveth to the heart its desire, to the eyes their delight; therewith had they enough.

Nor did it vex them that they were thus alone in the wild woodland; what should they want with other company? They were there together, a third would but have made unequal what was equal, and oppressed that fellowship which was so fair. Even good King Arthur never held at his court a feast that might have brought them greater joy and refreshment. Search through all the lands, and ye might not have found a joy, however great, for which these twain would have bartered a glass finger ring.

They had a court, they had a council, which brought them nought but joy. Their courtiers were the green trees, the shade and the sunlight, the streamlet and the spring; flowers, grass, leaf and blossom, which refreshed their eyes. Their service was the song of the birds, the little brown nightingales, the throstles, and the merles, and other wood birds. The siskin and the ringdove vied with each other to do them pleasure; all day long their music rejoiced ear and soul.

Their love was their high feast, which brought them a thousand times daily the joy of Arthur's Round Table and the fellowship of his knights. What might they ask better? The man was with the woman and the woman with the man, they had the fellowship they most desired, and were where they fain would be.

In the dewy morning they gat them forth to the meadow where grass and flowers alike had been refreshed. The glade was their pleasure ground; they wandered hither and thither, hearkening each other's speech and waking the song of the birds by their footsteps. Then they turned them to where the cold clear spring rippled forth, and sat beside its stream, and watched its flow till the sun grew high in heaven, and they felt its heat. Then they betook them to the linden: its branches offered them a welcome shelter, the breezes were sweet and soft beneath its shade, and the couch at its feet was decked with the fairest grass and flowers.

There they sat side by side, those true lovers, and told each other tales of those who ere their time had suffered and died for love. They mourned the fate of the sad Queen Dido; of Phyllis of Thrace; and Biblis, whose heart brake for love. With such tales did they beguile the time. But when they would think of them no more, they turned them again to their grotto and took the harp, and each in their turn sang to it softly lays of love and of longing; now Tristan would strike the harp while Isolt sang the words, then it would be the turn of Isolt to make music while Tristan's voice followed the notes. Full well might it be called the Love Grotto.

At times they would ride forth with the crossbow to shoot the wild game of the woodland, or to chase the red deer with their hound Hiudan, for Tristan had taught him to hunt hart and hind silently, nor to give tongue when on their track. This would they do many days, yet more for the sake of sport and pleasure than to supply themselves with food, for in sooth they had no care save to do what might please them best at the moment.

While they thus dwelt in the woods, King Mark in his palace was but sorrowful, for he grieved ever for his honor and for his wife, and his heart grew heavier day by day.

In these days, more to solace himself than for love of adventure, he bethought him to ride forth to the chase, and by chance he came into that very wood where Tristan and Isolt had their dwelling. The huntsmen and their dogs came upon a herd of deer and separated a strange stag from among them. He was white, with a mane like to that of a horse, and larger than stags are wont to be. His horns were small and short, scarce grown, as if he had but lately shed them; and they chased this stag hotly till evening, but he fled from thence to the wood of the grotto, whence he came, and thus escaped.

King Mark was greatly vexed, and the huntsmen even more, that they had lost the quarry (for the beast was passing strange in form and color), and they were all ill pleased. So they turned not homeward, but encamped in the wood for the night, thinking to take up the chase on the morrow.

Now, Tristan and Isolt had heard all day long the sound of the chase, for the wood rang with the horns and the baying of the hounds. They thought it could be no one but Mark, and their hearts grew heavy within them, for they deemed they were betrayed.

The next morning the chief huntsman arose ere the flush of dawn was in the sky; he bade his underlings wait till the day had fully broken and then follow him. In a leash he took a brachet, which served him well and led him on the right track. It guided him onward through many rough places, over rocks and hard ground, through barren lands and over grass where yestereven the stag had fled before him. The huntsman followed straight on the track till at last the narrow path came to an end, and the sun shone out clearly; he was by the spring in Tristan's glade.

That same morning had Tristan and his ladylove stolen forth, hand in hand, and come full early, through the morning dew, to the flowery meadow and the lovely vale. Dove and nightingale saluted them sweetly, greeting their friends Tristan and Isolt. The wild wood birds bade them welcome in their own tongue—'twas as if they had conspired among themselves to give the lovers a morning greeting. They sang from the leafy branches in changeful wise, answering each other in song and refrain. The spring that charmed their eye and ear whispered a welcome, even as did the linden with its rustling leaves. The blossoming trees, the fair meadow, the flowers and the green grass, all that bloomed laughed at their coming; the dew which cooled their feet, and refreshed their heart, offered a silent greeting.

When the twain had rejoiced them enough in the fair morning air they betook them again to their grotto, fearing lest the hunt might come their way, and one of the hounds discover their hiding place. After a while they laid them down on the couch, apart, and Tristan laid his unsheathed sword between them; so they fell asleep.

Now, the huntsman of whom I spake but now, who had followed the trail of the stag to the spring, he spied in the morning dew the track left by Tristan and his lady, and he bethought him 'twas but the trail he was following. So he dismounted and followed, till he came to the door of the grotto; 'twas fastened with two bolts, so that he might go no further.

Marveling much, he turned aside, and sought all around and over the hill, till by chance he found a little window, high up in the wall of the grotto. Fearing greatly, he looked through, and saw nought but a man and a woman. Yet the sight moved him to wonder, for he thought that of a truth the woman came of no mortal race, none such had ever been born into this world. Yet he did not stay long at gaze, for he spied the unsheathed sword, and drew back in terror; he deemed that here was magic at work, and was affrighted to remain. So he made his way down the hill and rode back toward the hounds.

Now, King Mark had become aware that his chief huntsman had ridden forth after the stag, and had hastened to meet him.

"Sir King," said the huntsman, "I will tell thee a marvel; I have but now found a fair adventure!"

"Say, what adventure?"

"I have found a Love Grotto!"

"Where and how didst thou find it?"

"Sire, here, in this wilderness."

"What? Here, in this wild woodland?"

"Yea, even here."

"Is there any living soul within?"

"Sire, a man and a goddess are within. They lie side by side on a couch and seem to slumber. The man is even as other men, but I doubt me for his companion, if she be mortal! She is more beautiful than a fairy. Never was any so fair of mortal flesh. And between them lieth a sword, bare, bright, and keen. I know not what it may betoken."

The king quoth, "Lead me thither."

The master huntsman led him forthwith on the track of the game to the spot where he had dismounted. The king alighted on the grass, and followed the path the huntsman showed him. So came King Mark to the door, and turned aside and climbed the hill even to the summit, making many a twist and turn as the huntsman had told him. And he, too, found at last the window and looked through, and saw the twain lie on the crystal couch, sleeping as before; and he saw them even as the huntsman had said, apart, with the naked sword blade between them, and knew them for his nephew and his wife.

His heart grew cold within him for sorrow, and e'en for love, for the strange chance brought him alike grief and joy —joy, from the thought that they were indeed free from guilt; sorrow, since he believed what he saw.

And he spake in his heart: "Nay, what may this mean? Are they indeed guilty, as I deemed; then what doeth the sword here? One would say they are in truth no lovers. Are they verily guilty or not?" And one while his heart said *Yea* and another while *Nay*.

Then Love, the Reconciler, crept near to King Mark, and laid the golden lie before his eyes, and the *Nay* shone in fair colors into his heart; but the *Yea*, the very truth, it pained him so sore he would not look upon it, for the tempting vision of their golden innocence drew him on to the Easter Day of gladness, where in the light of dawn lay all his joy.

He gazed on his heart's delight, Isolt, and deemed that never before had he seen her so fair. She lay sleeping, with a flush as of mingled roses on her cheek, and her red and glowing lips apart; a little heated by her morning wandering in the dewy meadow and by the spring. On her head was a chaplet woven of clover. A ray of sunlight from the little window fell upon her face, and as Mark looked upon her he longed to kiss her, for never had she seemed so fair and so lovable as now. And when he saw how the sunlight fell upon her, he feared lest it harm her, or awaken her, so he took grass and leaves and flowers, and covered the window therewith, and spake a blessing on his love and commended her to God, and went his way, weeping.

A sorrowful man, the king returned to the huntsman, and bade him lead his hounds homeward; he would hunt no more in that woodland.

Scarcely had the king departed when Tristan and Isolt awoke from their slumber. Then they looked around them and marveled to see that the sun shone in but at two windows, and not at three, as it was wont to do. And when they saw the third was darkened they arose with one accord and went out of the grotto, and found the window covered with grass and flowers. Then they looked on the sand before the doorway, and found there the tracks of men's footsteps, and feared greatly lest Mark had been there, and had discovered their hiding place. They might in no wise be certain, yet it comforted them to think that even if he had seen them, there would have been nought to rouse his anger.

Then King Mark, when he had returned, called his kinsmen and his council together, and told them what he had found, and said henceforth would he believe nothing against Tristan and Isolt. His lords saw how it stood with the king, and that his desire was to recall the twain, so like wise men they gave counsel according to the desire of the heart, and bade him send messengers to fetch his wife Isolt and his nephew Tristan, since they had done nought against his honor, and he would henceforth believe no evil of them.

So they sent for Kurwenal, and bade him ride to the woodland and say that the king sent greeting and love to Tristan and the queen, and bade them come again, and none should speak evil of them.

So Kurwenal rode thither and bare Mark's message, and the lovers were glad at heart, more that men should again hold them in honor than for aught else. They took their journey back to court as before, yet never again in all their days were they so happy as they had been aforetime, nor might they again find solace and bliss in each other's love.

Now King Mark and his courtiers were in all things anxious to do them honor, yet they might no longer be openly friendly as before, for Mark, the doubter, prayed them straitly for God's sake, and for his, to keep a watch on their looks and words, and no longer to show each other favor and confidence as of yore; and this grieved the lovers sorely.

But King Mark was joyful: he had as much happiness as his heart desired with his lady Isolt; he would that all should show her open honor, and nothing rejoiced him more than that she should be hailed as queen and lady wherever he was king and lord. 'Tis the blindness of love that will close its eyes to that which it would not see. For in truth he knew that his wife's heart and soul were given to Tristan, yet would he not know it.

To whom then shall the shame or his dishonor be given? For in truth 'twere wrong to say that Tristan and Isolt deceived him; he saw with his eyes, and knew, unseeing, that she loved him not; and yet he loved her!

Alas! many a Mark and many an Isolt doth one see today
—men who are blind, or whose hearts and eyes are blind.
Many are there who hug their blindness, and will not see
that which lieth before their eyes, but hold for a lie that which
their heart knoweth to be the truth. And would we look upon
it fairly, then ought we scarce to blame the woman, if she let
the man see that which she doth think and do. For so soon
as a man seeth the shame, then is he no longer deceived, but
hath at his own will turned his back upon the truth. And in
truth the wondrous beauty of Isolt had so fettered King
Mark's eyes and senses that he could not see in her aught
that should displease him, for he loved her so well that he
overlooked all the sorrow she might cause him.

But to Isolt separation from Tristan was even as death; the
more her husband forbade her to show favor and kindness toward him, the more her heart clung to him. For this is ever
the way of women; children of Mother Eve are they all; 'twas
she who brake the first commandment. For our Lord God
bade her do as she would with fruit, flowers, and grass, all
that was in the fair garden of Paradise save one tree only
(and the priests say 'twas the fig tree), the which was forbidden her on peril of death. Yet she plucked the fruit, and
brake the commandment, and lost Paradise.

Now is it my firm belief that Eve would never have desired
to eat of that tree had it not been forbidden to her. Even so,
the first thing that she did showed of what mind she was, for
'twas the thing that she was forbidden. Of every fruit might
she eat at her pleasure, yet would she have none save that for
which she must pay so heavily.

Yet what greater honor may a woman have than that she
fight against her love and her desire for the sake of honor?
For in sooth the strife shall end in that her womanhood and
her honor alike be justified; and he who is beloved of such a
lady findeth himself elect to all bliss. He hath Paradise in his

heart, and need vex himself with no fear lest the serpent be hidden amongst the flowers, or that a thorn will pierce his hand if he pluck a rose, for thorns and thistles alike are banished from that garden.

But alas! such happiness was not for Tristan and Isolt; the watch they must keep upon their words and looks was bitter to them both, and never had they sought so earnestly for means whereby they might come together; yet when they found them 'twas but to their sorrow and bitter grief.

It was midday, and the sun shone hotly, so that the queen would no longer abide in the palace, but took her way forth to the orchard. There, under the cool shade of a tree, she bade her maidens prepare a couch that she might rest awhile. This they did, spreading the couch with purple and fine linen, and Queen Isolt bade them leave her, all save Brangoene alone.

Then, since the place was lonely, and none were abroad at that hour, she sent Brangoene secretly to Tristan, bidding him come and speak with her. This she did, and Tristan did even as Adam when Eve proffered him the fruit—he took it, and ate death thereof with her.

But Brangoene went away sadly, bidding the chamberlain see that none enter the queen's apartments, and sat herself down by one of the doors, sorrowing to think that her caution and her counsel might not serve her lady better.

Scarcely had the chamberlain taken his stand before the door ere King Mark came toward him, and asked impatiently for the queen.

"She sleepeth, sire," answered her maidens; and Brangoene, as she sat, hid her face in her hands, for her heart failed her.

But the king said, "Where doth the queen sleep?" And they told him, in the garden. And Mark went thither and found his heart sorrow, for there lay his wife and his nephew, clasped in each other's arm, cheek to cheek, and lip to lip. So were Mark's doubts at an end; he suspected no more, for he knew.

Silently he turned and went his way, and calling the lords of his council, told them how Tristan and the queen were even now together, and bade them go, and take the twain, and judge them according to the law of the land.

But even as Mark turned to go, Tristan awoke, and saw him, and said within himself: "Alas! what hast thou done, faithful Brangoene? I wot well this shall be our death! Awake, Isolt, unhappy love, heart's queen, we are betrayed!"

"Betrayed?" she spake. "How may that be?"

"My lord the king stood but now above us; he saw us, and I saw him. Now hath he gone to bring witnesses; he worketh for our death. Heart's lady, fair Isolt, now must we part, never again may we rejoice in each other as aforetime. Now bethink thee of the true love that hath been betwixt us, and see that it remain ever steadfast; let me not out of thine heart! For whatever befall mine, thou shalt never depart from it. Isolt must ever dwell in Tristan's heart! See, love, that neither time nor distance change thy mind toward me. Forget me not, whatever befall. Sweet love, fair Isolt, kiss me, and bid me farewell!"

She stepped a little back, and spake, sighing: "Our hearts and our souls have been too long and too closely knit together that they may ever learn forgetfulness. Whether thou art far or near, in my heart shall be nothing living save Tristan alone—my love and my life. Body and soul have been thine this long while; see that no other woman ever separate thee from me, so that our love and our faith be not ever steadfast and true as they have been betwixt us these many years. And take thou this ring; let it be a token to thee of faith and love, that at any time if thou lovest other than me thou mayest look upon it and remember how thou abidest in mine heart. Think of this parting, how near it goeth to heart and life! Remember the many heavy sorrows I have suffered through thee, and let none be ever nearer to thee than Isolt! Forget me not for the sake of another! We two have loved and sorrowed in such true fellowship unto this time, we should not find it overhard to keep the same faith even to death. Yet methinks 'tis needless to remind thee thus. If Isolt were ever one heart and one faith with Tristan, that is she now, that must she ever be. Yet would I fain make one prayer to thee: whatever land thou seekest, have a care for thyself —*my* life; for if I be robbed of that, then am I, *thy* life, undone. And myself, *thy* life, will I for thy sake, not for mine, guard with all care. For thy body and thy life, that know I well, they rest on me. Now bethink thee well of me, thy body, Isolt. Let me see my life in thee, if it may well be so, and see thou thy life in me! Thou guardest the life of both. Now come hither and kiss me. Tristan and Isolt, thou and I, we twain are but one being, without distinction or difference. This kiss shall be a seal that I thine, and thou mine, remain even to death but one Tristan and one Isolt!"

Now that they had set the seal on their covenant, Tristan departed thence, with bitter sorrow; his self, his other life, Isolt, remained weeping sorely. Never aforetime had their parting been thus sorrowful.

Herewith came the king, and with him a company of his lords and counselors, yet they came too late, for they found but Isolt alone.

Then they drew the king aside, and said, "Sire, herein hast thou wronged both thy wife and thine honor. Now, as many a time before, hast thou accused the queen needlessly and for nought. Thou wrongest thyself. How canst thou be joyful the while thou dost shame thy wife, and make her and thyself the mock of the land? Yet hast thou found no wrong in her. Why slander the queen who hath not betrayed thee? For thine own self and thine honor do so no more." Thus they counseled him; and Mark held his peace, and went thence unavenged.

Tristan betook him to his lodging, and bade his folk make ready and come with him swiftly to the haven. There he went aboard the first ship he found, and sailed with his men to Normandy. But there he abode not long, for he sought a life that should bring him some comfort for his sadness. He fled from death that he might seek death, and so free him from the death of the heart—his separation from Isolt. What profit to flee from death if he bare death with him? What profit if the torment that drave him forth from Cornwall yet lay, day and night, upon him?

He bethought him that if his sorrow were ever to be lessened it must needs be by deeds of knighthood; so hearing that there was war in Almayne, he journeyed thither, and served scepter and crown so faithfully that the Roman Empire never won under its banners a warrior who wrought such mighty deeds. Many an adventure had he, the which I will not recount, for if I were to tell all the deeds that have been written of him, the tale would indeed be marvelous! But the many fables men tell of him I cast to the winds; 'tis toil and labor enow to record the truth.

Tristan's life and death, the fair-haired Isolt, she had sorrow and grief enough. Her heart well-nigh broke as she watched his ship sail thence; but his life kept her in life—apart from him she might neither live nor die. She watched the sail flutter in the wind, and spake in her heart: "Alas, alas! Sir Tristan, my heart clingeth to thee, my eyes follow thee, and thou speedest from me! Why go thus quickly? Knowest thou not that thou dost flee thy life in fleeing from Isolt? Thou canst no more live a day without me than I can live without thee. Our lives are so interwoven that thou bearest my life with thee; and though in sooth thou leavest thine, yet may neither of us rightly die nor fully live! So am I, poor Isolt, henceforth neither dead nor living! What may I do, alas? I am here, and I am there, yet am I in neither place. I see myself on the sea, and know myself on the land. I sail hence with Tristan, and sit here beside King Mark!" So she bemoaned herself.

When Tristan had been half a year and more in Almayne he became heavy at heart, hearing nought of his lady, and thought to return to the land where he might hear some rumors of her doings. So he gat him back to Normandy, and from thence to Parmenie, thinking that he would find comfort and counsel with Rual. But alas! he and his wife were both dead; yet his sons welcomed Tristan gladly, and were joyful at his coming. They kissed his hands and feet, eyes and mouth, many a time. "Lord," they said, "in thee hath God given us back both father and mother. Now abide here with us, and take again all that was thine, and let us serve thee even as our father served thee, who was thy man, as we would gladly be! Our father and mother are alike dead, but God hath looked upon our need, and sent thee back to us!"

Then they showed Tristan the tomb, and he stood and wept awhile beside it, and said, "Now if faith and honor may be buried in the earth, here do they lie entombed. Yet if faith and honor are aught akin to God, as men say, then doubt I not that these twain are now crowned above, even as the children of God are crowned."

The sons of Rual, even as their father, laid themselves and all they had at Tristan's service, and vexed themselves in all things to do his will; and thus he abode with them many days.

Now was there a dukedom, betwixt Brittany and England, which was called Arundel, and lay upon the sea coast. The ruler of the land was an old man, but a brave and courteous. The story saith that his neighbors had made war upon him, and had robbed him of possessions by sea and land. Right willingly had he avenged himself, but as yet he lacked the power to do so. One son and one daughter had the duke. The son had received knighthood three years past, and had won much praise and honor for his valiant deeds. His sister was a fair maiden, Isolt of the White Hand was she called, and her brother's name was Kahedîn. The duke's name was Jovelîn.

A rumor came to Parmenie that there was fighting in the dukedom of Arundel, and Tristan, thinking thereby to forget his sorrow, journeyed thither, and found the duke in his castle of Karke. Thither went he with all his friends, and the duke received him with the welcome befitting a noble warrior, for he knew Tristan well by report—all the islands of the Western Sea were full of his fame. The duke was joyful of his coming, and Kahedîn, his son, was minded to show him all the honor he might, and would ever be in his company. Friendship was sworn betwixt the two, and they kept that oath faithfully, even unto their death.

Tristan bade the duke tell him how matters stood with him; what was the might of his enemies, and where they most straitly beset his land; and when he knew that they had in truth a mighty force against them, he sent secretly to Parmenie, to Rual's sons, telling them he was in need of aid; and they came swiftly, with five hundred men, and great store of food and drink, for the duke's foemen had laid the land waste.

When Tristan knew of their coming, he went to meet them, and led them under cover of night into the land. One half he bade abide at the castle of Karke, and keep their presence secret till he and Kahedîn had need of them. With the other half he rode to a castle which the duke had bidden him guard, and commanded them to lie hidden, even as those at Karke.

With the daylight Tristan and Kahedîn rode to the border, burning and sacking every fortress on their path, so that the cry went abroad through all the land that Kahedîn had ridden forth openly to dare the enemy. And when the former heard this they gathered their men together and came out to meet them, and fell in with them beneath the walls of Karke. When the battle was at its height Tristan's knights who had lain hidden within the castle fell upon them suddenly, and thus taken by surprise, the foe could do nought but fly, or yield themselves prisoners, or die on the field.

When they had thus taken the leaders captive, Tristan and Kahedîn, with all their knights, rode into the enemy's land. There was no fortress so strong that it might resist them, and all the goods and all the prisoners they won they sent to Karke, till the land was once more in their power, and the duke was well avenged.

Then Tristan bade Rual's sons return to Parmenie, and thanked them much for the aid they had given him. The prisoners he bade receive their lands again from the hands of Duke Jovelîn, and swear to remain his men, and abstain henceforth from making war upon him; and to this all the princes agreed. Hereafter was Tristan held in great honor at court and through all the land, and all men alike were fain to do his bidding.

Now Kahedîn's sister, Isolt of the White Hand, was a fair and noble maiden, the flower of the land for beauty and virtue. As Tristan beheld her, the old sorrow awoke in his heart. She reminded him of the other Isolt, the Princess of Ireland; nor might he hear or speak her name but that his sorrow might be read in his face. Yet he loved the grief that lay at his heart, and saw the maiden gladly, in that she called to his mind the faith he had sworn to the fair-haired Isolt. Isolt was alike his sorrow and his joy; she brought him comfort, and she vexed him sore. The more his heart yearned for the one Isolt, the more gladly he beheld the other.

And he said in his heart, "Yea, God, how the name doth lead me astray! Truth and falsehood betray alike mine eyes and my soul. *Isolt* rings laughing in mine ear at all times, yet know I not who Isolt may be; mine eyes behold her, and yet they see her not. Isolt is far from me, and yet is she near. Once more am I bewitched, and Cornwall hath become Arundel; Tintagel, Karke; and Isolt hath taken the form of Isolt! I deemed when men spake of this maiden as *Isolt,* that I had found my love again—and yet was I deceived. Overlong do I desire the sight of Isolt; now am I come where Isolt is, and find her not! I see her day by day, yet see her not; therefore make I my moan. I have found Isolt, yet not the fair-haired Isolt, who was so kindly cruel. The Isolt who vexeth thus my heart is she of Arundel, not Isolt the fair; she, alas! mine eyes behold not. And yet she whom I now behold, and who is sealed with her name, her I must ever honor and love, for the sake of the dear name that so oft hath given me joy and gladness unspeakable."

So Tristan spake oft with himself, and the maid, Isolt of the White Hand, marked his troubled glances, and saw how they rested upon her, and her heart went out toward him, for she heard how throughout the land all men praised him; and her eyes strove to answer the thought in him, till the man began to marvel in his heart whether here he might not find an ending to his woe.

Then he upbraided himself for falsehood. "Ah, faithless Tristan! wouldst thou love *two* Isolts, when thine other life, Isolt, will have but one Tristan? She will have none other love but me; shall I woo another? Woe to thee, Tristan; lay aside this blind folly, and put the thought far from thee."

So was his heart turned again to the love that was his true heritage, and he thought but of his old grief.

Yet was he ever courteous to the maiden Isolt, and whatever her pleasure might be, that would he do. He told her knightly tales, he sang for her, and wrote and read, even as she bade him. And in those days he made the noble "Lay of Tristan," which men in all lands love and prize, and shall

prize while the world endures. For often it chanced when all
the folk sat together, Tristan, Isolt, and Kahedîn, the duke
and the duchess, with all the lords and ladies of the court,
that he wove fair verses, and roundels, and courteous songs,
and ever he sang this refrain:

> *"Isolt ma drue, Isolt m'amie,*
> *En vous ma mort, en vous ma vie!"*

But since he was so fain to sing thus, all who hearkened
deemed that he meant their lady, the maiden Isolt, and were
beyond measure joyful. And none more than Kahedîn. Many
a time and oft did he set Tristan beside his sister, and she,
when she smiled on Tristan and gave him her hand, did it as
if to pleasure her brother—yet was it to pleasure herself.

Yet day by day Tristan's sorrow grew heavier; he desired
but one Isolt, Isolt of Ireland; and Isolt of the White Hand, she
would have none but Tristan. Her heart and soul were his, his
grief was hers, and as she saw him grow pale and sigh for
sorrow, so she herself sighed and grew pale, till at length she
showed her love to him so openly, in sweet gestures, looks,
and words, that he scarce knew what he might do, and his
heart was tossed on a sea of doubt.

And as time passed on, and never word or message came
from Queen Isolt, he began to think whether his sorrow and
his faith were not all in vain.

"Ah, sweet friend, love Isolt!" he said, "now is our life too
far apart. 'Tis no longer as erewhile, when we had but one
joy, one sorrow, one love, and one life between us. Now is
our fate unlike. I am sad, and thou art joyful. My heart yearn-
eth for thy love, but thy longings for me, they are methinks
but feeble. Alas! alas! that which I have lost for thee dost
thou hold; thou art at home with thy lord Mark, and thy
friends around thee, and I am alone, a stranger in a strange
land. Little comfort may I have henceforth from thee, and

yet my heart clingeth to thee. Little need hast thou of me! Why dost thou ask not what befalls me? Ah! sweet Queen Isolt, hadst thou departed from me as I from thee, surely had I sent to learn tidings of her who was my life. And yet it may be that she hath sought me, and found me not, for he who seeketh a wanderer hath no fixed goal for his search. She may well have sought secretly through Cornwall and England, through France and Normandy, even to my land of Parmenie, and finding me not, she thinketh of me no more." [2]

Thus his doubt of Isolt of Ireland, and the love shown him by Isolt of the White Hand wrought on Tristan's heart, and vexed him day and night, till at last, for the friendship he bare to Kahedîn, and for the sweetness and beauty of Isolt the maiden, he determined to wed her. So the duke proclaimed a great feast, and the folk came from far and wide, and Isolt of the White Hand and Tristan were made man and wife by the bishop of the land, in the minster at Karke. And yet, for the love which he bare to Isolt of Ireland, which might not be stilled, was she but his wife in name. Yet none but they two knew of it, and Isolt's doubts were laid at rest, for Tristan told her how he had made a vow, many a year agone, should he ever wed, to leave his wife a maiden for a year.

Now Kahedîn, Isolt's brother, had loved, from his youth up, a lady of the land, and she, too, loved him well; yet her parents, against her will, had given her in marriage to another knight, the lord of Gamaroch, which lay near to the land of Arundel. And there, in his castle of Gamaroch, did her husband keep her strictly guarded, for he knew well that she loved him not; nor would he go abroad save that he bare the keys of the castle with him.

Then Kahedîn in his sorrow took counsel with Tristan, and Tristan bade him, if he could by any means win speech

[2] End of Gottfried's poem.

with his lady from without, to pray her to make molds in wax of the keys while her husband slept, and throw the molds into the moated ditch below the castle wall. This she did, and with the aid of a cunning smith they made keys that would fit the locks.

So when next Nampotenis, for so was the knight called, rode abroad, and left his wife in guard, Kahedîn and Tristan came secretly, and unlocked the castle gates, and entered. The lady received them with much joy; but as they crossed the moat the wind loosened the circlet from Kahedîn's helmet and it fell to the ground; but neither of the twain were aware of it.

Then Kahedîn and his lady spake together through the hours of the night, and Tristan kept watch without till the dawning. With the morning light they rode away, and deemed that none knew of their coming.

But when Nampotenis came again in the morning, he beheld in the moat the circlet that had fallen from Kahedîn's helmet, and knew well it was none of his or of his knights', and deemed that forsooth his wife's lover had been with her. Then with stern words he bade her confess the truth, and because she greatly feared his wrath and cruelty, she told him all; and Nampotenis forthwith called his men together, and pursued after the two knights, and overtook them in the forest.

They had no thought that they were pursued, and were taken at unawares, and ere they wist their foes were upon them. Nampotenis fell on Kahedîn and ran him through the body with his spear, so that he fell dead. But Tristan in wrath drew out his sword and ran upon Nampotenis and smote him dead, and put all his men to flight. Yet ere they fled had one of them smitten Tristan through the thigh with a poisoned spear. With great sorrow did Tristan bear his dead comrade back to Karke, and they buried him in the minster.

Isolt of the White Hand dressed Tristan's wound, and bade the leeches of the land do what they might to heal him, but nought that they might do was of any avail, for the venom was so potent their skill might not prevail against it.

Then Tristan saw well how it stood with him, and he said to himself, "Now might I but send to my lady Isolt, methinks she would cure me now, even as her mother did aforetime; otherwise must I die of this hurt." Then secretly he sent for Kurwenal, and prayed him to go with all speed to Tintagel and seek out Isolt the queen. "Bear with thee this ring, and show it to her as a token from me, and say how that I lie sorely wounded, and must needs die an she come not to mine aid. And if for love of me she will come, then I pray thee to set a white sail to the ship; but if she cometh not, then let the sail be black, for I shall know she loveth me no more."

Then Kurwenal departed, even as Tristan bade him, and came to Tintagel, and told Isolt the queen secretly all that Tristan had bade him say. She made ready in haste, and wrapped her in her veil, and stole to the harbor, and sailed away ere any might know of it.

Now Tristan bade them bear him day by day to the shore that he might watch for the ship from Cornwall till his weakness grew so great he might do so no longer; then he bade his wife, Isolt, watch from the window of his chamber and bear him tidings when Kurwenal should return.

But Isolt of the White Hand had hearkened secretly when her husband spake to Kurwenal, and her heart was hot within her for anger 'gainst the other Isolt, for she knew well who it was that Tristan loved. So when at last she spied the ship that bare Isolt the queen thither, she said to her husband, "Yonder cometh the ship wherein Kurwenal sailed hence."

"What manner of sail doth it bear?" spake Tristan.

" 'Tis black as night," answered Isolt of the White Hand, yet she lied, for the sail was white as snow.

Then Tristan spake no word, but turned his face to the wall, and said in his heart, "God keep thee, my love Isolt, for I shall look on thee no more," and with that he loosed his hold of the life he had held till then, and his soul departed.

Now the ship wherein was Isolt of Ireland drew nigh to the haven; and as they came to shore they heard the bells toll from the minster and the chapels, and the voice of weeping and lamentation in the streets. "What meaneth this woe?" asked Isolt the queen, "and wherefore do ye toll the bells?" Then an old man answered, and said, "Fair lady, a great misfortune hath befallen our land. Tristan, the bravest of knights, he who drave out our enemies and restored our duke to his own, is but now dead. He hath died of a wound from a poisoned spear; but now have they borne his body to the minster."

Then Isolt answered no word, but turned her on the way to the minster, and went thither swiftly; and all looked upon her, and marveled at her beauty and her woe. And when she came to the minster, Tristan lay dead on the bier, and beside him sat Isolt of the White Hand. Then Isolt of Ireland looked upon her: "Why sittest thou here beside the dead, thou who hast slain him? Arise, and get thee hence!" And Isolt of the White Hand arose and drew aside, for she feared the queen.

But Isolt of Ireland spake no word more, but laid her down on the bier by her lover, and put her arms around him, and sighed once, and her soul departed from her body.

Now tidings had been brought to King Mark how that Isolt the queen had fled with Kurwenal, and he took ship and pursued after her swiftly, but ere he came to shore at Arundel she lay dead beside Tristan. And there Kurwenal told Mark all that had chanced, and the secret of the love potion, and how it was by no will of their own but through the magic of the love drink that the twain had wronged him. And Mark spake, weeping: "Alas! Tristan, hadst thou but trusted in me, and told me all the truth, then had I given Isolt to thee for wife."

Then he bade them embalm the bodies, and he bare them back with him to Tintagel, and laid them in marble tombs on either side of the chapel wherein the kings of his line lay buried. And by the tomb of Tristan he bade them plant a rose tree, and by that of Isolt a vine, and the two reached toward each other across the chapel, and wove branches and root so closely together that no man hereafter might separate them.

THE YOUTH OF

ALEXANDER THE GREAT

FOREWORD

In the realm of secular story the cycles of Arthur and Charlemagne—the Matter of Britain and the Matter of France—
were rivaled by a third cycle which was called the Matter of
Rome, but might more aptly be called the Matter of Classical
Antiquity. Pyramus and Thisbe, Paris and Helen, Aeneas and
Dido were almost as famous as Tristan and Isolt. The siege
and capture of Troy were celebrated by medieval poets along
with Arthur's fatal battle of Camlan and the slaughter of Roland and Oliver at Roncevaux. And of all the names of antiquity, one of the most familiar was that of Alexander the
Great. Of him Chaucer wrote in the "Monk's Tale" "that
every wight that hath discretion hath heard somewhat or all of
his fortune." This was certainly true of the Middle Ages, and
it applied not only to Western Europe but to all the lands

which extended eastward to the Indian Ocean. The literature concerned with the great conqueror of the fourth century B.C. was prodigious, and the languages in which it was written would make a long list.

As with the legends of Arthur and Charlemagne, there was at the core a historic personage and a military triumph, and in Alexander's case the triumph consisted of the conquest of the whole of the Middle East, Persia and Northwest India. It was an earth-shaking event which 2,300 years later has left traces in all the Alexandrias of our atlases and in the Alecs and Saundersons of our birth registers. As with Arthur and Charlemagne, historic fact was soon mingled with rumor, propaganda and ancient myths. Nothing was too fantastic to include in the farrago. The most conflicting views were taken of Alexander's character; on the one hand he was exalted as a model of the virtues—courage, liberality, magnanimity and even chastity; on the other, he was charged with cruelty, drunkenness and ambition, while his ascent to the skies, borne up by gryphons, was interpreted as an example of the deadliest of sins, pride.

The earliest compilation of this material which had a great influence in the West, the first romance of Alexander, was written in Greek at Alexandria about 300 A.D. and was passed off as the work of Callisthenes, one of the conqueror's generals; hence it is called the Pseudo-Callisthenes. Latin versions followed. The earliest vernacular romance was composed in the Dauphiné about 1100 by one Alberic, about the same time that the earliest manuscripts of the Charlemagne romances were made and the first signs of the spread of Arthurian stories outside Celtic lands appear. Alberic's poem was twice expanded in Northern France, the second time in a poem in twelve-syllable lines, which as a result have come to be called Alexandrines. About 1270 an anonymous Picard author took this version and added here and there passages of his own composition, and it is from the resulting compilation that the selections in this book on the youth of Alexander have been translated.

It is easy to distinguish the parts of this thirteenth-century poem which represent elaborations of Alberic—the portents which accompanied the hero's birth, the denial that he was the son of an enchanter, his precocity, his tutors and his education. The dream of the serpent came directly from the Alexandrine poem, and the gryphon flight was an episode of Alexander's maturity, arbitrarily transferred to the period of his youth.

Needless to say, history has been overlaid by a mass of prodigies and marvels, and it gives one quite a start to read that Homer and Ptolemy were among Alexander's tutors, teaching him Latin, falconry and fencing! We can be sure that the poet did not take his own information very seriously, and, like Shakespeare or Walter Scott, would have acknowledged his anachronisms with a shrug. We need no great perspicacity to realize that the story of the gryphon flight, so popular as a subject for medieval art, has been treated, not in a solemn tone to illustrate the sin of pride, but with a keen eye for comic effect, all the more amusing because of the humiliating role assigned to the sages of antiquity. And it is primarily as humor, unconscious as well as conscious, that the account of Alexander's nativity and youthful exploits is included in this book.

R. S. L.

THE STORY*

I wish to treat the history of Alexander in verse, and to write in French so that I may be of some profit to lay folk. Some there are who know how to begin well but do not know how to bring their work to a fine conclusion. They resemble a little donkey who when he is born is a comely creature, and endears himself to many people, but the older he grows, the uglier and more repulsive he is. Just so these bastard racon-

* Translated by R. S. Loomis.

teurs ruin good stories, and though they wish to be prized at court above the best, when they have said their say it is not worth a penny, and their work has to be patched together again.

But if anyone wishes to soften his heart toward good manners, let him raise his head to hear these verses and learn what he ought to do and what he ought to drop, how he should praise his friends, keep those he has and win others, how he should handle his enemies so roughly that not a single one would dare to show a proud front to him, and how he should keep them in terror as a hawk holds a lark.

When Alexander, the son of Philip, was born, the day was marked by many great signs, for the heavens underwent violent changes. The sun and moon lost their light and the day was darkened, the ground cracked open wide, and a wild storm raged on the sea. The king, his father, was filled with alarm. Before the child's birth, it thundered, lightnings descended, the air was troubled, and a rain fell as red as blood. Cities were swallowed up in the earth. People were terror-stricken and said that Alexander must have been begotten by a master enchanter in the form of a dragon. But that was a lie, for he put the matter to the test and there was no warrior so mighty as he. He was indeed the son of the glorious King Philip, and became lord of Greece, was acclaimed a powerful king, and possessed the castles and strongholds of Macedonia. His mother was Olympias; there was never a fairer lady. From her Nature endowed him with such virtues that he was sweet and humble and full of generosity.

When the child was born, the king rejoiced and so did knights and men-at-arms, both small and great throughout the land. The queen, who had suffered the pains and the travail, was filled with delight at the fulfillment of her desire. The great tempest which had preceded stopped at once. Nurses were brought to watch over the child, ladies all of gentle birth, and they nourished him well until he was weaned. In a short while he walked and was able to speak, and when he had reached the age of reason, he was given tutors, the most adept according to the customs of the heathen.

Five masters the king appointed to teach the child, the wisest he could find in his realm. If you want to know their names, I can give them: Aristotle, Clichon, Ptolemy, Homer, and Natanabus the enchanter. First they put him to letters so that he could speak Latin, and for his further improvement they made him debate. All the seven liberal arts they made him learn and remember so that he never found his peer. They made him hunt in the woods and along the river banks so that he need never fear that any master huntsman would ever mock at his taking a stag or a boar. He learned the art of feeding birds, keeping them healthy, and watching their molting, and he could fly falcons, sparrow hawks, and goshawks along the good river banks, so that when he went to disport himself he took plenty of birds. He was taught to play chess and tables till he could checkmate his opponent. They instructed him in fencing, so that he knew how to cover his head, to thrust, to wound his antagonist, and to parry. Then they taught him to bear arms, to spur his horse, to strike with sword, and to handle his lance. He learned how to recognize a man worthy of honor, to cherish and love him, and to hate and destroy a wicked man. Thus he was able to treat each person with the respect due him. They taught him to strike the tambor and the harp, to sing to the rote, the vielle, and the gigue, to play songs and lays and to compose them by his talent in all keys.

As the writing tells, at the age of ten Alexander was lying in a bed adorned with paintings; a costly embroidered silk, lined with marten's fur, was his coverlet. At night there came to him a dream, a mysterious vision, that he was eating an egg, and it rolled from his hands and broke on the paved floor. A dreadful serpent issued from it; never had man seen so loathsome a shape. It passed round the bed three times, then withdrew to its shell and fell dead at the entrance. That was a great marvel!

Frightened by the dream, Alexander awoke and was so shaken that he did not know whether he was asleep or awake. The chamberlain gave him his clothes, and when he was dressed he went and whispered his dream in his father's ear. When the king heard it, he was filled with wonder, and sent his messengers as far as the Red Sea, wherever he could find a wise man to interpret the dream. The first to arrive was Aristotle of Athens. When they were all assembled, the chamber was full. The king related the dream, and each of the sages endeavored to give a sure and reasonable answer.

First a Greek spoke, who considered himself the flower of many sciences, of divining by lot, of necromancy, of astronomy, and of the interpretation of authors. "Now listen," said he to great and small. "I will prove myself a master in expounding this dream. The egg is a thing of little strength. The evil dragon which issued from it is a proud man who will wage many wars, overcome kings and emperors, subdue princes and vassals, conquer cities and towers, and seize lands and fiefs. But he will not be able to take advantage of it, his labors will count for little, and when he returns his power will dwindle away."

When Philip heard that, his color changed with anger, for he thought that Alexander would always be a coward. Next spoke Salios de Namier, a wise man in the laws. "Listen, lords," said he, "to what I will tell you. No man, it seems to me, can derive profit from a thing which in a dream breaks easily. The egg is such a thing. The fierce and dreadful dragon which issued from it is a proud man who will conquer lands, and reign by force over savage countries. But he will be unable to gain what he desires, for those who ought to aid him will desert him, and he will be obliged to return in frustration, as the dragon did."

This reply filled Philip with dismay. After these two, Aristotle of Athens spoke, rising to his feet and striving to speak well. "Harken, lords, to a sure explanation. The egg is not a thing of no worth. It signifies the world, both sea and shore, and the yolk is the inhabited land. The dragon which came out of it, I tell you plainly, is Alexander, who will endure great suffering but will be lord of all the world, and his men will hold his realm after him. Then he will return to Macedonia, dead, as the dragon returned to his shell."

When Philip heard this, he made great joy, and held Aristotle in high esteem, and gave to him all his gold and silver. Alexander was clever and, if the writing does not lie, he learned more in twenty days than another lad in a hundred. One day near the beginning of September he was spurring through a wood together with the masters who were instructing him. He called Aristotle: "Master, come here. I will tell you something I have in mind to do, and I ask you to keep it secret. The king has two gryphons which are so strong that the smaller one could carry two men an acre and is heavier than an ox and a cow. They are gluttons for food. They will carry me flying to the sky, and I shall survey the lands which will belong to me and shall know how it feels to be a bird when it flies up in the warm air."

Aristotle answered: "This is a very delightful request I hear! I will not be responsible for such folly. If we lose you, we shall not be happy. We shall all be hanged, if I know anything about it; yes, before the sun goes down."

"Master," said Alexander, "leave this matter alone. I do not like men who scold. Let me do what I like this time, whether it is wise or foolish, for I will not give up the flight for all the gold in the world."

Then he commanded a squire, whom he saw standing by, to

shut up the gryphons in a cellar and to see that they tasted no food until the third day. "Then," he said, "I shall be able to see how they can fly." The squire did not dare to disobey and came galloping to those who had charge of the monsters; he had the cellar opened and the gryphons shut inside. Alexander himself went and caused a chair to be made with speed, with boards carefully fitted and a canopy overhead. It was so contrived that he could not be tipped out when he was seated in it to survey the world. Then he had two buckskins brought and stretched over the chair so that the heat of the sun could not scorch him. Then he caused a third hide to be cut in half to make heavy straps. Then he ordered the two gryphons to be brought, had them bound firmly round the body and under the wings with the straps, and thus they were attached to the chair. He took two long spits, sharpened with an adz, had a plucked capon fixed on the end of each, and had them project beyond the length of the straps and arranged so that he could turn them in any direction he wished, up or down. He now entered the chair and had himself locked in.

He showed the meat to the gryphons, and they began beating their wings to reach it. Those who were looking on could not guess what he wished to do, but they saw him departing and wept for fear. The king heard the clamor and asked what the matter was. They told him and he looked to see his child borne away to the sky. He could not keep from swooning. The peers and the barons, as they saw Alexander rising aloft, wrung their hands and tore their hair. No one could console the boy's mother. The king ordered all the tutors to be imprisoned at once, and unless they gave him back his child before nightfall he would have them hanged or beheaded on the morrow.

The queen stood in the upper room of the tower, gazing at her son whom the gryphons were carrying away. She wept and cried loudly, but he did not hear her, and when he did not turn back she had no hope that she would ever see him again. As she was lamenting, a kindly man took her and comforted her with soft words. The king gave orders that the tutors should never be freed from prison for any ransom, and that if Alexander did not come back they should be hanged or burned to coal. But the youth, like a fool, was soaring away toward the heaven faster than an eagle. Great was the mourning throughout the household.

Alexander was now so high that they could no longer see him. He hoped to reach the sky but he could not, and the return journey seemed to him long. He could ascend no higher, for he could not endure the heat of the sun; the feathers of the gryphons began to scorch and they began to swoop downward. Whether he would or no, Alexander was forced to descend. He turned the spits downward and skillfully adjusted them so that the beasts could smell the meat and strained to reach and swallow it. At last he made them settle down softly in a meadow. Because the the sun's heat had shrunk the hides, with great pain he extricated himself from the chair. He left the spits for the gryphons, and when they had devoured the meat, they began to roar so that they made the valleys and the mountains echo clearly. Alexander went to his father to give his pledge for his tutors, but when the king saw him, he began to rebuke and mock him for keeping up his childish tricks. But the queen embraced him and was overcome with joy, for she had thought never to take him in her arms again. He was eleven years old when he performed this rash exploit. That he was able to soar to the sky signified that he would be able to possess and rule the whole world.

AUCASSIN AND

NICOLETE

———

FOREWORD

Lightly, daintily, as a butterfly flickering on its sunlit way, *Aucassin and Nicolete* sings its songs and tells its story, with an enchantment all its own. It fulfills its own happy promise that no one hearing it, however sad or sick or weary,

But is healèd, but is glad
'Tis so sweet.

This *chante-fable,* or song-story, as it calls itself, survives in only one thirteenth-century manuscript. No medieval allusions to it are known, and its certain influence has been noted in only one later romance, yet it is today one of the best known of all medieval stories. In Andrew Lang's justly famous translation, its sweetness has been kept but without sacrifice of its soft raillery, its whimsical juxtaposition of absurdities, even of parody, with high romance. Its unknown author, familiar as he was with a wide range of antecedent romantic poetry, wrote this idyll of "teen-age" love with an exquisite awareness of both its amusing excesses and its tender poignancy. In our own twentieth century, it is still so well loved that no collection of medieval tales seems complete without it, and new editions of the old French text and translations in many languages continue to accumulate. Its power to enchant is almost incredibly evident when it has been given, in recent years, in the King-Coit Children's Theatre in New York City. This dramatic presentation can hardly have been surpassed in its perfect charm even by that played in 1779 at Versailles before the King and Queen of France.

The original author unquestionably had dramatic intention and skill, even if he did not achieve genuine dramatic form. His song-story pauses for songs, for description and narration, yet it hovers "on the threshold of romantic comedy." Its forty-one sections, alternating between lyrical verse and cadenced prose, are each one attributed: the songs to a singer, the prose to those who tell the tale and speak its parts. As never more than two speaking parts are recorded in any one episode, and the talk is alive with suggestions for dramatic impersonation and mimetic action, it is probable that the singer and the narrator were intended to become the actors of the dialogues. Though the action wanders as wildly as in any romance of adventure—from Aucassin's castle in Beaucaire, Provence, through strange forests and across perilous seas, through the ludicrous land of Torelore, to Carthage, which Nicolete recognizes as her childhood home, then back to Beaucaire—the scenes are always clearly placed and the action easily followed. If the performers were, as would be probable, those nomad entertainers who were, by the early thirteenth century, adding to their acrobatic tricks and storytelling the occasional role of actors, they would necessarily have depended, in the absence of all scenic·devices, on their play-text to make plain its course. In *Aucassin* significant statements always make clear just what its personages are doing and where they are.

But whether *Aucassin* was written for actors to act or for dramatic recitation only, its principal characters have a fresh and endearing reality. The rambling plot uses motifs already well worn in romances: the love of a Christian knight for a foreign slave, cruel parents, Saracens who steal children and separate lovers, dire perils on sea and land; but it is all given unity and cohesion by the young lovers who, together or apart, appear in every scene. Nicolete, radiant in beauty, is no abstraction, no remote inactive figure; a spirited, quick-witted girl, she gets herself out of prison, dares dangers and wounds, escapes a royal marriage to go, in minstrel disguise, to seek and win her lost love. The author may have had in mind other tales of similar young lovers, some medieval version of Ovid's tale of *Pyramus and Thisbe,* or the twelfth-century French romance of *Floire et Blanchefleur,* or perhaps some Arabic tale come to France by way of Moorish Spain, but his lovers are livelier individuals, more acutely drawn, more perceptive of the vagaries of youth. The beautiful boy Aucassin is a stubborn adolescent who won't eat, won't fight, won't even protect himself in deadly battle till he recalls that, headless, he can speak no more with Nicolete. He is violent, now fiercely railing against his cruel father, now capturing an enemy and forcing him to swear to fight always against that father, now beating the ridiculous King of Torelore as he lies in pretended childbed. Again, Aucassin is gentle and generous with the surly oxherd, and always, with Nicolete or without her, he is young love at its primal moment of longing and utter tenderness. There may be a touch of literary satire in the picture of this lovesick yet sturdy youth who, unlike the current heroes of romance, scornfully rejects all knightly duties, but psychologically his complete, compulsive obsession by one and one thing only, rings true. It drives him to outbursts against conventional social and religious thinking: Why can't he have the slave girl since he loves her and she is so fair, so sweet? Why should he fear to be damned if she is with him? In a sophisticated poem of the time, the *Roman de la Poire*

(1260), a lover asserts that the lips of his lady would give him more joy than God in Heaven; but nothing anywhere else matches in length and vigor Aucassin's explosive outcry against heaven where, to his mind, go only the pious old, the sick, the wretchedly poor, or his praise of hell with its luxuries, its noble knightly warriors, its gay ladies, its poets and music-makers. There with Nicolete he would gladly go. His youth is crying out, impudently, passionately, against age, against the whole medieval creed of ascetic renunciation as the one means to salvation. It is a famous protest and it quivers still with the sense of ardent life and feeling.

The gifted, sensitive author of *Aucassin and Nicolete* gave it the gifts of genius. His sweet lyrics—moving in an odd archaic rhythm in groups of seven-syllabled lines linked by assonance but each lyric section ending with a short four-syllabled line—were set to music; the melodic phrases are copied in the manuscript. Words and music are inseparably linked. So, too, were linked the lyrics and the prose sections, for each in turn was apt to add something to the narrative. The author's mind moved readily through old forms of lyric and narrative verse, through *pastourelles* where shepherds speak in rustic ways, through troubadour dawn songs, remembered here in the sentinel's warning to Nicolete, through some farcical *fabliau* which may have suggested the absurdities of Torelore, through the motifs of old romance. The scenes of his own romance have the bright, pure clarity of color, the decorative design, that medieval artists gave to their glowing illuminations in books or to the stained-glass windows that translated legends into light. Yet this verbal artist has done what they could not do: given his story atmosphere and glamour through changing lights and shadows, moonlight on dew-wet grass, daisies dark beside Nicolete's white feet, black shadow by a donjon tower, starlight through the leafy branches of Nicolete's little bower. He introduced human contrasts that increase both the brightness and the shadow. Nicolete, so "bright of brow," and Aucassin, exquisite young things as they are, make vivid contrast with the poorly clad, rough-

spoken serfs. The ugliest of these, scoffing at the rich young
Aucassin's grief for a lost hound, tells with harsh realism his
own tale of a lost ox, of cruel poverty and bitter injustice. The
whole text shows that this thirteenth-century writer of idyllic
romance, like William Morris in the nineteenth, was a man of
warm heart, of true social vision, and an adorer of medieval
beauty.

L. H. L.

———————

THE STORY*

Who would listen to the lay,
Old in time, of heart so gay,
'Tis how two young lovers met,
Aucassin and Nicolete,
Of the pains the lover bore
And the sorrows he outwore,
For the goodness and the grace,
Of his love, so fair of face.

Sweet the song, the story sweet,
There is no man hearkens it,
No man living 'neath the sun,
So outwearied, so foredone,
Sick and woful, worn and sad,
But is healèd, but is glad
　　　'Tis so sweet.

So say they, speak they, tell they the Tale:

How the Count Bougars de Valence made war on Count
Garin de Biaucaire, war so great, and so marvelous, and so

* Translated by Andrew Lang, with a few revisions by the editors.

mortal that never a day dawned but always he was there, by the gates and walls and barriers of the town with a hundred knights and ten thousand men-at-arms, horsemen and foot-men: so burned he the Count's land, and spoiled his country, and slew his men. Now the Count Garin de Biaucaire was old and frail, and his good days were gone over. No heir had he, neither son nor daughter, save one young man only; such an one as I shall tell you. Aucassin was the name of the damoi-seau: fair was he, goodly, and great, and featly fashioned of his body and limbs. His hair was yellow, in little curls, his eyes blue and laughing, his face beautiful and shapely, his nose high and well set, and so richly seen was he in all things good, that in him was none evil at all. But so suddenly overtaken was he of Love, who is a great master, that he would not, of his will, be dubbed knight, or take arms, or follow tourneys, or do whatsoever him beseemed. Therefore his father and mother said to him: "Son, go take thine arms, mount thy horse, and hold thy land, and help thy men, for if they see thee among them, more stoutly will they keep in battle their lives and lands, and thine, and mine."

"Father," said Aucassin, "I marvel that you will be speaking. Never may God give me aught of my desire if I be made knight, or mount my horse, or face battle wherein knights smite and are smitten again, unless thou give me Nicolete, my true love, that I love so well."

"Son," said the father, "this may not be. Let Nicolete go, a slave girl she is, out of a strange land, and the Captain of this town bought her of the Saracens and carried her hither, and hath reared her and let christen the maid, and took her for his daughter in God, and one day will find a young man for her, to win her bread honorably. Herein hast thou nought to make or mend, but if a wife thou wilt have, I will give thee the daughter of a king, or a count. There is no man so rich in France, but if thou desire his daughter, thou shalt have her."

"Faïth! my father," said Aucassin, "tell me where is the place so high in all the world, that Nicolete, my sweet lady and love, would not grace it well? If she were Empress of Constantinople or of Germany, or Queen of France or England, it were little enough for her; so gentle is she and courteous, and debonaire, and compact of all good qualities."

Here singeth one:

Aucassin was of Biaucaire
Of a goodly castle there,
But from Nicolete the fair
None might win his heart away
Though his father, many a day,
And his mother said him nay,
"Ha! fond child, what wouldest thou?
Nicolete is glad enow!
Was from Carthage cast away,
Paynims sold her on a day!
Wouldst thou win a lady fair
Choose a maid of high degree
Such an one is meet for thee."
"Nay of these I have no care,
Nicolete is debonaire,
Her body sweet and the face of her
Take my heart as in a snare,
Loyal love is but her share
            That is so sweet."

Then speak they, say they, tell they the Tale:

When the Count Garin de Biaucaire knew that he would avail not to withdraw Aucassin his son from the love of Nicolete, he went to the Captain of the city, who was his man, and spake to him, saying: "Sir Count, away with Nicolete thy daughter in God; cursed be the land whence she was brought into this country, for by reason of her do I lose Aucassin, that will neither be dubbed knight, nor do aught of the things that fall to him to be done. And wit ye well," he said, "that if I might have her at my will, I would burn her in a fire, and yourself might well be sore adread."

"Sir," said the Captain, "this is grievous to me that he comes and goes and hath speech with her. I had bought the maiden at mine own charges, and nourished her, and baptized, and made her my daughter in God. Yea, I would have given her to a young man that should win her bread honorably. With this had Aucassin thy son naught to make or mend. But, since it is thy will and thy pleasure, I will send her into that land and that country where never will he see her with his eyes."

"Have a heed to thyself," said the Count Garin; "thence might great evil come on thee."

So parted they each from other. Now the Captain was a right rich man, so had he a rich palace with a garden in face of it; in an upper chamber thereof he let place Nicolete with one old woman to keep her company, and in that chamber put bread and meat and wine and such things as were needful. Then he let seal the door, that none might come in or go forth, save that there was one window, over against the garden, and strait enough, where through came to them a little air.

Here singeth one:

Nicolete as ye heard tell
Prisoned is within a cell
That is painted wondrously
With colors of a far countrie,
And the window of marble wrought,
There the maiden stood in thought,
With straight brows and yellow hair
Never saw ye fairer fair!

On the wood she gazed below,
And she saw the roses blow,
Heard the birds sing loud and low,
Therefore spoke she wofully:
"Ah me, wherefore do I lie
Here in prison wrongfully:
Aucassin, my love, my knight,
Am I not thy heart's delight,
Thou that lovest me aright!
'Tis for thee that I must dwell
In the vaulted chamber cell,
Where there's naught to make me cheer.
By the Son of Mary dear,
I will stay no longer here,
    If I may flee!

Then speak they, say they, tell they the Tale:

Nicolete was in prison, as ye have heard soothly, in the chamber. And the noise and bruit of it went through all the country and all the land, how that Nicolete was lost. Some said she had fled the country, and some that the Count Garin de Biaucaire had let slay her. Whosoever had joy thereof, Aucassin had none, so he went to the Captain of the town and spoke to him saying:

"Sir Captain, what hast thou made of Nicolete, my sweet lady and love, the thing that best I love in all the world? Hast thou carried her off or ravished her away from me? Know well that if I die of it, the price shall be demanded of thee, and that will be well done, for it shall be even as if thou hadst slain me with thy two hands, for thou hast taken from me the thing that in this world I loved the best."

"Fair Sir," said the Captain, "let these things be. Nicolete is a captive that I did bring from a strange country. Yea, I bought her at my own charges of the Saracens, and I bred her up and baptized her, and made her my daughter in God. And I have cherished her, and one of these days I would have given her a young man, to win her bread honorably. With this hast thou naught to make, but do thou take the daughter of a king or count. Nay more, what wouldst thou deem thee to have gained, hadst thou made her thy leman, and taken her to thy bed? Plentiful lack of comfort hadst thou got thereby, for in Hell would thy soul have lain while the world endures, and into Paradise wouldst thou have entered never."

"In Paradise what have I to win? Therein I seek not to enter, but only to have Nicolete, my sweet lady that I love so well. For into Paradise go none but such folk as I shall tell thee now: Thither go these same old priests, and halt old men and maimed, who all day and night cower continually before the altars, and in the crypts; and such folk as wear old mantles and old tattered frocks, and naked folk and shoeless, and covered with sores, perishing of hunger and thirst, and of cold, and of little ease. These be they that go into Paradise; with them have I naught to do. But into Hell would I fain go; for into Hell fare the goodly clerks, and goodly knights that fall in tourneys and great wars, and stout men-at-arms, and all men noble. With these would I rather go. And thither pass the sweet ladies and courteous that have two lovers, or three, and their lords also thereto. Thither go the gold, and the silver, and cloth of vair, and cloth of gris, and harpers, and makers, and the prince of this world. With these I would gladly go, let me but have with me Nicolete, my sweetest lady."

"Certes," quoth the Captain, "in vain wilt thou speak thereof, for never shalt thou see her; and if thou hadst word with her, and thy father knew it, he would let burn in a fire both her and me, and thyself might well be sore adread."

"That is even what irketh me," quoth Aucassin. So he went from the Captain sorrowing.

Here singeth one:

Aucassin did so depart
Much in dole and heavy at heart
For his love so bright and dear,
None might bring him any cheer,
None might give good words to hear,
To the palace doth he fare
Climbeth up the palace stair,
Passeth to a chamber there,
Thus great sorrow doth he bear,
For his lady and love so fair.
"Nicolete, how fair art thou,
Sweet thy footfall, sweet thine eyes,
Sweet the mirth of thy replies,
Sweet thy laughter, sweet thy face,
Sweet thy lips and sweet thy brow,
And the touch of thine embrace,
All for thee I sorrow now,
Captive in an evil place,
Whence I ne'er may go my ways
      Sister, sweet friend!"

So say they, speak they, tell they the Tale:

While Aucassin was in the chamber sorrowing for Nicolete his love, even then the Count Bougars de Valence, that had his war to wage, forgat it no whit, but had called up his horsemen and his footmen; so made he for the castle to storm it. And the cry of battle arose, and the din, and knights and men-at-arms armed them, and ran to walls and gates to hold the keep. And the townsfolk mounted to the battlements, and cast down bolts and pikes. Then while the assault was great and even at its height, the Count Garin de Biaucaire came into the chamber where Aucassin was making lament, sorrowing for Nicolete, his sweet lady that he loved so well.

"Ha! son," quoth he, "how caitiff art thou, and cowardly, that canst see men assail thy goodliest castle and strongest. Know thou that if thou lose it, thou losest all. Son, go to, take arms, and mount thy horse, and defend thy land, and help thy men, and fare into the battle. Thou needst not smite nor be smitten. If they do but see thee among them, better will they guard their substance, and their lives, and thy land and mine. And thou art so great, and hardy of thy hands, that well mightst thou do this thing, and to do it is thy devoir."

"Father," said Aucassin, "what is this thou sayest now? God grant me never aught of my desire, if I be dubbed knight, or mount steed, or go into the battle where knights do smite and are smitten, if thou givest me not Nicolete, my sweet lady, whom I love so well."

"Son," quoth his father, "this may never be: rather would I be quite disinherited and lose all that is mine, than that thou shouldst have her to thy wife, or to love *par amours*."

So he turned him about. But when Aucassin saw him going he called to him again, saying: "Father, go to now, I will make with thee fair covenant."

"What covenant, fair son?"

"I will take up arms, and go into the battle on this covenant, that, if God bring me back sound and safe, thou wilt let me see Nicolete my sweet lady, even so long that I may have of her two words or three, and one kiss."

"That will I grant," said his father.

At this was Aucassin glad.

Here one singeth:

> Of the kiss heard Aucassin
> That returning he shall win,
> None so glad would he have been
> Of a myriad marks of gold
> Of a hundred thousand fold.

Called for raiment brave of steel,
Then they clad him heel to heel,
Twyfold hauberk doth he don,
Firmly braced the helmet on.
Girt the sword with hilt of gold,
Horse doth mount, and lance doth wield,
Looks to stirrups and to shield,
Wondrous brave he rode to field.
Dreaming of his lady dear
Setteth spur to the destrere,
Rideth forward without fear,
Through the gate and forth away
To the fray.

So speak they, say they, tell they the Tale:

Aucassin was armed and mounted, as ye have heard tell. God! how goodly sat the shield on his shoulder, the helm on his head, and the baldric on his left haunch! And the damoiseau was tall, fair, featly fashioned, and hardy of his hands, and the horse whereon he rode swift and keen, and straight had he spurred him forth of the gate. Now believe ye not that his mind was on kine, or cattle of the booty, nor thought he how he might strike a knight, nor be stricken again: nor no such thing. Nay, no memory had Aucassin of aught of these; rather he so dreamed of Nicolete, his sweet lady, that he dropped his reins, forgetting all there was to do, and his horse that had felt the spur, bore him into the press and hurled among the foe, and they laid hands on him all about, and took him captive, and seized away his spear and shield, and straightway they led him off a prisoner, and were even now discoursing of what death he should die.

And when Aucassin heard them, "Ha! God," said he, "sweet Saviour. Be these my deadly enemies that have taken me, and will soon cut off my head? And once my head is off, no more shall I speak with Nicolete, my sweet lady, that I love so well. Natheless have I here a good sword, and sit a good horse unwearied. If now I keep not my head for her sake, God help her never, if she love me more!"

The damoiseau was tall and strong, and the horse whereon he sat was right eager. And he laid hand to sword, and fell a-smiting to right and left, and smote through helm and nasal, and arm and clenched hand, making a murder about him, like a wild boar when hounds fall on him in the forest, even till he struck down ten knights, and seven he hurt, and straightway he hurled out of the press, and rode back again at full speed, sword in hand. The Count Bougars de Valence heard say they were about hanging Aucassin, his enemy, so he came into that place, and Aucassin was ware of him, and gat his sword into his hand, and lashed at his helm with such a stroke that he drave it down on his head, and he being stunned, fell groveling. And Aucassin laid hands on him, and caught him by the nasal of his helmet, and gave him to his father.

"Father," quoth Aucassin, "lo! here is your mortal foe, who hath so warred on you with all malengine. Full twenty years did this war endure, and might not be ended by man."

"Fair son," said his father, "thy feats of youth shouldst thou do, and not seek after folly."

"Father," saith Aucassin, "sermon me no sermons, but fulfill my covenant."

"Ha! what covenant, fair son?"

"What, Father, hast thou forgotten it? By mine own head, whosoever forgets, will I not forget it, so much it hath me at heart. Didst thou not covenant with me when I took up arms, and went into the battle, that if God brought me back safe and sound, thou wouldst let me see Nicolete, my sweet lady, even so long that I may have of her two words or three, and one kiss? So didst thou covenant, and my mind is that thou keep thy word."

"I!" quoth the father. "God forsake me when I keep this covenant! Nay, if she were here, I would let burn her in the fire, and thyself shouldst be sore adread."

"Is this thy last word?" quoth Aucassin.

"So help me God," quoth his father, "yea!"

"Certes," quoth Aucassin, "this is a sorry thing meseems, when a man of thine age lies!"

"Count of Valence," quoth Aucassin, "I took thee?"

"In sooth, sir, didst thou," saith the Count.

"Give me thy hand," saith Aucassin.

"Sir, with good will."

So he set his hand in the other's.

"Now givest thou me thy word," said Aucassin, "that never whilst thou art living man wilt thou avail to do my father dishonor, or harm him in body, or in goods, but do it thou wilt?"

"Sir, in God's name," saith he, "mock me not, but put me to my ransom; ye cannot ask of me gold nor silver, horses nor palfreys, vair nor gris, hawks nor hounds, but I will give you them."

"What?" quoth Aucassin. "Ha, knowest thou not it was I that took thee?"

"Yea, sir," quoth the Count Bougars.

"God help me never, but I will make thy head fly from thy shoulders, if thou makest not troth," said Aucassin.

"In God's name," said he, "I make what promise thou wilt."

So they did the oath, and Aucassin let mount him on a horse, and took another and so led him back till he was all in safety.

Here one singeth:

When the Count Garin doth know
That his child would ne'er forego

Love of her that loved him so,
Nicolete, the bright of brow,
In a dungeon deep below
Childe Aucassin did he throw.
Even there the Childe must dwell
In a dun-walled marble cell.
There he waileth in his woe
Crying thus as ye shall know.

"Nicolete, thou lily white,
My sweet lady, bright of brow,
Sweeter than the grape art thou,
Sweeter than sack posset good
In a cup of maple wood!
Was it not but yesterday
That a palmer came this way,
Out of Limousin came he,
And at ease he might not be,
For a passion him possessed
That upon his bed he lay,
Lay, and tossed, and knew not rest,
In his pain discomforted.
But thou camest by the bed,
Where he tossed amid his pain,
Holding high thy sweeping train,
And thy kirtle of ermine,
And thy smock of linen fine,
Then these fair white limbs of thine,
Did he look on, and it fell
That the palmer straight was well,
Straight was hale—and comforted,
And he rose up from his bed,
And went back to his own place,
Sound and strong and full of face!

My sweet lady, lily white,
Sweet thy footfall, sweet thine eyes,
And the mirth of thy replies,
Sweet thy laughter, sweet thy face,
Sweet thy lips and sweet thy brow,
And the touch of thine embrace.
Who but doth in thee delight?
I for love of thee am bound
In this dungeon underground,
All for loving thee must lie
Here where loud on thee I cry,
Here for loving thee must die
   For thee, my love."

Then say they, speak they, tell they the Tale:

Aucassin was cast into prison as ye have heard tell, and
Nicolete, of her part, was in the chamber. Now it was summertime, the month of May, when days are warm, and long, and
clear, and the night still and serene. Nicolete lay one night on
her bed, and saw the moon shine clear through a window, yea,
and heard the nightingale sing in the garden, so she minded
her of Aucassin her lover whom she loved so well. Then fell
she to thoughts of Count Garin de Biaucaire, that hated her to
the death; therefore deemed she that there she would no
longer abide, for that, if she were told of, and the Count knew
whereas she lay, an ill death would he make her die. Now she
knew that the old woman slept who held her company. Then
she arose, and clad her in a mantle of silk she had by her, very
goodly, and took napkins, and sheets of the bed, and knotted
one to the other, and made therewith a cord as long as she
might, so knitted it to a pillar in the window, and let herself
slip down into the garden, then caught up her raiment in both
hands, behind and before, and kilted up her kirtle, because of

the dew that she saw lying deep on the grass, and so went her way down through the garden.

Her locks were yellow and curled, her eyes blue and smiling, her face featly fashioned, the nose high and fairly set, the lips more red than cherry or rose in time of summer, her teeth white and small; her breasts so firm that they bore up the folds of her bodice as they had been two apples; so slim was she in the waist that your two hands might have clipped her, and the daisy flowers that brake beneath her as she went tiptoe, and that bent above her instep, seemed black against her feet, so white was the maiden. She came to the postern gate, and unbarred it, and went out through the streets of Biaucaire, keeping always on the shadowy side, for the moon was shining right clear, and so wandered she till she came to the tower where her lover lay. The tower was flanked with buttresses, and she cowered under one of them, wrapped in her mantle. Then thrust she her head through a crevice of the tower that was old and worn, and so heard she Aucassin wailing within, and making dole and lament for the sweet lady he loved so well. And when she had listened to him she began to say:

Here one singeth:

Nicolete the bright of brow
On a pillar leanest thou,
All Aucassin's wail doth hear
For his love that is so dear,
Then thou spakest, shrill and clear,
"Gentle knight withouten fear
Little good befalleth thee,
Little help of sigh or tear,
Ne'er shalt thou have joy of me.
Never shalt thou win me; still
Am I held in evil will

Of thy father and thy kin,
Therefore must I cross the sea,
And another land must win."
Then she cut her curls of gold,
Cast them in the dungeon hold,
Aucassin doth clasp them there,
Kissed the curls that were so fair,
Them doth in his bosom bear,
Then he wept, even as of old,
All for his love!

Then say they, speak they, tell they the Tale:

When Aucassin heard Nicolete say that she would pass into a far country, he was all in wrath.

"Fair sweet friend," quoth he, "thou shalt not go, for then wouldst thou be my death. And the first man that saw thee and had the might withal, would take thee straightway into his bed to be his leman. And once thou camest into a man's bed, and that bed not mine, wit ye well that I would not tarry till I had found a knife to pierce my heart and slay myself. Nay, verily, wait so long I would not: but would hurl myself on it so soon as I could find a wall, or a black stone; thereon would I dash my head so mightily, that the eyes would start, and my brain burst. Rather would I die even such a death, than know thou hadst lain in a man's bed, and that bed not mine."

"Aucassin," she said, "I trow thou lovest me not as much as thou sayest, but I love thee more than thou lovest me."

"Ah, fair sweet friend," said Aucassin, "it may not be that thou should love me even as I love thee. Woman may not love man as man loves woman, for a woman's love lies in the glance of her eyes, and the bud of her breast, and her foot's tiptoe, but the love of man is in his heart planted, whence it can never issue forth and pass away."

Now while Aucassin and Nicolete held this parley together,

the town's guards came down a street, with swords drawn beneath their cloaks, for the Count Garin had charged them that if they could take her they should slay her. But the sentinel that was on the tower saw them coming, and heard them speaking of Nicolete as they went, and threatening to slay her.

"God!" quoth he, "this were great pity to slay so fair a maid! Right great charity it were if I could say aught to her, and they perceive it not, and she should be on her guard against them, for if they slay her, then were Aucassin, my damoiseau, dead, and that were great pity."

Here one singeth:

> Valiant was the sentinel,
> Courteous, kind, and practiced well,
> So a song did sing and tell
> Of the peril that befell.
> "Maiden fair that lingerest here,
> Gentle maid of merry cheer,
> Hair of gold, and eyes as clear
> As the water in a mere,
> Thou, meseems, hast spoken word
> To thy lover and thy lord,
> That would die for thee, his dear;
> Now beware the ill accord,
> Of the cloaked men of the sword,
> These have sworn and keep their word,
> They will put thee to the sword
> Save thou take heed!"

Then speak they, say they, tell they the Tale:

"Ha!" quoth Nicolete; "be the soul of thy father and the soul of thy mother in the rest of Paradise, so fairly and so courteously hast thou spoken me! Please God, I will be right ware of them, God keep me out of their hands."

So she shrank under her mantle into the shadow of the pillar till they had passed by, and then took she farewell of Aucassin, and so fared till she came unto the castle wall. Now that wall was wasted and broken, and some deal mended, so she clomb thereon till she came between wall and fosse, and so looked down, and saw that the fosse was deep and steep, whereat she was sore adread.

"Ah God," saith she, "sweet Saviour! If I let myself fall hence, I shall break my neck, and if here I abide, tomorrow they will take me and burn me in a fire. Yet liefer would I perish here than that tomorrow the folk should stare on me for a gazing-stock."

Then she crossed herself, and so let herself slip into the fosse, and when she had come to the bottom, her fair feet and fair hands that had not custom thereof, were bruised and frayed, and the blood springing from a dozen places, yet felt she no pain or hurt, by reason of the great dread wherein she went. But if she were in pain to win there, in worse was she to win out. But she deemed that there to abide was of none avail, and she found a pike sharpened, that they of the city had thrown out to keep the hold. Therewith made she one stepping place after another, till, with much travail, she climbed the wall. Now the forest lay within two crossbow shots, and the forest was of thirty leagues this way and that. Therein also were wild beasts, and beasts serpentine, and she feared that if she entered there they would slay her. But anon she deemed that if men found her there they would hale her back into the town to burn her.

Here one singeth:

Nicolete, the fair of face,
Climbed upon the coping stone,
There made she lament and moan
Calling on our Lord alone

For His mercy and His grace.
"Father, King of Majesty,
Listen, for I nothing know
Where to flee or whither go.
If within the wood I fare,
Lo, the wolves will slay me there,
Boars and lions terrible,
Many in the wild wood dwell,
But if I abide the day,
Surely worse will come of it,
Surely will the fire be lit
That shall burn my body away,
Jesus, Lord of Majesty,
Better seemeth it to me,
That within the wood I fare,
Though the wolves devour me there
Than within the town to go,
      Ne'er be it so!"

Then speak they, say they, tell they the Tale:

Nicolete made great moan, as ye have heard; then commended she herself to God, and anon fared till she came unto the forest. But to go to sleep in it she dared not, by reason of the wild beasts, and beasts serpentine. Anon crept she into a little thicket, where sleep came upon her, and she slept till prime next day, when the shepherds issued forth from the town and drove their beasts between wood and water. Anon came they all into one place by a fair fountain which was on the fringe of the forest; thereby spread they a mantle, and thereon set bread. So while they were eating, Nicolete wakened, with the sound of the singing birds, and the shepherds, and she went unto them, saying, "Fair boys, our Lord keep you!"

"God bless thee," quoth he that had more words to his tongue than the rest.

"Fair boys," quoth she, "know ye Aucassin, the son of Count Garin de Biaucaire?"

"Yea, well we know him."

"So may God help you, fair boys," quoth she, "tell him there is a beast in this forest, and bid him come chase it, and if he can take it, he would not give one limb thereof for a hundred marks of gold, nay, nor for five hundred, nor for any ransom."

Then looked they on her, and saw her so fair that they were all astonied.

"Will I tell him thereof?" quoth he that had more words to his tongue than the rest; "foul fall him who speaks of the thing or tells him the tidings. These are but visions ye tell of, for there is no beast so great in this forest, stag, nor lion, nor boar, that one of his limbs is worth more than two deniers, or three at the most, and ye speak of such great ransom. Foul fall him that believes your word, and him that telleth Aucassin. Ye be a fairy, and we have none liking for your company; nay, hold on your road."

"Nay, fair boys," quoth she, "nay, ye will do my bidding. For this beast is so mighty of medicine that thereby will Aucassin be healed of his torment. And lo! I have five sols in my purse; take them, and tell him: for within three days must he come hunting it hither, and if within three days he find it not, never will he be healed of his torment."

"My faith," quoth he, "the money will we take, and if he come hither we will tell him, but seek him we will not."

"In God's name," quoth she; and so took farewell of the shepherds, and went her way.

Here singeth one:

Nicolete, the bright of brow,
From the shepherds doth she pass

All below the blossomed bough,
Where an ancient way there was,
Overgrown and choked with grass,
Till she found the crossroads where
Seven paths do all way fare,
Then she deemeth she will try,
Should her lover pass thereby,
If he love her loyally.
So she gathered white lilies,
Oak leaf that in green wood is,
Leaves of many a branch I wis,
Therewith built a lodge of green,
Goodlier was never seen,
Swore by God who may not lie,
"If my love the lodge should spy,
He will rest awhile thereby
If he love me loyally."
Thus his faith she deemed to try,
"Or I love him not, not I,
     Nor he loves me!"

Then speak they, say they, tell they the Tale:

Nicolete built her lodge of boughs, as ye have heard, right fair and neatly, and wove it well, within and without, of flowers and leaves. So lay she hard by the lodge in a deep coppice to know what Aucassin will do. And the cry and the bruit went abroad through all the country and all the land, that Nicolete was lost. Some told that she had fled, and some that the Count Garin had let slay her. Whosoever had joy thereof, no joy had Aucassin. And the Count Garin, his father, had taken him out of prison, and had sent for the knights of that land, and the ladies, and let make a right great feast, for the comforting of Aucassin his son. Now at the high time of the feast, was Aucassin leaning from a gallery, all woful and discomforted. Whatsoever men might devise of mirth, Aucassin had no joy thereof, nor no desire, for he saw not her that he loved. Then a knight looked on him, and came to him, and said: "Aucassin, of that sickness of thine have I been sick, and good counsel will I give thee, if thou wilt hearken to me—"

"Sir," said Aucassin, "gramercy; good counsel would I fain hear."

"Mount thy horse," quoth he, "and go take thy pastime in yonder forest, there wilt thou see the good flowers and grass, and hear the sweet birds sing. Perchance thou shalt hear some word, whereby thou shalt be the better."

"Sir," quoth Aucassin, "gramercy; that will I do."

He passed out of the hall, and went down the stairs, and came to the stable where his horse was. He let saddle and bridle him, and mounted, and rode forth from the castle, and wandered till he came to the forest, so rode till he came to the fountain, and found the shepherds at point of noon. And they had a mantle stretched on the grass, and were eating bread, and making great joy.

Here one singeth:

> There were gathered shepherds all,
> Martin, Esmeric, and Hal,
> Aubrey, Robin, great and small.
> Saith the one, "Good fellows all,
> God keep Aucassin the fair,
> And the maid with yellow hair,
> Bright of brow and eyes of vair,
> She that gave us gold to ware.
> Cakes therewith to buy ye know,
> Goodly knives and sheaths also.
> Flutes to play, and pipes to blow,
>   May God him heal!"

Here speak they, say they, tell they the Tale:

When Aucassin heard the shepherds, anon he bethought him of Nicolete, his sweet lady he loved so well, and he deemed that she had passed thereby; then set he spurs to his horse, and so came to the shepherds.

"Fair boys, God be with you."

"God bless you," quoth he that had more words to his tongue than the rest.

"Fair boys," quoth Aucassin, "say the song again that anon ye sang."

"Say it we will not," quoth he that had more words to his tongue than the rest; "foul fall him who will sing it again for you, fair sir!"

"Fair boys," quoth Aucassin, "know ye me not?"

"Yea, we know well that you are Aucassin, our damoiseau, natheless we be not your men, but the Count's."

"Fair boys, yet sing it again, I pray you."

"Hearken! by the Holy Heart," quoth he, "wherefore should I sing for you, if it likes me not? Lo, there is no such rich man in this country, saving the body of Garin the Count, that dare drive forth my oxen, or my cows, or my sheep, if he finds them in his fields or his corn, lest he lose his eyes for it, and wherefore should I sing for you, if it likes me not?"

"God be your aid, fair boys, sing it ye will, and take ye these ten sols I have here in a purse."

"Sir, the money will we take, but never a note will I sing, for I have given my oath, but I will tell thee a plain tale, if thou wilt."

"By God," saith Aucassin, "I love a plain tale better than naught."

"Sir, we were in this place, a little time agone, between prime and tierce, and were eating our bread by this fountain, even as now we do, and a maid came past, the fairest thing in the world, whereby we deemed that she should be a fay, and all the wood shone round about her. Anon she gave us of that she had, whereby we made covenant with her, that if ye came hither we would bid you hunt in this forest, wherein is such a beast that, an ye might take him, ye would not give one limb of him for five hundred marks of silver, nor for no ransom; for this beast is so mighty of medicine, that, an ye could take him, ye should be healed of your torment, and within three days must ye take him, and if ye take him not then, never will ye look on him. So chase ye the beast, an ye will, or an ye will let be, for my promise have I kept with her."

"Fair boys," quoth Aucassin, "ye have said enough. God grant me to find this quarry."

Here one singeth:

Aucassin when he had heard,
Sore within his heart was stirred,
Left the shepherds on that word,
Far into the forest spurred
Rode into the wood; and fleet
Fled his horse through paths of it,
Three words spake he of his sweet,
"Nicolete the fair, the dear,
'Tis for thee I follow here
Track of boar, nor slot of deer,
But thy sweet body and eyes so clear,
All thy mirth and merry cheer,
That my very heart have slain,
So please God to me maintain
I shall see my love again,
        Sweet sister, friend!"

Then speak they, say they, tell they the Tale:

Aucassin fared through the forest from path to path after
Nicolete, and his horse bare him furiously. Think ye not that
the thorns him spared, nor the briars, nay, not so, but tare his
raiment, that scarce a knot might be tied with the soundest
part thereof, and the blood sprang from his arms and flanks
and legs, in forty places, or thirty, so that behind the Childe
men might follow on the track of his blood in the grass. But
so much he went in thoughts of Nicolete, his lady sweet, that
he felt no pain nor torment, and all the day hurled through
the forest in this fashion nor heard no word of her. And when
he saw Vespers draw nigh, he began to weep for that he found
her not. All down an old road and grassgrown he fared, when
anon looking along the way before him, he saw such an one as
I shall tell you. Tall was he, and great of growth, loathly and
marvelous to look upon: his head huge and black as charcoal,
and more than the breadth of a hand between his two eyes,
and great cheeks, and a big nose and broad, big nostrils and
ugly, and thick lips redder than a collop, and great teeth yellow and ugly, and he was shod with hosen and shoon of bull's
hide, bound with cords of bark over the knee, all about him a
great cloak, twyfold, and he leaned on a grievous cudgel; and
Aucassin came unto him, and was afraid when he beheld him.

"Fair brother, God aid thee."

"God bless you," quoth he.

"As God he helpeth thee, what makest thou here?"

"What is that to thee?"

"Nay, naught, naught," saith Aucassin; "I ask but out of
courtesy."

"But for whom weepest thou," quoth he, "and makest such
heavy lament? Certes, were I as rich a man as thou, the whole
world should not make me weep."

"Ha! know ye me?" saith Aucassin.

"Yea, I know well that ye be Aucassin, the son of the Count, and if ye tell me for why ye weep, then will I tell you what I make here."

"Certes," quoth Aucassin, "I will tell you right gladly. Hither came I this morning to hunt in this forest; and with me a white hound, the fairest in the world; him have I lost, and for him I weep."

"By the heart our Lord bare in his breast," quoth he, "are ye weeping for a stinking hound? Foul fall him that holds thee high henceforth! for there is no such rich man in the land, but if thy father asked it of him, he would give thee ten, or fifteen, or twenty, and be the gladder for it. But I have cause to weep and make dole."

"Wherefore so, brother?"

"Sir, I will tell thee. I was hireling to a rich villein, and drove his plow; four oxen had he. But three days since came on me great misadventure, whereby I lost the best of mine oxen, Roger, the best of my team. Him go I seeking, and have neither eaten nor drunken these three days, nor may I go to the town, lest they cast me into prison, seeing that I have not wherewithal to pay. Out of all the wealth of the world have I no more than ye see on my body. A poor mother bare me, that had no more but one wretched bed; this have they taken from under her, and she lies in the very straw. This ails me more than mine own case, for wealth comes and goes; if now I have lost, another tide will I gain, and will pay for mine ox whenas I may; never for that will I weep. But you weep for a stinking hound. Foul fall whoso thinks well of thee!"

"Certes, thou art a good comforter, brother, blessed be thou! And of what price was thine ox?"

"Sir, they ask me twenty sols for him, whereof I cannot abate one doit."

"Nay, then," quoth Aucassin, "take these twenty sols I have in my purse, and pay for thine ox."

"Sir," saith he, "gramercy. And God give thee to find that thou seekest."

So they parted each from other, and Aucassin rode on; the night was fair and still, and so long he went that he came to the lodge of boughs, that Nicolete had builded and woven within and without, over and under, with flowers, and it was the fairest lodge that might be seen. When Aucassin was ware of it, he stopped suddenly, and the light of the moon fell therein.

"God!" quoth Aucassin, "here was Nicolete my sweet lady, and this lodge builded she with her fair hands. For the sweetness of it, and for love of her, will I alight, and rest here this night long."

He drew forth his foot from the stirrup to alight, and the steed was great and tall. He dreamed so much on Nicolete his right sweet lady, that he slipped on a stone, and drave his shoulder out of his place. Then knew he that he was hurt sore; natheless he bore him with what force he might, and fastened with the other hand the mare's son to a thorn. Then turned he on his side, and crept backwise into the lodge of boughs. And he looked through a gap in the lodge and saw the stars in heaven, and one that was brighter than the rest; so began he to say:

Here one singeth:

> "Star, that I from far behold,
> Star, the Moon calls to her fold,
> Nicolete with thee doth dwell,
> My sweet love with locks of gold,
> God would have her dwell afar,
> Dwell with Him for evening star,

> Would to God whate'er befell,
> Would that with her I might dwell.
> I would clip her close and strait,
> Nay, were I of much estate,
> Some king's son desirable,
> Worthy she to be my mate,
> Me to kiss and clip me well,
> 　　　Sister, sweet friend!"

So speak they, say they, tell they the Tale:

When Nicolete heard Aucassin, right so came she unto him, for she was not far away. She passed within the lodge, and threw her arms about his neck, and clipped and kissed him.

"Fair sweet friend, welcome be thou."

"And thou, fair sweet love, be thou welcome."

So either kissed and clipped the other, and fair joy was them between.

"Ha! sweet love," quoth Aucassin, "but now was I sore hurt, and my shoulder twisted, but I take no force of it, nor have no hurt therefrom since I have thee."

Right so felt she his shoulder and found it was twisted from its place. And she so handled it with her white hands, and so wrought in her surgery, that by God's will who loveth lovers, it went back into its place. Then took she flowers, and fresh grass, and leaves green, and bound these herbs on the hurt with a strip of her smock, and he was all healed.

"Aucassin," saith she, "fair sweet love, take counsel what thou wilt do. If thy father let search this forest tomorrow, and men find me here, they will slay me, come to thee what will."

"Certes, fair sweet love, therefore should I sorrow heavily, but, an if I may, never shall they take thee."

Anon gat he on his horse, and his lady before him, kissing and clipping her, and so rode they at adventure.

Here one singeth:

Aucassin the frank, the fair,
Aucassin of the yellow hair,
Gentle knight, and true lover,
From the forest doth he fare,
Holds his love before him there,
Kissing cheek, and chin, and eyes,
But she spake in sober wise,
"Aucassin, true love and fair,
To what land do we repair?"
"Sweet my love, I take no care,
Thou art with me everywhere!"
So they pass the woods and downs,
Pass the villages and towns,
Hills and dales and open land,
Came at dawn to the sea sand,
Lighted down upon the strand,
Beside the sea.

Then say they, speak they, tell they the Tale:

Aucassin lighted down and his love, as ye have heard sing. He held his horse by the bridle, and his lady by the hands; so went they along the sea shore, and on the sea they saw a ship, and he called unto the sailors, and they came to him. Then held he such speech with them, that he and his lady were brought aboard that ship, and when they were on the high sea, behold a mighty wind and tyrannous arose, marvelous and great, and drave them from land to land, till they came unto a strange country, and won the haven of the castle of Torelore. Then asked they what this land might be, and men told them that it was the country of the King of Torelore. Then he asked what manner of man was he, and was there war afoot, and men said: "Yea, and mighty!"

Therewith took he farewell of the merchants, and they commended him to God. Anon Aucassin mounted his horse, with his sword girt, and his lady before him, and rode at adventure till he was come to the castle. Then asked he where the King was, and they said that he was in childbed.

"Then where is his wife?"

And they told him she was with the host, and had led with her all the forces of that country.

Now when Aucassin heard that saying, he made great marvel, and came into the castle, and lighted down, he and his lady, and his lady held his horse. Right so went he up into the castle, with his sword girt, and fared hither and thither till he came to the chamber where the King was lying.

Here one singeth:

Aucassin the courteous knight
To the chamber went forthright,
To the bed with linen dight
Even where the King was laid.
There he stood by him and said:
"Fool, what mak'st thou here abed?"
Quoth the King: "I am brought to bed
Of a fair son, and anon
When my month is over and gone,
And my healing fairly done,
To the minster will I fare
And will do my churching there,
As my father did repair.
Then will sally forth to war,
Then will drive my foes afar
　　　　From my countrie!"

Then speak they, say they, tell they the Tale:

When Aucassin heard the King speak on this wise, he took all the sheets that covered him, and threw them all abroad about the chamber. Then saw he behind him a cudgel, and caught it into his hand, and turned, and took the King, and beat him till he was well-nigh dead.

"Ha! fair sir," quoth the King, "what would you with me? Art thou beside thyself, that beatest me in mine own house?"

"By God's heart," quoth Aucassin, "thou ill son of an ill wench, I will slay thee if thou swear not that never shall any man in all thy land lie in of child henceforth for ever."

So he did that oath, and when he had done it, "Sir," said Aucassin, "bring me now where thy wife is with the host."

"Sir, with good will," quoth the King.

He mounted his horse, and Aucassin gat on his own, and Nicolete abode in the Queen's chamber. Anon rode Aucassin and the King even till they came to that place where the Queen was, and lo! men were warring with baked apples and with eggs and with fresh cheeses, and Aucassin began to look on them, and made great marvel.

Here one singeth:

> Aucassin his horse doth stay,
> From the saddle watched the fray,
> All the fight and fierce array;
> Right fresh cheeses carried they,
> Apples baked, and mushrooms gray,
> Whoso splasheth most the ford
> He is master called and lord.
> Aucassin doth gaze awhile,
> Then began to laugh and smile
>> And made game.

Then speak they, say they, tell they the Tale:

When Aucassin beheld these marvels, he came to the King, and said, "Sir, be these thine enemies?"

"Yea, sir," quoth the King.

"And will ye that I should avenge you of them?"

"Yea," quoth he, "with all my heart."

Then Aucassin put hand to sword, and hurled among them, and began to smite to the right hand and the left, and slew many of them. And when the King saw that he slew them, he caught at his bridle and said: "Ha! fair sir, slay them not in such wise."

"How," quoth Aucassin, "will ye not that I should avenge you of them?"

"Sir," quoth the King, "overmuch already hast thou avenged me. It is nowise our custom to slay each other."

Anon turned they and fled. Then the King and Aucassin betook them again to the castle of Torelore, and the folk of that land counseled the King to put Aucassin forth, and keep Nicolete for his son's wife, for that she seemed a lady high of lineage. And Nicolete heard them, and had no joy of it, so began to say:

Here singeth one:

Thus she spake, the bright of brow:
"Lord of Torelore and King,
Thy folk deem me a light thing,
When my love doth me embrace,
Fair he finds me, in good case,
Then am I in such derray,
Neither harp, nor lyre, nor lay,
Dance nor game, nor rebeck play
    Were so sweet."

Then speak they, say they, tell they the Tale:

Aucassin dwelt in the castle of Torelore, in great ease and great delight, for that he had with him Nicolete his sweet love, whom he loved so well. Now while he was in such pleasure and such delight, came a troop of Saracens by sea, and laid siege to the castle and took it by main strength. Anon took they the substance that was therein and carried off the men and maidens captives. They seized Nicolete and Aucassin, and bound Aucassin hand and foot, and cast him into one ship, and Nicolete into another. Then rose there a mighty wind over sea, and scattered the ships. Now that ship wherein was Aucassin, went wandering on the sea, till it came to the castle of Biaucaire, and the folk of the country ran together to wreck her, and there found they Aucassin, and they knew him again. So when they of Biaucaire saw their damoiseau, they made great joy of him, for Aucassin had dwelt full three years in the castle of Torelore, and his father and mother were dead. So the people took him to the castle of Biaucaire, and there were they all his men. And he held the land in peace.

Here singeth one:

> Lo ye, Aucassin hath gone
> To Biaucaire that is his own,
> Dwelleth there in joy and ease
> And the kingdom is at peace.
> Swears he by the Majesty
> Of our Lord that is most high,
> Rather would he they should die
> All his kin and parentry,
> So that Nicolete were nigh.
> "Ah sweet love, and fair of brow,
> I know not where to seek thee now,
> God made never that countrie,
> Not by land, and not by sea,

> Where I would not search for thee,
> If that might be!"

Then speak they, say they, tell they the Tale:

Now leave we Aucassin, and speak we of Nicolete. The ship wherein she was cast pertained to the King of Carthage, and he was her father, and she had twelve brothers, all princes or kings. When they beheld Nicolete, how fair she was, they did her great worship, and made much joy of her, and many times asked her who she was, for surely seemed she a lady of noble line and high parentry. But she might not tell them of her lineage, for she was but a child when men stole her away. So sailed they till they won the city of Carthage, and when Nicolete saw the walls of the castle, and the countryside, she knew that there had she been nourished and thence stolen away, being but a child. Yet was she not so young a child but that well she knew she had been daughter of the King of Carthage; and of her nurture in that city.

Here singeth one:

> Nicolete, the good and true,
> To the land has come anew,
> Sees the palaces and walls,
> And the houses and the halls!
> Then she spake and said: "Alas!
> That of birth so great I was,
> Cousin of the Amiral
> And the very child of him
> Carthage counts King of Paynim,
> Wild folk hold me here withal;
> Nay Aucassin, love of thee
> Gentle knight, and true, and free,

> Burns and wastes the heart of me.
> Ah God grant it of his grace,
> That thou hold me, and embrace,
> That thou kiss me on the face
> Love and lord!

Then speak they, say they, tell they the Tale:

When the King of Carthage heard Nicolete speak in this wise, he cast his arms about her neck.

"Fair sweet love," saith he, "tell me who thou art, and be not adread of me."

"Sir," said she, "I am daughter to the King of Carthage, and was taken, being then a little child, it is now fifteen years gone."

When all they of the court heard her speak thus, they knew well that she spake sooth: so made they great joy of her, and led her to the castle in great honor, as the King's daughter. And they would have given her to her lord a King of Paynim, but she had no mind to marry. There dwelt she three days or four. And she considered by what means she might seek for Aucassin. Then she got her a viol, and learned to play on it, till they would have married her on a day to a great King of Paynim, and she stole forth by night, and came to the sea-port, and dwelt with a poor woman thereby. Then took she a certain herb, and therewith smeared her head and her face, till she was all brown and stained. And she let make coat and mantle and smock and hose, and attired herself as if she had been a harper. So took she the viol and went to a mariner, and so wrought on him that he took her aboard his vessel. Then hoisted they sail, and fared on the high seas even till they came to the land of Provence. And Nicolete went forth and took the viol, and went playing through all that country, even till she came to the castle of Biaucaire, where Aucassin lay.

Here singeth one:

At Biaucaire below the tower
Sat Aucassin, on an hour,
Heard the bird, and watched the flower,
With his barons him beside,
Then came on him in that tide,
The sweet influence of love
And the memory thereof;
Thought of Nicolete the fair,
And the dainty face of her
He had loved so many years,
Then was he in dole and tears!
Even then came Nicolete
On the stair a foot she set,
And she drew the viol bow
Through the strings and chanted so;
"Listen, lords and knights, to me,
Lords of high or low degree,
To my story list will ye
All of Aucassin and her
That was Nicolete the fair?
And their love was long to tell
Deep woods through he sought her well,
Paynims took them on a day
In Torelore and bound they lay.
Of Aucassin naught know we,
But fair Nicolete the free
Now in Carthage doth she dwell,
There her father loves her well,
Who is king of that countrie.
Her a husband hath he found,
Paynim lord that serves Mahound!
Ne'er with him the maid will go,

For she loves a damoiseau,
Aucassin, that ye may know,
Swears to God that never mo
With a lover will she go
Save with him she loveth so
In long desire."

So speak they, say they, tell they the Tale:

When Aucassin heard Nicolete speak in this wise, he was right joyful, and drew her on one side, and spoke, saying: "Sweet fair friend, knew ye nothing of this Nicolete, of whom ye have thus sung?"

"Yea, sir, I know her for the noblest creature, and the most gentle, and the best that ever was born on ground. She is daughter to the King of Carthage that took her there where Aucassin was taken, and brought her into the city of Carthage, till he knew that verily she was his own daughter, whereon he made right great mirth. Anon wished he to give her for her lord one of the greatest kings of all Spain, but she would rather let herself be hanged or burned, than take any lord, how great soever."

"Ha! fair sweet friend," quoth the Count Aucassin, "if thou wilt go into that land again, and bid her come and speak to me, I will give thee of my substance, more than thou wouldst dare to ask or take. And know ye that for the sake of her, I have no will to take a wife, howsoever high her lineage. So wait I for her, and never will I have a wife, but her only. And if I knew where to find her, no need would I have to seek her."

"Sir," quoth she, "if ye promise me that, I will go in quest of her for your sake, and for hers, that I love much."

So he sware to her, and anon let give her twenty livres, and she departed from him, and he wept for the sweetness of

Nicolete. And when she saw him weeping, she said: "Sir, trouble not thyself so much withal. For in a little while shall I have brought her into this city, and ye shall see her."

When Aucassin heard that, he was right glad thereof. And she departed from him, and went into the city to the house of the Captain's wife, for the Captain her father in God was dead. So she dwelt there, and told all her tale; and the Captain's wife knew her, and knew well that she was Nicolete that she herself had nourished. Then she let wash and bathe her, and there rested she eight full days. Then took she an herb that was named *Eyebright* and anointed herself therewith, and was as fair as ever she had been all the days of her life. Then she clothed herself in rich robes of silk whereof the lady had great store, and then sat herself in the chamber on a silken coverlet, and called the lady and bade her go and bring Aucassin her love, and she did even so. And when she came to the palace she found Aucassin weeping, and making lament for Nicolete his love, for that she delayed so long. And the lady spake unto him and said: "Aucassin, sorrow no more, but come thou on with me, and I will show thee the thing in the world that thou lovest best; even Nicolete thy dear love, who from far lands hath come to seek of thee." And Aucassin was right glad.

Here singeth one:

> When Aucassin heareth now
> That his lady bright of brow
> Dwelleth in his own countrie,
> Never man was glad as he.
> To her castle doth he hie
> With the lady speedily,
> Passeth to the chamber high,
> Findeth Nicolete thereby.
> Of her true love found again

Never maid was half so fain.
Straight she leaped upon her feet:
When his love he saw at last,
Arms about her did he cast,
Kissed her often, kissed her sweet
Kissed her lips and brows and eyes.
Thus all night do they devise,
Even till the morning white.
Then Aucassin wedded her,
Made her lady of Biaucaire.
Many years abode they there,
Many years in shade or sun,
In great gladness and delight.
Ne'er hath Aucassin regret
Nor his lady Nicolete.
Now my story all is done,
> Said and sung!

HAVELOK THE DANE

FOREWORD

In addition to the three famous "Matters" of romance that
have been noted before in this book as the Matter of France,
of Britain, of Antiquity, there were many other medieval romances, some too miscellaneous for any grouping, others that
might by analogy be called the Matter of England. Such romances as *King Horn, Havelok the Dane, Beves of Hampton,
Guy of Warwick* and others were known in both French and
English versions and enjoyed long-lasting popularity. As the
names of the last two titular heroes suggest, these romances
were all, in part at least, localized in England, and contain
names and themes reminiscent of the period of Viking conquests. Those terrible "red sea-birds," the Vikings of the
North, who, in the ninth century, pillaged the coasts of England, later on settled themselves there so extensively that

over a thousand Scandinavian place names can be identified on the map; the dialects of such northern counties as Lincoln, Derby, and York in the old Danelaw, became saturated with words of Scandinavian origin. Though descendants of these settlers ultimately became true Englishmen at heart, they preserved ancestral memories and worked some of them into legends that they developed in this English home. When the author of *Havelok the Dane,* writing in Lincolnshire before 1300, concluded his English romance with references to his Danish hero's coronation in London as King of England, to the sending home of his Danish followers, and to his long life and rule in England, the poet was probably thinking of that great historic Dane, King Cnut, of whom the same things had been true during his English rule from 1016-38.

The two earliest extant accounts of Havelok's story were written in England in French in the twelfth century. Geffrei Gaimar's was in his chronicle history of the English; the other, the *Lai d'Haveloc,* took the form of a courtly Breton *lai,* a type about which more will be said in connection with *Sir Orfeo.* Both versions place the story in the far-off days of King Arthur, but this was simply a way of gaining interest for a hero much less famous than Arthur. Havelok's own name—corresponding to the Irish Abloc, the Old English Anlaf, the French (H)aveloc, the Norse Olaf—and his nickname Cuaran would seem to identify him with that famous Olaf Cuaran (d.981), the Norse king of Dublin and frequent invader of England. But nothing save the names connects the two; in fact no convincing historical prototype for Havelok has been found. It seems safer to consider him a folk hero whose legend developed according to familiar story patterns of a hero's exile from and return to his home and kingdom, of his life as a male Cinderella who serves as a scullion, who has incredible prowess, and who is finally revealed by a mysterious light or a king's mark on his shoulder.

The specific localization of the Havelok legend in Lincolnshire even in twelfth-century accounts is important; in them, as in all later versions, it was to Grimsby on the Humber

River, to the place to be named for him, that Grim brought Havelok; it was to Lincoln that the royal boy went to earn his living. These traditions were kept vigorously alive. The town seal of Grimsby, dating from the time of Edward I (d.1307), shows the figures and names of *Gryem, Habloc* and his wife, *Goldeburgh*. A Lincolnshire chronicler, Robert Mannyng of Brunne (d. 1338), who set himself to write English history for simple, unlearned men, refers to the stone in Lincoln Castle that Havelok threw, to the chapel there where the hero had been married, and complains sharply because he, the writer, can find no serious historian who gives an account of Havelok or of Grim. But he himself knew a written English story in rime about Havelok, in fact had quoted from it in an earlier work, and this must have been the same version that we know as the immensely vigorous, bluff and hearty romance of *Havelok the Dane*.

For this its author used his own Lincolnshire dialect, and seems to have been especially at home in Lincoln; he makes its ancient bridge the scene of Havelok's early efforts to get a job, and refers to the green where Godrich was executed as being still there. The poet was preëminently a man of the people, probably a minstrel like those he pictures gathering for Havelok's feast in Denmark, some of them reading aloud romances in books, some of them singing and chanting or playing musical instruments. He was utterly unlike such writers as Chrétien de Troyes, Gottfried von Strassburg, or the author of *Aucassin*. They had belonged to the intelligentsia of their times and had written primarily for courtly audiences. The *Havelok* poet had in mind men like himself, of humble origin and experience. He begins with a forthright demand for a cup of good ale, and probably envisaged himself as reading or telling the tale in a tavern or the kitchen of a manor house. He uses familiar devices for effective oral recitation; he repeats and summarizes his narrative; he prays dramatically for himself, his listeners, his good characters; the bad ones he curses vehemently. He salts his story with shrewd proverbial sayings —on how hope tricks the foolish, speed companions success,

or on the effectiveness of meed. His comparisons are to familiar, homely things: a goaded beast, the fierce dogs of a mill
house, swift sparks from fire, the stillness of stone. He pictures, not castles and knights, but such settings and characters
as would please the common people. Grim, a baron in the *Lai
d'Haveloc,* for him becomes a rough-handed but kind-hearted
fisherman who sells his little Danish farm with its woolly
sheep and bearded goats, to provide the boat in which, with
Havelok and his family, he will escape to England. Grim's
catches, his labors as a fisherman, like those of the hero as a
scullion, are faithfully enumerated. Havelok's physical prowess
is everywhere lauded; he can carry the heaviest loads, can be
the champion at all village sports, and is invincible with his
fists. There is a great deal of physical violence, of brutality in
the story, especially when the wicked are punished, but that is
oddly offset by a special tenderness for little children, for the
hero as a small boy, for Havelok's own concern for little lads.
The poet expresses a genuine piety and reverences loyalty
both to God and man. Grim's loyalty to his helpless little
prince, and the loyalty of Grim's sons and daughters to Havelok and his young wife when they are in need, are movingly
related. To the sons are given homely names found in no
other version: Red Robert, William Wendut, Hugh Raven,
names that might have belonged to Lincolnshire peasants. The
archvillains of the story are the two disloyal usurpers who
alike break their plighted word to the dying royal fathers of
Goldborough in England and Havelok in Denmark and steal
the realms of the children they had sworn to protect. Each
villain, however, is given a fair trial, a judicial if horrible exe-
cution. Despite the violence of life as depicted in the poem, it
breathes respect for law and portrays Athelwold of England as
an ideal king who kept such law and order in his realm that
traders might go safely everywhere, who punished evildoers,
whether knight or cleric, and protected the weak and helpless.
There is little that is romantic in the romance; Havelok is
horrified when he is married to a wife he is too poor to support. Words of affection are few. The storyteller was con-

cerned with action, not with sentiment, with the forceful ways of men with men. Swiftly, with distinctive realism of detail and shrewd practicality of spirit, he put into 3001 lines of rimed couplets a story in which not only a king's son but humble people play vigorous parts.

L. H. L.

THE STORY*

Listen, good folk, wives, maidens, and men, and I will tell you the tale of Havelok, the mightiest man at need that ever rode a horse. But fill me a cup of good ale ere the story begins. And may Christ shield us all from hell! *Benedicamus domino!*

In the old days there lived a king who made good laws and was dear to old and young. He loved God and Holy Church, truth and righteous men, but he hated robbers, and all the outlaws he could find he hanged high on the gallows. In his time a man with red gold in his bag found none to trouble him; pedlars could fare through all England and boldly buy and sell, and no one harmed them who was not quickly brought to nought. The land was at peace and great was the praise of the king. He was England's flower. He followed his foes till they dared not move; he pitied the fatherless; he imprisoned the knight, were he ever so great, who did widows wrong; he destroyed the limbs of those wrought shame to maidens. He was strong and unafraid, swift in fight as a flame. He was generous, and the bread on his table was never too fine to give, for Christ's sake, to the poor who travel afoot.

The king's name was Athelwold and he had no heir save one fair little maid, too young to walk or speak. When a sick-

* Translated and slightly abridged by L. H. Loomis.

ness came upon him that he knew was his death, he sent a call for all his lords from Roxburgh to Dover, to come to him in Winchester where, no longer able to sleep or eat, he lay in his hard bonds. There, sobbing and lamenting, they greeted him, but he bade them be still. "Wailing is of no help," he said. "I am brought to my death. Now I pray you, who is to have charge of my daughter who will be your lady after me?"

When they answered that Earl Godrich of Cornwall was a true man, wise and much feared, the king was pleased. He ordered a fair cloth to be brought, and Mass book, chalice, paten, and corporal to be laid on it. On these he made Godrich swear to care for the maiden till she had learned courtesy and was old enough to speak of love; and then he should give her to the tallest, fairest, and strongest man alive. When this oath was taken, the king gave England and his daughter into the earl's keeping. He then prayed, took the sacrament, and did penance with a severe scourging, so that blood ran from his tender flesh. He gave away all his goods so that there was not enough left for his shroud and coffin. When he had said, *"In manus tuas,"* he died before them all, and great was the mourning.

After the king was laid in earth, Earl Godrich seized all England for his own and put knights whom he could trust into the castles. He made the people swear good faith to him, and sent justices through the land and appointed sheriffs, beadles, magistrates, and sergeants of the peace, with long glaives, to keep the wild woods from wicked men. He had everything at his own will, and soon England stood in fear of him, as the beast fears the goad.

In time Goldborough, the king's daughter, came to be the loveliest of women, and wise in all good ways. Many a tear was shed for her, but when Earl Godrich heard men say that she was fair and chaste and the rightful heir, he said to himself, "Why should she be queen over me? Why should she have all England and me and mine in her hand? Should I give this land to a foolish girl? I have been too soft with her. But it shall not be as she thinks: 'Hope often tricks a fool.' "

With that, not caring a straw for his oath, like a wicked Judas, he took her from Winchester to Dover on our seacoast. In the castle he fed and clothed her miserably and let no one come near to avenge her wrongs. May Jesus Christ, who freed Lazarus from death's bonds, release her and may she see him hanged who brought her, all innocent, to such woe!

Leaving her there in prison, our story goes on. In Denmark there was a rich and powerful king, named Birkabeyn, who had a son, Havelok, and two daughters. He loved the three as his own life. But it chanced that death, which will not forbear for rich or poor, for king or emperor, was to seize him when most he wished to live. He called priests, canons, and monks to prepare him for death; then his knights chose his own friend, the rich Earl Godard, to rule till the prince could be made king. Godard swore by the altar, the Mass-gear, the bells men ring, that he would care so faithfully for the children as to please their kindred, and give Denmark over when Havelok was of age. But Birkabeyn was no sooner buried than Godard took the heir and his sisters, Swanborow and Elfled, and put them in a castle where none could reach them. Before they were three years old they had often wept bitterly for cold and hunger. When in course of time Godard was sure of his hold on the land and the people, he planned a great treachery against the children. The devil take him!

Godard went to the tower where the children were wailing. The boy, who was brave enough, fell on his knees and greeted him fairly.

"What is the matter with you?" said Godard. "Why do you wail and howl?"

"We hunger," answered Havelok; "we have not half enough to eat, nor knight nor knave to serve us. Woe for us that we were born! Alas, is there no wheat for bread? We are nearly dead with hunger."

But Godard cared nothing, not a straw, for their woe. As if in sport, he took the little girls, wan and green they were, and cut their throats. In their blood they lay, sprawled by the wall. Terrified, Havelok saw the knife at his own heart. Little as he was, he knelt before that Judas, and said, 'Lord, have pity! My homage and all Denmark will I give you if you will let me live. On the book will I swear never to bear shield or spear to harm you, and today will I flee from Denmark and never come again. I will vow Birkabeyn was not my father."

Now when this devil heard that, somewhat did he begin to soften. He drew back the knife, still warm with the children's blood, and a miracle it was, that for pity he went his way. But though he would not kill the boy himself, he grieved that Havelok was not dead. Staring as if he were mad, he mused alone and then he sent for a fisherman whom he knew would do his will.

"Grim, my thrall," he said, "you know that all I bid you, you must do. Tomorrow I will make you free and rich if you will take a child when you see the moon tonight, and cast him in the sea. The sin of it will I take for my own."

Then Grim took the child, and bound him fast; he wrapped him in an old cloth, gagged him with foul rags so that he could not speak or breathe, and cast him in a black bag. Lifting him on his back, he bore him to his cottage and gave him over to Dame Leve, whom he told what his lord commanded. When she heard that, she started up and threw the boy down so hard that his head cracked against a great stone. Then might Havelok well say, "Alas, that ever I was born a king's son!"

In this fashion the child lay until midnight, when Grim bade Leve bring a light so that he might put on his clothes. As she was handling them, she saw a clear light, bright as day, shining about the child. From his mouth came a ray like a sunbeam. It was as though wax candles burned within the house.

"Jesus Christ!" said Dame Leve, "what light is this in our dwelling? Rise up, Grim, and see what it means."

Both of them hastened to the boy and unbound him, and shortly, as they turned back his shirt, they found on his right shoulder a king's birthmark, very bright and fair.

"God knows, this is the heir who will be Lord of Denmark," cried Grim, and he fell down at Havelok's feet, and sorely grieved. "My lord, have pity on me and on Leve here! Both of us are your churls, your hinds. Well will we feed you till you can ride and bear helmet, shield, and spear, and never shall Godard know, that vile traitor! Through no other man than you, my lord, will I have freedom."

Then was Havelok a blithe lad, and he sat up and asked hungrily for bread. Dame Leve said, "Good is it for me that you can eat. I will fetch you bread and cheese, butter and milk, pasties and cheese cakes, and with all such, lord, will we feed you in this great need. Oh, true it is as men swear, 'Where God will help, nothing can harm.' "

Then Havelok ate ravenously a whole loaf and more, and when he was fed, Grim made a good bed, undressed him, and laid him in it. "Sleep fast," he said, "and do not fear the night, for from sorrow you are brought to joy."

Now as soon as it was daybreak, Grim took his way to Godard, that wicked steward of Denmark, and, telling him the boy was dead, asked for his reward and freedom.

Godard looked at him grimly. "So you will be an earl now, will you?" he said. "Get you gone, you foul churl of the dirt, and be forever thrall, as you have been before. You have done wickedly. For a little more I will send you to the gallows."

Overlate, as he ran away, Grim bethought him how he

could escape from that traitor. "What shall I do? Should
Godard know that Havelok lives, he will hang us both. Better
is it for us to flee the land and save all our lives."

Then Grim sold all his grain, his woolly sheep, his horned
cattle, horses, swine, and bearded goats, the geese and farm-
yard hens; everything that he could, he sold, and turned it
into money. He tarred his ship and put in a mast, strong
cables, good oars, and a sail—not a nail was lacking. When he
had made all ready, he took young Havelok, himself, and his
wife, his three sons, and his two pretty daughters, and rowed
out to high sea. When he was about a mile from land the
north wind came, which men call "bise," and drove them unto
England, that afterward was to be Havelok's. But first he suffered shame and sorrow before it was his. If you listen, you
will straightway hear the story.

Now Grim landed at the north end of Lindsey in the
Humber and, drawing up his ship on the sand, he made
there a little earth house. Because he owned it, the place there
took the name of Grim, and men call it Grimsby and so
shall do until doomsday.

Grim was a wise fisherman, and with net and hook he
caught many a good fish: sturgeon, whale, turbot, salmon, seal,
and eels; also cod and porpoise, herring, mackerel, flounder,
plaice and skate. He made baskets for himself and his three
sons, for carrying the fish they sold. To town and farm he
went, and never did he come home with empty hand. When
he caught a big lamprey, he took it straight to Lincoln. Often
he went from end to end of that good town till he had sold
everything and counted his pennies. When he came home he
brought with him wastel bread and horn-shaped cakes, and
his bags full of grain and meat. Hemp, too, he would have, and
strong ropes for the nets he cast in the sea.

Thus did Grim live, and for twelve years or more he fed his
family well. But Havelok came to know that, while he lay at

home, Grim was sorely toiling for his food, and he thought, "No longer am I a child, but well grown, and easily can I eat more than Grim can ever get. I eat more than Grim and his five children. God knows, this must not be. I will go now and learn to labor for my meat. Work is no shame! Gladly will I bear the baskets, and it will not grieve me, though the burden is great as an ox."

On the morrow when it was day, Havelok sprang up, cast on his back a basket stacked high with fish, and he alone carried as much as the four men. He sold every bit and brought home each piece of silver, keeping back not a farthing. And never, thereafter, did he lie at home, but went forth each day so that he would learn his trade.

Now it chanced that there came a great dearth of wheat, and Grim did not know how he would feed his family; there were no more good fish. Great fear did he have because of Havelok, on whom was all his thought. Then Grim said to him, "Havelok, I think we will soon die of hunger, for our meat is long since gone, and the famine lasts. It is better that you go hence, ere it be too late. You know the way to Lincoln, and there is many a good man from whom you can win your food. But alas for your nakedness! I will make you, son, a coat from my sail, so you will take no cold."

Taking down the shears from the nail, Grim made the coat, and Havelok put it on. With no other kind of dress, and barefoot, he went to Lincoln. He had no friend there, and did not know what to do. For two days he fasted, but on the next he heard a man calling, "Porters, porters, come here!" Like a flash all the poor folk sprang forward and Havelok shoved nine or ten into the mud, and, leaping to the earl's cook, who was buying meat at the bridge, he bore the food to the castle, and for this service he got a farthing cake. On another day when the cook called the porters, Havelok knocked down sixteen good lads who stood in his way, and ran with his fish basket and began snatching up the fish. He lifted up a whole cartload of cuttlefish, of salmon and plaice, great lampreys, and eels, and he spared not his heels or his toes, till he came to the castle and men took the burden from his head. The cook looked at him and, thinking he was a strong fellow, asked, "Will you stay with me? I will feed you gladly. Your food and hire are well earned."

"God knows I ask no other hire, dear sir. Give me enough to eat and I will fetch fuel and water, make the fire burn clear, skin eels, and wash your dishes well."

When the cook had said, "I ask no more," and told him to sit down, Havelok was still as a stone till he had eaten enough. Then he went to the well and, filling a great tub, bore it alone to the kitchen. He would let no one fetch water, or bear meat from the bridge; he alone bore the peat, the sedges and the wood, and drew all the water that was needed. He took no more rest than as if he were a beast, and of all men was he meekest. He was always laughing and blithe of speech, for his troubles he could well conceal. No child was so little that Havelok would not play with him, and young or old, knights or children, quiet or bold, all who saw, loved him. His fame went far, how he was meek and strong and fair, as God made him, but almost he was naked. He had nought to wear but one wretched coat, not worth a faggot. Then the cook took pity on him and bought him new clothes, hose and shoes, and he put them on quickly. When he was clothed, no one on earth looked fairer, and no one looked more fit to be a king. When all the earl's men were together at the Lincoln games, Havelok stood like a mast, shoulders taller than any. At wrestling he overthrew every one, and yet for all his strength he was gentle, and despite a man's misdeeds to him, he never laid hand on him for ill. Virgin he was, and would no more lie with a whore than with a witch.

It came to pass then that Earl Godrich made barons and

earls, and all the men of England come to Lincoln, to be at the Parliament. With them came many a champion, and some nine or ten young men began to sport, while servants and bondsmen with their goads, just as they had come from the plow, gathered to watch. No horseboy but was there. The beam of a tree lay at their feet and the strong young men began mightily to put the stone. Strong was he who could lift it to his knee, but no priest could lift it breast-high. A champion was he reckoned who could put it one inch beyond another.

Now as the crowd stood and stared, making a great noise over the best throw, Havelok looked on. Never before had he seen stone-putting, and of it he was very ignorant. His master bade him try what he could do, and half afraid he started, caught the heavy stone, and hurled it the first time twelve feet beyond all other throws. The champions that saw it shouldered each other and laughed. "We stay here too long," they said, and would play no more. Now the wonder could not be hid, and very shortly through all England went the tale of how Havelok had put the stone. In castle and hall, the knights told of it and how he was strong and tall, till Godrich, hearing them, thought to himself, "Through this knave shall I and my son win England. On the Mass-gear King Athelwold made me swear that I would give his daughter to the highest, strongest, fairest man alive. Though I went to India, where could I find one so tall and skillful as Havelok? It is he who shall have Goldborough."

Planning this wicked treason, for he believed Havelok a churl's son, Godrich sent quickly for Goldborough to come to Lincoln, and told her, though she vowed she would wed none save a king or a king's son, that on the morrow she must wed his cook's knave. When the day came, that Judas called to him Havelok and asked him if he would marry.

"No, on my life!" quoth Havelok. "What should I do with

a wife? I could not feed nor clothe her, and where would I
take a woman? I have nothing: no house nor cot, no stick nor
blade of grass, no food nor clothes, but one old white coat.
These clothes I wear are the cook's, and I am his servant."

Godrich started up and struck him savagely. "Unless you
take her whom I give you for wife, I will hang or blind you."
Then Havelok was afraid and granted that which was asked;
and Goldborough too, when that wicked traitor threatened
her, dared not hinder the marriage. She thought it was the will
of God who makes the wheat to grow and who had made her
a woman. So they were married and pennies were thick on
the book, and all was done fair and well at the Mass. The
good clerk who married them was the Archbishop of York,
whom God had sent to that Parliament.

When the marriage was done, then Havelok knew not
what to do, where to stay, or where to go, for plainly he saw
that Godrich—may the devil take him!—hated them. Because
Havelok knew full well that harm would come to his wife,
he decided that they should flee to Grim and his three sons,
since there they could best hope to be fed and clothed. On
foot they went, since they knew no help for it, and held the
right way till they came to Grimsby. Now Grim had died, but
his five children were still alive and they made great joy to
welcome Havelok. They fell on their knees and cried, "O welcome, dear lord, and welcome to your fair wife. Blessed be
the time when in God's law you married her. Happy are we
now to see you alive. We have horses and cattle, a ship on
the sea, gold, silver, and many things which our father Grim
charged us to give to thee. Stay here, and all is yours. You
will be our lord and we will serve you both. Our sisters will do
whatever she bids; they will wash and wring her clothes, and
bring water for her hands, and make the bed for you both."

Joyously then they broke sticks and set the fire ablaze. So
that there should be no lack of meat, they spared neither

goose nor hen, duck nor drake, and also they fetched wine and ale. Many times the wassail cup was passed. But at nightfall, with sad heart Goldborough lay down, for to one all unfitting had she been wed. A light, fair and bright like flame, suddenly filled the room, and she saw that it came from the mouth of him who slept beside her. Terrified, she thought, "What means this? He will be a nobleman, I think, a nobleman before he dies." Then she saw on his shoulder a red-gold cross, and the voice of an angel said, "Goldborough, let be thy sorrow. That fair cross shows that he who has wedded thee is a king's son, and that thou shalt be a queen. Of Denmark and of England he shall be king."

When she had heard these words of the heavenly angel, she was too blithe to hide her joy, and she kissed Havelok as he slept unknowing. He started up from his sleep.

"Dear one," he said, "hear a most wonderful dream. I thought I was in Denmark, on a hill so high that I could see all the world. And as I sat there, my arms were so long that I could hold all Denmark. But when I would draw my arms to me, all who lived there clave to them, and the keys of the strong castles fell at my feet. Again I dreamed that I flew over the salt sea to England and all the Danish folk, except the bondsmen and their wives, went with me. I closed all England in my hand, and gave it, Goldborough, to you. Beloved, what can this mean?"

"May Christ turn your dreams to joy," she answered. "As if I saw it, I believe you will yet wear England's crown, and within a year you will have the whole of Denmark and all who dwell there. But do not delay your going. 'Speed companions success.' Take with you Grim's sons, for they are eager and love you heartily. Delay has often done harm."

When the day came, Havelok rose and went, before he did anything else, to church, there to kneel and call on Christ and the Cross. "O Thou who dost rule the wind and the

water, the wood and the field," he cried, "of Thy mercy pity
me, Lord. Give me vengeance on the foe who killed my
sisters before my eyes and bade Grim drown me in the sea.
With wicked wrong he holds my land who has made me a
beggar, though I never did him harm. Let me pass safely
across the sea, O Lord, and bring me to that land which Godard holds, the land that by right is mine."

Laying his offering on the altar, Havelok returned home
and found Grim's sons going out to their fishing so that
Havelok might have good eating. He called to him Robert the
Red, the eldest brother, and William Wendut, and Hugh
Raven, and told the story of his father, and of how his sisters
were killed, and how Grim had saved him. "And now," he
said, "that I am come of age and am able to wield weapons, I
shall never be glad till I see Denmark. I pray you come with
me, and rich men will I make you. Each one shall have ten
castles and all their lands.[1]

[In this fashion it came to pass that Grim's sons with
Havelok and Goldborough sailed to Denmark, where they
came to Earl Ubbe, who had been a friend of Havelok's father.] Havelok thus besought him, "I ask leave from you and
from no other magistrate to sell my wares as I go from town
to town."

To Ubbe, Havelok then gave a gold ring, with a stone in
it worth a hundred pounds. 'Wise was he who first gave
meed,' and wise was Havelok who gained so much for his
gold ring. Ubbe would not have given up the ring for anything. He saw that Havelok was very strong, broad-shoul-
dered, deep-chested, tall, and thought him fitter for the bearing of shield and spear than for buying and selling. Yet he
promised Havelok should have his boon if he would come
that day with Goldborough to dine with Ubbe. And Havelok,

[1] A gap of 180 lines occurs here because a leaf has been lost from
the manuscript. The passage told of Havelok's return to Denmark.

though fearful for her, led her to the court. Red Robert, who would have died to keep her from harm, went with her, also William Wendut, good in any need. "A good thing it is for him who feeds a good man."

Ubbe and his knights and men started up, and over them all, like a tall hill, towered Havelok. Then Ubbe loved Havelok, seeing him so fair and courteous, and when it was time to eat, he brought in his own wife and said jestingly, "Lady, you and Havelok must eat together, and Goldborough, fair as a flower on a tree, with me. By St. John, no other woman in Denmark is so beautiful!"

The blessing was said, and before them was put the best food that ever king or emperor ate. Cranes, swans, venison, salmon, lamprey, sturgeon were set before them, together with spiced wine and white wine and red; not even the youngest page had to drink ale. Weary would this good company be if I told you all. When the time came for going, Ubbe bethought him, "If I let them go alone, woe will be because of this woman. For her sake men will kill her lord." So he called forth ten knights and sixty men with their bows and lances and sent them all to Bernard Brown, the magistrate of the town, and bade him guard Havelok and Goldborough as his own life.

Now Bernard was no niggard, and he prepared fine fare for Havelok's supper. But just as they were about to sup, a man in a loose jacket, and sixty others with drawn swords and long knives in hand, demanded entrance to the house. Bernard started up, threw a mail coat on his back, seized an ax, and leaped like a mad man to the door. He cried out that if he opened the door, he would kill them.

"Think you we are afraid?" said a varlet. "We will go in at this door despite you, you churl."

They seized a boulder and let it fly, breaking the door asunder. Havelok saw that, and withdrawing the big bar, threw open the door. "Come fast," he cried, "and cursed be he who flees hence!"

Then one of the men drew his sword and with two other robbers tried to kill Havelok, but he lifted up the bar and at one blow slew the three, so that their brains lay spilled in the starlight. Four more he killed ere the others took counsel, and divided into two parties to rush on him like dogs on a baited bear. They were strong and quick, and soon they had wounded him in more than twenty places. Seeing how the blood ran from his sides like water from a well, Havelok was maddened, and with the bar he felled twenty to the ground. Then a great din arose. Standing far from him, no more daring to be near to him than to a boar or a lion, they hurled at him stones and spears. Hugh Raven heard that uproar and feared lest men wrought harm to Havelok because of his wife. Catching up an oar and a long knife, he ran thither like a deer, and saw how these madmen stood around Havelok, beating him just as a smith hammers on his anvil.

"Oh, woe," he cried, "that ever I was born to see this grief! Robert! William! Where are you? Get each of you a cudgel and let not one of these dogs flee before our lord is avenged. Follow fast after me. I have a stout oar. Cursed be he who hits not hard!"

"Yes, yes," answered Robert, "we have the moonlight to see by." He gripped a staff big enough to carry an ox, and William Wendut took a bar bigger than his thigh, and Bernard had his ax. Wildly they leaped forth to the fight and dreadful wounds they gave the rogues; ribs were broken, arms, knees, legs; skulls were cracked, backs beaten to a pulp. Of the sixty thieves, not one was left alive. They got what they deserved. When the morrow dawned, they lay heaped on one another, like dead dogs. Some were slung into ditches, some dragged there by the hair.

Tidings came quickly to Ubbe, and he leaped on a steed

and with his knights rode forth to the town. He called Bernard out of his house, and he came all tattered and torn, with his clothes well-nigh gone.

"O lord," he cried, "at moonrise tonight more than sixty robbers came here to rob and kill me. Quickly they broke the door and would have bound me, had not Havelok and the good men started up and, seizing some a bar, some a stone, driven them out like dogs from a mill house. A thousand men is Havelok worth alone! Save for him I should be dead now. But great is his hurt, for they gave him such wounds that the least might fell a horse, and much I fear he will die. In the side, in the arm, in the thigh, in more than twenty places has he wounds, though when he first felt the pain there was never a boar that fought as he did. No skull was too hard for him to smash. As a hound follows a hare, he followed the thieves, and not a cursed one did he spare till each one lay stone still. Had he not done so, they would have cut him to pieces."

"Speak you the truth, Bernard?" asked Ubbe; and all the townsmen who stood about swore that he did. "The thieves would have taken all his goods," they said, "had not this man of a far land slain them. Who else could stand alone in the night against seventy stalwart men? They were led by Giffin Galle."

"Fetch Havelok quickly," answered Ubbe, "that I may see his wounds. If he can be healed, I myself will dub him knight; and did they live, he should hang those vile men, Cain's kin and Eve's. I care not a sloe for them."

Now Havelok was brought before Ubbe, who had great sorrow for his wounds, till a leech saw them and said they could be healed. Then Ubbe ceased all grief. "Come forth now with me," he said, "you and Goldborough and your three servants. I will be your warrant. No friends of those you have killed are to lie in wait to slay you, for I will lend you a room in my high tower until you are whole again. Nothing shall be between us save a wall of fir wood, and speaking loud or low, you shall hear and see me when you will. And no knight or clerk of mine shall bring shame to your wife more than to mine."

With rejoicing, Ubbe brought them soon to his city, Havelok and his wife and his three men. And it was about the middle of the first night there, that Ubbe saw a great light as of day in that tower, and he wondered what it might be, whether they were drinking together or what; at that hour he thought none would be up save rascals and thieves. He went and peered in through a crack, and saw the five lying fast asleep, and still as stone. From Havelok's mouth came the sunny gleam, and to see it Ubbe called more than a hundred of his knights and men. The brightness was as if a hundred candles burned there. On his left side Havelok lay with his bright bride in his arms, both bare to the breast; never was a fairer pair. A good sport did it seem to the knights to look upon them, and on Havelok's naked shoulder they were aware of a cross, clear and brighter than gold in the light. Sparkling it shone, like a carbuncle, giving enough light to choose a penny by. Then both high and low knew that it was a king's mark, and that they gazed on Birkabeyn's own son. "He is Birkabeyn's heir," they said; "never in Denmark was brother so like to brother as this fair man is like the king."

They fell at his feet, and there was not one who did not weep for joy. They were as glad as if he had been drawn back from the grave. They kissed his feet, his toes, his toenails, so that he woke; and at first he was angered, for he thought they would kill him.

Then said Ubbe, "Lord, be not afraid. Good is it for me, dear son, that I see you. Homage I offer you, for in very truth ought I to be your man. You are come of Birkabeyn, and though you are young, you shall be King of Denmark; tomorrow you shall take homage of earl, baron, warrior, and thane.

With rejoicing shall you be made a knight; you are so brave a man."

Very blithe was Havelok for that, and he thanked God heartily. When dawn came and the night shadows were gone, Ubbe summoned all his lords to come before him, if they loved their own lives and those of their wives and children. There was not a man who did not go to learn what the justice wished, and presently he said to them, "Listen all of you, freemen and serfs, to a thing I will tell you. You know full well how on his death day all this land was Birkabeyn's, and how he, by your counsel, gave over his three children, Havelok and his two daughters, and all his possessions into Godard's charge. On the book and the Mass-gear the earl swore to care for them, but he let his oath go altogether. He killed the maidens, and would have slain the boy had not God saved him. Godard would not kill the boy with his own hand but made Grim swear to drown him. But Grim saw Havelok's beauty and knew him for the right heir, and quickly fled from Denmark into England. There for many winters has Havelok been fed and fostered. Now look where he stands! In all this world he has no peer. Be right glad of him, and come hither quickly to do homage to your lord. I myself will do it first, and all of you afterward."

On his knees then Ubbe knelt down fairly, and everyone saw how he became Havelok's man. After him came every baron in that town, and the warriors, the thanes, the knights, and swains, so that at the day's end there was not one man of whom Havelok had not fealty. Ubbe summoned then by writs all governors of castles, boroughs, towns, and when all had sworn homage to Havelok, with a bright sword Ubbe dubbed him a knight and nobly made him king. Great was the joy then; there were spear fights and buckler play, wrestlings, stone puttings, harping and piping, gambling, romance reading in the book, and the singing of old tales, and gleemen strik-

ing on the tabor. There men could see the bulls and boars
baited by lively dogs, and watch also every other sport. There
was great gift-giving of clothes and great plenty of food. The
feast lasted forty days. The king knighted Robert and William
Wendut and Hugh Raven and made all three barons, and gave
them lands and other possessions so rich that each one kept
twenty knights day and night in his retinue.

When the feast was done, the king kept a thousand armed
knights and five thousand men. I will not lengthen the story,
but when Havelok had all the land in his power, he vowed,
and his men with him, that they would never cease fighting
until they had revenge on Godard. They did not delay setting
forth, and Robert, who was master of the army, was first to
come upon Godard. With a large company he was off on a
hunt. Robert cried out, saying Godard should come with him
to the king. But with his fist Godard struck him a mighty
blow in the teeth before Robert seized his long knife and
smote him through the arm. When Godard's men saw that,
and ten of them were shortly killed by Robert's brothers, they
started to flee. But Godard cried, "O my knights, what do you
do? I have fed you, and will feed you still. Help me in this
need. Shame will be upon you, if you let Havelok do his
will."

Then his men went forward again and killed one of the
king's knights and a peasant, and wounded ten others. But
quickly the king's men killed them all save only Godard; him
they bound fast, though he roared like a bull caught in a hole
and baited with dogs; they threw him upon a scurvy mare
with his face to the tail. So was he brought to Havelok, to
whom he had brought hunger, cold, and misery before the boy
was twelve. As "Old sin makes new shame," so did he pay
dearly for the wrongs he had wrought. The king called Ubbe
and all his lords and thanes together, rich and poor, high and
low, and bade them speak Godard's doom. Sitting around the

wall, they gave a true judgment. "We doom," they said, "that Godard be flayed alive, drawn to the gallows at the tail of this wretched horse, and hanged. And it shall be written there: 'This is that wicked man who thought to take from the king his land, and who killed the king's sisters.' The doom is doomed; we say no more."

With this judgment given, Godard was shriven by the priest, then quickly a man came with a knife of ground steel, and from top to toe he flayed Godard, who shrieked so loudly for mercy, men could hear him a mile away. The old horse was brought, and with a sail rope Godard was bound to her tail and drawn to the gallows, not by the road, but over the fallow field. By the neck he was hanged. Curses on anyone's pity. The man was false.

Now, after Godard was dead, the king took quickly all his land, houses and goods, and gave them to Ubbe, saying, "Here I give you power in all your land, in all your fees." [2]

When in after years Havelok returned to England he swore that at Grimsby, because of the good Grim had done while poor and in evil state, he would make a priory of black monks to serve Christ till doomsday. But when Godrich of Cornwall heard that Havelok as King of Denmark had come with a strong army to England, and that Goldborough, the fair and rightful heir, was at Grimsby, he was most sorrowful. Quickly he called forth, on pain of their lives, every man who could ride a horse or bear a weapon, be it hand ax, scythe, spike, spear, dagger, or long knife, and ordered them to come to Lincoln on the seventeenth of March. If there were any rebel who would not come, he swore by Christ and St. John to make him and his children thralls. Because the English

[2] The English poem here omits a part of the story told in the *Lai d'Haveloc*. After four years as King of Denmark, Havelok and his wife with a great fleet go to England to regain her heritage.

feared him as a hack fears the spur, they came all together on the day set them.

"Listen," he said, "for I have not gathered you for sport. At Grimsby strangers have come and taken the priory; they burn the churches, bind the priests, and strangle both monks and nuns. What will ye counsel? If they rule thus for long, they will gain mastery of us all, to kill or enslave us. Let us go forth quickly. Help yourselves and me by killing these dogs. Nevermore shall I be glad or ever receive the sacrament or be shriven till he is driven from the land. Follow fast after me, for I will be the first to strike with the drawn sword. Cursed be he who stands not fast beside me."

"Yea, yea," cried Earl Gunter; and "Yea," said Earl Reyner of Chester, and so did all who stood there. Then could one see the bright coats of mail cast on, and the high helmets, and so did they hasten to arms that in as short a while as one could count a pound, they had leaped on their steeds and were faring toward Grimsby.

Now Havelok had found out each thing concerning their start, and with all his army he came against them. He struck off the head of the first knight he met, Robert killed another, William Wendut cut off the arm of a third, and Hugh Raven cut an earl's head in two. Ubbe came upon Godrich, and grimly they fought till both fell headlong to the earth. Then they drew their swords and, drenched in sweat, they fought so madly that the least blow would have shattered a flint. From morning the fight lasted till at sunset Godrich gave Ubbe such a cruel wound in the side that he would have fallen, had not Hugh Raven borne him away. Before he was rescued, a thousand knights had been slain on each side, and of the common soldiers such slaughter was made that there was not a pool on the field but was so full of blood that streams of it ran down to the hollow. And now Godrich, like a lion, did so rush on the Danes, they fell like grass before the scythe. When Havelok saw how his people died, he forced on his steed. "Godrich," he cried, "why act you so? You know full well that Athelwold made you swear on the Mass book and the chalice you would give England to his daughter when she came of age. Yield it now without fighting. I will forgive you all injury, for I see how great is your strength and your valor."

"That will I never do! I will kill you and hang her high," said Godrich, and he gripped his sword and struck Havelok so mightily that he cleft Havelok's shield in two. When that shame was done him before his army, Havelok felled Godrich to the earth. But not for long did Godrich lie at his feet; he started up and smote Havelok, so that he tore from his coat of mail more rings than I can tell, and the blood streamed down to his feet. Then wildly went Havelok at his foe, and heaving high his sword, he struck off Godrich's hand. When he had so shamed the traitor, he bound him in fetters of steel and sent him to the queen, whom it well behooved to hate him. But, since Godrich was a knight, Havelok commanded that no one should beat or do him shame, until the knights had righteously doomed him.

Now the English, when they knew that Goldborough was England's rightful heir and that Havelok had wedded her cried together for his mercy and offered him homage. But Havelok commanded that first the queen should be brought, to see if they would know and accept her. Six earls fared quickly after her and brought her there, that lady, peerless in courtesy beneath the moon. Sorely weeping, the English fell on their knees before her. "Christ's mercy and yours," they cried; "much wrong have we done, being faithless to you. For England ought to be yours and we your men. Not one of us, young or old, but knows that Athelwold was king here and you his heir."

"Since ye grant it now," said Havelok, "I will that ye sit down and, as Godrich has wrought, look that ye judge him righteously, for justice spares neither clerk nor knight. Then if you wish and advise it, according to the law of the land, I will take your homage."

So they sat them down, for none dared hinder the trial, and they condemned Godrich to be bound endwise on a filthy ass, with his head to the tail, and in shameful dress, thus to be led through Lincoln, to a green that is there yet, I think, and to be bound to a stake with a great fire about, until he was burned to dust. To warn other wretches, they also judged that, for his sin, his children should lose forever the heritage that was his.

Now was this doom quickly fulfilled and Goldborough rejoiced and gave thanks to God that the wicked traitor was burned who planned to destroy her. And Havelok then took homage of all the English and made them swear to keep good faith to him, against any man alive.

When he had surety of them all, he called to him the Earl of Chester, a young unmarried knight, and said, "Sir Earl, if you will take my counsel, well will I do by you. By St. David, I will give you for a wife the fairest thing alive, Gunnild of Grimsby, daughter of Grim who fled with me from Denmark to save me from death. I advise that you marry her, for she is fair and noble, and I will show that she is dear to me; for always while I live, for her sake, you, too, will be dear to me."

The earl would do nothing against the king, and on that same day he wedded her. Never came two together in bed who were to live better lives. They begot five fine sons. When Gunnild had been brought to Chester, Havelok did not forget Bertram, the earl's cook.

"Friend, you shall have rich reward," he cried, "for the good deeds you did to me in my need. For when I had only my coat, and had no bread, no food, nor anything of my own, you fed and clothed me well. You shall have for that now the earldom of Cornwall and all Godrich's land in town and field; moreover, I desire that you should wed Grim's daughter, Levive the lovely. Courteous she seems, and fair as a flower; the hue of her cheek is like the new rose on the bush when fairly it lies in the warm, bright sun."

Then Havelok girded Bertram with the sword of the earldom, and with his own hand made him a knight, and giving him arms, wedded him soon to that sweet maid. They lived happily ever after and begot many children. Then Havelok feasted well his Danes and gave them rich lands and goods, and soon after with his army he went to London for his crowning, so that English and Danes there, high and low, saw how proudly he bore it. The feast of his crowning lasted with great joy for forty days or more, and then, when he saw the Danes were ready to fare into Denmark, he gave them leave to go and committed them to St. John. He commanded that Ubbe, his justice, should so rule Denmark that no complaint should come to him.

When they were gone, Havelok remained in England and for sixty years he was king there with Goldborough for his Queen. So great was their love that all the world spoke of the pair. Neither one had joy away from the other, and never were they angry, for always was their love new. Fifteen sons and daughters they had, of whom God willed that each one should be a king or queen. "Good is it for him who begets a good child."

Now have you heard the tale all through of Havelok and Goldborough, how they were born, how they were wronged in their youth, and how they were avenged. Every bit have I told you. For that I would beseech each one of you who have heard it, that with good will, you say a Paternoster for him who has made the rime and who, for its sake, has waked many a night. May Christ at the end bring his soul to God!

SIR ORFEO

———

Classical Greek stories not infrequently passed on to the Middle Ages by way of such famous Roman poets as Virgil and Ovid or the sixth-century philosopher Boethius. All three authors related the legend of Orpheus of Thrace who, driven by unendurable woe, dared in dark Hades to seek his dead bride, Eurydice. There, his ineffably sweet singing and harping made tortures cease "And made Hell grant what Love did seek." Eurydice was restored to him, but he, unable to obey the command not to look back upon her, even at the very verge of light and life, lost her forever. The Latin writers made of this tragic Greek legend an exalted tribute to the godlike power of music and an unforgettable example of that unrestraint by which so often in human life man loses what he most desires.

The Middle Ages, in taking over classical stories, inevitably

refashioned them, reclothed them in the rich habiliments of
medieval knights and ladies or the humble garb of poor folk,
gave them contemporary medieval settings, customs, concepts.
Knowing little and caring less for the historical realities of antiquity but fascinated by surviving legends of ancient Troy or
Thebes, by such mythic tales as that of Orpheus, son of a
muse, medieval poets, from the twelfth century on, modernized to their own taste and culture the ancient classical stories
and combined them with traditions unknown to the Greek or
Roman world. Epic gave place to romance, learned Latin to
vernacular French. Before 1200 French poets were referring
to a *Lai d'Orphey* and once even described it as sung by an
Irish harper. The French word *lai,* related to the Irish *laid,* a
song, came in time to mean a short, highly romantic narrative
of which Breton minstrels made such use that their Breton lays
became famous. A gifted courtly poet, Marie de France (ca.
1170), in the preface to her own twelve narrative lays, declares with delightful mendacity that she will tell true stories
of which the Bretons had made lays. In her own lays, as in
most of those still known to us, Celtic fairy lore, of a type
familiar in Irish, Welsh and Breton tales, is a chief ingredient;
truth, in the sense of factual experience, is the least. In the
early fourteenth century, an English poet, writing in a south-
western dialect, and musing over the Breton lays known to
him, spoke of their taste for fairy lore, for wondrous happen-
ings of long ago, for gallant deeds, and, above all, for love
stories. This preface, attached to both *Sir Orfeo* and to an
English version of Marie de France's *Lai de Fresne,* is a happy
description of the type.

The French *Lai d'Orphey* had probably, even in the twelfth
century, begun to fuse classical and Celtic elements. In the
English poem the fusion is complete. The dim, dark Hades of
Greek myth has become the radiant Otherworld of the Celts,
here approached through a rocky subterranean entrance. The
land within is bright as summer sun, its royal palace of shining magnificence. The only reminiscence of the Greek land of
the dead is in the human forms Orfeo sees, still in the atti-

tudes in which death took them. Orfeo keeps the superlative
gift of music of his Greek prototype, but he presents himself
as a poor minstrel to the resplendent King and Queen of
Fairyland. These personages have lost entirely the awesome-
ness of the classical Rulers of the Dead. The fairy host that
appeared to Heurodis in her dream beneath the fairy tree, the
fairy hunt and dance seen by Orfeo, were Celtic additions to a
story of which the very structure had been affected by contact
with an ancient Irish legend, the *Wooing of Etain*. It cannot
be by chance that both tell of the visit of an Otherworld king
to a mortal woman, of his vow to abduct her after a brief delay, of his doing so despite the armed guards her royal husband had set to guard her, of the latter's sight of her among
fairy women, and his going himself to the fairy Otherworld.
Both stories make use of the motif of the Rash Promise, a
favorite in Celtic fiction. The wholly happy ending in *Sir
Orfeo* is oddly anticipated in a story told by a British author,
Walter Map (ca. 1182), about a Breton knight who, grieving
for his dead wife, saw her in a company of fairy women, carried her off, and lived happily with her and their children for
many years.

But neither classical nor Celtic legends account entirely for
the English *Sir Orfeo* which was composed in the early fourteenth century and copied soon after in that notable collection of Middle English verse, the Auchinleck manuscript
(1330-40), now in Edinburgh. *Sir Orfeo* was thoroughly infused with English interests and feeling. In the Auchinleck
version Thrace is patriotically identified with Winchester, and
Orfeo, become a good English king, bids his people summon a
Parliament after his death, to choose his successor. He goes
from his palace to spend desolate years on a rough English
heath; when a hawking party rides by, he sees familiar English
birds, mallards, cormorants, herons, fly before the swooping
falcons; when he confronts the fairy king, with English blunt-
ness he bids him keep his word. The final recognition scene is
filled with English heartiness, with the laughter, the music-
making of the feast, the swift, warm welcome given to the

ragged old harper for Orfeo's sake, the joy of the steward who knocks the table over in his excitement, the joy of all the shouting lords as they recognize their king. They are true men all. The English poet may lack the suave elegance of Marie de France, the polished refinements of her French couplets, but in his own sometimes roughened couplets, there is distinctive warmth and charm. His is no "untutored simplicity," no unawareness of the arts of contrast and suspense. He may not know much about classical mythology, may mistake the goddess Juno for a king, but in the telling of his tale he has the art of swift and vividly concrete narration; he gives to his characters simple and natural speech and gesture. They owe little to foreign antecedents. The poem has no trace in it of those courtly love concepts which for so long had influenced nearly all expression of romantic emotion. The husband here, looking upon his anguished wife, upon her who had always been so lovely and so still, speaks to her with a perfect tenderness. It is enhanced, not lessened, by a reminiscence of the grave, beautiful words of the Biblical Ruth (I, 16) when Orfeo vows to his wife: "Whither you go, I go with you; whither I go, you too will come."

L.H.L.

THE STORY*

Often we read lays for the harp that were written to tell us of wondrous things. Some were about joy, some of woe, some of treachery and guile, of jests and ribaldry, some of fairy things, but mostly they told of love. In Brittany they are written, where these stories were first known; when the Bretons heard of an adventure of old times, they took their harps and gladly made a lay of it and gave it a name. I can tell some

* Modernized by L. H. Loomis.

but not all of them. Right now I will tell you, my lords, of
Sir Orfeo. He was a King of England, a stalwart, hardy man,
generous and courteous. His father was born of King Pluto,
his mother of Juno, and once they were thought to be gods.
Of all things, Orfeo loved harping most and honored every
good harper. But nowhere was any harper better than he himself. Hearing him, feeling the joy and melody of his playing,
a man might think he was in Paradise.

This King lived in Thrace, a mighty place now called
Winchester. He had a noble Queen named Heurodis, the fairest of ladies and full of love and gentleness. In the month of
May, with its warm and happy days, when winter showers are
ended, when fields bloom and trees blossom, Queen Heurodis
and two of her maidens went forth one morning to an orchard
to see the flowers and hear the singing birds. They sat down
together under a grafted tree and there on the grass the
Queen fell asleep. Not daring to waken her, the maidens let
her sleep until the afternoon. But when she wakened, she
burst into tears, screamed and writhed about, scratching her
face so that it bled, and tearing her rich dress to pieces. She
was altogether out of her wits. Not daring to stay, the maidens ran to the palace for help. Knights and ladies, and more
than sixty maidens, ran to the orchard, took up the Queen,
and quickly carried her to bed.

When Orfeo heard of all this, he was never more sad. With
ten knights he came to her chamber, and as he looked at her,
was filled with pity.

"Dear life," he said, "what troubles you? Why do you shriek,
you who have always been so still? Your white body is rent
by your nails. Your once rosy face is pale as death, your small
fingers have blood upon them. Your lovesome eyes glare at
me as if I were your foe. I beg you, stop this piteous outcry
and tell me what thing has happened to you and what can
help you now?"

At last she lay still, and weeping, said, "Alas, my lord, Sir Orfeo, since our first days together, never once have we been separate; as my life I have loved you, and so have you loved me. But now we must be apart. Do you your best alone, for I must go."

"Alas!" said he, "then I am lost. Where will you go, and to whom? Whither you go, I go with you; whither I go, you too will come."

"No, no, my lord, it is not so. The truth is this: When I slept this morning in our orchard, two fair knights, fully armed, bade me come in haste to speak with their lord and king. I said I would not and I could not. They rode fast away but quickly their king came with more than a hundred knights and a hundred damsels, all riding on snow-white steeds and in clothes milk-white. Never before have I seen creatures so fair. The King's crown was not of silver or of red gold: it was a precious jewel, shining like the sun. He made me, whether I would or not, ride beside him on a palfrey. He brought me to his palace, showed me castles and towers, rivers, forests, parks in flower, splendid horses. He brought me again to our own orchard and there he said, "Lady, tomorrow be here beneath this very tree; you are to go and live with us forever more. If you try to prevent us, it matters not where you are, you will be brought away though your limbs be torn apart; nothing can save you."

King Orfeo cried out: "Alas, alas, and woe is me! Sooner would I lose my life than thus to lose my wife, my Queen." He asked for counsel from every man, but there was no one who could help him.

On the morrow at midmorning Orfeo took his weapons, and with ten hundred knights, each one armed and grim, went with the Queen to the tree. They made a shield-wall and said they would die there, every man, ere the Queen be taken. Yet she was snatched away, taken magically, and no one knew

where she had gone. What crying, what weeping and woe was
then! The King went to his chamber and swooned so often
upon the stone floor as he made his laments, that very nearly
he lost his life.

He called together his barons, earls and lords of renown,
and to them he said, "Lords, I here ordain before you my high
steward to keep my kingdom hereafter. In my place he shall
stand. I have lost my Queen, fairest of all ladies, and will
never again look upon a woman. To the wilderness I will go,
to live with wild beasts in forests old. When you learn that I
am dead, call then a Parliament and choose a new king. Do
the best you can with all that is mine."

The hall was filled with wailing and weeping. Young and
old, for tears, could hardly speak a word. On their knees they
prayed him not to go, but he bade them cease, saying, "This
thing must be."

With that he forsook his kingdom. Putting on a pilgrim's
mantle, without kirtle or hood, and taking with him nothing
but his harp, he went forth, barefooted and all alone, from the
castle gate. Sad cries and woe enough there was when he, who
had been crowned a king, so wretchedly left the town. Into the
wilderness, through wood and heath he went, finding nothing
but misery there. He who wore soft furs and slept on a
purple bed, lies now on the hard ground and covers himself
with leaves and grass. He who possessed castle and towers,
rivers, forests, flowering fields, now, as the frost and snow begin, must make his bed of moss. He before whom noble
knights and ladies knelt, sees before him only wild snakes
gliding by. In place of the plenty he once had, of meat and
drink and all delicious things, he must now dig and delve ere
he find roots enough for food. On wild fruit and poor berries
he lived in summertime; in winter, roots, grasses and bark of
trees were all that he could find. Through such hardships his
body wasted away and was scarred. Lord, who can tell what

this King suffered for ten years and more? His beard, black and rough, grew to his waist. His harp, his one solace, he hid within a hollow tree. But straightway, when the day was bright, he took it out and harped upon it for his own content. As its sound went through the woods, for joy the wild beasts gathered round, the birds clung to the briar bushes as they listened to the music of his harping. But when he stopped, no creature stayed with him.

Sometimes, in summer's noontime heat, Orfeo saw the King of Faërie and his company passing on a hunt; faintly he heard their cries, their horn-blowing, their barking dogs, but never did he see them catch a beast, nor ever know whither they went. Again he saw a great host, ten hundred well-armed knights, fierce and brave of look, with swords in hand, and banners floating wide, but where they would go, he never knew. At other times he saw knights and ladies, richly garbed, dance together with cunning skill while tabors, trumpets, and every kind of music was played beside them.

On one special day he saw sixty ladies together, not a man among them, and all riding forth as gay, as gentle, as birds on a branch. Each one bore a falcon on her wrist, for they were going hawking along the river. Game birds were there in plenty, mallards, herons, cormorants. The waterbirds rose, the falcons swooped, and each one slew his prey. Orfeo laughed to see it. "By my word," he said, "there is good sport. I will go thither, for this sport I too was wont to see."

He rose, and as he drew near he saw his own Queen, the Lady Heurodis. Eagerly he looked at her and she at him, but not one word did either speak. When she saw how miserable he was who had been so rich, so exalted, her tears flowed. The other ladies, seeing this, made her ride on. With him she could not stay.

"Alas, and woe is me," he said. "Why does death not slay me now? Why can I not die? Too long has my life lasted when I dare not speak one word to my own wife, nor she to me. Why does my heart not break? But whatsoever happens now, wherever these ladies ride, the selfsame way I too will go. For life, for death, I care not now."

Quickly then he put on his pilgrim's cloak, and with his harp on his back he hastened on; no stump or stone could stop him. In at a rock where the ladies rode, he waited not a moment to follow after.

After he had gone three miles or more, he came to a fair land all bright as on a summer's day, and green and flat and smooth. No hill, no dale was there. A royal castle, wondrously high, stood in the midst, its outer wall as clear and bright as crystal. It had a hundred towers with strong battlements, and from the moat rose buttresses richly arched with red gold. All kinds of animals were carved on the vaulting, and the spacious halls were built of precious stones; the meanest pillar was of burnished gold. Always that land was bright, for when it should be dark at night the jeweled stones shone as brightly as the sun at noonday. No one could tell or think how wonderful it was; to Orfeo it seemed the very court of Paradise.

The ladies alighted at this castle, and Orfeo wanted to follow them in. He knocked at the gate and the porter asked him what he wished. "Lo, I am a minstrel," he said. "If it be your lord's will, I will cheer him with my playing." The porter at once undid the gate and brought him within the castle.

Orfeo looked about him and saw lying there within the wall people supposed to be dead, but they were not so. They had all been brought there. Some stood without their heads; some had no arms; some, wounds right through the body; some lay, fast-bound; some full-armed, on their horses sat; some had been strangled as they ate, or drowned in water or shriveled up by fire; wives lay in childbed, dead or mad. A great many lay just as they do when they rest at noon. As each one was when the fairies took him from this world, so he was when they brought him here. Orfeo saw his love, his wife, beneath a tree. He knew her by her clothes.

When he had seen all this, he knelt down before the King. "My lord," he said, "if it be your will, you should hear my minstrelsy."

"What man are you," answered the King, "who come hither though neither I nor anyone else ever sent for you. Since my reign first began, never, never have I found anyone so foolish as to dare to come here unless I sent for him."

"My lord, believe me," he replied, "I am only a poor minstrel and many a lord's house I seek, for that is our custom. Even when we are unwelcome, we must proffer our music-making."

He sat down before the King, and taking his sweet-sounding harp in hand and tuning it with skill, he played such blissful notes as brought everyone in the palace to hear him and to lie down at his feet. The King, listening, sat very still. Joy he had in this music, and so had his stately Queen. When Orfeo's harping ceased, the King spoke to him at once. "Minstrel, your music has pleased me much. Ask whatever you will of me and I will give it to you generously."

"Sir," replied Orfeo, "give me, I beseech you, that lady so fair of face who sleeps beneath the grafted tree."

"No, no," cried out the King, "that cannot be. A sorry couple you two would be—you so lean and rough and black, and she so lovesome, without one flaw. A hateful thing it would be to see her in your company."

"O gentle King," said Orfeo then, "a yet more hateful thing it were to hear you speak a lie. Just now you said that what I asked, that should I have. Of necessity, you must keep your word."

"Since it is so," returned the King," take her by the hand and go. And may you have joy of her."

Orfeo knelt and said his great thanks. His wife's hand he took and they went quickly away from that land by the same road that he had come. Then at last to Winchester they came, to his very own city, but no one knew that it was he. For fear of being known, he dared go no further than the town's end and there, as though he were a poor minstrel, he found refuge with a beggar for himself and his wife. He asked for tidings of the land and who held it in his hand. The poor beggar told him every bit, how ten years ago the Queen was stolen away by fairies, and how the King went into exile, no one knew where, and how the steward held the land, and many other things besides.

On the morrow about noontide, making his wife stay where she was, Orfeo borrowed clothes from the beggar, hung his harp on his back, and went into the city so that he might be seen. Earls and barons, ladies and burgesses looked at him amazedly. "How long is the hair that hangs on him; his beard reaches to his knee! He is withered like a tree."

In the street as he went along he met his steward and loudly cried to him: "Sir Steward, have pity upon me. I am a harper come from heathendom. Help me now in this distress."

The steward answered: "Come, come with me. Of whatever I have, you shall have part. Every good harper is welcome to me for the sake of my lord, Sir Orfeo."

In the castle the steward sat at table and many lords sat beside him. Trumpeters and drummers, harpers and fiddlers, made much music. Listening, Orfeo sat silent in the hall. When at last they all were still, he took his harp, tuned it, and then he harped the most blissful notes that ever man heard. Every one loved his music.

The steward looked and recognized the harp at once. "Minstrel," he cried, "where did you get this harp and how? I pray you tell me without delay."

"Lord, in an unknown land once I passed through a wilderness, and there in a dale I found a man torn to pieces by lions and eaten by sharp-toothed wolves. Beside him I found this harp. It was ten years ago."

"O woe is me," wept the steward. "That was my lord, Sir Orfeo. What shall I do, wretch that I am, now that I have lost such a lord as he? Alas, that ever I was born, alas for him, for his hard lot and for his wretched death!" Swooning, he fell to the ground. His barons lifted him and told him how it always is—there is no remedy for death.

King Orfeo knew then that his steward was a true man and loved him as he ought to do. Standing up, the King thus spoke: "Steward, hearken now to this. If I were in truth King Orfeo and had suffered much in the wilderness, and had won my Queen away out of the fairy land, and had left her at the town's end with a beggar, and had come here poorly clad to test your good will, and found you true, never should you regret it. With all certainty, you should be King after me. But if you had heard blithely of my death, you would at once have lost your office."

Then all who sat therein knew that it was King Orfeo. The steward knocked over the table and fell down at his feet. So, too, did every lord, and with one voice they shouted: "You are our lord, sire, and our King." Rejoicing, they took him to a chamber, bathed him and shaved his beard and attired him as a king for all to see. With a great procession and all kinds of minstrelsy, they brought the Queen to town. Lord, what music-making there was! And how they wept for joy to see the two all safe and sound! King Orfeo was newly crowned with his Queen, Heurodis. Long afterwards they lived, and then the steward was made King.

Breton harpers heard this tale of wonder and made of it a pleasant lay. They named it with the King's name and it is called *Orfeo*. Good is the lay and its music sweet.

Thus did Sir Orfeo come out from his sorrow. God grant us all that we fare as well.

SIR GAWAIN AND

THE GREEN KNIGHT

———

FOREWORD

This romance is the gem, the "pearl among peas," to borrow from of its own apt imagery, of all English romances. Save for Chaucer's *Troilus and Criseyde*, likewise written in the last quarter of the fourteenth century, *Sir Gawain and the Green Knight* is unsurpassed.

For Chaucer, the Gawain poet's London-born and far more cosmopolitan contemporary, tales of "th'olde dayes of the Kyng Arthour" were already a bit outdated, already subjects for a little derisive humor. But it was not so for that "Master Anonymous," as the Gawain poet has been called, who chose in his own romance to celebrate one of the oldest of Arthurian heroes, and to make him, for times still to come, unforgettable and significant. Though thus late-born, this Arthurian poem has about it the golden glow of a poet's perfect identification with his material.

Of this unknown "Master" we know only what can be learned from a single manuscript, now in the British Museum, which contains four poems, all now attributed to the same writer: the *Pearl*, in the form of an exquisitely fashioned elegy; two forceful homilies; and *Sir Gawain*. They reveal a poetic personality and power of the first rank, but no record, no allusion, has yet established his name or status. That he lived in northwestern England is shown by his dialect and by his easy use of the ancient alliterative type of verse, newly revived in that region in the mid-fourteenth century. Provincial by London standards as were both his dialect and his verse form, he used them in masterly fashion, and his poems betray wide reading in Latin, French and English writings. The *Pearl* and *Sir Gawain* notably reveal his familiarity with courtly life. Not even Chaucer's *Troilus* is more courtly than is *Sir Gawain*.

Much of the glamour of medieval romances resided and still resides in their portrayal of the splendors of castle life, the gorgeous festivities, the sumptuous feasts, the great hunts, with which, in the bright intervals between warfare, wealthy aristocrats amused themselves. From such descriptions came much of that beauty which Shakespeare himself found in the "chronicles of ladies dead and lovely knights." The *Gawain* poet writes with delight of such things, of the stately royal feast at Camelot, of the more riotous revelries at Sir Bercilak's shining many-towered castle. The poet's sharply varied hunting scenes sprang from a knowledge expert and precise of game, of terrain, of usages. As a connoisseur of luxuries—from delicate, costly trifles of embroidery and jewel-craft, to rich fabrics and splendid armor—the poet lingers over their description as if, one by one, he were handling them with a personal pleasure. When he reports the debonair conversations of Gawain with the lovely lady sent to tempt him, the lightsome play of words, despite their deeper undertones, suggests the adroit advances, the retreats, of a courtly dance. The initial horror of the Green Knight's decapitation at Arthur's feast is gallantly relieved by Arthur's own likening of it to the craft, the diversion, of the interludes which were often played before a courtly audience.

But it is not only in the presentation of medieval "Merry England" that the poem excels, but also in the surprising realism of its setting, and in the new level of meaning with which it is infused. In general, medieval poets celebrated only the joys of spring and summer; winter was too harsh a time to sing about. But the *Gawain* poet chose to evoke for his story midwinter in northern England with its bitter rigors, its howling winds, its freezing rains and snows. Not until Keats wrote the *Eve of Saint Agnes* was the sense of cold to be more intensely realized by any poet. Twice in *Sir Gawain* a dramatic contrast is made between the warm, indoor joys of human life and fellowship, and the stark loneliness, the icy desolation without. It needs no sense of the past, no modern mythologizing, to recognize how powerfully both the cruel winter season and the wild, rugged landscape become factors in the spiritual drama of Gawain's testing and thus enhance the sense of its reality. Perfect as he had been in the tests of herohood and courtesy and loyalty up to the moment when he kept the lady's girdle, it is when he prepares to leave Bercilak's castle to face the inhuman, incredible head-cutting test that Gawain's breaking point, his final wrong choice, is most vividly circumstanced by the icy dawn, the blizzard snows. Realistically, psychologically, the moment and the choice are perfectly conceived; the young hero gains in human credibility what he loses in ideal perfection.

The three plot themes of the romance were not inventions of the poet; all were old until his genius minted them anew. The introductory story of a Challenger who proposes a head-cutting contest as a supreme test of courage derived ultimately from *Bricriu's Feast,* an Irish narrative of the ninth century, full of mythic, pagan features. By the twelfth century this fantastic but striking episode had been absorbed into courtly French Arthurian romance, but no version, then or later, preserved as many of the original elements of the Irish story as did *Sir Gawain,* presumably by way of those oral as well as written versions to which the poem itself refers. The three temptations of Gawain, dramatically paralleled by Bercilak's three hunts and, like them, increasing in exigency, owe something to Welsh traditions but more to a French type of story early associated with Lancelot. In the thirteenth century it was motivated by Morgan la Fay, the most famous enchantress of Arthurian story; she, bent on destroying Lancelot's loyalty to Queen Guinevere, sends her own fair damsel to seduce him. The *Gawain* poet, though perhaps not the first to combine the Challenge and the Temptation stories, in fitting them to the personality of the gay and gallant young Gawain, endowed them with new life and vivid dialogue. He also bound them together by a motif originally belonging to a twelfth-century *fabliau:* that promised Exchange of Winnings, which leads to the denouement of the romance.

The dexterous integration of the three plots resulted in one of the best narratives in medieval fiction. Swiftly told within 2530 lines, the action still pauses now and then for gentle meditations on the glory of ancient Troy and the Trojans who had founded Britain, on the eternal passing of the seasons, on the golden five-pointed pentangle as symbol of the endless interlocking of truth. The poem is seasoned with humor, as when the author begins by saying that the adventure of which he is going to tell was a "tall" story, one of the strangest, even for Arthur's day. Again, palpably amused at the thought of a goddess grown old, he presents Morgan le Fay as a squat, ugly, overdressed old woman, though she is still, as a goddess, possessed of malign powers. Above all, he gives to Gawain, so long before a famous character in Arthurian story, a new and memorable quality of spiritual distinction. The "fine issue" of his story here is not the proof of herohood or of chastity, but of a failure, even in the best of knights, to keep a perfect integrity. In keeping the girdle that might save his life, Gawain broke his promise and betrayed his own good faith. The reproach of Bercilak, however compassionate, still strikes the heart: "A little you failed and loyalty you lacked . . . you loved your life." Romantic, remote as in some ways this fairy fiction for medieval adults may seem today, its significance, as something beautifully created and deeply felt, remains. Its meaning lies plain. When a man loves something more than the sanctity of his own promise, his own honor, no fame, no other virtue, can hide the fault. Overwhelmed with shame and contrition, Gawain returns to Arthur's court, to confess publicly a failure for which he blames only himself. In so doing he gains a new nobility, a deeper fellowship with his kind, a deeper significance for those who read his story today.

L.H.L.

THE STORY*

When the last assault had been delivered, and the siege of Troy was over, and the city was destroyed by fire and laid in ashes, Prince Aeneas sailed away with his noble kindred, and they conquered new realms and made themselves lords of well-nigh all the riches of the Western Isles. Romulus made his way swiftly to Rome, and built that city splendidly, and called it after himself by the name which it still bears. Ticius went to Tuscany and built dwellings there, and Langobard did the like in Lombardy. And far over the French flood[1] Felix Brutus, with joy in his heart, founded a broad realm on the hills of Britain. In that kingdom there have been many wars and tumults and wonders, with shifts of good fortune and of ill.

And when Britain had been founded by this noble Prince,

---

* From *The Story of Sir Gawain and the Green Knight,* translated by M. R. Ridley (1950), by permission of Edmund Ward (Publishers) Ltd.
[1] I.e., the English Channel.

a bold race of men was bred there, lovers of battle, who wrought much strife as the years passed. And more marvels befell in that land than are told of in any other. But of all that dwelt here as Kings of Britain, King Arthur, they tell us, was the noblest. And so I mean to tell of an adventure, which some men hold a marvel; among all the tales about Arthur it is one of the strangest. If you will listen for a short while I will tell you this lay, even as I heard it told in the court, and as it is recorded in writing; and I shall tell the brave tale in our English fashion, with the letters truly linked.[2]

King Arthur lay at Camelot [3] at Christmas, with many of his lords, great knights, all the noble brotherhood of the Round Table, and they kept high revel with carefree merrymaking. There were many tourneys, with gallant jousting of knights, and after the jousting they rode to the court for song and dance; the festival went on full fifteen days, with all the banqueting and jollity that could be devised. There was nothing but the gayest happiness among lords and ladies, in hall and in chamber, at their pleasure, with cheerful noise of merrymaking by day, and dancing at night. All the splendor of the world was gathered in that castle, the noblest knights, servants of Christ, and the loveliest ladies that ever drew breath, and the lord that ruled them the noblest king upon earth. They were all in the prime of their age, the most fortunate band of people under heaven, and it would have been hard to find in any castle on earth so hardy a company.

On New Year's Day there was a great banquet, with double portions, for the whole company. First, Mass was sung in the chapel, with loud chanting of the priests and the rest, and they celebrated the octave of Christmas. When the service came to an end, the King came into the great hall with his knights, and some hurried forward with the New Year's gifts

---

[2] I.e., in alliterative verse.

[3] A legendary city, which Malory took to be Winchester.

held high above their heads, and there was a busy contest for them; those that won a prize were glad, but even the ladies who won nothing laughed at their failure. So they made merry till it was time for dinner, and then they washed and went to their appointed seats, the noblest, as was right, at the high table. In the center of the dais sat the Queen, Guenevere, with her clear gray eyes, loveliest of ladies, splendidly gowned. Over her chair was spread the finest silk, over her head a canopy of rich scarlet from Toulouse, and behind her a tapestry of cloth of gold from Turkestan, adorned with the most precious of costly jewels. No man could say that he ever looked on a fairer lady.

But Arthur would not sit down to eat till all the rest were served. He was so glad in his youth, and boyish in his eagerness, and his young blood ran high and his mind was restless, so that he never could be idle or sit still for long. But there was something else that kept him from his seat, a custom that his high heart had devised, that on a great festival such as this he would eat no meat till he had heard some strange tale of adventure, of the deeds of princes, or feats of arms, some great wonder which he might listen to and believe; or it might be that some strange knight would come, and ask him to name one of his own true knights to joust with him, each staking his life on his skill, and granting the other such advantage as fortune should bring him. This was the King's custom when he held court at each great feast with his noble company. So he waited, standing proudly, full of high spirits, and talking merrily with all.

There the King stood, talking courteously of this thing and that across the high table to where Sir Gawain sat by Guenevere's side. On her other hand, with Arthur's seat between, sat Agravain *à la dure main*. These were both Arthur's nephews and trusty knights. At the end of the table sat Bishop Baldwin, and Ywain, Urien's son, also sat with them. These were

set on the dais and duly served, and the rest of the knights
and ladies sat at the long tables down the hall. Then the first
course was brought in. The trumpeters raised their trumpets,
so that the banners that hung from them flashed in the light,
and blew a blast; then the roll of the kettledrums and the
wild music of the pipes made the hall ring, and many a
heart thrilled to the music. With that there were brought in
all manner of the richest dainties, plenty of fresh meats and
stews of many kinds, so that the servants could hardly find
room to set the silver dishes on the tables before the guests.
Each guest helped himself as he liked, without stint. There
were twelve dishes for each pair of diners, and good ale and
wine that gleamed bright in the goblets.

So the tables were set with the choicest fare, and the trumpets sounded a fresh fanfare as a sign that the feast might
begin. But the notes had hardly died away when there swung
in at the hall door a fearsome warrior, the tallest of all on
earth. From the neck to the waist he was so thick-set and
squarely built, and he was so long in flank and limb, that one
might have thought he was half a giant; but he was in fact a
man, as mighty as any horse could bear in saddle, but yet
shapely in his mightiness, burly in back and breast, but slen-
der in the waist and with clean-run limbs. They were all
amazed at his color, for they saw that he was bright green all
over.

His clothes were green, too. He wore a plain close-fitting
coat of green, and over that a gay green mantle, lined with
close-trimmed white fur. The hood of the mantle was the
same, green outside and lined with white fur, and he had
thrown it back off his hair so that it lay on his shoulders. His
legs were clothed in long green hose, close-fitting, so that you
could see the play of the muscles under them. On his heels
were bright golden spurs, fastened with striped silken straps,
and his feet in the stirrups were shod with long green shoes.

His coat and his mantle and his fine silken saddlecloth were embroidered with birds and butterflies in green and gold, and adorned besides with precious stones like emeralds. The pendants of his horse's breast-piece, and the crupper, and the studs on the bit, and the stirrups, all were of green enamel and encrusted with green stones. He rode a huge green horse; his mane and his tail, green as the rest of him, were curled and combed and plaited with thread-of-gold and adorned with emeralds. His forelock was plaited in an intricate knot, bound with green ribbon, and from it hung golden bells, that rang sweetly as he moved his head. The knight had long waving green locks that hung down over his shoulders, and a great beard that covered his chest, and both locks and beard were cut evenly round at the level of his elbows, so that he looked as though he were wearing a short tunic, buttoned up to the neck.

They all looked at him in wonder, as he sat there on his great horse, flashing and bright as the lightning; and they thought that if it came to fighting there could be no man in the world who could withstand him, so mighty a warrior he seemed. But he wore no armor, no helmet, nor hauberk, nor gorget; he carried no shield, nor lance, nor sword. In one hand he held a bunch of holly, the tree that stays greenest of all when the leaves fall from others in autumn. But in the other hand he grasped his one weapon, and a terrible enough weapon it was, a prodigious battle-ax, with a spike sticking out beyond the head. The spike had been forged of green steel and of gold, and the head was a full ell-yard long, burnished and bright and keen as the keenest razor. The haft was stout wood, with an iron band winding round it, chased in green, and a thong, too, knotted at the head and looped round the haft, ornamented with tassels and buttons of green.

The Green Knight rode up the hall, right to the dais, fearless of danger. He greeted no one as he rode, but looked straight before him over their heads, and the first words he spoke were: "Where is the ruler of this company? It is he that I want to see and to have plain speech with him." And with that he let his eyes rove over the company, and scanned each man to see who might seem to be a knight of renown.

Long they gazed at him, astonished what this marvel might mean, the Green Knight on the green horse, greener than grass, both gleaming more like a piece of jewelry, green enamel on gold, than like flesh and blood. They all scanned him, to see what it was that stood there, and walked round him, wondering what his purpose was. They had seen many marvels, but never before such a marvel as this, and they thought he must be some phantom from the land of Faërie. And all were amazed at his words, and some were afraid to answer, and some waited in courtesy for the King to make reply. So they sat still as stones, and there was heavy silence through the great hall, as though they were all asleep.

There was Arthur's adventure for him, plain before his eyes. He stood before the dais, fearless, and gave the stranger a ready salutation. "You are welcome, sir, to this place. I am the master of this house, and my name is Arthur. Light down from your horse, I pray you, and stay and eat with us, and after that let us know what your will is."

But the Green Knight answered him: "Not so; so God help me, who sits throned above the skies, it was none of my errand to wait any while in this dwelling. But your renown, my lord, is spread wide about the world, and the warriors that live in your castle are held to be the best, the stoutest to ride out in their steel-gear, bravest and worthiest of all men on earth, valiant to contend with in all fair contests, and here, I have heard it told, all the true ways of courtesy are known. It is that which has drawn me hither today. You may be sure by this branch which I bear in my hand that I come in peace, seeking no danger. For if I had made my journey with battle in my thoughts, I have a hauberk at home, and a helmet, a shield and a sharp spear, bright-shining, and other weapons too, and I can wield them. But since I look for no war, I wear the softer clothes of a traveler. If you are as bold as all men tell, you will grant me freely the sport that I ask for."

Arthur said, "Sir knight, even if it is just a combat that you crave, we can find a man to fight you."

"No," said he. "I am telling you the truth, it is no fight that I am seeking. All who are sitting around the hall are no more than beardless children, and if I were buckled in my armor, and riding my war charger, there is no man here who could match his feeble might against mine in combat. All I ask in this court is just a Christmas game, seeing that it is the time of Noel and New Year, and here are many young warriors. If there is any man in this hall who counts himself bold enough, hot in blood and rash in brain, stoutly to change stroke for stroke with me, I will give him, as a free gift, this battle-ax. It is heavy enough, and he can wield it as he pleases. I shall abide the first blow, unarmed as I am now. If any man is bold enough to test what I say, let him come swiftly to me and grasp this weapon—I quit-claim it forever, and he can keep it for his own—and I shall stand up to his stroke, steady on the floor of this hall. But you must proclaim my right to have a free blow at him in return, though I will grant him the respite of a year and a day. Now let us see quickly, dares any man speak?"

They had been astonished at first, when he rode into the hall, but they were stiller than ever now, both high and low. The Green Knight turned in his saddle, and his angry eyes roved savagely over the rows of sitting men, and he bent his bristling eyebrows, that flashed green as he moved, and he waved his beard as he sat and waited for someone to rise. And when no one answered to his challenge he coughed scornfully, and gave himself a great stretch with an air of insulting them, and started to speak.

"Well," said he, "is this Arthur's house, of which the renown runs through so many kingdoms? What has happened to your conceit and your boasted conquests, the fierceness of your wrath and your high words? All the revels and the renown of the famous Round Table are overturned with one word of one man, for you are all cowering for fear, and no one has lifted a finger." And he threw back his head, and laughed loud in their faces. The King felt the insult, and shame made the blood rush to his fair forehead and cheek, as the tempest of his anger rose, and he felt the anger also of his knights rising all round him. And he moved boldly forward, and stood by the Green Knight's stirrup, and spoke.

"Sir, by heaven, what you ask is foolishness. If it is folly that you seek, it is folly you shall rightly find. There is not a man in this hall that is afraid of your big words. Give me your battle-ax, for God's sake, and I will grant you myself the boon you have asked for." He gave him his hand, and the knight got proudly down from the saddle to the floor. Arthur took the ax in his hand, and grasped the helve, and swung it this way and that, trying the weight to see what the feel of it would be when he struck. The stout warrior stood there before him, towering head and shoulders above any man in the hall. He stood grimly stroking his beard, and not a muscle in his stern face moved as he drew down his coat, no more daunted or dismayed for the stroke that was coming than if someone on the seat beside him had offered him a goblet of wine.

Then Gawain, from where he sat by the Queen's side, leaned forward and spoke to the King. "I pray you, my lord, in plain words, let this combat be mine. Bid me rise from my seat and stand by you, so that without discourtesy to my liege

lady the Queen I can leave her side; and I will give you my
counsel before all this noble company. In truth it is not
seemly, when such a challenge is thrown out in your hall, that
you yourself should be so eager to take it up, when there are
sitting all round you so many of your knights. There are none
in the world firmer of will, or stauncher fighters on a stricken
field. I may be the weakest of all of them, and the feeblest of
wit; there is nothing about me to praise except that you are
my uncle, and all the virtue that is in me is the blood I share
with you. But since this business is so foolish, and beneath
your dignity as King, and since I have made my request first,
grant it to me. Whether I have spoken fittingly or not, I leave
to this company to decide. Let them speak their minds freely."

So the knights whispered together, and they were all of one
mind, that the crowned King should be relieved of the challenge, and Gawain given the game.

Then the King commanded Gawain to rise from his place;
and he rose quickly, and came and knelt before the King,
and grasped the great ax. And the King let him take it, and
lifted up his hand and gave him the blessing of God, and
cheerfully bade him be hardy both of heart and hand. "Take
care, cousin," he said, "over your blow; and if you direct it
aright I am well sure that you will stand up to the blow that
he will deal you later."

Gawain went to the Green Knight with the battle-ax in
hand, and the Knight waited for him, calm and undismayed,
and spoke to Gawain. "Before we go forward with this business, let us say over again our covenant. First, I ask you, sir,
tell me truly your name."

"I am called Gawain," he said, "I that am to deal you this
buffet, whatever happens later; and a year from today I will
come, and no man else with me, and you shall deal me another blow in return, with what weapon you will."

And the Green Knight answered, "Sir Gawain, so may I

thrive as I am wondrously eager that you shall let drive at me. By God, sir, I am glad that it is from your hand that I am to get what I asked for here; and you have rehearsed exactly, point by point, all the covenant that I sought of the King, except this—Promise me, on your honor, that at the year's end you yourself will come and seek me out wherever you think I may be found, and take from me the wages for whatever you deal me today before this noble company."

"Where am I to look for you?" said Gawain. "Where do you live? By God who made me, I know nothing of your dwelling, nor from what king's court you come, nor your name. Tell me truly your name, and where you live, and I will use all the skill I have to win my way thither; and that I swear on my troth as true knight."

"That is enough for New Year," said the Green Knight; "I need no more. If, when you have done me the courtesy of your blow, I tell you my house and my home and my own name, you will know all about me and be able to keep tryst. And if I do not speak, you will be all the better off, for you can stay in your own land, and seek no further. But enough words! Take your grim tool in your hand, and let us see what kind of a man you are with the ax!"

"Gladly, sir knight," said Gawain, and ran his finger along the edge of the ax.

The Green Knight at once took up his stand, with his head a little bent, and his long hair thrown forward over the crown of his head, so that the naked flesh of his neck showed ready for the stroke. Gawain gripped his ax, and put his left foot forward to get his balance; then he hove up the ax above his head and brought it down swiftly and surely on the bare flesh, so that the sharp steel shore clean through the flesh and the bones and clove his neck in two, and the bright blade drove on and bit into the ground. The fair head fell from the neck and rolled among the feasters, who pushed it away with their feet. The blood spurted from the body and shone bright on the green mantle. The Green Knight did not fall nor even stagger, but strode firmly forward among the knights, and laid hold of his fair head and lifted it up. Then he turned to his horse, gathered the reins, put his foot in the stirrup-iron and swung himself into the saddle. He held his head by the hair, in his hand, and settled himself in his seat as calmly as though nothing had happened to him, though he sat there headless; and he turned himself about, his gruesome bleeding trunk, and many were in dread of him before he had ended what he had to say.

For he held the head in his hand, and turned it so that it faced full at the guests on the high table. And the eyelids lifted, and the eyes gazed at them wide open; and the lips moved, and the head spoke.

"Sir Gawain, be prompt to come as you have promised and seek faithfully till you find me, as you have sworn now in this hall in the hearing of these knights. Make your way to the Green Chapel, I charge you, to receive such a blow as you have just dealt—well you deserve it—to be promptly paid on the morning of next New Year's Day. For men know me as the Knight of the Green Chapel. Seek therefore to find me and fail not, but come, or be called recreant for ever."

With that he gave a roar, and wheeled his horse, and flung out at the hall door with his head in his hand; and the sparks flashed from the flints beneath his horse's hooves. To what land he went no man knew, any more than they had known whence he had come to them. The King and Gawain laughed together at the strangeness of the adventure, but all men there kept it in their hearts for a marvel.

And, indeed, Arthur himself was amazed in his heart, but he did not let it be seen. He turned to Queen Guenevere, and said to her courteously and loud so that all could hear, "Dear lady, let nothing dismay you. This is Christmastide, and this was no more than a diversion, fitting the season, like the interludes that come between the singing and dancing of the lords and ladies. None the less, now I can set me down to my dinner, for I have seen my marvel, I cannot deny it." Then he glanced at Gawain, and said to him, "Now, sir, hang up your ax; it has had enough work for one day." So they hung the ax up on the arras behind the dais, so that all men could see it, and show it in witness of the wonder they had seen that day.

Then the King sat down in his own seat between Guenevere and Agravain, and the knights took their places again, and the servants served them all manner of meats, and the minstrels played while the feast went forward. And all was joy and merriment till the day drew to an end.

Now take good heed, Sir Gawain, that you do not shrink, but go through to the end with this perilous venture that you have taken upon you.

So this adventure was the first gift that the New Year brought to Arthur. He had longed to hear of some daring deed, and there was no tale for him when the company sat down to meat, but now they had more than words, stern enough work and plenty of it on their hands. Gawain was glad when the venture fell to him in the great hall that New Year's Day, but it seemed a graver thing as the year drew to its end. For though men are gay when strong wine gladdens their hearts, a year passes swiftly, and never brings round the same thing twice, and the end seldom matches the beginning. So this Yule passed and the year after it, as season followed season in order. After Christmas came meager Lent, that tries the flesh with spare diet of fish and even plainer fare. But all over the world the winter began to give back before the onset of the spring weather. The cold drew down into the ground and the clouds lifted, and the rain came down in showers bright and warm, and fell on the fair meadowland, and the flowers began to come out, and the fields and the woods put on their green dresses, and the birds got ready to build, and sang a full-throated song of joy for the kindly summer that was to come on all the hillsides. The buds swelled and were ready to break into bloom along the rich luxuriant hedgerows, and the woods in their finery were filled with the sweet singing of the birds.

Then came summer with his gentle breezes, and the west wind breathed softly on seeds and herbs. Very lovely were the plants that then grew, and the drops of dew fell from the leaves, waiting for a gleam of the bright sun. Then came autumn, bringing fruit and corn to fullness and urging all things to be ripe before the winter came. High up from the face of the land it whirled the dust that the drought had made, and the fierce winds drove clouds across the sun. The leaves floated down from the trees and lighted on the ground, and all the grass grew gray that had been earlier so green, and all that grew up in the spring ripened and then rotted. So by many passing days the year drew on towards its close, and the winter came round again, as is the way of the world.

When the Michaelmas moon was come with its promise of winter, then Gawain began to think of the hard journey that lay before him.

He stayed at Arthur's court till All Saints' Day, and on that day the King held a feast in his honor, with high revel of all the Round Table. And all the courtly knights and the lovely ladies were full of grief for Gawain, but none the less they spoke only of mirth, and made the gay speeches of courtesy with little joy in their hearts. After meat Gawain spoke gravely to his uncle about his journey, and said to him in plain words, "Now, my liege lord, I must ask your leave to depart. You know all about this business that I have on my hands, and I am not going to tell you over again the troubles of it. But I am bound to start on my venture no later than tomorrow morning, to seek out the Green Knight, as God will guide me."

Then all the best men in the castle came together, Ywain and Arrak, and many others, Sir Dodinal de Sauvage, the Duke of Clarence, Lancelot of the Lake, and Lionel, and the good Lucan, the royal butler, and Sir Bors and Sir Bedevere, strong men of their hands, and many other noble knights, with Mador de la Port. All this company came round the King to give counsel to Gawain, with anxious care in their hearts. There was much deep grief in the hall that so worthy a knight as Gawain should have to go on this errand, to abide so dangerous a blow and give no blow of his own sword in answer. Gawain alone stayed full of cheer, and he said to them, "Why should I shrink from it? A man must stand up to his fate, whether it brings him good or ill."

He stayed with them all that day, and the next morning he made himself ready. Early he asked for his arms and they were all brought to him. First there was spread smoothly over the floor a carpet of rich scarlet silk of Toulouse, and much gilded armor lay gleaming on it. The great knight stepped on to it, and handled his steel armor, and he was clothed in a doublet of rich cloth of Turkestan, and then in a close-fitting tunic, fastened up to the neck, and lined within·with pure white fur. They then put the steel shoes on his feet, and clad his legs in the steel of the finely-wrought greaves, with knee-pieces hinged to them, polished bright, and fastened about his knees with buckles of gold. Then the fine thigh-pieces, that fitted close to his strong sinewy thighs, and were laced close with thongs. And then the mail shirt with its bright rings of linked steel was put over his tunic, and then the burnished arm-pieces with the bright elbow-pieces, and the gauntlets of steel-plate and all the splendid gear that was to guard him on his venture. Over all was his rich surcoat, and on his feet his bright golden spurs were fastened, and his true-tempered sword was girt at his side with a silken girdle.

When he was fully arrayed, his harness was splendid to look on, for the smallest buckle or loop gleamed bright with gold. So in full armor he heard the Mass, celebrated at the high altar. Then he came to the King and to his fellow knights of the court, and courteously took his leave of the lords and ladies, and they embraced him and brought him on his way, commending him to Christ. By this time Gringolet, his horse, was all ready for him. The saddle shone brightly with many gold fringes, and all the breast-cloths, and the skirts of the caparison, the crupper, and the horse-cloth matched the saddlebows, and all was studded with rich golden studs on a red background, so that it glittered and sparkled like rays of sunlight. Then he took his helmet in his hands and kissed it quickly. It was stapled strongly and padded inside; it sat high on his head, fastened behind, and with a light drapery over the visor, embroidered and set about with the finest gems on a broad silken strip. Down the seams there were figures of birds, parrots preening themselves, and turtle-doves, and truelove knots intertwined, a work that many maidens in the castle had spent seven winters in accomplishing. And even more precious was the golden circlet that ringed the helmet, with the device on it done in flashing diamonds.

They then brought him his shield, that was bright gules, with the pentangle* charged on it in pure gold. He took it by the baldric and slung it round his neck, and it was the last fitting touch in his splendid array. And why the pentangle was Gawain's special emblem must be explained, even though the story waits. It is a sign that Solomon devised of old, as a token of fidelity, of which it is a fit emblem. For it is a figure that has five points, and each line in it overlaps and locks with another, and wherever you start on it it is endless, and everywhere the English call it the endless knot. So it was fitting for Gawain and was his famous device, since Gawain was known for a good knight, faithful in five ways and five times in each way. He was like refined gold, pure from any vileness, and radiant with all virtues. Therefore he bore the pentangle as his emblem, as the truest and gentlest in speech of all the knights.

First, he was faultless in his five wits; and then he never failed in the might of his hands and the skill of his five fingers. He put all his trust in the five wounds that Christ bore on the cross. And whenever he stood in the press of fight he kept steadfast in his mind, through all the tumult, that he drew all his might in battle from the five joys that the gracious Queen of Heaven had of her Child. For this reason he had, on the upper half of the inside of his shield, a picture of the Virgin painted, so that when he looked at it his courage never failed. And the fifth five that Gawain had were the five virtues: generosity, and love of his fellow men, and cleanness, and courtesy that never failed, and, lastly, pity, that is above all other virtues; these five were deeper in Gawain's heart and more surely part of him than of any other knight. With these five he was girded, and each was joined with the others; there are five fixed points in the pentangle, and no line runs into another nor yet is sundered from the rest; and there is no place, wherever a man begins, at which he can come to an end of the figure. Therefore on Gawain's bright shield the device was charged, splendidly, gold upon gules. That is the pure pentangle, as wise men call it.

So was Gawain made ready for his venture; he took his lance in his hand and bade them all farewell, he thought forever.

He set spurs to Gringolet, who sprang forward, striking the

sparks from the flints with the steel of his hooves. And all who saw the noble knight set out sighed in their hearts, and said one to another in their sorrow for Gawain, "By Christ, it is grievous thing that you, Gawain, so noble a knight, will be lost to the world. It would be hard to find his peer upon earth. It would have been wiser to go about this business more warily, and have made him a duke of the realm. In all the land there is no greater leader of men, and he had better have been that great leader than brought to nothing, his head cut off by a knight from elfland, and all for vanity and pique. Who ever knew a king to take such counsel, like knights in their trifling games at Christmas?" And their eyes were full of tears as the noble knight rode out that day from their dwelling. He made no tarrying, but swiftly went his way, and rode many wandering roads.

He rode through the realm of Logres,[4] as God guided him, toward a task that seemed no more a Christmas game. Often he spent the long nights companionless, finding no fortune that he liked; and by wood and hill he had no one but his horse to bear him company, and no one to talk to but God only. So he rode forward till he came to North Wales, and he held the isles of Anglesey on his left hand, and he passed over the fords by the forelands, over by the Holy Head,[5] till he struck the shore again in the wild land of Wirral;[6] therein there lived but few that were loved by either God or man. And all the time as he went on his way he asked all that he met whether they had heard tell of a green knight anywhere thereabouts or of a green chapel. And they all said no, that never in their lives had they seen a man of that color. Gawain took strange roads by many a dreary hillside, and many shifts

[4] England south of the Humber.
[5] Not Holyhead in Anglesey.
[6] In Cheshire.

of fortune he was to know before he came to the sight of the Green Chapel.

Many a steep cliff he overpassed as he journeyed, far sundered from his friends, in country where he was a stranger. And at each ford and river passage that he came to, it was seldom that he did not find a foe blocking his path, and one so foul and fell that he must needs fight him. So many wonders the knight met among the hills that it would be hard to tell the tenth part of them. Sometimes he fought with dragons, sometimes with wolves, and then again with trolls of the forest that lived among the crags; with bulls and bears and boars, and ogres that panted after him and pursued him from the high fells. And had he not been a strong fighter and a stubborn, and had not God preserved him, beyond doubt he would many times have been slain and left there dead. But his fights wearied him less than the winter weather, when the cold clear rain fell from the clouds and froze into hail before it reached the faded ground below. More nights than he cared for he slept in his armor among the bare rocks, half dead with the cold and the sleet, while the cold stream came rattling down from the crest high above him, and hung over his head in icicles. So in peril and pain and hardship the knight rode this way and that over the countryside, till the morning of Christmas Eve; and he made his prayer to Mary that she would guide him as he rode, and bring him to some dwelling of men.

On that same morning he rode gaily along a hillside into a deep forest that was wonderfully wild, with high hills rising on each hand and woods below of huge gray oaks, hundreds together, and a tangle of hazel and hawthorn, with rough shaggy moss hanging over them. Many birds sat shivering on the bare twigs, piping a pitiful little song as the cold nipped them.

The knight on Gringolet passed on his way beneath them, through swamp and mire, all by himself, and troubled about how he was to keep Christmas, if he could not manage to see the due service of the Lord, who on that same night was born of a maiden to heal all our sorrows. And so with a sigh he said, "I beseech you, Lord Christ, and Mary, gentlest mother so dear, to bring me to some shelter where I may devoutly hear the Mass and matins tomorrow. Humbly I ask it, and say straightway my Pater Noster and Ave and Credo." He rode on, praying as he rode, and confessed his sins, and crossed himself, saying, "The Cross of Christ be my good speed."

He had crossed himself but three times when he was aware through the trees of a dwelling circled by a moat, standing on a mound that rose from a piece of meadowland, shut in under the boughs of many great trees that closed in round the moat. It was a castle, the fairest that ever a knight owned, built in a clearing with a park all round it, and round the park a stout palisade of spikes that took in more than two miles of forest land. Gawain looked at the stronghold from that side, and saw it shimmering and shining through the fair oaks, and then he reverently took off his helmet and gave devout thanks to Jesus and St. Julian, gentle Lord and gentle saint, who had thus shown him kindness and heard his prayer. "Now," said he, "grant me good lodging." And with that he touched Gringolet with his golden spurs, and made his way, as chance would have it, to the chief gate, which brought him swiftly to the end of the drawbridge, and he saw the bridge firmly pulled up, and the gates shut fast, and the solid walls that feared no blast of tempest.

Gawain came to a halt on Gringolet by the bank of the deep double ditch that circled the castle. The wall ran down into the water wonderfully deep, and towered up to a huge height above it, wrought of hard hewn stone right up to the cornices, and with bantels[7] of the best under the battlements. There were fair turrets fashioned between, with many loopholes well devised to shut fast. Gawain had never seen a better barbican. Further in he saw the hall rising high, with towers all about, whose pinnacles rose high aloft, with carven tops cunningly wrought. On the tower roofs his eye picked out many white chimneys that gleamed like chalk cliffs in the sunlight. And there were so many pinnacles, gaily painted, scattered about everywhere and climbing one above another among the embrasures of the castle, that it looked as though it were actually cut out of paper. The knight on his horse thought he would do well if he could contrive to come within the wall and rest pleasantly in that dwelling through the holy season. He called aloud, and soon there came on the wall a courteous porter, who greeted the knight errant, and asked what he desired.

"Good sir," said Gawain, "will you take my message to the lord of the castle, and tell him that I ask for shelter?"

"Yes, by St. Peter," said the porter; "but I know without asking that you will be welcome, sir knight, to stay here with my master as long as you will."

Then he came down from the wall and came out swiftly, and others with him, to welcome the knight. They let down the great bridge, and came courteously out, and knelt down on the cold ground to give such greeting to the knight as they thought due to him. They gave him passage through the great gate, set full open, and he forthwith told them to rise, and rode in over the bridge. Some came and held his saddle while he got off, and then other willing servants took Gringolet to stable. Then came knights and squires to bring this guest with all joyous welcome into the hall. When he took his helmet from his head, they were ready to take it from his hand in their eagerness to serve him, and they took his sword and his

[7] Horizontal courses of masonry jutting out from the wall.

shield. And as they pressed round him, proud men who took pride to honor so princely a guest, he greeted them courteously one by one. Then they brought him, splendid in his armor, into the great hall, where the flames of the fire leapt and gleamed brightly on the hearth. Then the lord of the castle himself came from his own room to give gracious greeting to the knight who stood there. And he said, "You are welcome to all that you can wish. All that is here is yours, to use at your pleasure." "I thank you," said Gawain; "may Christ reward you." And they embraced one another like old friends.

Gawain looked at the host who greeted him so kindly, and thought the owner of the castle looked a valiant warrior. He was a huge man, in the full flower of his age, with a shining beard that covered his chest, the color of beaver's fur. He stood there, stern and stalwart, with his feet firmly planted. His face was fell as fire, and he was forthright in his speech. He was the right man, Gawain thought, to be the lord of the noble company in his halls. He turned back to his room, and gave orders that a man should be assigned to Gawain who would serve him well. There were plenty of servants ready to do his bidding, and they brought him to a bedroom, bright and shining, where the bed and all the hangings were of the finest. There were bed-hangings of gleaming silk, with clear gold hems, and coverlets elaborately wrought with embroidered panels of white fur on them. There were curtains running on ropes with rings of red gold, and tapestries of Toulouse and Turkestan hanging on the walls, and others that matched them for carpets underfoot.

There with gay speeches they unarmed him, took off his plate armor and his bright mail tunic, and the gay raiment below it. Then quickly they brought him all manner of garments, to be his own, so that he could choose which he liked, and have others to change into. When he had made his choice, and arrayed himself in a robe that fitted him well with flowing skirts, through which glowed the gay colors of surcoat and hose, they thought he looked as fresh as the spring, and the handsomest knight that ever had been. Wherever in the world he came from, they thought, he must be a warrior without equal on any stricken field.

A chair was set before the hearth where the fire of charcoal was burning, and it was prepared for Sir Gawain with cushions and quilted coverings, cunningly wrought. Then they put a gay mantle round his shoulders, of brown silk, richly embroidered and lined with the finest ermine, and a hood of the same. He sat down in the chair and eagerly warmed himself, and his spirits rose. Then they brought out trestles and set up a table, and put a clean white cloth on it, and on that an overcloth, and a saltcellar, and silver spoons. Gawain washed his hands and sat down to eat. And the quiet well-trained servants served him, with many excellent stews, well seasoned, and doubled portions of them, as was his right, and various kinds of fish, some baked in bread, some grilled on the embers, some boiled and some in well-spiced stews, and all with the subtlest of sauces that tickled his palate.

Sir Gawain said courteously that it was as fine a feast as he had ever eaten, but they all retorted, as courteously but with smiles, that this was a meal fit only for a fast day, but that soon they would show him a real feast. And Gawain ate his meal, and drank the good wine, and made merry.

Then, without pressing him or seeming discourteously inquisitive, they asked him questions about himself, till he told them what court he came from, the court of which Arthur was sole monarch, the great King who was lord of the Round Table, and that he himself who sat in their hall was Gawain, whom fortune had brought to them that Christmas. And when his host knew what knight it was that he was entertaining, he laughed loud in his pleasure. And all in the castle took delight to come as soon as they could into the presence of a knight who was famed above all men in the world for all noble virtues, for prowess in arms and perfection in courtly manners.

Each man whispered to his neighbor, "Now we can watch the finished arts of courtesy, and the delicate turn of phrase of courtly conversation; we shall learn just by listening what profit there is in speech, since we have given welcome to a knight who is the paragon of good breeding. God has shown us His favor in bringing such a guest as Gawain under our roof at the season when men sit and sing cheerful carols of His birth. Gawain will give us all a lesson in what knightly manners mean, and anyone who listens to him will have a chance of learning how to talk with the lady that he loves."

By the time that dinner was ended and the noble company rose, it had drawn near to nightfall. The chaplains took their way to the chapel, and rang the bells sweetly, as summons to evensong at that holy season. The lord of the castle went to the chapel, and his lady with him, into their special pew, and Gawain soon gladly followed them. The lord caught him by his robe and led him to his seat, and greeted him warmly, calling him by his name, and said that he was the most welcome to his castle of all knights in the world; and Gawain thanked him heartily and they embraced.

They sat quietly together till the service was ended, and then the lady wished to meet the knight, and she came out of the pew with many fair maidens attending her. She was the fairest of all of them, with her smooth skin, and the lovely color of her cheeks, the grace of her movements and her gracious ways. She was lovelier even than Guenevere, Sir Gawain thought, as he made his way down the chancel to salute her. She was escorted on her left hand by another lady, older than she, indeed, an ancient dame and held in honor, it seemed, by the knights around her.

Very unlike were the two ladies, for the younger was fresh in her beauty, and her color was clear red in lip and smooth cheek, but the other was yellow and withered, and her cheeks were rough and wrinkled and flabby. The one wore kerchiefs on her head, with many lustrous pearls, that showed her bosom and her fair throat, that shone as white as snowdrifts on the hills. The other wore a gorget close up round her neck, and her swarthy chin was wrapped in white veils, and her forehead was all enfolded in silk that muffled her close, and she wore a turreted headdress tricked out with trinkets, so that nothing could be seen of her but her black brows and her two eyes and her nose and her naked lips, that were flabby and ugly to see. And she was short and thick-set, and clumsy in figure. She was a worshipful lady, maybe, but not a lovely one. Far sweeter was the other whom she escorted.

When Gawain saw that fair lady, that looked kindly at him, he asked leave of the lord and went to meet them. He saluted the elder, bowing low, and he took the other in his arms and gave her the kiss of greeting, and spoke courteously to her.

They desired his better acquaintance, and at once he offered himself as their true servant, if they would have him. They then took him between them and, talking as they went, they brought him to their sitting room, to the hearthside, and ordered the servants to bring spiced wine; and the servants made haste to obey. And the lord often sprang up in high spirits and bade them all make merry. He took his hood off and threw it up and caught it on a spear point, and waved it at them, telling them it was a prize for whoever could devise the merriest sport for Christmastime. "And," said he, "by my faith, I am ready to challenge the best of you before I have to go without my hood; and my friends will help me." So with laughing words the lord made merry, to entertain

Gawain with games in the hall that night, till he gave order for the lights to be brought. Then Gawain took his leave and went to his bed.

Next day was Christmas Day, when all men remember the time when the Lord God was born on earth to live and die for our salvation, and there is gladness in every dwelling upon earth for His sake. So it was in the lord's castle that day, and they had all manner of dainties, and dishes cunningly cooked that the servants at mealtime brought to the high table. The old ancient lady sat at the head, and the lord took his place beside her. Gawain and the fair lady sat together in the center, in the place of honor, and they were served first, and after them all in the hall, each according to his degree. There was feasting and mirth and much rejoicing, so that it would be hard to tell it all, even if one were to describe it point by point. But it is sure that Gawain and the fair lady took such delight in their companionship, their merry converse with each other and courteous interchange of speech, that no knight and lady ever enjoyed themselves more. All about them was the noise of trumpets and kettledrums, and the shrill music of the pipes, and the buzz of talk; but they had eyes and ears only for each other.

They kept high festival that day and the next day, and the third day after. The third day was St. John's Day, the last of the feast, and as full of gaiety as the rest. They knew that they must all be about their daily business in the gray of the next dawn, so they kept up the revels till the small hours, drinking wine and dancing and singing all through the night. And at last with the dawn they took their leave, each to go his own way.

Gawain said good morning to his host, and his host took him to his own room to the fireside, and thanked him for the honor he had done him by coming to his castle at that high season, and gracing it with his noble presence. "I know, sir, that all my life long it will make me warm at heart that Gawain has been my guest at God's own festival."

"I thank you, sir," said Gawain, "but it is I that have had the honor from you, and may the King above reward you for it. And I am your man, to work your will at your bidding, in all things high or low, and I hold myself in duty bound to that." Then the lord strove earnestly to get Gawain to stay with him longer, but Gawain answered that he could by no means consent.

Then the lord asked Gawain straight out what grim task had driven him at that season of festival to ride out so boldly by himself from the King's court, even before the joys of Christmas were wholly over in the dwellings of men.

"Truly," said Gawain, "you are right. It is a great business and a pressing, that has called me out from my own dwelling. I have it laid on me to seek out a place that I do not know whither in the wide world to ride to find it. I would give all the land in Logres, if only, by God's grace, I might come near to it on New Year's morning. Therefore, sir, I ask you now, tell me truly if you have ever heard tell of the Green Chapel, and where in the world it is, and of the Green Knight that dwells there. There was a tryst established by a sure covenant between us that I was to meet that man at that place if I lived so long. And of the New Year that is our trysting day it wants now a very little, and, by God's Son, I would rather look on that knight's face, if God would grant it me, than have any other good fortune on earth. So, I think, by your leave, I must go my way, since I have barely three days to be about my business; and I would rather drop dead here at your feet than fail my tryst."

Then the lord laughed, and he said, "There is no doubt now that you must stay and not go your way, for I will guide you to your goal by the end of the three days, and the Green Chapel need trouble you no more. You shall lie at ease in your bed late into each day, and ride out on the first day of the year, and come to the place of your tryst by the mid-morning, to achieve what you will when you get there. Stay here with me till New Year's Day, and then rise up and depart. One of my men shall set you on your way, and the Green Chapel is not two miles from here."

Gawain was glad, and laughed merrily. "Now I thank you for this beyond everything else that you have done for me. Since my venture is all but achieved, I will, as you wish, stay with you, and do whatever else you like."

Then the lord took him and set him down and let the ladies be summoned to give him the more pleasure. And they had a merry time, the four of them by themselves. The lord chattered in his delight as though he was almost out of his wits and did not know what he was at. Then he said to the knight, crying aloud, "Now that you have thought well to do as I asked you, will you also hold to a promise that I will ask?"

"Surely, sir," said Gawain, "while I am your guest in your castle, I will obey any command you give."

"You have had a weary journey," said the other, "and have wandered from far, and after that you have stayed awake all night with me and you are not yet well rested, and you have not had enough of either food or sleep. You shall stay in your room tomorrow, and lie at your ease till Mass time, and come down to your meal when you choose, and my wife shall sit with you and entertain you till I come home again. You will stay here and I will get up early and go hunting."

Gawain bowed to him and granted all he asked.

"Further," said the lord, "we will make a promise between us. Whatever game I kill in the forest, it shall be yours, and whatever good fortune you come by here, give me that in exchange. Let us agree on our honors to make good this exchange, whether it is of trifles or of something better."

"Before God," said Gawain, "I will do it, and it does me good to see you in such a merry mood."

"Let someone bring us wine to drink," said the other, "and the bargain is struck." So he said and they all laughed, and drank their wine and talked gaily together, the two knights and the two ladies. And then they stood up and with elaborate courtesy and many fair words they quietly said good night to one another and kissed, and by the light of many bright torches each was escorted to his soft bed. And just before they parted for the night they reminded each other of their bargain.

Quite early, before the dawn came, the folk in the castle rose, and those that were for the road summoned their grooms, and the grooms made haste to saddle their horses, got ready all their gear, and packed their bags. Then they dressed in their finest riding clothes, and mounted, and took hold of their reins, and went each his way. And the lord of the castle was up as early as any of them, ready dressed for the hunt with many of his knights. He heard Mass, and then ate a hasty breakfast, and was ready with his horn for the hunting field. Before there was even a glimmer of dawn over the land he and his men were mounted, and the kennel men coupled the hounds, and opened the kennel doors, and called the hounds out, blowing clear on the horns the three long notes. The hounds bayed as they heard them, and made a great clamor, as the huntsmen whipped in and turned back those that went straying off on false scents. There were a hundred hunters, the best horsemen in the country. The keepers of the deer hounds went to their hunting stations, and cast off the couples, and the horns rang loud and clear through the forest.

At the first sound of the hunt all the wild creatures trembled, and the deer huddled together in the valley, half mad for fear, and then hastened to the high ground, but they were turned back by the beaters who shouted aloud at them. They let the harts go their way, and the noble bucks, with their high-held heads and their fine antlers, for the lord had given orders that in the close season there was to be no hunting of the male deer. But the hinds were ringed in with shouts of "Hay!" and "Ware!" and the does were driven down with great clamor to the bottoms of the valleys. There you might see, as the bowmen loosed, the curving flight of the arrows. At each turn in the wood there flashed a shaft, that bit into the brown hides with its broad head, and the deer cried out as they fell bleeding in death along the hillsides. The hounds coursed hard after them, and the hunters with their horns followed the hounds, with blasts on the horns that rang as though the cliffs were splitting. Any beasts that escaped the bowmen were pulled down and killed after they had been harassed from the high ground and driven down to the streams in the valleys. The men at the low-lying stations were skilled, and the greyhounds so strong that they gripped the deer and tore them down as soon as they came in sight. The lord was carried away with joy of the hunting, and now he galloped, and now he dismounted to watch the death of a deer, and he drove hard all day till the night fell.

Meantime, while the lord took his delight in hunting along the woods, the good knight Gawain lay in his soft bed, keeping snug till the light of day gleamed on the walls of his room, with the curtains round him and the gay coverlet over him. And as he lay there dozing he heard a little timid noise at his door, and then heard it quickly open. He brought his head up out of the clothes and lifted a corner of the curtain and took a cautious glance to see what this might be. It was the lady, lovely to look on, that closed the door behind her very softly and quietly, and stole toward the bed.

Gawain did not know what to do, so he lay down again quietly and behaved as though he was still asleep. The lady crept noiselessly over the floor to the bed, and lifted the curtain, came inside and sat down on the edge of the bed, and stayed there a long time, to watch him when he woke. Gawain lay there a long time wondering what this might mean, for it seemed to him very strange; but then he said to himself, "Perhaps it would be better to ask straight out what she desires." So he woke up and stretched himself, turned toward her and opened his eyes, and pretended to be astonished, and crossed himself, to preserve himself from any harm. The lady sat there, with her lovely pink and white cheeks, and her sweet lips, and laughed at him.

"Good morning, Sir Gawain," said she gaily, "you are a careless sleeper, that lets a lady slip thus to your bedside without hearing her. Now you are caught, and unless we can make a truce I shall imprison you in your bed, be sure of that." And she laughed as she made fun of him.

"Good morning, sweet lady," said Gawain cheerfully. "Everything shall be done to me as you like, and I am well content, for I yield myself as your prisoner, and pray you for favor; that, I think, is the best I can do, and there is no way out of it." So he laughed back at her. "But," said he, "fair lady, will you then grant me a boon and release your prisoner for long enough to let him get up and out of his bed and get himself dressed? Then I should be in better case to talk with you."

"No, no, dear knight," said the sweet lady, "you are not to get out of your bed. I have a better idea than that. I shall tuck you up where you are, and then talk with my knight that I have caught. You are Sir Gawain, whom all men hold in honor wherever in the world you ride your ways, and you win great praise among lords and among ladies and among all men that live, for your honor and your courtesy. And now here you are, and we are by our two selves. My lord and his men are hunting afar, the knights in the castle are in their beds and so are my maidens, and the door is shut and close latched. And since I have here in this house the knight that is the honored favorite of all the world, I shall spend my time well while it lasts in talking to him. You are welcome to my person to do with as you please. I am perforce, and must remain, your servant."

"Faith," said Gawain, "that rejoices my heart, even though I am far below what you have said of me. I am unworthy, and I know it, of the honor that you do me. But, if you will it, it would be pure joy to me to put myself wholly at your service, to do your pleasure whether in word or deed."

"Good faith, Sir Gawain," said the lady, "if I held light the goodness and the prowess that please all others, that would be poor courtesy. There are ladies enough who would give all the jewels and the gold that they possess to have you, dear knight, in their power, as I have you, to talk to you and hear your courtly answers, and have you comfort them and soothe their cares. I give praise to the Lord who rules the heavens that I have by His grace here under my hand the desire of all the world."

So the lovely lady spoke sweetly to him, and he made courteous answer.

"Madam," said Gawain, "Mary reward you for the noble generosity you have shown me. There are many who just copy other men, and the courtesy they show me is far beyond my deserts; but your kindness comes from your own heart, that does not know how to be less than courteous to any man."

"Nay," said the lady, "it is far otherwise. Were I the fairest and noblest of all women alive, and had I all the wealth of the world in my hands, so that I could choose as I would from all the men on earth a lover to my liking, there is no man I would choose before you, seeing all that I have found in you of beauty and courtesy and gay spirits, all that I had heard of you before, and now find to be true."

"My noble lady," said Gawain, "you could have chosen far better, but none the less I am very proud that you hold me so high. I am your servant, and I hold you my queen; I offer myself as your true knight, and may Christ reward you for accepting my service."

Thus they spoke of many things till past midmorning, and the lady behaved as though she loved him dearly. But Gawain met her with his perfect courtesy, yet a little distantly, and she thought, "Even if I were the loveliest maiden on earth, he left his love-making behind him when he set out on this journey," for she remembered the grim task that lay before him, and the stroke that might strike him down, which he could not escape. So she spoke of leaving him, and he did not stop her.

She bade him good day, and glanced at him with a laugh, and as she stood by him she surprised him with make-believe severity. "I thank you for my entertainment. But I begin to wonder whether you are Gawain at all."

"Why so?" he asked anxiously, fearing that in some way his words had failed in courtesy.

"Bless you!" she said, "so good and courteous a knight as Gawain is famed to be, the very pattern of knightly manners, could not have talked so long with a lady without asking her for a kiss, even if only by some trifle of a hint at the end of a speech."

"Be it as you wish," said Gawain. "Surely I will kiss you at your bidding. That is no more than your knight's duty; and besides, I should hate to displease you, so you need not ask twice."

Then she came to him, and bent sweetly down, and put

her arms round him and kissed him. They commended each other to the keeping of Christ, and she quietly opened the door and went out.

Gawain rose and hastened to dress, called his servant, and chose his raiment. When he was arrayed he went gladly to Mass, and then to the meal that was ready for him, and made good cheer all day till the moon rose. There was never a knight had a gayer time, with two such worthy ladies to entertain him, the elder and the younger, and the three of them had much happiness together.

Meantime the lord of the castle was off all day at his hunting, chasing the hinds over heath and through woodland. And by the time that the sun drew down to the west they had killed does and hinds almost beyond counting. Then all the hunters flocked together at the end of the day and made a quarry of all the deer, and cut them up. Each man had his due portion, and on a hide they laid out parts to feed the hounds. Then they blew the kill, and the hounds bayed, and they took up the carcasses, and turned homeward, winding as they rode many clear notes on the horns. And as daylight ended, the whole company was back in the great castle where the knight lived secure. There they found ease, and bright fires kindled. And as the lord came in Gawain met him, and they were glad to greet each other again.

Then the lord commanded all the company to gather in the great hall, and the ladies to come down with their maidens. And then before them all he bade men bring in the venison. And he called laughingly to Gawain and told him the tally of all the swift deer, and showed him what fine condition they had been in. "How does this please you?" said he. "Have I done well? Have I deserved your thanks by my skill in the field?"

"Indeed," said Gawain, "this is the finest kill in a day's hunting that I have seen in seven years in wintertime."

"I hand it over to you," said the knight, "for by our covenant you can claim it for your own."

"True," said Gawain, "and I say the same to you. What I have with honor won in this house I make it over to you with as good will." And he threw his arms round his neck and gave him a kiss as near to the sweetness of the lady's as he could manage. "There are my winnings," he said; "they are all that I can show for my day, but I would hand them over as freely if they were worth more."

"Good," said the other, "and I thank you. Maybe it is the richer prize of the two, if only you would tell me where you were clever enough to win it."

"That was not in the covenant," said Gawain, "so ask me no more; you have been given all that is due you, and do not suspect otherwise." They laughed and made merry, and went to supper, where new delicacies were laid ready for them.

Then they sat by the fireside in the lord's own room, and servants brought them goblet after goblet of choice wine. And in their laughing talk they made again the same agreement that they made the day before, that, whatever changes fortune should bring in their winnings, they would exchange their new gains when they met the next night. And they pledged each other to this as before in a special goblet of wine. Then they said good night, and they all went happily to their beds.

By the third cockcrow the lord was out of his bed, and so were his knights. They heard Mass and took breakfast, and then the company rode out to the woods, before the dawn light came, to hunt the boar. With huntsmen and horns they rode through the flat lands and uncoupled the hounds to draw the thorn brakes.

Then they called on the huntsman to draw the thickets by the side of a marsh, and he called by name to the hounds that first gave tongue, and cheered them on with cries of excitement, and the other hounds when they heard them came swiftly to the same place, and at once picked up the scent, twenty couple at once; and there rose such a babel and din of the pack in full cry that the rocks rang aloud with it. The hunters cheered them on with horn and voice, and they all came together between a pool in the wood and a jagged crag.

By the side of the marsh under the crag, where rocks had fallen and lay about in confusion over a knoll, the hounds pressed on to force the boar to break covert, and the men after them. They made casts round the knoll, and the foot of the crag, knowing well that the boar was there, and the first to give tongue was one of the bloodhounds. Then they beat the bushes to rouse him out, and out he swung, bringing disaster to those that stood in his path, a magnificent beast, an old boar that had long ago left the herd, fierce and huge. He was a grim sight, and when he grunted in fury many hearts quailed. At his first rush he hurled three men to the ground, and then without doing more hurt he charged away at full gallop. They hallooed with shouts of "Hi!" and "Hay! Hay!" and put the horns to their lips and blew the recall. There was much merry din of men and of hounds as they sped shouting after the boar. Often he stood at bay, wounding the pack on all sides, and he ripped up many of the hounds with his tusks, and they whined and yelped piteously.

Then men pressed forward to shoot him, and loosed their shafts and hit him again and again. But the points could do nothing with the tough hide that covered his shoulders, and the barbs could not bite into his flesh, even when the arrow was shot so hard that the smooth shaft splintered, but the heads bounced off again wherever they hit. None the less the blows of the arrows hurt him, and he grew fighting mad and charged out on the men, goring them. And many were afraid and shrank back. But the lord on a fast horse made after him, blowing the blast of the recall on his bugle, and rode through the undergrowth in full pursuit of the boar till the sun shone out clear in the sky.

Meantime Gawain lay at ease in his bed in the castle, under the gay coverings, and the lady did not forget to come to say good morning to him. She came early, and was at him to get him to change his mood. She came and drew back the curtain and peeped in at the knight. Sir Gawain gave her courteous welcome, and she returned his greeting eagerly and sat down beside him quietly, and laughed, and with a loving look she spoke to him. "Sir, if you are indeed Gawain, of all knights the most nobly courteous, it seems strange to me that you know so little of the manners of polite society, and if anyone instructs you in them, forthwith you cast them out of your mind. You have forgotten already the lesson I taught you only yesterday in the plainest words that I could manage."

"What was that?" said Gawain, "for I do not know what you mean, and if it is true, the blame is mine."

"I gave you a lesson in kissing," said the fair lady, "and how to claim a lady's favor when it is plainly there for the asking, as a courteous knight should."

"Dear lady," said he, "take back that speech. I dare not make that request for fear of being refused, since if I were refused I should know that I had been wrong to ask it."

"Faith," said she gaily, "you will certainly not be refused. And even if anyone were so mannerless as to deny you, you are strong enough, surely, to take what you want, consent or none."

"That," said Gawain, "is true enough. But in the land where I come from it brings no luck to use force, or to take any gift that is not given of free will. But I am here at your bidding to kiss or be kissed at your pleasure. You may take my kisses when you like, and cease when you choose."

The lady bent down and kissed him, and they talked long

of the griefs and joys of love. "I have wanted to put a question to you," said the lady, "if you will not be angry with me, and to ask the reason for something. In all the records of chivalry the two things chiefly praised are true love and the lore of knightly warfare. And the tale of their striving in honor of their loves is the title and the theme of the stories of the deeds of all true knights. For their true loves they have ventured their lives, and endured long days of woe, and then avenged themselves by their valor, and ended their sorrows, and brought happiness to their ladies in their bowers by their proven prowess. That is all so, and yet here are you, so young and fresh and brave, famous everywhere for your courtesy and your valor, the finest-looking knight of your time, whose fame and whose honor is spread all over the world, and here am I, coming and sitting beside you twice over, and yet I have heard not one single word from your lips that had anything to do with love. Surely you, that are so courteous and so ready with your vows of knightly service, ought to be eager to instruct a young creature, like me, and give her some notion of the rules and the art of the game of true love. It cannot be that you do not know, for your renown in such things is world-wide. Is it that you think that I am too dull and stupid to understand your sweet speeches? Shame on you, Sir Gawain! Here I come all by myself, and sit by your side to learn. Please, give me my lesson while my lord is away."

"Faith," said Gawain, "God reward you for all your kindness. It makes me glad at heart and full of joy that so noble a lady should come to me, and take the trouble to entertain so poor a man as I am, even though I am your knight. That you should show me any favor at all is a delight to me. But for me to take on myself the hard task of teaching you the primer of the arts of love—you, who have already, I know, double the skill in them that I have, or ever shall have while I live, or a hundred men like me—that would be, dear lady, the silliest kind of folly. But I will do your bidding with all my powers, as I am in duty bound, and always be your faithful servant, so God preserve me!"

Thus the fair lady tested him, and tempted him to wrong, whatever else she wished of him. But he kept her at a distance so skillfully that he failed in neither courtesy nor honor, and there was no sin on either side, and nothing but happiness for both of them. They laughed together and talked long, and then she kissed him, and took her leave and departed.

Then Gawain bestirred himself, and rose and dressed and went to Mass, and then their dinner was prepared and daintily served, and Gawain sat and talked with the ladies all the rest of the day.

But the lord rode hard across country after his doomed boar, that rushed over the slopes and broke in his jaws the backs of the best of the hounds whenever he stood at bay, till the bowmen shifted him and made him change his ground in spite of all he could do, such showers of arrows fell on him from the company that gathered round him. At last he was so wearied that he could run no more, but made what haste he could to a hole in a level bank by a rock where the stream ran past. There he got the bank at his back, and began to paw the ground, and the foam dripped from the corners of his mouth as he whetted his white tusks. And the bold men who stood round were by now weary of him and of harassing him from a distance, but there was not a man who dared to close in on him, for he looked as dangerous as ever. He had wounded many of them already, and they shrank from coming within reach of his rending tusks, for he was still fierce and furious and full of fight.

But then came up the lord himself, spurring his horse, and saw the boar standing at bay. He got down from his horse, and left it standing there, and drew his bright sword, and went forward with long strides, passing through the ford to where the grim beast was waiting for him. The boar watched him coming with his weapon in hand, and his bristles rose and he snorted so fiercely that many feared for the knight. The boar made straight at him and the man and the beast fell locked together and the water swirled about them. But the beast had the worst of it, for the man watched his mark well at the first charge, and drove the sharp steel firmly into his throat, right up to the hilt, and pierced the heart. The boar snarled and gave up the fight and made away across the stream, but a hundred hounds fell on him, biting furiously, and the men drove him to open ground, where the hounds finished him off.

Then there was loud hallooing, and the blowing of the kill on the loud horns, and the hounds bayed over the boar as their masters bade, they who had been the chief huntsmen in that long chase. Then one who was wise in woodcraft cut up the boar. He cut off the head, and fed the hounds with some of the flesh. Then they slung the carcass on a stout pole, and set off for home. The head was borne before the lord himself, who had slain the beast in the ford by the skill and the strength of his hands.

It seemed a long time before he could see Sir Gawain again, and when they got back to the castle, and came into the hall, he called him, and spoke merrily to him, full of joy. And the ladies were summoned, and all the company. Then he showed them the flesh of the boar, and told them the whole story of the hunt, the huge size and the fierceness of the boar, and the struggle he had with him in the wood to which he had fled. And Gawain praised his prowess and the deed he had achieved, for he had never in his life, he said, seen such a carcass. Then he handled the huge head, and said, by way of praising the lord, that it was a grim sight and he was half afraid of it, even in death.

"Well, Sir Gawain," said the lord, "the prize is your own, as you know, by the sure covenant whereby we bound ourselves."

"True," said Gawain; "and just as faithfully I will now in turn give you my takings." And as he spoke he put his arms round his neck and gave him a kiss, and then at once another, and said, "Now we are quits, and we have both paid all our dues since the time that I came to your castle up till tonight."

"By St. Giles," said the lord, "you are the best man I know. If you carry on so profitably with this business, you are going to be a wealthy-man before you know it."

Then they set out the trestles and put the tables on them, with tablecloths over them. Then the clear lights glimmered out along the walls as men put the waxen torches in place, and served supper in the hall. And a cheerful noise of merrymaking sprang up round the fires, and all the time at supper and afterward they sang songs and Christmas carols and danced, with laughter and every kind of good cheer. All the while Gawain sat by the lady, and she behaved so sweetly to him, with little side glances of love between themselves, that Gawain was all bewildered and at odds with himself, for he could not courteously keep her again at a distance, but felt that he must join her in her courtly dalliance, even if it were to turn out amiss.

When they had enjoyed themselves in the hall as long as they wished, the lord brought them to his room, and they sat down by the hearth. There they drank wine, and talked, and proposed to make the same terms again for New Year's Eve. But Gawain said he must take his leave and ride away in the morning, for it was drawing near the time of the tryst that he had to keep. But the lord said no, and bade him stay quietly at home, and said, "As I am true knight, I pledge my honor that you shall come to the Green Chapel, to do

what you have to do there, in the dawn of the New Year long
before prime.[8] Therefore lie late in your room and take your
ease, and I will go hunting in the woods, and stand by our
bargain, and exchange my winnings with you when I come
back again. I have tested you twice, and I find you true to
your word. 'Third time is best time'; let us remember that in
the morning, but let us make merry while we can, and think
of nothing but delight. Sorrow is always waiting for a man
when he is set on finding it."

Gawain agreed that he would stay, and they drank a last
draught happily together, and then the lights were brought
and they went to their beds. Gawain lay and slept quietly
and sound all night, but the lord, who was full of his hunting, was up and about with the dawn.

After they had heard Mass they ate a hasty breakfast, and
the lord asked for his horse and went out to meet his knights,
who were ready for him, dressed and mounted before the
gates of the hall. It was a glorious morning; the hoarfrost
sparkled bright on the ground, and the sun rose fiery red
against the cloudrack, and his bright rays cut through the
mists overhead. The huntsmen uncoupled by the side of a
coppice, and the rocks in the wood rang to the notes of the
horns. Some of the hounds picked up the scent of the fox
where he was lying, and they dashed this way and that across
it as they were trained. One of them gave tongue on it, the
huntsman called to him, and all the rest made after him,
panting in full cry on a high scent. The fox ran before them,
and soon they made him break covert, and as soon as they saw
him they bayed furiously. He twisted and turned through
many a rough patch of undergrowth, and doubled back, and
often waited in the bottom of a hedge to listen. In the end
he jumped over a little ditch by a thorn hedge, and stole

[8] Prime: (the service for) the first hour of the day, i.e. 6 a.m.
or sunrise.

away very quietly by the side of a spinney, and he would have tricked the hounds and got away, but before he was aware of it he ran full into a hunting stand where three fell on him fiercely at once. He swerved at once and bravely swung off on a new track, and with despair in his heart made off into the wood.

Then it was good to hear the cry of the hounds when the whole pack was running together, hot on the scent. There was such clamor when they got a sight of him that it sounded as though the clustering crags had crashed down together. When the hunters viewed him they hallooed and turned him, cursing him for a thief, and the hounds were hard on him, so that he had no rest. When he broke for the open they fell on him so that he had to swing in again. So the cunning fox led them, the lord and his men, all round and about, over hill and dale, till noon.

Meantime Gawain at home slept soundly through the cold morning within the fair curtains. But the lady could not sleep, for she was still set in her heart on making love to him. She rose quickly and made her way to his room, clad in a lovely robe down to her feet, lined with the finest furs. She wore no gay color on her head but the well-cut gems that hung about her headdress in clusters of twenty. Her sweet face was unveiled, and her throat was bare, for the robe was cut low both back and front. She came in and closed the door behind her. Then she threw open a window, and called to Gawain and mocked him gaily.

"Gawain, Gawain, how can you sleep so sound on so bright a morning?"

Gawain was deep sunk in sleep, but at this he woke and heard her.

He had been deep in gloomy dreams, and muttering as he dreamed, like a man troubled with a throng of dreary thoughts, how that day he had to meet his destiny at the

Green Chapel, when he encountered the Green Knight, and
had to stand up to his stroke and make no resistance. But
when that gracious lady came in he came to his waking senses,
and swam up out of his dreams, and made haste to answer
her greeting. The lady came to him, laughing sweetly, and
bent over him and softly kissed him, and he welcomed her
with good cheer. And when he saw her so lovely and so gaily
arrayed, with her flawless beauty and her sweet color, joy
welled up and warmed his heart. And they smiled gently at
each other, and fell into gay talk, and all was joy and happiness and delight between them. It would have been a perilous time for both of them, if Mary had not taken thought for
her knight. For that noble princess urged him so, and pressed
him so hard to confess himself her lover, that at last he must
needs either accept her love or bluntly refuse her. And he
was troubled for his courtesy, for fear that he should behave
like a churl, but more afraid of a wound to his honor, if he
behaved badly to his host, the lord of the castle. And that at
any rate, he said to himself, should not happen. So he laughed
a little, though kindly, and put aside all the fond loving
words that sprang to her lips.

And she said, "You are to blame, Gawain, if you have no
love for the woman that holds you so near her heart, of all
women on earth most sorely stricken, unless it is that you already have a lover that pleases you better, and you plighted
your troth to her so surely that you will not break faith—and
that is what I am coming to believe. Tell me the truth now,
for God's sake, and do not hide it, nor make any pretense."

With a kindly smile, said Gawain, "By St. John I have no
lover, nor will have one now."

"That," said she, "hurts more than anything else you could
say. But I have my answer, and it wounds. Give me one kiss,
and I will leave you. There is nothing left for me but sorrow,
for I love you dearly." She stooped with a sigh and gave him

a sweet kiss, and then she stood up, and said as she stood by
him, "Now, my dear, as I go away, do at least this for me;
give me some gift, if it·is only your glove, that I can have
something to remind me of you and lessen my grief."

"I wish I had here," said Gawain, "for your sake, the most
precious thing I have in the world. You have deserved ten
times over a richer gift of thanks than any I could offer. But to
give you a love gift would avail but little, and it is not fitting
for your honor to have a glove as a keepsake of Gawain, and
I am here, in lands far from my home, on a venture, and I
have no men with me bringing my bags with things that
would be worthy of you. It saddens me, dear lady, that I can
do so little to show my love to you, but each man must do
the best he can as he finds himself; do not take it amiss nor
be sorry."

"Well," said the lovely lady, "Gawain, noblest of knights,
even if I can have nothing of yours, you shall have something
of mine." And she held out to him a rich ring of the red
gold, with a bright jewel blazing on it that flashed as bright
as the sunrays. It was worth a king's ransom, but Gawain refused it and said at once, "I will take from you, fair lady; no
gifts to keep at this time; there is nothing I have to offer
you, and so I will take nothing."

She persisted, and asked him again and again to take it, but
he swore on his honor that he would not, and she was sorry
that he denied her, and she said, "If you refuse my ring, because it seems too rich, and you will not be so beholden to
me, then I will give you my girdle, which is a cheaper gift."
And she took hold of a belt that was fastened round her
waist, clasped over her tunic under the bright mantle. It was
fashioned of green silk, and trimmed with gold, embroidered
only round the edges and adorned with pendants. That she
offered to him, and besought him to take it, unworthy gift
though it was.

But he said that he would accept nothing, neither gold nor keepsake, before God gave him grace to achieve the adventure that he had taken on himself. "And so," he said, "do not be angry with me, but cease your asking, for I cannot grant it; I am deeply in your debt because of all your kindness to me, and for ever and through all things I am your true servant."

"Now are you refusing this silk," said she, "because it seems so cheap a gift? It seems so, I know, a small thing and of little value. But if a man knew the powers that are knit into its fabric, he might hold it at a higher rate. Any man that is girt with this green girdle, when it is close clasped around him, there is no man under heaven that can cut him down, and he cannot be slain by any skill upon earth."

Then Gawain thought about it again, and it came into his head that this was the very thing for the peril that lay before him, when he came to the chapel to meet his doom, and that if he could escape death he would owe much to the charmed girdle. So he was more patient with her as she pressed it on him, and let her speak on. She offered it to him again, and prayed him earnestly to take it, and in the end he consented, and she gave it him eagerly. But she besought him for her sake never to reveal it, but to keep it loyally hidden from her lord. And he promised her that no man should ever know of it, but themselves only. And he thanked her many times and deeply from the bottom of his heart. And she kissed him the third time.

Then she took her leave and left him there, knowing that she could get no more of him. When she was gone, Gawain arrayed himself at once, in his finest apparel, and put away the love lace that the lady had given him, hiding it away securely where he could easily find it again.

Then promptly he made his way to the chapel, and went quietly to a priest and prayed him to teach him how to amend his life and how his soul might be saved when he went thence. He made his confession and told all his misdeeds, less and more, and asked for forgiveness, craving absolution. And the priest absolved him, setting him as clean from his sins as though the day of judgment were to come the next day. And then he made merrier with the ladies on that day than ever before, with dancing and singing and all manner of delight, till the night fell. Each man in the castle had courteous words from him, and said that he had never seen Sir Gawain in such spirits since first he came to their castle.

Let us leave him there at his ease, with love all about him, and go back to the lord who was still out in the country at the head of his hunt.

By now he had killed the fox that he had hunted all day. As he jumped a hedge to get a view of the rascal, and heard the pack that sped after him, he had seen the fox making his way through a tangled thicket, and all the pack in full cry at his heels. He watched him and waited carefully and drew his bright sword and aimed at him. The fox swerved from the steel, and would have drawn back, but a hound was on him before he could recover, and there right before the horse's hooves they all fell on him and worried him.

The lord dismounted in haste and grasped the fox, snatching him quickly from the hounds' mouths, and held him high over his head and hollaed at the top of his voice, while the hounds bayed fiercely round him. The huntsmen hurried to his call, blowing the recall till they came in sight of their lord. And the whole hunt gathered, and all who had horns blew them, and the rest that had no horns hallooed. It was the merriest cry that ever was heard, this requiem that was raised for Reynard's soul! They gave the hounds their reward, and patted and stroked their heads, and then they skinned the fox, and then turned homeward, for it was near nightfall, blowing great blasts on the horns as they rode.

At length the lord got down at his own castle, and found

there a fire burning brightly on the hearth, and Gawain beside it, full of delight after the day of joy he had had with the ladies. He was wearing a mantle of rich blue stuff that fell to his feet, and a surcoat that suited him well, and a hood that fell over his shoulders, both of them lined with soft white fur. He met his host in the middle of the hall, and greeted him merrily, and said to him courteously, "Tonight I will be the first to make good our covenant, that we made with so happy an outcome, and sealed it with the draught of wine." Then he embraced the lord and gave him three kisses, as loving and eager as he could make them.

"By God!" said the lord, "you are doing well at your new trade, if you made a cheap bargain."

"No matter for the bargain," said Gawain at once, "so long as I have paid you in full what I owed you."

"Marry," said the other, "mine are poor winnings to set beside yours, for I have hunted all day and I have nothing to show for it but this miserable fox skin—the devil take it!— and that is a poor exchange for the precious things that you have pressed on me, three such warm and loving kisses."

"None the less," said Gawain, "I thank you."

And the lord told him all the tale of the hunt as they stood there.

With mirth and with minstrelsy, and with the dishes of their choice set before them, and the laughter of the ladies and the jokes that Gawain and his host exchanged, they made as merry as any men could who were neither silly nor drunk. The lord and his company talked and laughed together till the time came to say good night and go to their beds.

Then Gawain made his farewells in courteous form, first to his host, and thanked him. "For all the kindly sojourn that I have had here, and the honor you have done me at this high season, may God reward you. I give myself to you for one of your own men, if you will have me. And now farewell, for, as you know, I must be on my way tomorrow morning, if you will assign me one of your men, as you said you would, to guide me on the way to the Green Chapel, to find there on New Year's Day whatever fate God has in store for me."

"Faith," said the lord, "I will give you with good will all that I promised." And he appointed one of his men to set Gawain on his way, and bring him over the hills, so that he should have no trouble with his road, and guide him through woodland and brake by the shortest track. Gawain thanked him for his kindness, and then he took his leave of the noble ladies.

He spoke to them with sorrow at parting, and kissed them both, and talked to them, thanking them again and again, and they replied to him in the same way. They sighed sadly and commended him to the keeping of Christ. And then he said good-bye courteously to the company. Each man that he met he thanked for the kindness and the service that he in particular had done for him, and all the trouble he had taken. And each man was as sorry to say good-bye to Gawain as though they had had him living among them all his life. Then they brought him with lights to his room, and left him to go content to bed. Perhaps he slept less soundly than before, for he had much on his mind for the morrow to keep him awake.

Let him lie there peacefully, for now he is near the goal that he has been seeking. If you will listen, I will tell you how they fared.

And New Year's Day drew near, and the night passed, and day drove hard on the heels of the dark. And all the wild weather in the world seemed to be about the castle. There were clouds above that sent their cold breath down to the ground, and there was bitter cold from the north, torturing all ill-clad men. And the snow shivered down bitingly, and pinched all the wild creatures. And the whistling wind swooped down from the heavens and in the dales drove the snow into great drifts.

Sir Gawain listened as he lay in his bed, and for all that he kept his eyes shut it was little he slept. And as each cock crew he knew that his hour was coming nearer. Swiftly he got up, before the dawn, by the dim light of a lamp that gleamed in his room, and he called to his servant, who answered him straightaway, and bade him bring his mail shirt and saddle his horse. The servant rose and brought Gawain his clothes, and dressed him in his full armor. First he put on him warm garments to keep out the bitter cold, and then his war harness, body-piece and plates for arms and legs, all polished and shining—for the whole time that Gawain had been staying in the castle his man had kept it carefully—and every ring in his splendid mail shirt shone as clean from the rust as on the first day when the armorer had made it. Gawain put this armor on, as gleaming a warrior as any between Britain and the far land of Greece, and he thanked his man, and told him to bring his horse.

And while he put on the glorious clothes—his coat, with the badge clearly worked on velvet, trimmed and set about with precious stones, with embroidered seams, and lined inside with fur—yet he did not leave off the love lace, the lady's gift. That, you may be sure, Gawain for his own sake did not forget. When he had belted on his sword round his hips, then he wound twice round his waist, swiftly and close, the green silken girdle, fit for a fair knight and shining out against the splendid scarlet of the cloth. But it was not for its richness that he wore it, or for pride in its pendants that glittered with the gleam of polished gold, but to save his life, when he had to stand in the face of danger, and, by his covenant, not stir a weapon in his own defense. And now the brave knight was ready to go out to his fate.

There was Gringolet ready waiting for him, his great warcharger. He had been stabled and fed as well as ever in his life, and was full of spirit, ready to gallop just for the joy of galloping. Gawain went to him and looked at his glossy coat, and said quietly to himself, "There is a company of men in this castle whose thoughts are full of courtesy. Joy befall the lord who maintains them, and, for his dear lady, may she all her life long have all the love that she desires. Whenever for charity they entertain a guest and give him such hospitality as they have showed me, may the high God that rules the heavens above reward them, and all you also. And if I have any while longer to live on earth, I will freely requite you."

Then he set foot in the stirrup and swung himself into the saddle, and his man gave him his shield, and he slung it over his shoulders. Then he touched Gringolet with his golden spurs, and Gringolet stopped curvetting and sprang forward. Behind Gawain rode his squire with his lance, and as he rode out he commended the castle to Christ's keeping and wished it all good fortune.

The drawbridge was lowered, and both sides of the great gates were unbarred and thrown open. The knight crossed himself and rode over the planks, and thanked the porter who kneeled before him, bade him good day and commended him to the safekeeping of God. So Gawain rode his way with the one squire who was to guide him on his road to the dolorous place where he was to abide the grim onslaught. They passed by banks where all the boughs were bare, and the icy cold seemed to cling to the cliffs under which they rode. The clouds rode high, but there was ill weather under them. The mist drizzled on the moor and was heavier on the tops of the hills, so that each had a cap and a cloak of mist about it. The streams swirled and broke about their banks, and foamed white as they came down in spate. It was a hard wandering way they had to find when it lay through woods, till it came to the hour of dawn. Then they were high on a hill, and the white snow lay all round them. And his squire bade Gawain halt.

"Now I have brought you hither, my lord, and you are not far from the place which you have asked for and sought so earnestly. But now I shall tell you the truth, since each day that I have known you the more I have grown to love you; if you would do as I advise, you would fare the better. The place that you press forward to is held full perilous. In that waste land there dwells a man as evil as any on earth. He is stalwart, and grim, and a lover of blows, and mightier than any man on middle-earth, huger than Hector of Troy or any four knights of Arthur's house. And this is what he does at the Green Chapel. There is never a man passes that way, however proud of his prowess in arms, but he smites him down and kills him. He is a violent man, and he knows no mercy in his heart, and whether it be churl or noble that passes, monk or Mass priest, cleric or lay, he loves to kill them as well as he loves his own life. And so I tell you, as surely as you sit there in the saddle, and I tell you the truth, if once you come there, no matter if you had twenty lives, you are a dead man, if the knight has his will with you. He has dwelt here a long time, and fought many combats, and there is no guard against his grim blows.

"Therefore, for God's sake, sir, leave the man well alone, and go some other way and ride to another country, where Christ may be your speed. And I will turn home again, and I promise you besides that I will keep our secret truly, and never let drop a word that you flinched from meeting any man."

"All the thanks of my heart," said Gawain, slowly, "and

good luck to you, who wish me well. I am sure that you would truly keep my secret; but however close you kept it, if I now turned aside, and made haste to flee in the way you tell me to, then I should be a coward knight, and there could be no excuse. I will go on to the chapel, whatever chance may befall, and have such speech as I think well with this same knight, come weal or woe, as Fate will have it. And though he may be a grim creature to deal with, and stand there with his club, yet God can always contrive salvation for his servants."

Then said the squire, "Now that you go so far, and say plainly that you will bring doom on your own head, and throw away your life, I will not hinder nor keep you from it. Take here your helm on your head and your spear in your hand, and ride down this same path by the side of yonder rock, till you come down to the bottom of the wild valley. Then look a little to your left over the field, and you will see in that glade the chapel you seek, and by it the huge knight that dwells there. So fare you well, in God's name, Gawain the noble! For all the gold on the earth I would not go with you, nor bear you company one foot further through the wood." And with that he wheeled his horse and drove the spurs into him and set him over the field at a gallop, leaving Gawain there alone.

"By God," said Gawain, "I will not moan nor shed tear. I am altogether ready to do the will of God, and to His good pleasure I have given myself."

Then he spurred Gringolet, and picked up the track, and made his way along the bank by the side of a shaw, and rode along the rough bank right down to the dale. Then he looked about him, and saw how wild it was, and saw no sign of a shelter anywhere about, but high banks and sheer on both hands, with outcrops of gnarled rough knuckles of rock, and it looked as though the higher crags were grazing the clouds.

Then he reined in Gringolet and halted, and turned on this side and that, looking for the chapel.

He saw nothing like it anywhere, and he thought this strange. Then a little way away over the field he saw a small mound, a smooth swelling knoll, by the waterside where a cascade fell down, and the water of the brook bubbled in the basin as though it were boiling. Gawain gave Gringolet his head and came to the mound, and got down quietly and fastened the reins to the rough bough of a lime tree. Then he walked over to the mound, and strode all round it, wondering what it was. There was a hole in one end, and one on each side, and it was all overgrown with patches of grass; whether it was only an old cave or just a split in a rock, he could not make out.

"Well!" said he, "is this the Green Chapel? This is the kind of place where the devil might say matins at midnight! It is a desolate place, and this chapel, if it is the chapel, is evil looking, all overgrown. It is the right place for the knight in green to perform his devotions after the devil's fashion. I am beginning to think in my heart that it is the fiend that has appointed me this tryst, to destroy me here. It is an unchancy chapel, bad luck to it, the least hallowed church that ever I came into!"

With helm on head and lance in hand he came up to the mound, and then he heard, from a rock high up on a hill beyond the brook, a wondrous loud noise. Hark! it re-echoed on the cliff with the sound of a scythe being whetted on a grindstone. Hark! it whirred and rasped, like water at a mill; it rushed and rang, fearful to hear. Then said Gawain, "By God, this device, I think, is meant to greet me and to sound the challenge for me as I come. God's will be done. To say 'Woe is me!' does not help in the least. And though I may have to give up my life, no mere noise is going to scare me."

Then Gawain called aloud, "Who is master here, to keep tryst with me? For now am I, Sir Gawain, walking here and ready. If any man wants aught of me, let him come hither quickly, now or never, to work his will."

"Stay," said a voice from the bank above his head, "and swiftly you shall have all that I once promised you."

Yet the speaker went on for a while with the noise of his whetting before he would come down. Then he made his way down by the side of a crag, and came hurtling out of a crack in the rock with a grim weapon, a new Danish ax, with a massive blade on it, curving by the haft, whetted with a whetstone, and four foot long, measured by the thong that gleamed bright on the haft. There was the Green Knight, appareled as before, the same in his face and his limbs, his locks and his beard, except that this time he strode firmly on his feet, setting the haft to the ground beside him as he walked. And when he came to the water, not wanting to wade it, he used his ax as a jumping pole and leaped over, and came striding lissomely forward, fierce and fell, over the broad stretch of snow that lay all around.

Sir Gawain bent his head no farther than he must for courtesy, and greeted him. The other said, "Sir knight, now men may know that you are one who keeps tryst. Gawain, so God guard me, I tell you you are very welcome to my dwelling, and you have timed your travelings as a true man should. You know the covenants that we made between us. Twelve months ago today you took what chance gave you, and I was to give you prompt quittance this New Year's Day. Here we are in this valley by our two selves, and there are no men to part us, however tight we lock swaying in combat. Take your helm off your head, and take your wages, making no more resistance than I made then, when you whipped my head off at one blow."

"Nay," said Gawain, "by the Lord God who gave me life,

I shall have no grudge against you, not a grain, for any harm that may fall to me. But keep yourself to the one stroke, and I will stand still, and give you free leave to strike as you will." So he leaned his head down and bared his neck, showing the white skin, making as though he did not care, and giving no sign of fear.

Then the Green Knight got himself quickly ready, took firm hold of his grim tool to smite Gawain, and gathered every ounce of strength in his body together as he rose to the stroke, and drove at him as mightily as though he had a mind to destroy him. And if it had fallen as hard and as true as he seemed to intend, the doughtiest warrior alive would have been dead of the blow. But Gawain glanced sideways at the blade as it came swooping down to strike him to the earth, and he could not help his shoulders shrinking a little from the keen steel. And the Green Knight with a turn of his wrist swerved the blade aside, and then he told Gawain what he thought of him.

"You cannot be Gawain, that is held so good a knight, who never, they say, quailed for any host of men on hill or on dale. And now you flinched like a coward before you felt even a scratch. That is not what I have ever heard of Gawain. I did not flinch nor flee when you aimed your blow at me, and I made no evasions in Arthur's hall. My head fell at my feet, but did I flinch? Not I. And now you quail before any harm comes to you. So I deserve to be called a better knight than you are."

Said Gawain, "I shrank once, but I will not again, even if my head falls on the stones, though I cannot, like you, put it back again on my shoulders if it does! Get ready again, and come to the point. Deal me my doom, and do it out of hand. I will stand up to your stroke, and start away no more till your ax has struck me, and I pledge my troth to that."

"Have at you then," said the other, and hove up the ax,

and looked at him as fiercely as though he were mad with anger, and aimed a mighty blow at him; but just as the blade came down he held back before it could wound him. Gawain awaited the stroke steadfastly, and flinched this time not the least, but stood still as a stone or the stump of a tree that is anchored with a hundred roots round a rock in the ground.

Then merrily spoke the Green Knight: "Hm! Now that you have got your courage back, it is time to hit you in earnest. Throw back the hood that Arthur gave you, and see whether your neck can stand the blow that is coming."

To which Gawain, now full of wrath, replied in anger, "Drive on, fierce knight; you are too long over your threats. I wonder that you are not scared by your own fierceness."

"Faith," said the Green Knight, "if you are so furious, I will not delay, nor be slow in letting you have what you have come for. Ready!" Then he took his stance for the stroke, and set his lips and knit his brows. It was no wonder that Gawain, with no hope of rescue, little liked the look of him.

He lifted the ax lightly and let it deftly down just by the bare neck. And though he swung at him hard he did him no more hurt than to graze him on one side, so that the very tip of the blade just broke the skin, and the bright blood spurted over his shoulders to the ground. And when Gawain saw the blood red on the snow, he leapt forward more than a spear length, and seized his helm and set it on his head, and gave a twitch with his shoulders to bring his shield round in front of him, and flashed out his bright sword, and spoke fiercely—Never since his mother bore him had he been so gay, now that his trial was over.

"Stop your blows, sir, and deal me no more. I have endured one stroke in this place without making any return; but if you deal me another, be very sure that I will pay it back forthwith, and give you blow for blow again. There is only the one blow due to fall to me here—those were the terms of

the covenant made between us in Arthur's hall—so now, good
sir, hold your hand."

The Green Knight held off and rested on his ax, the haft
on the ground and his arms on the blade, and he watched
Gawain standing there, bold and fearless, full armed again,
and with never a thought of flinching. And he was glad to see
it, and he spoke cheerfully to him in a great voice, so that
his words rang clear like bells.

"Good knight, be not so wrathful. No man has here mis-
used you unmannerly, or treated you otherwise than as the
covenant allowed, which we made at the King's court. I
promised you a stroke, and you have had it and you can count
yourself well paid. That blow is full quittance of all that you
owe me. Had I wished, I could perhaps have dealt you a buffet more harshly, and done you injury. But, as it was, first I
threatened you with a feint, and gave you no wound. That
was for the agreement we made the first night at my castle,
and for the next day, when you kept troth loyally, and gave
me back, like a true man, your gains for the day. And the
second feint was for the next day after, when again you had
my dear lady's kisses and gave me them again. For those two
days I aimed the two strokes at you that were no more than
feints and did you no scathe. A true man pays his debts and
then need fear no danger. But the third time you failed in your
trust, and for that you had to take your third blow and the
wound.

"For it is my own green girdle that you are wearing, and it
was my own wife that gave it you. I know all about your
kisses, and the love-making of my wife, and how you bore
yourself, for it was I myself that brought it about. I sent her
to make trial of you, and surely I think that you are the most
faultless knight that ever trod upon earth. As a pearl for price
by the side of a white pea, so, by God's truth, is Gawain be-

side other gay knights. But just over the girdle, sir, you failed a little, and came short in your loyalty; yet that was not for any intrigue nor for love-making, but just that you loved your life, and I do not blame you for it."

Gawain stood in thought a long while, so overcome with grief that he groaned in his heart, and all the blood in his body seemed to rush to his face as he winced for shame at what the Green Knight said. And the first words that he said were, "Curse upon cowardice and covetousness both; there is evil power in them to destroy a man's virtue." Then he laid his hand to the knot of the girdle, and loosed it, and threw it savagely from him to the Green Knight, and said, "Lo, there is my broken faith, curse on it. I was afraid of your blow, so cowardice taught me to make terms with covetousness, and forget my true nature, the generosity and loyalty that belong to true knights. Now I have shown myself false, I that ever was afraid of any treachery or untruth, and hated them. I make my confession to you, sir knight, between the two of us. I have behaved very ill. Let me now do what I can to gain your good will; and afterwards I will show that I have learned my lesson."

The Green Knight laughed, and said to him friendlily, "Such harm as I took, I count it wholly cured. You have made such free confession that all your faults are cleansed, and besides you have done your penance at the edge of my blade. I hold you purged of all your offenses and as clean as if you had never failed in virtue since the day you were born. And I give you the gold-hemmed girdle that is green as my gown. Sir Gawain, you will be able to think back on this day's contest when you ride out among great princes. It will be a noble token of the meeting of two chivalrous knights at the Green Chapel. And now, this very New Year's Day, you shall come back with me to my castle, and we will finish off happily the rest of the revel that we left." He pressed him to come, and said, "We must put you on good terms again with my wife, who behaved as your enemy."

"Nay," said Gawain, and took hold of his helm and lifted it from his head, and thanked the Green Knight. "I have stayed too long already. All happiness be yours, and may the great God grant it you, He that brings honor to men. Commend me to your fair and gracious lady, and to that other also, those two whom I honor, who with their devices so cunningly beguiled me. But it is no marvel if a fool goes astray in his wits, and through the wiles of women comes to sorrow, seeing that Adam was deceived by Eve, and Solomon by many women, and Delilah brought doom on Samson, and David was overcome by the beauty of Bathsheba, and endured much sorrow. All these were brought down by the wiles of women. How far better it would be if we could love them well, but never believe them, if only a man could do it. For those were the noblest men of old, and prosperity came to them beyond all men under the vault of heaven, but they were all bemused and beguiled by the love of women. And so, I think, even if I too was deluded, there was some excuse for me.

"But for your girdle—and may God reward you for your kindness—that I will wear with the best will in the world, not for the sake of the splendid gold, nor the silk, nor the pendants that hang from it, nor its costliness, nor the lovely work in it, nor for the honor that I shall get when I am seen wearing it, but as a memorial of my sin. I shall look at it often when I ride out proudly, and I shall feel remorse in my heart for the fault and frailty of the erring flesh, which is so ready to catch the infection and the stain of ill-doing. So when pride stirs in my heart for my prowess in arms, one glance at the love lace will humble me. But there is one thing I would ask you—may it not displease you—since you are lord of the land where I have lived with you in your castle, and been treated with honor—may He requite you who upholds the heavens and is throned above the skies! Will you tell me your true name that you are called by? Then I will ask no more."

"I will tell you truly," said the other. "Bercilak de Haut-desert I am called in my own land. And it is the might of Morgan la Fay that has brought all this about. She dwells in my house, and she knows all the cunning of magical lore and the crafty ways of it, and has learned the mysteries of Merlin, for once she had dealings in love with that great wizard, who knows all your knights at home. And so Morgan the goddess is her name, and there is never a man so high and proud but she can humble and tame him.

"It was she who sent me to your splendid halls, to make trial of your pride, and to see whether there was truth in the report that runs through the world of the great renown of the Round Table. She sent this marvel to steal your wits away from you, and she hoped to have daunted Guenevere and brought her to death with dismay at that same strange figure that stood like a phantom before the high table, and spoke from the head that he held in his hand. She is that ancient lady whom you saw at my castle, and she is your own aunt, Arthur's half-sister, daughter of that Duchess of Tintagel on whom Uther later begat Arthur, that now is King. So now I ask you, sir knight, come back to my halls and meet your aunt again, and make merry with us. My company all love you, and by my faith I wish you as well as any man on earth for your true loyalty."

But Gawain still said no, and could not be persuaded. So they embraced and kissed and commended each other to the Prince of Paradise, and parted there in the snow. Gawain mounted and rode off, hasting to the King's castle, and the knight in the bright green went his own way.

And Gawain on Gringolet, with his life given back to him, rode through many wild ways, sometimes with a roof over his head at night, and sometimes sleeping under the stars. He had many adventures by the way, and won many victories. The wound in his neck was healed, and he wore the shining girdle about it, slantwise like a baldric to his other side, and fastened under his left arm in a knot, the token of his fault, to remind him of the stain of it. So he came to the court, sound and whole. And great joy rose in the castle when the great King knew that the good Sir Gawain was come, and rejoiced over it. And the King kissed the knight, and the Queen too, and then many a true knight thronged round him to greet him and ask him how he had fared. He told them all the wonders, all the hardships he had, the adventure at the chapel, and the way the Green Knight dealt with him, the love of the lady, and at last the love lace. And he bared his neck and showed them the wound that he took at the knight's hands as punishment for his failure in troth. When he came to the telling of this part he was tormented, and groaned for grief and sorrow, and the blood rushed to his cheeks with the shame of what he had to confess.

"See, my lord," said Sir Gawain, and laid his hand on the girdle, "this is the band that is sign of my fault, my disgrace, the mark of the cowardice and the covetousness that I yielded to, the token of my broken troth. And I must needs wear it as long as I live. For no man can hide his scar, nor rid himself of it; when once it is fastened upon him it will never depart."

The King comforted the knight, and all the court laughed kindly, and agreed, to cheer him, that all the lords and ladies of the Round Table, everyone of the brotherhood, should wear a slanting baldric of bright green, just like Gawain's. So that became a part of the glory of the Round Table, and ever after a man that wore it was honored. So the ancient books of romance tell us.

This adventure happened in the days of King Arthur, and the books about Britain, that Brutus founded, record it. And many other adventures like it have befallen since the siege and assault ceased at Troy and the bold knight Brutus first made his way to this land.

And may He that wore the crown of thorns bring us to His bliss.

THE BOOK OF BALIN

by Sir Thomas Malory

FOREWORD

In the first printing shop ever known in England, in July, 1485, William Caxton printed a volume destined to become one of the Great Books of English literature. As its editor, he gave it the title, *Le Morte Darthur,* by which it has ever since been known, though the title, in fact, applied only to the last of its stories of King Arthur and his knights. In a preface of great charm and interest Caxton described how he had been urged to print such a book, and how he had received a copy of its "histories," which Sir Thomas Malory had reduced from certain French books into English. This English version Caxton divided into twenty-one books. Of the whole compilation he said genially that readers are at their liberty to believe or not in its truth, but "for to pass the time this book shall be pleasant to read in . . . wherein they shall find many joyous and pleasant histories, and noble and renowned acts of humanity, gentleness, and chivalry . . . friendliness, hardiness, love, cowardice, murder, hate, virtue, and sin. Do after the good and leave the evil, and it shall bring you to good fame and renown."

Of the English author of this famous book, Sir Thomas Malory, few certain facts are known. Indubitably he was a Warwickshire knight and soldier; he spent years in prison; he died in 1471; on his tombstone appeared the simple tribute, *Valens Miles*. In recent years, however, a number of fifteenth-century indictments have been noted which charge him with serious crimes, violent robberies, brutal personal assaults. They would seem to indicate that from 1450-60 Malory suddenly began and subsequently led a turbulent life of crime. Though records of trial and conviction as sequels to these indictments are singularly lacking, though Malory himself vowed his innocence, though modern authorities on medieval legal practices grant that such indictments were wholly invalid as proofs of guilt, still Malory had to pay the hard penalty, whether the accusations were true or false, of spending many years in prison. It was there that he wrote his Arthurian stories, there that, as a knight-prisoner, he prayed for deliverance and for God's help. In view of the highly controversial character of medieval indictments and the general breakdown of law before and during the lawless Wars of the Roses (1455-85), it is best to turn from the man to his book, to that "last classic" of the Middle Ages, which is still so highly counted among the world's well-loved books. Because of the discovery in 1934 of a manuscript antedating Caxton's edition of Malory's own work, now edited by Professor Eugène Vinaver (Oxford, 1947, 3 volumes), we can learn more of what were the writer's original intentions, trace more clearly the stages through which his stylistic genius developed, but as it was Caxton's edition which made Malory famous, it is that version which, in modernized form, is printed here.

The *Book of Balin* was called by Caxton the second book of the *Morte Darthur;* he divided it into nineteen chapters with a rubric for each one. It is complete within itself and fully represents the vigor of Malory's writing. Its first sentence makes swift allusion to Arthur's early history; later allusions, chiefly in the form of prophecies by the wizard Merlin, refer to the coming adventures of the Sangreal and to Arthur's last battle at Salisbury. But these and other links, reaching backward and forward in the great Arthurian cycle, are not necessary to the understanding of the *Balin* romance. Arthur appears in it, not as a remote but as an immediate, mighty figure; his personal wrath against Balin motivates a series of fateful consequences for that hero. In Malory's source for this book, a thirteenth-century French prose romance now published as the *Roman de Balain* (edited by M. D. Legge, Manchester, 1942) but long known as part of the Merlin cycle, there was, as the literary fashion of that century dictated, a good deal of intricate interweaving of narrative threads, of leisurely divagations from the main theme, of romantic but needless embellishments, of too prolonged descriptions, especially of battles. Malory, a man of different race and period, himself enduring a "dolorous prisonment," gave to the story a new tone and power. Leaving out the superfluities in which a tragic theme had been enmeshed, cutting out three-fourths of the original, he released the basic concept of an essentially innocent man doomed to terrible mischance, and did it with a force realized but not matched in the modern poetic versions by Tennyson (1885) and Swinburne (1896). Not, perhaps, until Thomas Hardy wrote *Jude the Obscure* (1895) was the sense of fatalism in human life more movingly portrayed.

Step by step, yet swiftly too, the story mounts to its tragic climax when the two devoted brothers, Balin and Balan, each unaware of the other's identity, slay each other. Every scene in which Balin appears adds to his fuller characterization. He is poor, blunt, obstinate, too swift in private vengeance for cruel wrongs, but always brave and loyal, always honest and right-minded in intent. He speaks laconically: "I am not afeard. . . . Do it yourself!" or in bitter outcries: "God knoweth I did none other but as I would ye did to me"; "I would slay myself to make thee a liar." Sternly he rebukes the maiden who scorns his poor dress: "Worthiness . . . and good deeds are not in arrayment, but manhood and worship is hid within a man's person." The words are wholly Malory's and spring from a concept as forthright as was Robert Burns's "A man's a man for a' that." Malory omits the French hero's lamentations about fate, but deepens the feeling of the English Balin's sense of doom as he hears the triumphant horn-blowing as for a slain beast: "I am the prise and yet am I not dead."

The book is full of those marvels and mysteries, those heroic deeds and noble loyalties, those passions of love and vengeance, those strange "customs," which made the very substance of medieval fiction. Yet despite its inherited unrealities, such as that of the castle where all maidens passing by were required to bleed their blood to fill a silver dish, or the portents and dire consequences of Balin's Dolorous Stroke in the Grail Castle, Malory gave a kind of realism to his narrative. It may come from the simple naturalism of telling how men lodged "in a wood among leaves beside the highway, and took off the bridles of their horses and put them to grass," or even from the terrific nosebleed of an anguished lover! To the characters unnamed in his source Malory gave good names; and sometimes he individualized them by a single vivid word: Lanceor of Ireland is an "orgulous" knight, furiously ready to fight but not to reason why; Balin, like his story, is the "knight unhappy," a recurrent phrase in a prose full of haunting cadences. Did Milton, thinking of "knights of Logres or of Lyones,/Lancelot or Pelleas or Pellenore," recall Arthur's cry in Malory, "Oh, where is Balin and Balan and Pellinore?" Did one beautiful rhythm of English speech call to another across the centuries? Malory's genius for prose rhythms, his virile sense of life in the usages of familiar talk, his power to select, intensify, unite incidents based on a tragic theme, gave to his *Balin* a power and a beauty that, like Balin's own first adventure, can still "raise the heart." If its theme is of doom, its spirit is of courage. " 'Dread you not,' said Balin, 'we will do what we may.'" "Take the adventure that God will send you; . . . we will help each other as brethren ought to do."

L.H.L.

THE STORY

I

Of a damsel which came girt with a sword for to find a man of such virtue to draw it out of the scabbard.

After the death of Uther Pendragon reigned Arthur his son, the which had great war in his days for to get all England into his hand. For there were many kings within the realm of England, and in Wales, Scotland, and Cornwall. So it befell on a time when King Arthur was at London, there came a knight and told the king tidings how that the King Rience of North Wales had reared a great number of people, and were entered into the land, and burnt and slew the king's true liege people. "If this be true," said Arthur, "it were great shame unto mine estate but that he were mightily withstood." "It is truth," said the knight, "for I saw the host myself." Well, said the king, let make a cry, that all the lords, knights, and gentlemen of arms should draw unto a castle called Camelot in those days, and there the king would let make a council-general and great jousts.

So when the king was come thither with all his baronage, and lodged as they seemed best, there was come a damsel the which was sent on message from the great Lady Lile of Avelion. And when she came before King Arthur, she told from whom she came, and how she was sent on message unto him for these causes. Then she let her mantle fall that was richly furred; and then was she girt with a noble sword whereof the king had marvel, and said, "Damsel, for what cause are ye girt with that sword? It beseemeth you not." "Now shall I tell you," said the damsel; "this sword that I am girt withal doth me great sorrow and cumbrance, for I may not be delivered of this sword but by a knight, but he must be a passing good man of his hands and of his deeds, and without villainy or treachery, and without treason. And if I may find such a knight that hath all these virtues, he may draw out this sword out of the sheath, for I have been at King Rience's for it was told me there were passing good knights, and he and all his knights have assayed it and none can speed." [1] "This is a great marvel," said Arthur, "if this be sooth; I will myself assay to draw out the sword, not presuming upon myself that I am the best knight, but that I will begin to draw at your sword in giving example to all the barons that they shall assay every one after other when I have assayed it." Then Arthur took the sword by the sheath and by the girdle and pulled at it eagerly, but the sword would not out.

"Sir," said the damsel, "you need not to pull half so hard, for he that shall pull it out shall do it with little might." "Ye say well," said Arthur; "now assay ye all my barons, but beware ye be not defiled with shame, treachery, nor guile." "Then it will not avail," said the damsel, "for he must be a clean knight without villainy, and of a gentle strain of father side and mother side." Most of all the barons of the Round Table that were there at that time assayed all by row, but there might none speed; wherefore the damsel made great sorrow out of measure, and said, "Alas! I weened in this court had been the best knights without treachery or treason." "By my faith," said Arthur, "here are good knights, as I deem, as

[1] Succeed.

any be in the world, but their grace is not to help you, wherefore I am displeased."

II

How Balin, arrayed like a poor knight, pulled out the sword, which afterward was the cause of his death.

Then fell it so that time, there was a poor knight with King Arthur, that had been prisoner with him half a year and more for slaying of a knight, the which was cousin unto King Arthur. The name of this knight was called Balin, and by good means of the barons he was delivered out of prison, for he was a good man named of his body, and he was born in Northumberland. And so he went privily into the court, and saw this adventure, whereof it raised his heart, and he would assay it as other knights did, but for he was poor and poorly arrayed he put him not far in press.[2] But in his heart he was fully assured to do as well, if his grace happed him, as any knight that there was. And as the damsel took her leave of Arthur and of all the barons, so departing, this knight Balin called unto her, and said, "Damsel, I pray you of your courtesy, suffer me as well to assay as these lords; though that I be so poorly clothed, in my heart meseemeth I am fully assured as some of these others, and meseemeth in my heart to speed right well." The damsel beheld the poor knight, and saw he was a likely man, but for his poor arrayment she thought he should be of no worship without villainy or treachery. And then she said unto the knight, "Sir, it needeth not to put me to more pain or labor, for it seemeth not you to speed there as others have failed." "Ah! fair damsel," said Balin, "worthiness and good tatches[3] and good deeds are not

[2] In the crowd.
[3] Traits of character

only in arrayment, but manhood and worship is hid within man's person, and many a worshipful knight is not known unto all people, and therefore worship and hardiness is not in arrayment." "By God," said the damsel, "ye say sooth; therefore ye shall assay to do what ye may." Then Balin took the sword by the girdle and sheath, and drew it out easily; and when he looked on the sword it pleased him much. Then had the king and all the barons great marvel that Balin had done that adventure, and many knights had great despite of Balin. "Certes," said the damsel, "this is a passing good knight, and the best that ever I found, and most of worship without treason, treachery, or villainy, and many marvels shall he do. Now, gentle and courteous knight, give me the sword again." "Nay," said Balin, "for this sword will I keep, but it be taken from me with force." "Well," said the damsel, "ye are not wise to keep the sword from me, for ye shall slay with the sword the best friend that ye have, and the man that ye most love in the world, and the sword shall be your destruction." "I shall take the adventure," said Balin, "that God will ordain me, but the sword ye shall not have at this time, by the faith of my body." "Ye shall repent it within short time," said the damsel, "for I would have the sword more for your avail than for mine, for I am passing heavy for your sake; for ye will not believe that sword shall be your destruction, and that is great pity." With that the damsel departed, making great sorrow.

Anon after, Balin sent for his horse and armor, and so would depart from the court and took his leave of King Arthur. "Nay," said the king, "I suppose ye will not depart so lightly from this fellowship, I suppose ye are displeased that I have showed you unkindness; blame me the less, for I was misinformed against you, but I weened ye had not been such a knight as ye are, of worship and prowess, and if ye will abide in this court among my fellowship, I shall so ad-

vance you as ye shall be pleased." "God thank your highness,"
said Balin, "your bounty and highness may no man praise
half to the value; but at this time I must needs depart, beseeching you alway of your good grace." "Truly," said the
king, "I am right wroth for your departing; I pray you, fair
knight, that ye tarry not long, and ye shall be right welcome
to me, and to my barons, and I shall amend all miss that I
have done against you." "God thank your great lordship," said
Balin, and therewith made him ready to depart. Then the
most part of the knights of the Round Table said that Balin
did not this adventure all only by might, but by witchcraft.

III

*How the Lady of the Lake demanded the knight's
head that had won the sword, or the
maiden's head.*

The meanwhile, that this knight was making him ready to depart, there came into the court a lady that hight[4] the Lady of
the Lake. And she came on horseback, richly beseen, and
saluted King Arthur, and there asked him a gift that he
promised her when she gave him the sword. "That is sooth,"
said Arthur, "a gift I promised you, but I have forgotten the
name of my sword that ye gave me." "The name of it," said
the lady, "is Excalibur, that is as much to say as Cut-steel."
"Ye say well," said the king; "ask what ye will and ye shall
have it, an it lie in my power to give it." "Well," said the lady,
"I ask the head of the knight that hath won the sword, or else
the damsel's head that brought it; I take no force[5] though I
have both their heads, for he slew my brother, a good knight
and true, and that gentlewoman was causer of my father's
death." "Truly," said King Arthur, "I may not grant neither

---

[4] Was called.
[5] Do not care.

of their heads with my worship, therefore ask what ye will else, and I shall fulfill your desire." "I will ask none other thing," said the lady.

When Balin was ready to depart, he saw the Lady of the Lake, that by her means had slain Balin's mother, and he had sought her three years; and when it was told him that she asked his head of King Arthur, he went to her straight and said, "Evil be you found; ye would have my head, and therefore ye shall lose yours," and with his sword lightly he smote off her head before King Arthur. "Alas, for shame!" said Arthur, "why have ye done so? Ye have shamed me and all my court, for this was a lady that I was beholden to, and hither she came under my safe-conduct; I shall never forgive you that trespass." "Sir," said Balin, "me forthinketh[6] of your displeasure, for this same lady was the untruest lady living, and by enchantment and sorcery she hath been the destroyer of many good knights, and she was causer that my mother was burnt, through her falsehood and treachery." "What cause so ever ye had," said Arthur, "ye should have forborne her in my presence; therefore, think not the contrary, ye shall repent it, for such another despite had I never in my court; therefore withdraw you out of my court in all haste ye may."

Then Balin took up the head of the lady, and bare it with him to his hostelry, and there he met with his squire, that was sorry he had displeased King Arthur, and so they rode forth out of the town. "Now," said Balin, "we must depart, take thou this head and bear it to my friends, and tell them how I have sped, and tell my friends in Northumberland that my most foe is dead. Also tell them how I am out of prison, and what adventure befell me at the getting of this sword." "Alas!" said the squire, "ye are greatly to blame for to displease King Arthur." "As for that," said Balin, "I will hie me, in all the haste that I may, to meet with King Rience and de-

[6] I regret.

stroy him, either else to die therefore; and if it may hap me
to win him, then will King Arthur be my good and gracious
lord." "Where shall I meet with you?" said the squire. "In
King Arthur's court," said Balin. So his squire and he departed
at that time. Then King Arthur and all the court made great
dole and had shame of the death of the Lady of the Lake.
Then the king buried her richly.

IV

How Merlin told the adventure of this damsel.

At that time there was a knight, the which was the king's son
of Ireland, and his name was Lanceor, the which was an orgulous knight, and counted himself one of the best of the
court; and he had great despite at Balin for the achieving of
the sword, that any should be accounted more hardy, or more
of prowess; and he asked King Arthur if he would give him
leave to ride after Balin and to revenge the despite that he
had done. "Do your best," said Arthur, "I am right wroth
with Balin; I would he were quit of the despite that he hath
done to me and to my court." Then this Lanceor went to his
hostelry to make him ready. In the meanwhile came Merlin
unto the court of King Arthur, and there was told him the adventure of the sword, and the death of the Lady of the Lake.
"Now shall I say you," said Merlin; "this same damsel that
here standeth, that brought the sword unto your court, I shall
tell you the cause of her coming: she was the falsest damsel
that liveth." "Say not so," said they. "She hath a brother, a
passing good knight of prowess and a full true man; and this
damsel loved another knight that held her to paramour, and
this good knight her brother met with the knight that held her
to paramour, and slew him by force of his hands. When this
false damsel understood this, she went to the Lady Lile of

Avelion, and besought her of help, to be avenged of her own brother. . . ."

V

How Balin was pursued by Sir Lanceor, knight of Ireland, and how he jousted and slew him.

"And so this Lady Lile of Avelion took her this sword that she brought with her, and told there should no man pull it out of the sheath but if he be one of the best knights of this realm, and he should be hard and full of prowess, and with that sword he should slay her brother. This was the cause that the damsel came into this court. I know it as well as ye. Would God she had not come into this court, but she came never in fellowship of worship to do good, but always great harm; and that knight that hath achieved the sword shall be destroyed by that sword, for the which will be great damage, for there liveth not a knight of more prowess than he is, and he shall do unto you, my Lord Arthur, great honor and kindness; and it is great pity he shall not endure but a while, for of his strength and hardiness I know not his match living."

So the knight of Ireland armed him at all points, and dressed his shield on his shoulder, and mounted upon horseback, and took his spear in his hand, and rode after a great pace, as much as his horse might go; and within a little space on a mountain he had a sight of Balin, and with a loud voice he cried, "Abide, knight, for ye shall abide whether ye will or nill, and the shield that is to-fore you shall not help." When Balin heard the noise, he turned his horse fiercely, and said, "Fair knight, what will ye with me, will ye joust with me?" "Yea," said the Irish knight, "therefore came I after you." "Peradventure," said Balin, "it had been better to have holden you at home, for many a man weeneth to put his enemy to a rebuke, and oft it falleth to himself. Of what court be ye sent from?" said Balin. "I am come from the court of King Arthur," said the knight of Ireland, "that come hither for to revenge the despite ye did this day to King Arthur and to his court." "Well," said Balin, "I see well I must have ado with you, that me forthinketh for to grieve King Arthur, or any of his court; and your quarrel is full simple," said Balin, "unto me, for the lady that is dead did me great damage, and else would I have been loath as any knight that liveth for to slay a lady." "Make you ready," said the knight Lanceor, "and dress you unto me, for that one shall abide in the field." Then they took their spears, and came together as much as their horses might drive, and the Irish knight smote Balin on the shield, that all went to-shivers of his spear, and Balin hit him through the shield, and the hauberk perished, and so pierced through his body and the horse's croup, and anon turned his horse fiercely, and drew out his sword, and wist not that he had slain him; and then he saw him lie as a dead corpse.

VI

*How a damsel, which was love to Lanceor, slew
herself for love, and how Balin met with
his brother Balan.*

Then he looked by him, and was ware of a damsel that came riding full fast as the horse might ride, on a fair palfrey. And when she espied that Lanceor was slain, she made sorrow out of measure, and said, "O Balin, two bodies thou hast slain and one heart, and two hearts in one body, and two souls thou hast lost." And therewith she took the sword from her love that lay dead, and fell to the ground in a swoon. And when she arose she made great dole out of measure, the which sorrow grieved

Balin passingly sore, and he went unto her for to have taken the sword out of her hand, but she held it so fast he might not take it out of her hand unless he should have hurt her, and suddenly she set the pommel on the ground, and rove herself through the body. When Balin espied her deeds, he was passing heavy in his heart, and ashamed that so fair a damsel had destroyed herself for the love of his death. "Alas," said Balin, "me repenteth sore the death of this knight, for the love of this damsel, for there was much true love betwixt them both," and for sorrow might not longer behold him, but turned his horse and looked toward a great forest, and there he was ware, by the arms, of his brother Balan. And when they were met they put off their helms and kissed together, and wept for joy and pity. Then Balan said, "I little weened to have met with you at this sudden adventure; I am right glad of your deliverance out of your dolorous prisonment, for a man told me, in the castle of Four Stones, that ye were delivered, and that man had seen you in the court of King Arthur, and therefore I came hither into this country, for here I supposed to find you." Anon the knight Balin told his brother of his adventure of the sword, and of the death of the Lady of the Lake, and how King Arthur was displeased with him. "Wherefore he sent this knight after me, that lieth here dead, and the death of this damsel grieveth me sore." "So doth it me," said Balan, "but ye must take the adventure that God will ordain you." "Truly," said Balin, "I am right heavy that my Lord Arthur is displeased with me, for he is the most worshipful knight that reigneth now on earth, and his love will I get or else will I put my life in adventure. For the King Rience lieth at a siege at the Castle Terrabil, and thither will we draw in all haste, to prove our worship and prowess upon him." "I will well," said Balan, "that we do, and we will help each other as brethren ought to do."

VII

*How a dwarf reproved Balin for the death of Lanceor,
and how King Mark of Cornwall found them,
and made a tomb over them.*

"Now go we hence," said Balin, "and well be we met." The
meanwhile as they talked, there came a dwarf from the city of
Camelot on horseback, as much as he might, and found the
dead bodies, wherefore he made great dole, and pulled out his
hair for sorrow, and said, "Which of you knights have done
this deed?" "Whereby askest thou it?" said Balan. "For I
would wit it," said the dwarf. "It was I," said Balin, "that slew
this knight in my defense, for hither he came to chase me, and
either I must slay him or he me; and this damsel slew herself
for his love, which repenteth me, and for her sake I shall owe
all women the better love." "Alas," said the dwarf, "thou hast
done great damage unto thyself, for this knight that is here
dead was one of the most valiantest men that lived, and trust
well, Balin, the kin of this knight will chase you through the
world till they have slain you." "As for that," said Balin, "I
fear not greatly, but I am right heavy that I have displeased
my lord King Arthur, for the death of this knight." So as they
talked ogether, there came a king of Cornwall riding, the
which hight King Mark. And when he saw these two bodies
dead, and understood how they were dead, by the two knights
above said, then made the king great sorrow for the true love
that was betwixt them, and said, "I will not depart till I have
on this earth made a tomb," and there he pitched his pavilions and sought through all the country to find a tomb, and in
a church they found one was fair and rich, and then the king
let put them both in the earth, and put the tomb upon them,
and wrote the names of them both on the tomb. How here
lieth Lanceor the king's son of Ireland, t'ia at h's own request

was slain by the hands of Balin; and how his lady, Colombe, and paramour, slew herself with her love's sword for dole and sorrow.

VIII

How Merlin prophesied that two the best knights of the world should fight there, which were Sir Lancelot and Sir Tristram.

The meanwhile as this was a-doing, in came Merlin to King Mark, and seeing all his doing, said, "Here shall be in this same place the greatest battle betwixt two knights that was or ever shall be, and the truest lovers, and yet none of them shall slay other." And there Merlin wrote their names upon the tomb with letters of gold that should fight in that place, whose names were Lancelot de Lake and Tristram. "Thou art a marvelous man," said King Mark unto Merlin, "that speakest of such marvels; thou art a boistous man, and an unlikely to tell of such deeds. What is thy name?" said King Mark. "At this time," said Merlin, "I will not tell, but at that time when Sir Tristram is taken with his sovereign lady, then ye shall hear and know my name, and at that time ye shall hear tidings that shall not please you." Then said Merlin to Balin, "Thou hast done thyself great hurt, because that thou saved not this lady that slew herself, that might have saved her an thou wouldst." "By the faith of my body," said Balin, "I might not save her, for she slew herself suddenly." "Me repenteth," said Merlin; "because of the death of that lady thou shalt strike a stroke most dolorous that ever man struck, except the stroke of our Lord, for thou shalt hurt the truest knight and the man of most worship that now liveth, and through that stroke three kingdoms shall be in great poverty, misery and wretchedness twelve years, and the knight shall not be whole of that wound for many years." Then Merlin took his leave of

Balin. And Balin said, "If I wist it were sooth that ye say I should do such a perilous deed as that, I would slay myself to make thee a liar." Therewith Merlin vanished away suddenly.

And then Balan and his brother took their leave of King Mark. "First," said the king, "tell your name." "Sir," said Balan, "ye may see he beareth two swords, thereby ye may call him the Knight with the Two Swords." And so departed King Mark unto Camelot to King Arthur, and Balin took the way toward King Rience; and as they rode together they met with Merlin disguised, but they knew him not. "Whither ride you?" said Merlin. "We have little to do," said the two knights, "to tell thee." "But what is thy name?" said Balin. "At this time," said Merlin, "I will not tell it thee." "It is evil seen," said the knights, "that thou art a true man that thou wilt not tell thy name." "As for that," said Merlin, "be it as it be may, I can tell you wherefore ye ride this way, for to meet King Rience; but it will not avail you without ye have my counsel." "Ah!" said Balin, "ye are Merlin; we will be ruled by your counsel." "Come on," said Merlin, "ye shall have great worship, and look that ye do knightly, for ye shall have great need." "As tor that," said Balin, "dread you not, we will do what we may."

IX

How Balin and his brother, by the counsel of Merlin,
took King Rience and brought him
to King Arthur.

Then Merlin lodged them in a wood among leaves beside the highway, and took off the bridle of their horses and put them to grass and laid them down to rest them till it was nigh midnight. Then Merlin bade them rise, and make them ready, for the king was nigh them, that was stolen away from his host with a three score horses of his best knights, and twenty of them rode to-fore to warn the Lady de Vance that the king was coming; for that night King Rience should have lain with her. "Which is the king?" said Balin. "Abide," said Merlin, "here in a strait way ye shall meet with him;" and therewith he showed Balin and his brother where he rode.

Anon Balin and his brother met with the king, and smote him down, and wounded him fiercely, and laid him to the ground; and there they slew on the right hand and the left hand, and slew more than forty of his men, and the remnant fled. Then went they again to King Rience and would have slain him had he not yielded him unto their grace. Then said he thus, "Knights full of prowess, slay me not, for by my life ye may win, and by my death ye shall win nothing." Then said these two knights, "Ye say sooth and truth," and so laid him on a horse litter. With that Merlin was vanished, and came to King Arthur aforehand, and told him how his most enemy was taken and discomfited.[7] "By whom?" said King Arthur. "By two knights," said Merlin, "that would please your lordship, and tomorrow ye shall know what knights they are." Anon after came the Knight with the Two Swords and Balan his brother, and brought with them King Rience of North Wales, and there delivered him to the porters, and charged them with him; and so they two returned again in the dawning of the day. King Arthur came then to King Rience, and said, "Sir King, ye are welcome: by what adventure come ye hither?" "Sir," said King Rience, "I came hither by an hard adventure." "Who won you?" said King Arthur. "Sir," said the king, "the Knight with the Two Swords and his brother, which are two marvelous knights of prowess." "I know them not," said Arthur, "but much I am beholden to them." "Ah," said Merlin, "I shall tell you: it is Balin that achieved the sword, and his brother Balan, a good knight, there liveth not a better of prowess and of worthiness, and it shall be the great-

7 Defeated.

est dole of him that ever I knew of knight, for he shall not long endure." "Alas," said King Arthur," that is great pity; for I am much beholden unto him, and I have ill deserved it unto him for his kindness." "Nay," said Merlin, "he shall do much more for you, and that shall ye know in haste. But, sir, are ye purveyed," said Merlin, "for to-morn the host of Nero, King Rience's brother, will set on you or noon with a great host, and therefore make you ready, for I will depart from you."

x

How King Arthur had a battle against Nero and King Lot of Orkney, and how King Lot was deceived by Merlin, and how twelve kings were slain.

Then King Arthur made ready his host in ten battles,[8] and Nero was ready in the field afore the Castle Terrabil with a great host, and he had ten battles, with many more people than Arthur had. Then Nero had the vanguard with the most part of his people, and Merlin came to King Lot of the Isle of Orkney, and held him with a tale of prophecy, till Nero and his people were destroyed. And there Sir Kay the seneschal did passingly well, that the days of his life the worship went never from him; and Sir Hervis de Revel did marvelous deeds with King Arthur, and King Arthur slew that day twenty knights and maimed forty. At that time came in the Knight with the Two Swords and his brother Balan, but they two did so marvelously that the king and all the knights marveled of them, and all they that beheld them said they were sent from heaven as angels, or devils from hell; and King Arthur said himself they were the best knights that ever he saw, for they gave such strokes that all men had wonder of them.

In the meanwhile came one to King Lot, and told him while he tarried there Nero was destroyed and slain with all his peo-

[8] Divisions.

ple. "Alas," said King Lot, "I am ashamed, for by my default there is many a worshipful man slain, for an we had been together there had been none host under the heaven that had been able for to have matched with us; this faiter[9] with his prophecy hath mocked me." All that did Merlin, for he knew well that an King Lot had been with his body there at the first battle, King Arthur had been slain, and all his people destroyed; and well Merlin knew that one of the kings should be dead that day, and loath was Merlin that any of them both should be slain; but of the twain, he had liefer King Lot had been slain than King Arthur. "Now what is best to do?" said King Lot of Orkney; "whether is me better to treat with King Arthur or to fight, for the greater part of our people are slain or destroyed?" "Sir," said a knight, "set on Arthur, for they are weary and forfoughten and we be fresh." "As for me," said King Lot, "I would every knight would do his part as I would do mine." And then they advanced banners and smote together and all to-shivered their spears; and Arthur's knights, with the help of the Knight with the Two Swords and his brother Balan put King Lot and his host to the worse. But always King Lot held him in the foremost front, and did marvelous deeds of arms, for all his host was borne up by his hands, for he abode all knights. Alas, he might not endure, the which was great pity, that so worthy a knight as he was one should be overmatched, that of late time afore had been a knight of King Arthur's, and wedded the sister of King Arthur; and for King Arthur lay by King Lot's wife, the which was Arthur's sister, and gat on her Mordred, therefore King Lot held against Arthur. So there was a knight that was called the Knight with the Strange Beast, and at that time his right name was called Pellinore, the which was a good man of prowess, and he smote a mighty stroke at King Lot as he fought with all his enemies, and he failed of his stroke, and smote the horse's

[9] Impostor.

neck, that he fell to the ground with King Lot. And therewith anon Pellinore smote him a great stroke through the helm and head unto the brows. And then all the host of Orkney fled for the death of King Lot, and there were slain many mothers' sons. But King Pellinore bare the wite[10] of the death of King Lot, wherefore Sir Gawain revenged the death of his father the tenth year after he was made knight, and slew King Pellinore with his own hands. Also there were slain at that battle twelve kings on the side of King Lot with Nero, and all were buried in the Church of St. Stephen's in Camelot, and the remnant of knights and of others were buried in a great rock.

XI

Of the interment of twelve kings, and of the prophecy of Merlin, and how Balin should give the dolorous stroke.

So at the interment came King Lot's wife Morgause with her four sons, Gawain, Agravain, Gaheris, and Gareth. Also there came thither King Uriens, Sir Ewain's father, and Morgan le Fay, his wife, that was King Arthur's sister. All these came to the interment. But of all these twelve kings King Arthur let make the tomb of King Lot passing richly, and made his tomb by his own; and then Arthur let make twelve images of latten[11] and copper, and overgilt it with gold, in the sign of twelve kings, and each one of them held a taper of wax that burnt day and night; and King Arthur was made in sign of a figure standing above them with a sword drawn in his hand, and all the twelve figures had countenance like unto men that were overcome. All this made Merlin by his subtle craft, and there he told the king, "When I am dead these tapers shall burn no longer, and soon after the adventures of the

[10] Blame.
[11] Brass.

Sangreal [12] shall come among you and be achieved." Also he told Arthur how Balin the worshipful knight shall give the dolorous stroke, whereof shall fall great vengeance. "Oh, where is Balin and Balan and Pellinore?" said King Arthur. "As for Pellinore," said Merlin, "he will meet with you soon; and as for Balin he will not be long from you; but the other brother will depart, ye shall see him no more." "By my faith," said Arthur, "they are two marvelous knights, and namely[13] Balin passeth of prowess of any knight that ever I found, for much beholden am I unto him; would God he would abide with me." "Sir," said Merlin, "look ye keep well the scabbard of Excalibur, for ye shall lose no blood while ye have the scabbard upon you, though ye have as many wounds upon you as ye may have." So after, for great trust, Arthur betook[14] the scabbard to Morgan le Fay his sister, and she loved another knight better than her husband King Uriens or King Arthur, and she would have had Arthur her brother slain, and therefore she let make another scabbard like it by enchantment, and gave the scabbard Excalibur to her love; and the knight's name was called Accolon, that after had near slain King Arthur. After this Merlin told unto King Arthur of the prophecy that there should be a great battle beside Salisbury, and Mordred his own son should be against him. Also he told him that Basdemegus was his cousin, and germain unto King Uriens.

XII

How a sorrowful knight came before Arthur, and how Balin fetched him, and how that knight was slain by a knight invisible.

Within a day or two King Arthur was somewhat sick, and he let pitch his pavilion in a meadow, and there he laid him

[12] Holy Grail.
[13] Specially.
[14] Gave.

down on a pallet to sleep, but he might have no rest. Right so he heard a great noise of an horse, and therewith the king looked out at the porch of the pavilion, and saw a knight coming even by him, making great dole. "Abide, fair sir," said Arthur, "and tell me wherefore thou makest this sorrow." "Ye may little amend me," said the knight, and so passed forth to the castle of Meliot. Anon after there came Balin, and when he saw King Arthur he alighted off his horse, and came to the king on foot, and saluted him. "By my head," said Arthur, "ye be welcome. Sir, right now came riding this way a knight making great mourn, for what cause I cannot tell; wherefore I would desire of you of your courtesy and of your gentleness to fetch again that knight either by force or else by his good will." "I will do more for your lordship than that," said Balin; and so he rode more than a pace, and found the knight with a damsel in a forest, and said, "Sir knight, ye must come with me unto King Arthur, for to tell him of your sorrow." "That will I not," said the knight, "for it will scathe me greatly, and do you none avail." "Sir," said Balin, "I pray you make you ready, for ye must go with me, or else I must fight with you and bring you by force, and that were me loath to do." "Will ye be my warrant," said the knight, "and I go with you?" "Yea," said Balin, "or else I will die therefor." And so he made him ready to go with Balin, and left the damsel still. And as they were even afore King Arthur's pavilion, there came one invisible, and smote this knight that went with Balin throughout the body with a spear. "Alas," said the knight, "I am slain under your conduct with a knight called Garlon; therefore take my horse that is better than yours, and ride to the damsel, and follow the quest that I was in as she will lead you, and revenge my death when ye may." "That shall I do," said Balin, "and that I make vow unto knighthood"; and so he departed from this knight with great sorrow. So King Arthur let bury this knight richly, and made a mention on his tomb, how there was slain Herlews le Berbeus, and by whom the treachery was done, the knight Garlon. But ever the damsel bare the truncheon of the spear with her that Sir Herlews was slain withal.

XIII

How Balin and the damsel met with a knight which was in like wise slain, and how the damsel bled for the custom of a castle.

So Balin and the damsel rode into a forest, and there met with a knight that had been a-hunting, and that knight asked Balin for what cause he made so great sorrow. "Me list not to tell you," said Balin. "Now," said the knight, "an I were armed as ye be I would fight with you." "That should little need," said Balin, "I am not afeard to tell you," and told him all the cause how it was. "Ah," said the knight, "is this all? Here I ensure you by the faith of my body never to depart from you while my life lasteth." And so they went to the hostelry and armed them, and so rode forth with Balin. And as they came by an hermitage even by a churchyard, there came the knight Garlon invisible, and smote this knight, Perin de Mountbeliard, through the body with a spear. "Alas," said the knight, "I am slain by this traitor knight that rideth invisible." "Alas," said Balin, "it is not the first despite he hath done me"; and there the hermit and Balin buried the knight under a rich stone and a tomb royal. And on the morn they found letters of gold written, how Sir Gawain shall revenge his father's death, King Lot, on the King Pellinore. Anon after this Balin and the damsel rode till they came to a castle, and there Balin alighted, and he and the damsel went to go into the castle, and anon as Balin came within the castle's gate the portcullis fell down at his back, and there fell many men about the damsel, and would have slain her. When Balin saw that, he was sore aggrieved, for he might not help the damsel. Then he went up

into the tower, and leapt over walls into the ditch, and hurt
him not; and anon he pulled out his sword and would have
fought with them. And they all said nay, they would not fight
with him, for they did nothing but the old custom of the castle; and told him how their lady was sick, and had lain many
years, and she might not be whole but if she had a dish of
silver full of blood of a clean maid and a king's daughter; and
therefore the custom of this castle is, there shall no damsel
pass this way but she shall bleed of her blood in a silver dish
full. "Well," said Balin, "she shall bleed as much as she may
bleed, but I will not lose the life of her whiles my life
lasteth." And so Balin made her to bleed by her good will, but
her blood helped not the lady. And so he and she rested there
all night, and had there right good cheer, and on the morn
they passed on their ways. And as it telleth after in the
Sangreal, that Sir Percival's sister helped that lady with her
blood, whereof she was dead.

XIV

*How Balin met with that knight named Garlon at a
feast, and there he slew him, to have his blood
to heal therewith the son of his host.*

Then they rode three or four days and never met with adventure, and by hap they were lodged with a gentle man that was
a rich man and well at ease. And as they sat at their supper
Balin overheard one complain grievously by him in a chair.
"What is this noise?" said Balin. "Forsooth," said his host, "I
will tell you. I was but late at a jousting, and there I jousted
with a knight that is brother unto King Pellam, and twice
smote I him down, and then he promised to quit me on my
best friend; and so he wounded my son, that cannot be whole
till I have of that knight's blood, and he rideth away invisible;
but I know not his name." "Ah!" said Balin. "I know that

knight; his name is Garlon; he hath slain two knights of mine in the same manner; therefore I had liefer meet with that knight than all the gold in this realm, for the despite he hath done me." "Well," said his host, "I shall tell you, King Pellam of Listeneise hath made do cry in all this country a great feast that shall be within these twenty days, and no knight may come there but if he bring his wife with him, or his paramour; and that knight, your enemy and mine, ye shall see that day." "Then I behote[15] you," said Balin, "part of his blood to heal your son withal." "We will be forward to-morn," said his host. So on the morn they rode all three toward Pellam, and they had fifteen days' journey or they came thither; and that same day began the great feast. And so they alighted and stabled their horses, and went into the castle; but Balin's host might not be let in because he had no lady. Then Balin was well received and brought into a chamber and unarmed him; and there were brought him robes to his pleasure, and would have had Balin leave his sword behind him. "Nay," said Balin, "that I do not, for it is the custom of my country a knight always to keep this weapon with him, and that custom will I keep, or else I will depart as I came." Then they gave him leave to wear his sword, and so he went unto the castle, and was set among knights of worship, and his lady afore him.

Soon Balin asked a knight, "Is there not a knight in this court whose name is Garlon?" "Yonder he goeth," said a knight, "he with the black face; he is the marvelest knight that is now living, for he destroyeth many good knights, for he goeth invisible." "Ah well," said Balin, "is that he?" Then Balin advised him long: "If I slay him here I shall not escape, and if I leave him now, peradventure I shall never meet with him again at such a steven," [16] and much harm he will do an he live." Therewith this Garlon espied that this Balin beheld

---

[15] Promise.
[16] Occasion.

him, and then he came and smote Balin on the face with the back of his hand, and said, "Knight, why beholdest me so? For shame therefore, eat thy meat and do that thou came for." "Thou sayest sooth," said Balin; "this is not the first despite that thou hast done me, and therefore I will do what I came for," and rose up fiercely and clave his head to the shoulders. "Give me the truncheon," said Balin to his lady, "wherewith he slew your knight." Anon she gave it him, for alway she bare the truncheon with her. And therewith Balin smote him through the body, and said openly, "With that truncheon thou hast slain a good knight, and now it sticketh in thy body." And then Balin called unto him his host, saying, "Now may ye fetch blood enough to heal your son withal."

XV

How Balin fought with King Pellam, and how his sword brake, and how he gat a spear where-with he smote the dolorous stroke.

Anon all the knights arose from the table for to set on Balin, and King Pellam himself arose up fiercely, and said, "Knight, hast thou slain my brother? Thou shalt die therefor or thou depart." "Well," said Balin, "do it yourself." "Yes," said King Pellam, "there shall no man have ado with thee but myself, for the love of my brother." Then King Pellam caught in his hand a grim weapon and smote eagerly at Balin; but Balin put the sword betwixt his head and the stroke, and therewith his sword burst in sunder. And when Balin was weaponless he ran into a chamber for to seek some weapon, and so from chamber to chamber, and no weapon he could find, and always King Pellam after him. And at last he entered into a chamber that was marvelously well dight and richly, and a bed arrayed with cloth of gold, the richest that might be thought, and one lying therein, and thereby stood a table of clean gold with four pillars of silver that bare up the table, and upon the table stood a marvelous spear strangely wrought. And when Balin saw that spear, he gat it in his hand and turned him to King Pellam, and smote him passingly sore with that spear, that King Pellam fell down in a swoon, and therewith the castle roof and walls brake and fell to the earth, and Balin fell down so that he might not stir foot nor hand. And so the most part of the castle, that was fallen down through that dolorous stroke, lay upon Pellam and Balin three days.

XVI

How Balin was delivered by Merlin, and saved a knight that would have slain himself for love.

Then Merlin came thither and took up Balin, and gat him a good horse, for his was dead, and bade him ride out of that country. "I would have my damsel," said Balin. "Lo," said Merlin, "where she lieth dead." And King Pellam lay so, many years sore wounded, and might never be whole till Galahad the haut prince healed him in the quest of the Sangreal, for in that place was part of the blood of our Lord Jesus Christ, that Joseph of Arimathea brought into this land, and there himself lay in that rich bed. And that was the same spear that Longius smote our Lord to the heart; and King Pellam was nigh of Joseph's kin, and that was the most worshipful man that lived in those days, and great pity it was of his hurt, for through that stroke, turned to great dole, tray and tene.[17] Then departed Balin from Merlin, and said, "In this world we meet never no more." So he rode forth through the fair countries and cities, and found the people dead, slain on every side. And all that were alive cried, "O Balin, thou hast caused great damage in these countries; for the dolorous stroke thou gavest unto King Pellam three countries are destroyed, and doubt not

[17] Pain and sorrow.

but the vengeance will fall on thee at the last." When Balin was past those countries he was passing fain.[13]

So he rode eight days or he met with adventure. And at the last he came into a fair forest in a valley, and was ware of a tower, and there beside he saw a great horse of war, tied to a tree, and there beside sat a fair knight on the ground and made great mourning, and he was a likely man, and a well made. Balin said, "God save you, why be ye so heavy? Tell me and I will amend it, and I may, to my power." "Sir knight," said he again, "thou dost me great grief, for I was in merry thoughts, and now thou puttest me to more pain." Balin went a little from him, and looked on his horse; then heard Balin him say thus: "Ah, fair lady, why have ye broken my promise? For ye promised me to meet me here by noon, and I may curse thee that ever ye gave me this sword, for with this sword I slay myself," and pulled it out. And therewith Balin stert unto him and took him by the hand. "Let go my hand," said the knight, "or else I shall slay thee." "That shall not need," said Balin, "for I shall promise you my help to get you your lady, an ye will tell me where she is." "What is your name?" said the knight. "My name is Balin le Savage." "Ah, sir, I know you well enough, ye are the Knight with the Two Swords, and the man of most prowess of your hands living." "What is your name?" said Balin. "My name is Garnish of the Mount, a poor man's son, but by my prowess and hardiness a duke hath made me knight, and gave me his lands; his name is Duke Hermel, and his daughter is she that I love, and she me, as I deemed." "How far is she hence?" said Balin. "But six mile," said the knight. "Now ride we hence," said these two knights. So they rode more than a pace, till that they came to a fair castle well walled and ditched. "I will into the castle," said Balin, "and look if she be there." So he went in and searched from chamber to chamber, and found her bed,

[13] Exceedingly glad.

but she was not there. Then Balin looked into a fair little garden, and under a laurel tree he saw her lie upon a quilt of green samite and a knight in her arms fast halsing[19] either other, and under their heads grass and herbs. When Balin saw her lie so with the foulest knight that ever he saw, and she a fair lady, then Balin went through all the chambers again, and told the knight how he found her as she had slept fast, and so brought him in the place there she lay fast sleeping.

XVII

How that knight slew his love and a knight lying by her, and after, how he slew himself with his own sword, and how Balin rode toward a castle where he lost his life.

And when Garnish beheld her so lying, for pure sorrow his mouth and nose burst out a-bleeding, and with his sword he smote off both their heads, and then he made sorrow out of measure and said, "O Balin, much sorrow hast thou brought unto me, for hadst thou not showed me that sight I should have passed my sorrow." "Forsooth," said Balin, "I did it to this intent that it should better thy courage, and that ye might see and know her falsehood, and to cause you to leave love of such a lady; God knoweth I did none other but as I would ye did to me." "Alas," said Garnish, "now is my sorrow double that I may not endure, now have I slain that I most loved in all my life"; and therewith suddenly he rove himself on his own sword unto the hilts.

When Balin saw that, he dressed him thenceward, lest folk should say he had slain them; and so he rode forth, and within three days he came by a cross, and thereon were letters of gold written, that said, "It is not for no knight alone to ride toward

[19] Embracing.

this castle." Then he saw an old hoar gentleman coming toward him, that said, "Balin le Savage, thou passest thy bounds to come this way, therefore turn again and it will avail thee." And he vanished away anon; and so he heard an horn blow as it had been the death of a beast. "That blast," said Balin, "is blown for me, for I am the prise[20] and yet am I not dead." Anon withal he saw an hundred ladies and many knights, that welcomed him with fair semblant, and made him passing good cheer unto his sight, and led him into the castle, and there was dancing and minstrelsy and all manner of joy. Then the chief lady of the castle said, "Knight with the Two Swords, you must have ado and joust with a knight hereby that keepeth an island, for there may no man pass this way but he must joust or he pass." "That is an unhappy custom," said Balin, "that a knight may not pass this way but if he joust." "Ye shall not have ado but with one knight," said the lady.

"Well," said Balin, "since I shall thereto I am ready, but traveling men are oft weary and their horses too; but though my horse be weary, my heart is not weary; I would be fain there my death should be." "Sir," said a knight to Balin, "methinketh your shield is not good, I will lend you a bigger. Thereof I pray you." And so he took the shield that was unknown and left his own, and so rode unto the island, and put him and his horse in a great boat; and when he came on the other side he met with a damsel, and she said, "O knight Balin, why have ye left your own shield? Alas, ye have put yourself in great danger, for by your shield you should have been known; it is great pity of you as ever was of knight, for of thy prowess and hardiness thou hast no fellow living." "Me repenteth," said Balin, "that ever I came within this country, but I may not turn now again for shame, and what adventure shall fall to me, be it life or death, I will take the adventure that shall come to me." And then he looked on his armor, and un-

[20] Captive.

derstood he was well armed, and therewith blessed him and mounted upon his horse.

XVIII

*How Balin met with his brother Balan, and how
each of them slew other unknown, till
they were wounded to death.*

Then afore him he saw come riding out of a castle a knight, and his horse trapped all red,[21] and himself in the same color. When this knight in the red beheld Balin, him thought it should be his brother Balin, because of his two swords, but because he knew not his shield he deemed it was not he. And so they aventryd their spears and came marvelously fast together, and they smote each other in the shields, but their spears and their course were so big that it bore down horse and man, that they lay both in a swoon. But Balin was bruised sore with the fall of his horse, for he was weary of travel. And Balan was the first that rose on foot and drew his sword, and went toward Balin, and he arose and went against him; but Balan smote Balin first, and he put up his shield and smote him through the shield and tamed[22] his helm. Then Balin smote him again with that unhappy sword, and well-nigh had felled his brother Balan, and so they fought there together till their breaths failed. Then Balin looked up to the castle and saw the towers stand full of ladies. So they went unto battle again, and wounded every other dolefully, and then they breathed ofttimes, and so went unto battle that all the place there as they fought was blood red. And at that time there was none of them · both but they had either smitten other seven great wounds, so that the least of them might have been the death of the mightiest giant in this world.

[21] In red trappings.
[22] Pierced.

Then they went to battle again so marvelously that doubt it was to hear of that battle for the great blood-shedding, and their hauberks unnailed that naked they were on every side. At last Balan the younger brother withdrew him a little and laid him down. Then said Balin le Savage, "What knight art thou? For or now I found never no knight that matched me." "My name is," said he, "Balan, brother unto the good knight, Balin." "Alas," said Balin, "that ever I should see this day," an therewith he fell backward in a swoon. Then Balan yede[23] on all four feet and hands, and put off the helm off his brother, and might not know him by the visage it was so full hewn and bled; but when he awoke he said, "O Balan, my brother, thou hast slain me and I thee, wherefore all the wide world shall speak of us both." "Alas," said Balan, "that ever I saw this day, that through mishap I might not know you, for I espied well your two swords, but because ye had another shield I deemed ye had been another knight." "Alas," said Balin, "all that made an unhappy knight in the castle, for he caused me to leave my own shield to our both's destruction, and if I might live I would destroy that castle for ill customs." "That were well done," said Balan, "for I had never grace to depart from them since that I came hither, for here it happed to me to slay a knight that kept this island, and since might I never depart, and no more should ye, brother, an ye might have slain me as ye have, and escaped yourself with the life."

Right so came the lady of the tower with four knights and six ladies and six yeomen[24] unto them, and there she heard how they made their moan either to other, and said, "We came both out of one tomb, that is to say one mother's belly, and so shall we lie both in one pit." So Balan prayed the lady of her gentleness, for his true service, that she would bury them both in that same place there the battle was done. And she

[23] Went.
[24] Servants.

granted them, with weeping, it should be done richly in the best manner. "Now, will ye send for a priest, that we may receive our sacrament, and receive the blessed body of our Lord Jesus Christ?" "Yea," said the lady, "it shall be done"; and so she sent for a priest and gave them their rights. "Now," said Balin, "when we are buried in one tomb, and the mention made over us how two brethren slew each other, there will never good knight, nor good man, see our tomb but they will pray for our souls." And so all the ladies and gentlewomen wept for pity. Then anon Balan died, but Balin died not till the midnight after, and so were they buried both, and the lady let make a mention of Balan how he was there slain by his brother's hands, but she knew not Balin's name.

XIX

How Merlin buried them both in one tomb, and of Balin's sword.

In the morn came Merlin and let write Balin's name on the tomb with letters of gold, that "Here lieth Balin le Savage that was the Knight with the Two Swords, and he that smote the Dolorous Stroke." Also Merlin let make there a bed, that there should never man lie therein but he went out of his wit, yet Lancelot de Lake forbid[25] that bed through his noblesse. And anon after Balin was dead, Merlin took his sword, and took off the pommel and set on another pommel. So Merlin bade a knight that stood afore him handle that sword, and he assayed, and he might not handle it. Then Merlin laughed. "Why laugh ye?" said the knight. "This is the cause," said Merlin; "there shall never man handle this sword but the best knight of the world, and that shall be Sir Lancelot or else Galahad his son, and Lancelot with this sword shall slay the man that in the world he loved best, that shall be Sir Gawain." All this he let

[25] Destroyed.

write in the pommel of the sword. Then Merlin let make a bridge of iron and of steel into that island, and it was but half a foot broad, and there shall never man pass that bridge, nor have hardiness to go over, but if he were a passing good man and a good knight without treachery or villainy. Also the scabbard of Balin's sword Merlin left it on this side the island, that Galahad should find it. Also Merlin let make by his subtlety that Balin's sword was put in a marble stone standing upright as great as a mill stone, and the stone hoved always above the water and did many years, and so by adventure it swam down the stream to the City of Camelot, that is in English Winchester. And that same day Galahad the haut prince came with King Arthur, and so Galahad brought with him the scabbard and achieved the sword that was there in the marble stone hoving upon the water. And on Whitsunday he achieved the sword as it rehearsed in the book of Sangreal.

Soon after this was done Merlin came to King Arthur and told him of the dolorous stroke that Balin gave to King Pellam, and how Balin and Balan fought together the marvelest battle that ever was heard of, and how they were buried both in one tomb. "Alas," said King Arthur, "this is the greatest pity that ever I heard tell of two knights, for in the world I know not such two knights." Thus endeth the tale of Balin and Balan, two brethren born in Northumberland, good knights.

LIST OF SUGGESTED READINGS

———

GENERAL:
A. C. Baugh, *A Literary History of England* (New York, 1948), pp. 165-197.

ORIGINS OF ROMANCE:
E. K. Chambers, *The Medieval Stage* (Oxford, 1903), I, 23-77.
R. Crosby, "Oral Delivery in the Middle Ages," *Speculum,* XI (1936), pp. 88-110.

CHRÉTIEN DE TROYES, *Perceval:*
R. S. Loomis, *Arthurian Tradition and Chrétien de Troyes* (New York, 1949), pp. 7-24, 335-417, 430-433.

GOTTFRIED VON STRASSBURG, *Tristan and Isolt:*
Thomas of Britain, *The Romance of Tristram and Ysolt* (New York, 1951), pp. xv-xxxiii.

Gottfried von Strassburg, *Tristan and Isolt,* ed. A. Closs (Oxford, 1947).

THE YOUTH OF ALEXANDER:
G. Cary, *The Medieval Alexander* (Cambridge, 1956), pp. 9-30, 134 *f.*, 273 *f.*

AUCASSIN AND NICOLETE:
G. Frank, *Medieval French Drama* (Oxford, 1954), pp. 237-242.

HAVELOK THE DANE:
L. A. Hibbard, *Medieval Romance in England* (New York, 1960), pp. 195-199, 349.

SIR ORFEO:
I.. Hibbard, *Medieval Romance in England* (New York, 1924), pp. 195-199.

SIR GAWAIN AND THE GREEN KNIGHT:
Laura Hibbard Loomis, *Arthurian Literature in the Middle Ages,* ed. R. S. Loomis (Oxford, 1959), pp. 528-540.

SIR THOMAS MALORY, *Balin:*
King Arthur and His Knights, Selections from the Works of Sir Thomas Malory, ed. E. Vinaver (Boston, 1956), pp. vii-xx, 15-40, 166.

MODERN LIBRARY COLLEGE EDITIONS